Cases in Collective Bargaining & Industrial Relations

A Decisional Approach

Cases in Collective Bargaining & Industrial Relations

A Decisional Approach

Eleventh Edition

David A. Dilts

Professor of Economics
School of Business and Management Sciences
Indiana University Purdue University, Fort Wayne

McGraw-Hill Irwin

Boston Burr Ridge, IL Dubuque, IA Madison, WI New York San Francisco St. Louis
Bangkok Bogotá Caracas Kuala Lumpur Lisbon London Madrid Mexico City
Milan Montreal New Delhi Santiago Seoul Singapore Sydney Taipei Toronto

The McGraw-Hill Companies

McGraw-Hill Irwin

CASES IN COLLECTIVE BARGAINING & INDUSTRIAL RELATIONS:
A DECISIONAL APPROACH

Published by McGraw-Hill/Irwin, a business unit of The McGraw-Hill Companies, Inc., 1221 Avenue of the Americas, New York, NY, 10020.

This book is printed on acid-free paper.

2 3 4 5 6 7 8 9 0 DOC/DOC 0 9 8 7 6

ISBN-13: 978-0-07-298736-2
ISBN-10: 0-07-298736-7

Editorial director: *John E. Biernat*
Executive editor: *John Weimeister*
Editorial assistant: *Heather Darr*
Executive marketing manager: *Rhonda Seelinger*
Media producer: *Benjamin Curless*
Lead project manager: *Pat Frederickson*
Production supervisor: *Gina Hangos*
Lead designer: *Matthew Baldwin*
Cover image: © *Getty Images*
Typeface: *10/12 Times New Roman*
Compositor: *Laserwords Private Limited*
Printer: *R. R. Donnelley*

Library of Congress Cataloging-in-Publication Data

Dilts, David A.
Cases in collective bargaining & industrial relations : a decisional approach / David A. Dilts. -- 11th ed.
p. cm.
Rev. ed. of: Cases in collective bargaining & industrial relations : a decisional approach / Raymond L. Hilgert, David A. Dilts. 10th ed. c2003.
ISBN-13: 978-0-07-298736-2 (alk. paper)
ISBN-10: 0-07-298736-7 (alk. paper)
1. Collective labor agreements--United States--Cases. 2. Labor disputes--United States--Cases. 3. Industrial relations--United States--Case studies. I. Hilgert, Raymond L. Cases in collective bargaining & industrial relations. II. Title. III. Title: Cases in collective bargaining and industrial relations.
KF3408.A4H55 2007
344.7301'89--dc22

2006013613

www.mhhe.com

Preface

This 11th edition provides a convenient and extensive set of cases in a variety of union-management problem situations. The book probably is most utilized as a supplementary text in survey courses in labor relations and collective bargaining, labor economics, and industrial relations. The cases vary in length, complexity, and types of issues. As such, the collection is of sufficient magnitude and depth that the book is appropriate for advanced courses or case courses in collective bargaining and labor relations.

A major objective of the book has been to provide a means by which students can apply principles, concepts, and legal considerations they have learned to actual decision situations and confrontations between labor and management. These cases have been tested in seminars and classes and have been found to be challenging and fascinating learning instruments.

The cases are representative of the types of problems that perennially confront management and labor organizations. They test analytical abilities in dealing with challenging human relations and union-management problems in a way useful even for students who do not have a management or labor relations career in mind.

In an effort to reflect the impact of recent trends, the collection includes representative cases dealing with current issues in a variety of organizational environments in both the private and public sectors. About one-third of the cases in the 11th edition are new. Cases retained from previous editions provide continuity and balance, and they are timeless in their applications of union-management relationships.

Part One of the book presents National Labor Relations Board cases as restructured from published reports of the NLRB and court decisions. The format is to describe each situation from the perspective of an impartial writer reporting the facts and issues of the case. For the most part, the cases are written as follows: first, the background information of the case is presented, including relevant legal issues; then the position of the union(s) or person(s) and the position of the management or company are stated. An introductory discussion and important and substantive sections of the Labor Management Relations Act (as amended) are included at the outset of Part One to enable students to become familiar with the provisions of the Act as applicable throughout these cases. Legal obligations and responsibilities of unions and management under the Labor Management Relations Act continue to be among the most dynamic and important areas of collective bargaining today. Case studies such as those in Part One enable the student to appreciate the nature of this Act, its applications in various union-management situations, and the duties and legal obligations of management and union representatives in carrying out their responsibilities. To a considerable extent, similar duties and obligations are applicable in most public sector labor relations settings where other statutes provide the legal framework for collective bargaining.

Part Two consists of cases adapted from grievance-arbitration decisions with appreciation to the Bureau of National Affairs, Inc., Karen Silber, Permissions Editor, for permission to adapt certain published cases from *Labor Relations Reporter—Labor Arbitration Reports.* (Specific citations of cases utilized from these BNA publications are included in the instructor's manual.) Here, too, the approach has been to restructure the arbitration cases in a convenient format. Highlights and issues of each case are provided through relevant background information, including contractual provisions, policies, rules, and the like, that are pertinent. Principal contentions of the union and management sides are then presented. Cases in Part Two demonstrate the complexities and controversial areas that are both typical and unusual in the ongoing relationships between management and union personnel. Prior to the arbitration cases is an introductory overview of major considerations in the grievance-arbitration process from which these cases emanate.

In studying both the NLRB and labor arbitration cases—which have been selected without any intent of presenting "good" or "bad" or "right" or "wrong" union-management practice—the student should ask: "What are the problems or principal issues?" "What is at stake between the parties?" "What is justice or equity in the situation?" "What does the law require?" "What does the contract say on the issue(s)?" "How have previous NLRB decisions or previous labor arbitration decisions handled similar circumstances?" These questions, and the more specific questions at the conclusion of each case, urge students toward deeper analysis of issues. Decisions of the NLRB, the courts, and labor arbitrators for the cases are provided in an instructor's manual. Most students like to compare their decisions and approaches with those of authorities in the field, and instructors at their discretion may want to provide this information to their classes.

Index and classification tables are placed with both parts of the book. These tables cite major issues of each case; for the NLRB cases, legal provisions are indicated. Selected bibliographies in both parts provide suggestions for more detailed reading in areas either directly or indirectly involved in the case materials.

Although it is not possible to recognize everyone who has had a part in developing this book, general appreciation is extended to the reviewers of previous editions and to professors and students who have utilized the book. They have offered numerous insights and helpful suggestions and corrections for both the text and instructor's manual. Appreciation is extended to Donald Gardiner of the St. Louis office of the National Labor Relations Board, and to John Hornbeck of the Office of the General Counsel of the NLRB, whose assistance in regard to materials for Part One was invaluable. The cooperation of the Federal Mediation and Conciliation Service, principally LaFré Carter of the Washington, D.C., office of FMCS, in providing FMCS materials is similarly recognized. Karl A. Sauber, a labor relations attorney in St. Louis, again assisted with a number of helpful suggestions. The services of Karen Busch of the Washington University Olin Business School administrative staff, who word processed sections of the book and instructor's manual manuscripts, are gratefully acknowledged.

David A. Dilts

Dedication

In Memory of Ray Hilgert,
Friend, and Co-author

Contents

PART TWO

CASE PROBLEMS IN UNION-MANAGEMENT RELATIONS: CASES FROM GRIEVANCE ARBITRATION 163

Cases in Collective Bargaining & Industrial Relations

A Decisional Approach

Part **One**

Legal Aspects of Collective Bargaining: National Labor Relations Board Cases

Introduction to the Labor Management Relations Act (LMRA)

The purpose of this section is to briefly explain the principal provisions of the Labor Management Relations Act (LMRA) of 1947 as amended. A partial text of the Act follows. A selected bibliography is included at the end of this introductory section to provide the reader with a selection of reading materials to provide a more in-depth understanding of the Act. The student of collective bargaining and industrial relations may contact a regional or national office of the National Labor Relations Board (NLRB) to obtain various NLRB publications that explain detailed principles and procedures involved in administration of the law. For example, a publication included in the bibliography entitled *A Guide to Basic Law and Procedures under the National Labor Relations Act* is prepared by the Office of the General Counsel of the NLRB; this booklet is very helpful for understanding many of the day-to-day activities of the Board and some of its most recent thinking. Parts of this publication have been adapted and included here.

The LMRA of 1947, also known as the Taft-Hartley Act in recognition of the two major congressional authors of the law, is the principal labor legislation governing the rules of the game of collective bargaining for the private sector of the U.S. economic system.[1] The LMRA of 1947 constituted a major revision of the National Labor Relations (Wagner) Act of 1935. The Act since has been amended a number of times (1951, 1958, 1959, 1969, 1973, 1974, and 1980); the 1974 amendments focused primarily on health

[1] The Railway Labor Act of 1926 (as amended) governs collective bargaining in the rail and airline industries. Although the Railway Labor Act is not widely applicable and some of its provisions are considerably different from those in LMRA, its premises and procedures were drawn upon by the framers of the National Labor Relations (Wagner) Act of 1935, upon which the Act of 1947 subsequently was based. The student is encouraged to study the provisions of the Railway Labor Act, as well as a history of labor laws in the railroad industries that led to the passage of the Railway Labor Act of 1926. See Douglas L. Leslie, ***The Railway Labor Act*** (Washington, D.C.: Bureau of National Affairs, 1995).

care institutions. As it stands today, the Act is the fundamental legislative basis for private sector union-management relationships in the United States.[2] The LMRA is a complex statute. Of even greater complexity, however, is the body of administrative laws and decisions that has evolved over the years in hundreds of thousands of union-management cases. The Act is constantly being tested, evaluated, and reevaluated by the NLRB, the courts, and by the Congress of the United States in the light of changing times, new controversies and new decisions. It is not the purpose of this section to completely interpret the Act or to present it in its entirety. Rather, selected parts of the Act will be discussed to underscore the major elements of the Act governing the collective bargaining process. The analysis that follows is provided to give the reader a basis upon which to evaluate the cases in Part One of this text.

EXCERPTS AND COMMENTS ON THE TEXT OF THE LABOR MANAGEMENT RELATIONS ACT, 1947, AS AMENDED

Section 1. The Statement of Findings and Policy

The Act begins with an analysis of the reasons why Congress believed it was compelled to enact legislation. In order to make the statute effective, Congress also provided for the means and methods necessary to enforce the Act. The purpose of the Act is to promote the free flow of interstate commerce by prescribing and protecting rights of employers and employees.

[2] A major component of public sector labor relations is at the federal government employee level. Executive Order 10988, originally signed by President Kennedy in 1962, was replaced by Executive Order 11491, issued by President Nixon in 1970. (Executive Orders 11616 and 11636 issued by President Nixon in 1971, and Executive Order 11838, issued by President Ford in 1975, amended Executive Order 11491.) These orders provided federal employees with union representation and collective bargaining rights. Subsequently, in 1978, Title VII of the Civil Service Reform Act replaced these Executive Orders and consolidated into law provisions for civilian federal government employees to govern collective bargaining in the federal sector. Title VII of the Civil Service Reform Act (Public Law 95–454) closely parallels the LMRA in many fundamental areas, with many of its provisions similar to various provisions in LMRA governing union-management relations in the private sector. Federal government employees do not have the right to strike or to have a "union shop," and a number of key areas remain outside the scope of bargaining in the federal sector. For example, general compensation levels, benefit entitlements, and certain general conditions of employment are largely determined by congressional legislation; many areas of employee concern are handled under federal and civil service regulations. The Civil Service Reform Act created a new administrative agency, the Federal Labor Relations Authority (FLRA), whose functions are similar to those of the National Labor Relations Board (NLRB). Some cases decided in the federal sector have drawn for precedent and policy from decisions of the NLRB in the private sector. Included in the bibliography at the end of this introductory section are a number of sources to consult for public sector bargaining law, cases, and decisions.

The U.S. Postal Service was brought under partial coverage of the LMRA through enactment of the Postal Reorganization Act of 1970 (Public Law 91–375). This law granted the NLRB jurisdiction over the U.S. Postal Service for various aspects of bargaining unit determination, unfair labor practices, and related matters. The Postal Reorganization Act contains provisions for negotiation of collective bargaining agreements between the Postal Service and labor organization bargaining representatives. These provisions include a procedure for mediation and even binding arbitration of disputes when the parties are unable to reach a negotiated agreement.

This statement of public policy makes clear that the labor law of the land is designed to regulate both unions and employers in order to protect the public interest. The Act permits and protects employees to exercise their right to organize labor unions and to bargain collectively with their employers as a means of balancing economic power in the workplace. At the same time, the Act encourages union and employer practices that are fundamental to the friendly adjustment of industrial disputes, with the objective of eliminating some union and employer practices that impair the public interest by contributing to industrial unrest and strikes, which in turn impairs the free flow of interstate commerce.

The NLRB, which is the federal agency administering the Act, has consistently interpreted this section to mean that the public policy of the United States is to promote and encourage the principle of unionism.

Section 2. Definitions

This section of the Act defines various terms used in the statute, and also outlines the coverage of the Act. By its terms, the Act does not apply to employees in a business or an industry not in the interstate commerce. Interstate commerce is the authority for Congress to act. The Constitution (Article 4, section 4) reserves to Congress the power to regulate commerce among the states. In addition, the Act specifically states that it does not apply to the following:

Agricultural laborers.

Domestic servants.

Any individual employed by one's parent or spouse.

Government employees, including those of government corporations or the Federal Reserve Bank, or any political subdivision such as a state or a school district.[3]

Independent contractors who depend upon profits, rather than commissions or wages, for their income.

Individuals employed by an employer subject to provisions of the Railway Labor Act.

Supervisors are excluded from the definition of employees covered by the Act. Whether or not a person is a supervisor is determined by authority rather than by title. The authority required to exclude an employee from coverage of the Act as a supervisor is defined in Section 2(11) of the Act.

All employees properly classified as "managerial," not just those in positions susceptible to conflicts of interest in labor relations, are excluded from the protection of the

[3] About half the states have laws—which vary widely in scope and coverage—to provide collective bargaining rights and procedures for state and local government employees, including teachers and employees of government-operated health care facilities. For example, in 1984 the state of Illinois enacted a comprehensive labor relations law for its public employees, which contains many provisions that are comparable to provisions within Title VII of the Civil Service Reform Act for federal employees.

The following sources are recommended for a review of legislation governing collective bargaining for state, local, and municipal government employees: Richard Kearney, ***Labor Relations in the Public Sector,*** 2nd ed. rev. (New York: Marcel Dekker, 1992); John Piskulich, ***Collective Bargaining in State and Local Government*** (New York: Praeger, 1992); and Benjamin Aaron, Joyce Najita, and James L. Stern, ***Public Sector Bargaining,*** 2nd ed. (Washington, D.C.: Bureau of National Affairs, 1988).

Act. This was the thrust of a decision of the Supreme Court in 1974, in which the Court defined managerial employees as those with the right to effectively recommend the hiring or firing of employees. Therefore not all persons with supervisory responsibilities are managerial for purposes of the Act.

The 1974 amendments to LMRA (Public Law 93–360) brought all private health care institutions, whether or not operated for a profit, under the coverage of the Act. Section 2(14) defines a private health care institution as "any hospital, convalescent hospital, health maintenance organization, health clinic, nursing home, extended care facility, or other institution devoted to the care of sick, infirm, or aged person."

An *employer* is defined in the law as including "any person acting as an agent of an employer, directly or indirectly." A *person* is defined to include "one or more individuals, labor organizations, partnerships, associations, legal representatives, trustees, trustees in bankruptcy, or receivers."

The term *labor organization* means any organization, agency, or employee representation committee or plan in which employees participate and that exists for the purpose, in whole or in part, of dealing with employers concerning grievances, labor disputes, wages, rate of pay, hours of employment, or conditions of work.

Section 2(12) defines the meaning of the term *professional employee,* for which specific organizational rights are guaranteed in a later section.

Sections 3, 4, 5, 6. The National Labor Relations Board

Section 3 creates the NLRB as an independent regulatory agency to administer the Act. The NLRB consists of five members appointed by the President of the United States.

Section 3 also authorizes the appointment of a General Counsel of the Board, who is given supervisory authority over the Board attorneys and officers and employees in the regional offices of the Board.

Sections 4 and 5 outline certain compensation, procedural, and administrative authorities granted to the NLRB by the Congress.

However, the key section is Section 6, which gives the Board authority to establish rules and regulations necessary to carry out provisions of the LMRA. In effect, this section empowers the NLRB to administer and interpret the labor law as it deems appropriate to the case situations encountered.

In order to do this, the Board has developed various standards—for the most part, dollar sales or volume standards—by which it determines whether or not a business or some other form of enterprise is deemed to be interstate commerce and thus covered under the provisions of the Act.[4] The Board has developed detailed rules, policies, and procedures

[4] For example, the NLRB has used a standard of $500,000 total annual volume of business to determine whether a retail enterprise should be considered interstate. For ***nonretail businesses*** the Board uses two tests; (A) direct sales to consumers in other states or indirect sales through others, called outflow, of at least $50,000 a year; or (B) direct purchases of goods from suppliers from other states or indirect purchases through others, called inflow, of at least $50,000 a year.

Among the NLRB jurisdictional standards in effect at the time of writing this text are the following:

Office buildings: Total annual revenue of $100,000, of which $25,000 or more is derived from organizations that meet any of the standards except the indirect outflow and indirect inflow standards established for nonretail enterprises.

Public utilities: At least $250,000 total annual volume of business, or $50,000 direct or indirect outflow or inflow.

by which it determines appropriate collective bargaining units, holds representational elections, investigates labor disputes, and conducts other such matters. As with any body of law, the regulatory agency changed with its administration and the courts breathe life into the law. Prior to judicial and agency review and interpretation, law is only cold words on a page. The law is shaped into the living, substantive framework for conduct by those who must interpret and apply it to the facts and circumstances of the cases tried under its provisions. As such, the law changes and evolves over time. Specifically, the Board and courts are asked to rule on new and different applications of the law. Therefore, the current status of the law is simply a snapshot in time.

Newspapers: At least $200,000 total annual volume of business.

Radio, telegraph, television, and telephone enterprises: At least $100,000 total annual volume of business.

Hotels, motels, and residential apartment houses: At least $500,000 total annual volume of business.

Transit systems: At least $250,000 total annual volume of business.

Taxicab companies: At least $500,000 total annual volume of business.

Law firms and legal assistance programs: At least $250,000 gross annual revenues.

Employers that provide social services: At least $250,000 gross annual revenues.

Privately operated health care institutions: At least $250,000 total annual volume of business for hospitals; at least $100,000 for nursing homes, visiting nurses' associations, and related facilities; and at least $250,000 for all other types of private health care institutions defined in the 1974 amendments to the Act.

Associations: These are regarded as a single employer in that the annual business of all association members is totaled to determine whether any of the standards apply.

Enterprises in the territories and the District of Columbia: The jurisdictional standards apply in the territories; all businesses in the District of Columbia come under NLRB jurisdiction.

National defense: Jurisdiction is asserted over all enterprises affecting commerce when their operations have a substantial impact on national defense, whether or not the enterprises satisfy any other standard.

Private universities and colleges: At least $1 million gross annual revenue from all sources (excluding contributions not available for operating expenses because of limitations imposed by the grantor).

Symphony orchestras: At least $1 million gross annual revenue from all sources (excluding contributions not available for operating expenses because of limitations imposed by the grantor).

Ordinarily, if an enterprise does the total annual volume of business listed in the standard, it will necessarily be engaged in activities that "affect" commerce. The Board must find, however, based on evidence, that the enterprise does in fact affect commerce. The Board has established the policy that if an employer whose operations affect commerce refuses to supply the Board with information concerning total annual business, and so on, the Board may dispense with this requirement and exercise jurisdiction.

Section 14(c)(1) authorizes the Board, in its discretion, to decline to exercise jurisdiction over any class or category of employers where a labor dispute involving such employers is not sufficiently substantial to warrant the exercise of jurisdiction, provided that it cannot refuse to exercise jurisdiction over any labor dispute over which it would have asserted jurisdiction under the standards it had in effect on August 1, 1959.

Finally, the NLRB has adopted other standards and policies that it uses in determining its jurisdiction, depending upon various types of businesses and unique conditions involved. For example, the NLRB asserts jurisdiction over gambling casinos when these enterprises are legally operated and their total annual revenue from gambling is at least $500,000.

Section 7. Rights of Employees

This section, often referred to as the "employee bill of rights," is the portion of the Act in which Congress enumerated the rights employees must have for them to have a balance of economic power with their employers. It guarantees employees the right to self-organization; to form, join, or assist labor organizations; to bargain collectively through representatives of their own choosing; and to engage in (or refrain from) certain other concerted activities for the purpose of collective bargaining or other mutual aid or protection.

Examples of employee rights protected by Section 7 are:

Forming or attempting to form a union among the employees of a company.

Joining a union.

Assigning a union to organize the employees of any company.

Going out on strike for the purpose of attempting to obtain improved wages, hours, or other conditions of employment.

Refraining from joining a union (in the absence of a valid union shop agreement).

An individual does not have to be a member of a labor union or involved in promoting a labor union in order to have the rights enumerated in Section 7. Included in Part One are several cases in which individual employees claimed that what their employers had prohibited them from doing were "protected concerted activities."

UNFAIR LABOR PRACTICES: EMPLOYERS

Originally in the Wagner Act, Section 8 listed five unfair labor practices. These five unfair labor practices were only those activities of employers that were proscribed. With the 1947 amendment, unfair labor practices against unions were added. The unfair labor practices of employers are listed in Section 8(a) of the Act; those of labor organizations in Section 8(b). Section 8(e) lists an unfair labor practice that can be committed only by an employer and a labor organization acting together.

Section 8(a) (1) Employers are forbidden from engaging in practices that would interfere with, restrain, or coerce employees in the exercise of rights guaranteed by Section 7.

Section 8(a) (1) constitutes a broad statement against interference by the employer; employers violate this section whenever they commit any unfair labor practices. Thus, a violation of Section 8(a) (2), (3), (4), or (5) also results in a violation of Section 8(a) (1).

Various acts of an employer may independently violate Section 8(a) (1). Examples of such violations are:

Threatening employees with loss of jobs or benefits if they should join or vote for a union.

Threatening to close down the plant if a union should be organized in it.

Questioning employees about their union activities or membership in such circumstances as will tend to restrain or coerce the employees.

Spying on union gatherings, or pretending to spy.

Granting wage increases deliberately timed to discourage employees from forming or joining a union.

Threatening to terminate credit at the company store or to force employees to move out of company housing if the union wins bargaining rights for the employees.

Circulating antiunion petitions among employees.

Section 8(a) (2) Employers may not dominate or interfere with the formation or administration of any labor organization or contribute financial or other support to it.

In this regard, the Board distinguishes between "domination" of a labor organization and conduct that amounts to little more than illegal "interference." When a union is found to be "dominated" by an employer, the Board will normally order the organization completely disestablished as a representative of employees. But if the organization is found only to have been supported by employer assistance amounting to mere interference with the organization, the Board usually orders the employer to stop such support and to withhold recognition from the organization until it has been certified by the Board as a bona fide representative of employees.

In recent years, there has been a growth in various types of labor-management cooperative efforts such as quality circles, quality-of-worklife programs, total quality management, employee involvement groups, labor-management participation teams, and the like. In general, these types of efforts do not of themselves violate Section 8(a) (2), unless the effort leads to a circumvention of the negotiated labor agreement or some other interference with union or employee rights. At the time of writing of this text, a number of NLRB cases were in various stages of litigation. When finally decided, these cases may further clarify the permissible limits of activities of these forms of labor-management cooperation.

An employer violates Section 8(a) (2) by engaging in activities such as:

Assisting employees in organizing a union or an employee representation plan by providing financial support, legal counsel, or active encouragement.

Conducting a straw vote to determine whether employees favor an inside union, as opposed to one affiliated with one of the national unions.

Signing a union security contract with an inside union to forestall an organizing drive by an outside union.

Exerting pressure on employees to join a particular union.

Permitting a union to solicit dues checkoff authorizations from new employees as they go through the hiring process.

Permitting one union to solicit employees on company premises, while denying a competing union this same privilege.

Section 8(a) (3) This section prohibits discrimination in the hiring or tenure of employment or any term or condition of employment that tends to encourage or discourage membership in any labor organization. This provision, together with Section 8(b) (2), prohibits the closed shop, in which only persons who already hold membership in a labor organization may be hired. It also prohibits discriminatory hiring-hall arrangements by which only persons who have "permits" from a union may be hired. However, a proviso of this section permits an employer and labor union to agree to a union shop, where employees may be required to join a union after 30 days of employment (unless a union shop is prohibited by state law as provided for under Section 14[b] of the Act).

Section 8(a) (3) provides that an employee may be discharged for failing to pay the required union initiation fees and dues uniformly required by the exclusive bargaining representative under a lawful union shop contract. The section provides further, however, that no employer can justify any discriminatory action against an employee for nonmembership in a union if the employer has reason to believe that membership in the union was not open to the employee on the same terms and conditions that apply to others, or that the employee was denied membership in the union for some reason other than failure to pay regular dues and initiation fees.[5]

Some examples of types of discrimination in employment prohibited by Section 8(a) (3) include:

Discharging employees because they urged other employees to join a union.

Refusing to reinstate employees when jobs they are qualified for are open because they took part in a union's lawful strike.

Granting of "superseniority" to those hired to replace employees engaged in a lawful strike.

Demoting employees because they circulated a union petition among other employees asking the employer for an increase in pay.

Discontinuing an operation at one plant and discharging the employees involved, followed by opening the same operation at another plant with new employees, because the employees at the first plant joined a union.

Refusing to hire qualified applicants for jobs because they belong to a union. It would also be a violation if the qualified applicants were refused employment because they did not belong to a union, or because they belonged to one union rather than another.

Section 8(a) (4) Employers may not discharge or otherwise discriminate against employees because they have filed charges or given testimony under this Act. Examples of violations of this section are:

Refusing to reinstate employees when jobs they are otherwise qualified for are open because they filed charges with the NLRB claiming their layoffs were based on union activity.

Demoting employees because they testified at an NLRB hearing.

Section 8(a) (5) It is an unfair labor practice for an employer to fail to or refuse to bargain collectively with the representatives of the employees. The meaning of "bargaining collectively" is more specifically outlined in Section 8(d) of the Act. Section 8(d) has been applied and interpreted in many cases, and its provisions are among the most significant requirements of the Act.

[5] As a result of a case decided by the U.S. Supreme Court (***Communication Workers of America [CWA] v. Beck,*** June 29, 1988, 128 LRRM 2729), a nonmember of a union in a union shop bargaining unit who objects to paying a dues equivalent may be required to pay only that portion of the dues fee which is used for the actual and legitimate costs of representational activities of the union (e.g., collective bargaining, contract administration, and grievance adjustment).

Examples of employer violations of Section 8(a) (5) are:

Refusing to meet with representatives of a certified union because employees have threatened to go on strike.

Insisting that the union withdraw its demand for a union shop before the company would enter negotiations over a contract.

Insisting that members of the negotiating committee of the union be composed of employees of the company.

Refusing to discuss with union representatives an increase in the price of coffee served in the company cafeteria.

Announcing a wage increase without consulting the union.

Refusing to supply union negotiators with cost and other data concerning a group insurance plan covering the employees.

Subcontracting certain work to another employer without notifying the union that represents the affected employees and without giving the union an opportunity to bargain concerning the change in working conditions of the employees.

UNFAIR LABOR PRACTICES: LABOR ORGANIZATIONS

Experience under the Wagner ACT of 1935, illuminated the need to regulate certain behaviors of labor organizations. Therefore, the Congress included section 8(b) of the ACT to prescribe certain practices of labor organizations deemed harmful to collective bargaining. The 1947 and 1959 amendments to the Act made certain activities of labor unions unfair labor practices.

Section 8(b) (1) (A) A labor organization or its agents are forbidden "to restrain or coerce employees in the exercise of the rights guaranteed in section 7." The section also provides that it is not intended to "impair the rights of a labor organization to prescribe its own rules" concerning membership in the labor organization.[6]

Examples of restraint or coercion that violate Section 8(b) (1) (A) when done by a union or its agents include the following:

Mass picketing in such numbers that nonstriking employees are physically barred from entering the plant.

Committing acts of force or violence on the picket line, or in connection with a strike.

Threatening to do bodily injury to nonstriking employees.

Threatening employees that they will lose their jobs unless they support the union's activities.

Stating to employees who oppose the union that those employees will lose their jobs if the union wins a majority in the plant.

[6] The regulation of the internal affairs of labor organizations is covered by the Labor-Management Reporting and Disclosure Act (Landrum-Griffin Act) of 1959; this Act is administered by the U.S. Department of Labor.

Entering into an agreement with an employer that recognizes the union as exclusive bargaining representative when it has not been chosen by a majority of the employees.

Fining or expelling members for crossing a picket line that is unlawful under the Act or which violates a no-strike agreement.

Fining employees for conduct in which they engaged after resigning from the union.

Fining or expelling members for filing unfair labor practice charges with the Board or for participating in an investigation conducted by the Board.

Maintaining a seniority arrangement with an employer under which seniority is based on the employee's prior representation by the union elsewhere.

Refusing to process a grievance in retaliation against an employee's criticism of union officers.

Section 8(b) (1) (B) A labor organization is prohibited from restraining or coercing an employer in the selection of its own bargaining representative. The prohibition applies regardless of whether the labor organization is the majority representative of the employees in the bargaining unit. The prohibition extends to coercion applied by a union to a union member who is a representative of the employer in the adjustment of grievances.

This section is violated by such conduct as the following:

Insisting on meeting only with a company's owners and refusing to meet with the attorney the company has engaged to represent it in contract negotiations, and threatening to strike to force the company to accept demands.

Striking against several members of an employer association that had bargained with the union as the representative of the employers and secured the signing of individual contracts by the struck employers.

Insisting during contract negotiations that the employer agree to accept working conditions that will be established by a bargaining group to which it does not belong.

Fining or expelling supervisors for the way they apply the bargaining contract while carrying out their supervisory functions.

Section 8(b) (2) This section bars a union from causing or attempting to cause an employer to discriminate against an employee in violation of Section 8(a) (3). It also prohibits the union from attempting to cause an employer to discriminate against an employee whose membership in the union had been denied or terminated, except where this action was taken by the union because the employee failed to "tender" the regular initiation fees and/or periodic dues uniformly required as a condition of acquiring or retaining membership in the union, where a union shop agreement is in effect.

Contracts or informal arrangements with a union under which an employer gives preferential treatment to union members are violations of Section 8(b) (2). It is not unlawful for an employer and a union to enter into an agreement whereby the employer agrees to hire new employees exclusively through the union hiring hall so long as there is neither a provision in the agreement nor a practice in effect that discriminates against nonunion members in favor of union members or otherwise discriminates on the basis of union membership obligations. Both the agreement and the actual operation of the hiring hall must be nondiscriminatory; referrals must be made without reference to union membership or irrelevant or arbitrary considerations such as race.

Examples of violations of Section 8(b) (2) are:

Causing an employer to discharge employees because they circulated a petition urging a change in the union's method of selecting shop stewards.

Causing an employer to discharge employees because they made speeches against a contract proposed by the union.

Making a contract that requires an employer to hire only members of the union or employees "satisfactory" to the union.

Causing an employer to reduce employees' seniority because they engaged in antiunion acts.

Refusing referral or giving preference on the basis of race or union activities in making job referrals to units represented by the union.

Seeking the discharge of an employee under a union security agreement for failure to pay a fine levied by the union.

Section 8(b) (3) This section requires a labor organization to bargain in good faith with an employer about wages, hours, and other conditions of employment if it is the representative of that employer's employees. This section imposes on labor organizations the same duty to bargain in good faith that is imposed on employers by Section 8(a) (5). Both the labor organization and the employer are required to follow the procedures within Section 8(d) before terminating or changing an existing contract.

Section 8(b) (3) not only requires that union representatives bargain in good faith with employers but also requires that the union carry out its bargaining duty fairly with respect to the employees it represents. A union, therefore, violates Section 8(b) (3) if it negotiates a contract that conflicts with that duty, or if it refuses to handle grievances under the contract for irrelevant or arbitrary reasons.

Section 8(b) (3) is violated by any of the following:

Insisting on the inclusion of illegal provisions in a contract, such as a closed shop or a discriminatory hiring hall.

Refusing to negotiate on a proposal for a written contract.

Striking against an employer who has bargained, and continues to bargain, on a multiemployer basis to compel it to bargain separately.

Refusing to meet with the attorney designated by the employer as its representative in negotiations.

Terminating an existing contract and striking for a new one without notifying the employer, the Federal Mediation and Conciliation Service (FMCS), and the state mediation service, if any.

Conditioning the execution of an agreement upon inclusion of a nonmandatory provision such as a performance bond.

Refusing to process a grievance because of the race, sex, or union activities of an employee for whom the union is the statutory bargaining representative.

Section 8(b) (4) This section forbids secondary boycotts and certain types of strikes and picketing; it is a very complicated section. Secondary boycotts; sympathy strikes or boycotts to force recognition of an uncertified union; a strike to substitute another bargaining representative for one certified by the Board; strikes over so-called union jurisdictional disputes or work assignments; and several other types of third-party pressure tactics are forbidden under this section.

More specifically, Section 8(b) (4) prohibits a labor organization from engaging in strikes or boycotts or taking other specified actions to accomplish certain purposes or "objects" as they are called in the Act. The actions are listed in clauses (i) and (ii); the objects are described in subparagraphs (A) through (D). A union commits an unfair labor practice if it takes any of the kinds of action listed in clauses (i) and (ii) as a means of accomplishing any of the objects listed in the four subparagraphs.

Clause (i) forbids a union to engage in a strike, or to induce or encourage a strike, work stoppage, or a refusal to perform services by "any individual employed by any person engaged in commerce or in an industry affecting commerce" for one of the objects listed in subparagraphs (A) through (D). Clause (ii) makes it an unfair labor practice for a union to "threaten, coerce, or restrain any person engaged in commerce or in an industry affecting commerce" for any of the proscribed objects.

Section 8(b) (4) (A) prohibits unions from engaging in actions specified in clause (i) or (ii) to compel an employer or self-employed person to join any labor or employer organization, or to force an employer to enter a hot cargo agreement prohibited by Section 8(e). In general, a "hot cargo" agreement is any arrangement where the primary employer is compelled not to handle materials from a third-party company, generally a nonunion third party described in greater detail in the discussion of Section 8(e).

Section 8(b) (4) (B) contains the Act's secondary boycott prohibitions. A secondary boycott occurs if a union has a dispute with Company A and in furtherance of that dispute causes the employees of Company B to stop handling the products of Company A, or otherwise forces Company B to stop doing business with Company A. The dispute is with Company A, called the primary employer; the union's action is against Company B, called the secondary employer; hence, the term *secondary boycott.* Section 8(b) (4) (B) also prohibits secondary action to compel an employer to recognize or bargain with a union that is not the certified representative of its employees.

The prohibitions of Section 8(b) (4) (B) do not protect a secondary employer from the incidental effects of union action that is taken directly against the primary employer. Thus, it is lawful for a union to urge employees of a secondary supplier at the primary employer's plant not to cross a picket line there. Section 8(b) (4) (B) also does not prohibit union efforts to prevent an employer from contracting out work customarily performed by its employees, even though an incidental effect of such conduct might be to compel that employer to cease doing business with the subcontractor.

When employees of a primary employer and those of a secondary employer work on the same premises, a special situation is involved and the usual rules do not apply. A typical example of the shared site or "common situs" situation occurs when a subcontractor with whom a union has a dispute is engaged at work on a construction site alongside other subcontractors with whom the union has no dispute. Picketing at a common situs is permissible if directed solely against the primary employer, but it is prohibited if directed against secondary employers regularly engaged at the site. In some situations a company may set aside, or reserve, a certain plant gate, or entrance to its premises, for the exclusive use of a contractor. If a union has a labor dispute with the company and pickets the company's premises, including the gate so reserved, the union may be held to have violated Section 8(b) (4) (B).

Section 8(b) (4) (C) forbids a labor organization to use clause (i) or (ii) conduct to force an employer to recognize or bargain with a labor organization other than the one that is currently certified as the representative of its employees.

Section 8(b) (4) (D) addresses jurisdictional and work assignment disputes. It forbids a labor organization from engaging in actions described in clauses (i) and (ii) for the purpose of forcing any employer to assign certain work to "employees in a particular labor organization or in a particular trade, craft, or class rather than to employees in another labor organization or in another trade, craft, or class." The Act sets up a special procedure for handling disputes over work assignments under Section 10(k).

A proviso to Section 8(b) (4) makes clear that it is not unlawful for a person to refuse to enter the premises of an employer if the employees of that employer are engaged in a lawful strike ratified or approved by a representative of these employees. Another provision permits informational picketing in various circumstances, so long as such publicity and information picketing does not have the effect of inducing any individual employed by any person other than a primary employer to refuse to pick up, deliver, or transfer goods or to refuse to perform services at the establishment of the employer involved in the dispute.

The following union activities are considered to be unfair labor practices under this section:

Picketing a company after three of its four partners refused to comply with the union's demand that they become members (8[b] [4] [A]).

Picketing or threatening to picket a retail store to compel that employer to enter into an agreement whereby that employer will only use a delivery service firm which has an agreement with the union (8[b] [4] [A]).

Picketing the premises of an employer to compel him to cease doing business with another employer who has refused to recognize the union (8[b] [4] [B]).

Threatening an employer by telling her that her business will be picketed if she continues to do business with another employer whom the union has designated as "unfair" (8[b] [4] [B]).

Directing union members not to pick up and deliver products from a plant where the drivers had voted to be represented by a different union, which had received certification from the NLRB (8[b] [4] [C]).

Engaging in a strike to attempt to force the employer to assign to it the job of installing metal doors when the employer had assigned the work to the members of another union (8[b] [4] [D]).

Section 8(b) (5) A union may not require employees under a union shop agreement to pay an initiation fee that the Board finds excessive or discriminatory. The section states that the Board shall consider in determination of these types of fees the practices and customs of labor organizations in the particular industry and the wages currently paid to employees affected. For example, a local union would probably violate this section by raising its initiation fee from $25 to $500, when other locals of the same union charged from $15 to $100 and the starting rate for the job was $240 per week.

Section 8(b) (6) This section prohibits what is commonly known as featherbedding. Unions may not force an employer to pay or deliver, or to agree to pay or deliver, any money or thing of value for services that are not performed or not to be performed. This section has been narrowly interpreted by the Board and does not include situations in which the work is performed, although it may be "unnecessary."

Section 8(b) (7) This provision prohibits a union that has not been certified as the bargaining agent from picketing or threatening to picket an employer for the purpose of obtaining recognition by that employer or acceptance by his workers as their bargaining representative. Both recognitional and organizational picketing constitute unfair labor practices when: the employer has recognized a certified union and a new representation election would be barred under the Act (8[b] [7] [A]); a valid NLRB election has been conducted during the previous 12 months (8[b] [7] [B]); or a representation petition has not been filed with the Board "within a reasonable period of time not to exceed 30 days from the commencement of such picketing" (8[b] [7] [C]).

However, this section does not prohibit picketing for the purpose of truthfully advising the public (including consumers) that the company does not employ union members or have a contract with a union unless the effect of the picketing is to interfere with deliveries, pickups, and other services required by the picketed employer.

Section 8(e) This complicated provision forbids both labor organizations and employers to enter into agreements commonly known as hot cargo agreements. These are defined as agreements in which the employer will not handle, use, sell, transport, or deal in any of the products of another employer as required or forced by the labor organization.

Both the construction and garment industries are exempted from the conditions of this section. In the construction industry the parties may agree to a clause that restricts the contracting or subcontracting of work to be performed at the construction site. Typically, the union and the employer agree that subcontracted work will go to an employer who has a contract with the union. A union may strike, picket, or engage in any other lawful activity in order to obtain such an agreement with the employer. A labor organization in the garment (apparel and clothing) industry may not only strike, picket, or engage in other lawful activity to obtain such an agreement, but it may also engage in such activities in order to enforce it.

Section 8(f) This section creates an exception for the construction industry to the 30-day limitation on requiring employees to join the union under a union shop agreement. Where a hiring hall is utilized the unions in the construction industry provide labor by referral to various employers who are signatory to the labor agreement. Therefore, a union and employer in the construction industry may enter into an agreement whereby employees must join the union not later than 7 days after the date of hire, rather than 30 days, as provided in Section 8(a) (3) for all other employers. The parties may enter into such an agreement without having first established the majority status of the union, as required in Section 9.

FREE SPEECH

Section 8(c) This section of the Act provides that the expression of any views, argument, or opinion shall not constitute or be evidence of an unfair labor practice "if such expression contains no threat of reprisal or force or promise of benefit." Examples of actions this provision does not protect, and that would be ruled as unfair labor practices, are:

An implied threat by an employer that the organization of a union would result in the loss of certain benefits for employees.

A threat by an employer to close down a plant to move to another location, in the event of a union's winning an election.

A statement by a management official to an employee that the employee will lose her job if the union wins a majority in the plant.

A promise by management that benefits will be improved if a union does not win the representational election.

THE MEANING OF COLLECTIVE BARGAINING

Section 8(d) This section defines collective bargaining and what the parties' mutual obligations are with respect to negotiation and agreement. This definition imposes a mutual obligation upon the employer and the representative of the employees:

> to meet at reasonable times and confer in good faith with respect to wages, hours, and other terms and conditions of employment or the negotiation of an agreement or any question arising thereunder and the execution of a written contract incorporating any agreement reached if requested by either party, but such obligation does not compel either party to agree to a proposal or require the making of a concession.

The duty to bargain thus covers all matters concerning rates of pay, hours of employment, or other conditions of employment. These are called mandatory subjects about which the employer, as well as the employees' representative, must bargain in good faith, although the law does not require "either party to agree to a proposal or require the making of a concession." As determined by the NLRB, mandatory subjects of bargaining include but are not limited to such matters as pensions for present and retired employees, bonuses, group insurance, grievance procedure, safety practices, seniority, procedures for discharge, layoff, recall, or discipline, and the union shop. On nonmandatory subjects, that is, matters that are lawful but not related to "wages, hours, and other conditions of employment," the parties are free to bargain and to agree, but neither party may insist on bargaining such subjects to an impasse.

Section 8(d) also requires that the parties to a collective agreement follow certain steps in terminating or modifying the agreement. Among these requirements are that the party wishing to terminate or modify a labor contract must notify the other party to the contract in writing about the proposed termination or modification 60 days before the date on which the contract is scheduled to expire. This party also must, within 30 days after the notice to the other party, notify the Federal Mediation and Conciliation Service (FMCS) of the existence of a dispute if no agreement has been reached by that time, and further notify at the same time any state or territorial mediation or conciliation agency in the state or territory where the dispute occurred.[7]

The NLRB has interpreted this section to mean that union employees who go on strike without following the prescribed steps for terminating or modifying the contract lose protection of the law. They may not be reinstated by the Board if the employer discharges them.

REPRESENTATIVES AND ELECTIONS

Section 9 of the Act is a lengthy section that governs the procedural and legal requirements for the designation of representatives and election of union representatives. It provides for three types of elections among employees:[8]

> *Representation elections* to determine the employees' choice of a collective bargaining agent. These are held upon petition of an individual, employer, employees, or a labor organization. Typically, the NLRB will not hold an election unless the petitioner can show that at least 30 percent of the employees involved have indicated their support for the union, or for an election.
>
> *Decertification elections* to determine whether or not the employees wish to withdraw the bargaining authority of the union. These are held upon the petition of the employees or a labor organization.
>
> *Deauthorization polls* to determine whether or not the employees wish to revoke the authority of their union to enter into a union shop contract.

Section 9(a) This section provides that the union representative designated by a majority of employees appropriate for collective bargaining becomes the exclusive representative of the employees in bargaining. When a union majority representative has been chosen, it becomes unlawful for an employer to bargain with anyone else.

Sections 9(b) and 9(c) These sections outline in general terms the "rules of the game" for the holding of NLRB elections. Included in 9(b) is the mandate for the Board to decide what group of employees constitutes an appropriate unit for bargaining. The appropriate bargaining unit may extend to one or more employers, to one or more plants of the same employer, or it may be a subdivision of a plantwide unit such as a unit of skilled craftsmen. It is up to the Board to consider similarities of skills, wages, and working conditions; the history of collective bargaining in the company; the wishes of the employees; and any other factors that the Board may consider important in determination of the appropriate unit. Thus, employees who possess common employment interests concerning wages, hours, and conditions of employment usually are grouped together in a bargaining unit. However, Section 9(b) specifically limits the Board in its determination of a bargaining unit in several ways. It may not include professional and nonprofessional employees in the same unit, unless a majority of the professional employees vote to be included in the unit. It also prohibits the Board from including plant guards in the same unit with other

[7] Procedures of the FMCS are described in Appendix B to this introductory section.

[8] The Board also conducts "expedited elections" in connection with Section 8(b) (7) (C) and employer last-offer elections in connection with Section 209 of the Act.

employees, and from certifying a union of guards if it also includes members who are not guards. The Board also may not use "the extent to which employees have organized" as the controlling factor in deciding the appropriate bargaining unit (Section 9[c] [5]).

Section 9(c) (1) authorizes the NLRB to direct an election and certify the results thereof, provided the record shows that a question of representation exists.

An election may be held by agreement between the employer and the individual or labor organization claiming to represent the employees. In such an agreement the parties state the time and place agreed on, the choices to be included on the ballot, and a method to determine who is eligible to vote. They also authorize the NLRB Regional Director to conduct the election.

If the parties are unable to reach an agreement, the Act authorizes the NLRB to order an election after a hearing. The Act also authorizes the Board to delegate to its Regional Directors the determination on matters concerning elections. Under this delegation of authority the Regional Directors can determine the appropriateness of the unit, direct an election, and certify the outcome. Upon the request of an interested party, the Board may review the action of a Regional Director, but such review does not stop the election process unless the Board so orders. The election details are left to the Regional Director. Such matters as who may vote, when the election will be held, and what standards of conduct will be imposed on the parties are decided in accordance with the Board's rules and its decisions.

Section 9(c) (3) prohibits the holding of an election in any collective bargaining unit or subdivision thereof in which a valid election has been held during the preceding 12-month period.

In summary, Section 9 is one of the key sections that constantly confront both unions and management in collective bargaining relationships, particularly in the formative stages of a labor union in its efforts to gain representational status.

SPECIAL PROVISIONS FOR HEALTH CARE INSTITUTIONS

Representation election procedures are the same for health care facilities as for other establishments.[9,10] Similarly, as to unfair labor practices, the health care area is covered by the same statutory provisions as those that forbid employer or union discrimination

[9] In 1975, the NLRB issued its first guidelines for representational units in private health care institutions. In a series of cases—217 NLRB 131–138—these guidelines limited the number of bargaining units to avoid "proliferation" of units in health care organizations. In 1984, the NLRB ruled that it was no longer going to be held to a "community of interest" standard and would begin using a "disparity of interest" standard in health care bargaining unit determination. (See decision of the NLRB, St. Francis Hospital and IBEW Local 474, 271 NLRB No. 160.) However, in 1988, the NLRB developed and proposed new bargaining unit guidelines for acute-care hospitals. Up to eight bargaining units would be considered "appropriate" under the new rules. These are registered nurses, physicians, other professionals, technicians, skilled maintenance employees, office clerical employees, guards, and all other nonprofessional employees. In 1991, the U.S. Supreme Court upheld the NLRB's regulations recognizing up to eight categories of employee bargaining units in hospitals. Further, the Court affirmed the NLRB's authority to "engage in substantive rulemaking."

[10] In a 1994 decision of the U.S. Supreme Court (***NLRB v. Health Care and Retirement Corporation of America***), the Court held that one of the NLRB's previous tests for determining

against employees, failure to bargain in good faith, certain unlawful union picketing, and employer domination or support of a labor organization.

But with a goal of minimizing work stoppages at health care institutions and providing continuity of patient care, Congress in 1974 wrote into the Act another unfair labor practice—*Section 8(g)*. It prohibits a labor organization from striking or picketing a health care institution, or engaging in any other concerted refusal to work, without first giving the employer and FMCS a 10-day notice of such action. The section specifies, "The notice shall state the date and time that such action will commence. The notice, once given, may be extended by the written agreement of both parties."

Additionally, a series of special provisions for the health care industry were added to Section 8(d) of the Act. These health care amendments call for special dispute-settling procedures. A 90-day written notice must be served by employer or union of intent to terminate or modify a collective bargaining contract (30 days more than required by the Act elsewhere). If the dispute continues, the FMCS and similar state agencies must be notified at the 60-day point. If a dispute arises in bargaining for an initial contract, 30 days' notice must be given by the union to the employer, FMCS, and the appropriate agency. In either a contract termination-modification or initial contract dispute, under Section 213 of the Act, the FMCS may, if disagreement continues, invoke a 30-day no-strike, no-lockout period and set up a fact-finding board to make settlement recommendations, while continuing its mediation-conciliation efforts.

All else failing, the 10-day strike or picketing notice must be given as required by Section 8(g).

PREVENTION OF UNFAIR LABOR PRACTICES

Section 10 is very important in that it outlines the procedural requirements and limitations that are placed upon the Board and interested parties in processing unfair labor practice cases. The LMRA is not a criminal statute. The NLRB's actions are designed to stop unfair labor practices and to restore situations to their "original states"—those that prevailed before the violations occurred—insofar as possible. The orders of the Board serve basically to remedy the situation, not to punish persons who may have violated its provisions. The NLRB is authorized by Section 10(c) not only to issue a cease-and-desist order but "to take such affirmative action, including reinstatement of employees with or without back pay, as will effectuate the policies of this Act."

Sections 10(a), 10(b), 10(c), 10(d) These sections of the Act outline the general procedures by which the NLRB and its regional offices investigate, attempt to prevent, and/or remedy unfair labor practices. Generally, an unfair labor practice charge must be filed with an office of the NLRB within six months of the date of the occurrence of the alleged

whether or not nurses were supervisors was inconsistent with the LMRA. The Court held that concerning nurses, the Board had improperly interpreted and applied the meaning of the phrase "in the interest of the employer" within Section 2(11) of the Act to exclude nurses from supervisory status. Although the ultimate impact of this decision is not clear, at this writing it would appear that the NLRB will be required to adopt case-by-case tests and analyses of nurses' duties in order to determine whether certain nurses are properly classified as "professional employees" or "supervisors."

unfair labor practice. (As of 2005, 53 regional and other field offices of the NLRB were located in major cities in various sections of the country.) When a charge is received in the office of the Board, an agent will investigate to see whether formal proceedings are warranted.[11] If the regional office of the NLRB is unable to resolve the issue, and the complaint warrants a full hearing, an Administrative Law Judge (ALJ) from the Board's independent Division of Judges may be assigned to conduct a full, formal hearing to take testimony and examine the evidence. If the opinion of the ALJ is that the evidence presented is not sufficient to justify a finding that an unfair labor practice has been committed, the ALJ will issue an order dismissing the complaint. However, if the ALJ is of the opinion that an unfair labor practice(s) has occurred, he or she will make an appropriate finding and issue a remedial order. In effect, the findings and orders of the ALJ become recommendations to the NLRB. If there is no appeal of the ALJ's decision, the decision and remedial order (if any) of the ALJ become the decision and the order of the Board. If the case is appealed, the NLRB itself will review the determination made by the ALJ and either reverse, modify, or affirm the decision and order of the ALJ.

A remedial order issued by the NLRB usually will require the person, union, or company involved to cease and desist from the unfair labor practice(s) and to take affirmative action designed to remedy the effects of the unfair labor practice(s). Since the LMRA is not intended to designate criminal penalties, these orders will be designed to restore equity to the situation on the assumption that such equity is necessary to guarantee rights protected under the Act. Examples of affirmative actions required of employers are:

Disestablishing a union dominated by the employer.

Offering to hire employees denied employment because of their prounion attitudes or activities.

Offering to reemploy workers who were discharged for union activity; reimburse the employees for all lost wages, including interest; and restore full seniority and all other rights, including promotions, pay increases, pension privileges, and vacation rights that would have been received had the discriminatory discharges not occurred.

Upon request, bargaining collectively with a union as the exclusive representative of the employees in a certain described unit and signing a written agreement if an understanding is reached.

Examples of affirmative actions required of unions are:

Notification to the employee and the employer that the union does not object to the reinstatement or employment of certain persons who were discharged or denied employment as a result of certain discriminatory actions by the union.

Ordering the union to refund dues and fees illegally collected, including interest.

Directing the union to bargain collectively with a certain employer and sign a written agreement if an agreement is negotiated.

[11] In the event that the regional office refuses to issue a formal complaint, the person(s) who filed the charge may appeal this decision to the General Counsel of the NLRB, who has final authority to determine whether to issue a formal complaint (Section 3[d]).

Sections 10(e) and 10(f) These sections provide the legal avenues for the enforcement of Board orders and for appeal for relief from Board orders by an employer or union that believes that an order has been issued in error. Normally, the first appeal from an order of the regional office or ALJ will go to the full NLRB itself in Washington, D.C. The NLRB, in order to seek enforcement of its orders, may petition a federal district court or circuit court of appeals for appropriate relief or a restraining order. Appeals from a Board or district court order may be made to a federal appeals court, and ultimate appeal can be made to the U.S. Supreme Court. The large majority of cases, however, are not appealed to the federal courts but are decided at Board regional office and/or national NLRB levels.[12]

Section 10(j) This section empowers the NLRB to petition a U.S. District Court for appropriate temporary relief or a restraining order in certain unfair labor practice complaints.

Section 10(k) Special procedures for hearing and adjudicating jurisdictional disputes are provided for in this section.

Section 10(l) This section provides for special priority procedures, including court injunctions, to stop quickly certain acts, strikes, and boycotts that may result in "irreparable harm" to the employer. For the most part, these are directed against secondary boycotts and certain types of organizational picketing.

MISCELLANEOUS PROVISIONS

The remainder of the LMRA, although quite extensive in length, is not nearly so important to the duty to bargain collectively as are the provisions discussed to this point. Only brief mention will be made of the more salient miscellaneous provisions covered in the remaining sections that have not been mentioned previously.

Sections 11 and 12—Investigatory Powers and Penalties As the title suggests, Sections 11 and 12 outline the legal powers of investigation given the NLRB by the Congress and provide for penalties for violation of the Act.

Sections 13 to 18—Limitations Sections 13 through 18 state a series of limitations that the Act is not to be construed as interfering with or diminishing. Except where specifically provided for in the Act, Section 13 guarantees that the right to strike is still a right not to be diminished by the LMRA. Section 14(a) permits supervisors to be members of a labor organization, but states that employers are not required to bargain with supervisors as part of labor organizations. Section 14(b) permits so-called right-to-work laws in states where these laws are enacted. Specifically, Section 14(b) allows states to ban union shop contracts if they so choose. In 1985, Idaho became the 21st state to have a right-to-work law on its statute books. In 2001, Oklahoma became the 22nd state to have a right-to-work law on its

[12] Statistically over the years, about 65 percent of the unfair labor practice charges filed with the NLRB are dismissed by the regional offices of the Board or withdrawn by the parties. Of the remainder, over 90 percent usually are settled at the regional office level. Of the cases that are tried by an ALJ, about two-thirds are appealed to the full NLRB. Some 20 to 30 percent of Board decisions are appealed to Courts of Appeal; typically the NLRB is sustained in whole or part in over 80 percent of these cases. Only a few cases are reviewed by the Supreme Court, usually some five or fewer annually. Of the unfair labor practice complaints issued by the NLRB's General Counsel, about four-fifths are charges against employers.

statute book, although provisions of the Oklahoma law may be challenged in the courts. The majority of right-to-work states are located in the southern part of the United States.

Section 19 As amended in legislation passed in 1980, this section provides that any employee who has conscientious objections to joining or financially supporting a labor organization, based on the traditional tenets of a bona fide religion or sect, shall not be required to do so. However, such an employee may be required to make charitable contributions in an amount equal to union dues and initiation fees, and may be required to pay the costs incurred by the union of any requested grievance-arbitration procedure instituted on his/her behalf.[13]

The language in this section defining conscientious objection is not to be construed in such a way as to discriminate among religions or to favor any religious views.

Sections 201 through 205 These sections created and outline the functions of the FMCS and also a National Labor Relations Panel to advise the President on problems of industrial relations. The National Labor Relations Panel, consisting of representatives of management, labor, and the public, has been of limited influence in recent years.

Sections 206 through 210 The national emergency strike provisions, giving the President power to intervene in those disputes that are a national emergency. National emergencies are very narrowly defined in the Act and therefore these provisions have been invoked sparingly. These provisions have not been invoked since the late-1970s.

Section 301 This section provides that suits for violation of contracts between an employer and a union may be brought in the federal district courts. Unions are made responsible for the acts of their agents; however, money judgments assessed against a labor organization in a district court are enforceable only against the organization as an entity and not against individual members per se.

Section 303 Strikes and boycotts enumerated in and which violate Section 8(b)(4) are made illegal, as well as being unfair labor practices. Employers may sue to collect damages for injury resulting from such activities.

Summary

As the reader can appreciate, the Act is a relatively complex body of law. The expression of the Congressional intent in statutory language is but the first step toward the establishment of public policy. The public policy circuit is completed with the National Labor Relations Board and the judiciary interpreting and applying the congressionally authored language. The case law frames in specific meaning what those cold words on the page

[13] Section 19 was added to the Act in the 1974 amendments for health care institutions, but without the grievance-arbitration proviso. In a case decided in 1990 by the U.S. Court of Appeals for the Sixth Circuit (Cincinnati), that Court held that Section 19 "facially discriminated" among religions in violation of the First Amendment of the U.S. Constitution, "because it exempts from union membership only those employees who are members of bona fide religious organizations having the beliefs described in the statute." Thus Section 19 created "a denominational preference by conferring a benefit on members of the religious organizations described in the statute." According to this Court, when a law differentiates among religions, it "must be invalidated." At the time of writing of this text, it was not clear whether the U.S. Supreme Court would review this case on appeal (or another similar case) to decide upon the constitutional validity of Section 19 of LMRA.

mean in the context of heated human relations. Only through the examination and analyses of the cases decided by the NLRB and courts can a full appreciation of the law be had.

Other provisions of the statute are not analyzed here. This does not mean that these other provisions of the law are unimportant. In fact, they are important in specific, albeit rare, instances. What has been examined here are the highlights, that is, the provisions of the statute that give rise to the most litigation over the years, and that are of the greatest consequence to the day-in and day-out conduct of collective bargaining relations across this country.

Appendix **A**

Edited and Updated Excerpts from the Informational Pamphlet *The NLRB—What It Is, What It Does**

In recent fiscal years, the NLRB has received annually about 35,000 cases of all kinds. Over three-fourths are unfair labor practice charges. Over the years, charges filed against employers have outnumbered those filed against unions by about 2 to 1. Charges are filed by individual workers, employers, and unions.

WHAT IS THE STRUCTURE OF THE NLRB?

The NLRB has five Board Members and a General Counsel, each appointed by the President with Senate consent. The Board Members are appointed to five-year terms, the term of one Member expiring each year. The statute specifies that the President shall designate one Member to serve as Chairman of the Board. The General Counsel is appointed to a four-year term. Reappointments may be made.

Headquartered in Washington, the NLRB has 34 Regional Offices, 2 Subregional Offices, and 17 Resident or smaller field offices throughout the country.

The NLRB's judicial functions are by law separate from its prosecuting functions. The five-member Board acts primarily as a quasi-judicial body in deciding cases upon formal records, generally upon review from Regional Directors' or Administrative Law Judges' decisions. The General Counsel is responsible for the investigation and prosecution of charges of violations of the Act, and he has general supervision of the Regional Offices.

WHO ENFORCES BOARD ORDERS?

The NLRB has no statutory independent power of enforcement of its orders, but it may seek enforcement in the U.S. Courts of Appeals. Similarly, parties aggrieved by its orders may seek judicial review in the courts.

* Published by the NLRB, Washington, D. C. The NLRB has a website at the following address: **http://www.nlrb.gov/publicat.html**

Annually, the U.S. Courts of Appeals hand down numerous decisions related to enforcement and/or review of Board orders in unfair labor practice proceedings. Of these, about 85 percent affirm the Board in whole or in part.

HOW DO NLRB PROCEDURES WORK?

Upon the filing of an unfair labor practice charge with an NLRB Regional Office, members of the professional staff of that office investigate circumstances from which the charge arises, in order to determine whether formal proceedings are warranted. Approximately one-third of the unfair labor practice allegations are found, after investigation, to require legal disposition. In such a case, the Regional Office works with the parties in an attempt to achieve a voluntary settlement adequate to remedy the alleged violation. A very substantial number of cases are settled at this stage. If a case cannot be settled, then a formal complaint is issued, and the case is heard before an Administrative Law Judge.

NLRB Administrative Law Judges conduct formal hearings and issue decisions, which may be appealed to the five-member Board; if they are not appealed, the Administrative Law Judges' recommended orders become orders of the Board.

The NLRB's traditional emphasis on voluntary disposition of cases at all stages means that less than 5 percent of the unfair labor practice charges and other cases originally filed with the Regional Offices are litigated all the way through to a decision of the Board. Yet, despite the small percentage, the Board is still called on to decide on the order of 1,000 unfair labor practice cases and 500 representation cases each year.

In representation election cases, the Regional Directors have the authority to process all petitions, rule on contested issues, and direct elections or dismiss the requests, subject to review by the Board on limited grounds. The NLRB, through its Regional Offices, conducts thousands of representation elections a year, in which hundreds of thousands of employees exercise their free choice by secret ballot.

National Labor Relations Board—Statistical Information for Fiscal Year 2004*

The following statistics reflect the work of the various NLRB divisions during the 2004 fiscal year and are based on actions taken during that year and previous years.

Fiscal year 2004 saw an intake of 31,787 cases—a number close to that docketed during recent years, although considerably smaller than the NLRB caseloads during the late 1970s and early 1980s, which were 50,000 or more cases annually. During FY04, the intake of unfair labor practices cases was 29,966, a number somewhat higher than in several previous years. There were 4,545 representation petitions filed in FY04, a figure somewhat similar for several recent years.

The Board's Regional Offices conducted 2,764 representational elections during fiscal year 2004. Some 197,105 employees were eligible to vote in these elections. Unions won 52.0 percent of these elections, a percentage somewhat higher to that during most of

* These statistics are from the Sixty-ninth Annual Report of the NLRB, Tables 1, 4, 11, and 14, September 30, 2004.

the 1980s and 90s, but lower than the 55 percent or so during most of the 1970s. During FY04, the Board conducted 422 decertification elections. Unions were decertified in 65 percent of these elections, about the same percentage as in several previous years.

As remedies, the amount paid to employees as back pay in FY04 was about $207 million; some 2,000 employees were offered reinstatement. The amount paid to employees in FY99 as reimbursement for fees, dues, and fines was about $1,415,985.

Appendix B

The Federal Mediation and Conciliation Service (FMCS)*

FEDERAL MEDIATION AND CONCILIATION SERVICE MISSION

Promoting the development of sound and stable labor-management relations.

Preventing or minimizing work stoppages by assisting labor and management to settle their disputes through mediation.

Advocating collective bargaining, mediation, and voluntary arbitration as the preferred processes for settling issues between employers and representatives of employees.

Developing the art, science, and practice of dispute resolution.

And fostering constructive joint relationships of labor and management leaders to increase their mutual understanding and ability to resolve common problems.

The Federal Mediation and Conciliation Service (FMCS) is an independent agency of the Federal Government that uses mediation and other techniques to promote labor-management peace. Since we're a government agency our services are offered without charge.

Our specific mission is to prevent or minimize labor-management disputes having a significant impact on interstate commerce or national defense throughout the nation, both in the private and public sectors of the economy, excepting in the railroad and airline industries.

The Service was created by the Labor Management Relations Act of 1947 (LMRA—the Taft-Hartley Act). Mediation is an established process for resolving disputes between individuals or groups who sincerely seek a peaceful solution to their differences. It represents a rational alternative to the use of force.

The mediator is a neutral third party whose method and practice may vary. A mediator will listen, review, analyze, reason, explore, and suggest possible solutions to the problems that face representatives of both management and labor.

* Appendix B consists of adapted excerpts (some updated) from publications of the FMCS, Washington, D.C. Appendix C at the end of the Part Two introductory section will include additional FMCS material concerning preventive and grievance mediation and alternative dispute resolution.

Collective bargaining is an indispensable ingredient of a free industrial society. Mediation is a time-tested and productive tool that helps preserve and strengthen our collective bargaining system.

WHAT IS THE FEDERAL MEDIATION AND CONCILIATION SERVICE?

The Federal Mediation and Conciliation Service is an independent agency of the Federal Government created by Congress with a director appointed by the President. Its primary duty is to promote labor-management peace.

This responsibility is fulfilled by providing mediation assistance in preventing and settling collective bargaining controversies. For this purpose Federal mediators, known as commissioners, are stationed strategically throughout the country.

The Labor Management Relations Act requires that parties to a labor contract must file a dispute notice if agreement is not reached in 30 days—60 days in the health care industry—in advance of a contract termination or reopening date. The notice must be filed with the FMCS and the appropriate state or local mediation agency.

The notice alerts the service to possible bargaining trouble. If the case falls within the jurisdiction of the service, the regional office then assigns a mediator to check with the employer and union involved to see whether assistance is required.

It is a tribute to the nation's free collective bargaining system that in the overwhelming majority of cases in which notices are filed, the employers and unions reach agreements on their own without requiring mediation aid. Yet in those cases where third-party assistance is needed, it makes good sense to call in the mediator.

WHO ARE THE MEDIATORS?

Mediators are carefully selected and trained. About equal numbers have backgrounds with management and with labor, and many have had some experience with both.

Mediators are picked for the job because of their knowledge and demonstrated skill in collective bargaining. Regardless of background, they are required to maintain strict objectivity as representatives of the public interest.

HOW DOES THE MEDIATOR WORK?

While methods and circumstances vary, the mediator generally will confer first with one of the parties involved and then with the other to get their versions of the pending difficulties. Then with these problems firmly in mind, the mediator usually will call joint conferences with the employer and union representatives.

Mediators function informally, meeting separately and jointly with the parties to help them find some mutually acceptable solutions.

It is part of the job to listen, review, analyze, suggest, advise, reason, and explore all possible means of reaching an agreement.

The mediator can restart stalled negotiations, improve the bargaining atmosphere, encourage mutual discussions, explore alternative solutions, suggest specific contract clauses that have worked well elsewhere, and provide needed economic data and other information.

A mediator can help bring reason and a fresh viewpoint to the dilemma, and often points the way to a solution. In fact, some 95 percent of disputes receiving active mediation assistance are settled peacefully—without a strike. These are pretty good odds that mediation is a course worth trying.

Even when there is no stalemate or imminent deadline—but mounting difficulties clearly signal real trouble ahead—the mediator can be helpful. The mediator's training and skill often can spot difficulties early and help develop a remedy.

Mediation is a free and voluntary process. It can be requested by either party to a dispute, or the mediator may volunteer to help. There is no cost to either side, and mediation is available not only to private industry but also in public employment and other situations.

The mediator works hard to promote cooperation and understanding between management and labor not only during contract disputes but at other times as well in order to improve day-to-day relations in the workplace.

Through the use of FMCS technical services, unions and employers, with the assistance of the mediator, can improve the labor-management climate. The mediator can give advisory assistance on specific problems and encourage the use of joint labor-management committees. A skilled mediator can provide training and information to improve the knowledge and skill of both parties, can identify trends and developments, can encourage early bargaining to forestall deadline tensions, and will respond to the various needs of labor and management, including government employers and labor organizations, to improve their bargaining relationships.

In addition, the service helps employers and unions in selecting arbitrators to adjudicate labor-management disputes by maintaining a large roster of qualified arbitrators. When an employer and a union need an arbitrator, they need only to notify the service, and the service will provide a listing of qualified arbitrators in their area who are available to hear the dispute. When the parties have agreed on one name from the list, they notify FMCS and the service notifies the arbitrator.

The following aggregate statistics reflect the work of FMCS offices as summarized in a statistical report of the FMCS for fiscal year 2000.

Federal Mediation and Conciliation Service—Statistical Information for Fiscal Year 2000*

In FY00, the FMCS maintained 68 field offices throughout the United States. Slightly under 200 mediators were on staff. The FMCS received 38,242 formal notices of pending bargaining situations. Of these, 19,574 (about 50 percent) were assigned to mediators. Mediators actively participated and gave mediation assistance in 6,321 cases (about one-third of cases assigned). Mediators conducted 18,699 meetings with the parties in FY00. In the negotiation cases where FMCS mediators were monitoring or were active in mediating, there were only 400 work stoppages (about 2 percent of the FMCS cases assigned).

The above FMCS aggregate statistics for FY00 were generally similar to FMCS statistics for recent fiscal years.

* These statistics were provided in a memorandum from the Office of the General Counsel of the FMCS dated April 12, 2001.

Selected Bibliography

Better, Maurice B. *Contract Bargaining Handbook for Local Union Leaders.* Washington, D.C.: Bureau of National Affairs, 1993.

Cihon, Patrick J., and James O. Castagnera. *Labor and Employment Law.* 2nd ed. Boston: Wadsworth, 1993.

Diamond, Virginia. *Organizing Guide for Local Unions.* Silver Springs, Md.: George Meany Center for Labor Studies/Labor Heritage Press, 1992.

Dunlop, John T. *Industrial Relations Systems.* Boston: Harvard Business School Press, 1993.

The Federal Mediation and Conciliation Service. Washington, D.C.: Federal Mediation and Conciliation Service, U.S. Government Printing Office.

Feldacker, Bruce. *Labor Guide to Labor Law.* 3rd ed. Englewood Cliffs, N.J.: Prentice Hall, 1990.

Forces of Change: Report of the Mediator Task Force on the Future of FMCS. 2nd ed. Washington, D.C.: Federal Mediation and Conciliation Service, U.S. Government Printing Office, 1996.

Fossum, John A. *Labor Relations: Development, Structure, Process.* 6th ed. Burr Ridge, Ill.: Richard D. Irwin, 1995.

Franckiewicz, Matthew M. *Winning at the NLRB.* Washington, D.C.: Bureau of National Affairs, 1995. (Cumulative supplement, 1999).

Friedman, Sheldon, et al. *Restoring the Promise of American Labor Law.* Ithaca, N.Y.: ILR Press, 1994.

Garren, Brent; Elaine S. Fox; and John C. Truesdale. *How to Take a Case before the NLRB.* 7th ed. Washington, D.C.: Bureau of National Affairs, 2000.

Goldman, Alvin L. *Settling for More: Mastering Negotiating Strategies and Techniques.* Washington, D.C.: Bureau of National Affairs, 1991.

Gould, William B. Agenda for Reform, *The Future of Employment Relationships and the Law.* Cambridge, Mass.: MIT Press, 1993.

Gould, William B. *A Primer on American Labor Law.* 3rd ed. Cambridge, Mass.: MIT Press, 1997.

A *Guide to Basic Law and Procedures under the National Labor Relations Act.* Washington, D.C.: Office of the General Counsel of the NLRB, U.S. Government Printing Office.

Hardin, Patrick; James R. LaVaute; and Timothy P. O'Reilly. *The Developing Labor Law: The Boards, the Courts, and the National Labor Relations Act.* Washington, D.C.: Bureau of National Affairs, 1992. (Cumulative supplement, 1999).

Herman, E. Edward. *Collective Bargaining and Labor Relations.* 4th ed. Upper Saddle River, N.J.: Prentice Hall, 1998.

Hilgert, Raymond L. *Labor Agreement Negotiations.* 6th ed. Cincinnati: Dame/Thomson Learning, 2001.

Holley, William H., Jr., and Kenneth M. Jennings. *The Labor Relation Process.* 4th ed. Chicago: Dryden Press, 1991.

Jacobs, Eva E., ed. *Handbook of U.S. Labor Statistics.* 2nd ed. Lanham, Md.: Bernan Press, 1997.

Katz, Harry C., and Thomas A. Kochan. *An Introduction to Collective Bargaining and Industrial Relations.* 2nd ed. New York: McGraw-Hill, 2000.

Labor Law Reporter. Chicago: Commerce Clearing House.

Labor Relations Reference Manual. Washington, D.C.: Bureau of National Affairs.

Lawler, John. *Unionization and Deunionization: Strategy, Tactics, and Outcomes.* Columbia: University of South Carolina Press, 1990.

Leap, Terry L. *Collective Bargaining and Labor Relations.* 2nd ed. Upper Saddle River, N.J.: Prentice Hall, 1995.

Lebow, Richard N. *The Act of Bargaining.* Baltimore: Johns Hopkins University Press, 1996.

Leslie, Douglas. *Labor Law in a Nutshell.* 3rd ed. St. Paul, Minn.: West, 1992.

Lewicki, Roy J.; David M. Saunders; and John W. Minton. *Essentials of Negotiation.* Burr Ridge, III.: Richard D. Irwin, 1997.

Loughran, Charles S. *Negotiating a Labor Contract: A Management Handbook.* 2nd ed. Washington, D.C.: Bureau of National Affairs, 1992.

Mills, Daniel Quinn. *Labor-Management Relations.* 5th ed. New York: McGraw-Hill, 1994.

NLRB Decisions. Chicago: Commerce Clearing House.

Norris, Jeffrey A., and Michael J. Shershin, Jr. *How to Take a Case before the NLRB.* 6th ed. Washington, D.C.: Bureau of National Affairs, 1992.

Player, Mack. *Federal Law of Employment Discrimination in a Nutshell.* 3rd ed. St. Paul, Minn.: West, 1992.

Reynolds, Lloyd G.; Stanley H. Masters; and Colletta H. Moser. *Labor Economics and Labor Relations.* 11th ed. Upper Saddle River, N.J.: Prentice Hall, 1998.

Schlossberg, Stephen I., and Judith A. Scott. *Organizing and the Law.* Washington, D.C.: Bureau of National Affairs, 1991.

Sloane, Arthur A., and Fred Witney. *Labor Relations.* 9th ed. Englewood Cliffs, N.J.: Prentice Hall, 1997.

Strauss, George; Daniel Gallagher; and Jack Fiorito, eds. *The State of the Unions.* Madison, Wis.: Industrial Relations Research Association, 1991.

Taylor, Benjamin J., and Fred Witney. *Labor Relations Law.* 7th ed. Upper Saddle River, N.J.: Prentice Hall, 1996.

Twomey, David. *Labor and Employment Law.* 10th ed. Cincinnati: West/TTP, 1997.

Voos, Paula, ed. *Contemporary Collective Bargaining in the Private Sector.* Madison, Wis.: Industrial Relations Research Association, 1994.

Walton, Richard E.; Joel E. Cutcher-Gershenfeld; and Robert B. McKersie. *Strategic Negotiations: A Theory of Change in Labor-Management Negotiations.* Boston: Harvard Business School Press, 1994.

Weiler, Paul. *Governing the Workplace: The Future of Labor and Employment Law.* Cambridge, Mass.: Harvard University Press, 1990.

Zack, Arnold M., and Richard I. Bloch. *Labor Agreement in Negotiation and Arbitration.* 2nd ed. Washington, D.C.: Bureau of National Affairs, 1996.

Partial Text of the Labor Management Relations Act, 1947[1]:

(as amended by the Labor-Management Reporting and Disclosure Act of 1959,[2] by Public Law 93–360, 1974, and by Public Law 96–593, 1980)

[PUBLIC LAW 101-80TH CONGRESS]
[CHAPTER 120—1ST SESSION]
AN ACT

To amend the National Labor Relations Act, to provide additional facilities for the mediation of labor disputes affecting commerce, to equalize legal responsibilities of labor organizations and employers, and for other purposes.

Be it enacted by the Senate and House of Representatives of the United States of America in Congress assembled.

Short Title and Declaration of Policy

Section 1. (a) This Act may be cited as the "Labor Management Relations Act, 1947."

(b) Industrial strife, which interferes with the normal flow of commerce and with the full production of articles and commodities for commerce, can be avoided or substantially minimized if employers, employees, and labor organizations each recognize under law one another's legitimate rights in their relations with each other, and above all recognize under law that neither party has any right in its relations with any other to engage in acts or practices which jeopardize the public health, safety, or interest.

It is the purpose and policy of this Act, in order to promote the full flow of commerce, to prescribe the legitimate rights of both employees and employers in their relations affecting commerce, to provide orderly and peaceful procedures for preventing the interference by either with the legitimate rights of the other, to protect the rights of individual employees in their relations with labor organizations whose activities affect commerce, to define and proscribe practices on the part of labor and management which affect commerce and are inimical to the general welfare, and to protect the rights of the public in connection with labor disputes affecting commerce.

[1] Also Known as the Taft-Hartley Act.
[2] Also known as the Landrum-Griffin Act, Public Law 86–257.

Title I—Amendment of National Labor Relations Act

Section 101. The National Labor Relations Act is hereby amended to read as follows:

Findings and Policies

Section 1. The denial by some employers of the right of employees to organize and the refusal by some employers to accept the procedure of collective bargaining lead to strikes and other forms of industrial strife or unrest, which have the intent or the necessary effect of burdening or obstructing commerce by (a) impairing the efficiency, safety, or operation of the instrumentalities of commerce; (b) occurring in the current of commerce; (c) materially affecting, restraining, or controlling the flow of raw materials or manufactured or processed goods from or into the channels of commerce, or the prices of such materials or goods in commerce; or (d) causing diminution of employment and wages in such volume as substantially to impair or disrupt the market for goods flowing from or into the channels of commerce.

The inequality of bargaining power between employees who do not possess full freedom of association or actual liberty of contract, and employers who are organized in the corporate or other forms of ownership association substantially burdens and affects the flow of commerce, and tends to aggravate recurrent business depressions, by depressing wage rates and the purchasing power of wage earners in industry and by preventing the stabilization of competitive wage rates and working conditions within and between industries.

Experience has proved that protection by law of the right of employees to organize and bargain collectively safeguards commerce from injury, impairment, or interruption, and promotes the flow of commerce by removing certain recognized sources of industrial strife and unrest, by encouraging practices fundamental to the friendly adjustment of industrial disputes arising out of differences as to wages, hours, or other working conditions, and by restoring equality of bargaining power between employers and employees.

Experience has further demonstrated that certain practices by some labor organizations, their officers, and members have the intent or the necessary effect of burdening or obstructing commerce by preventing the free flow of goods in such commerce through strikes and other forms of industrial unrest or through concerted activities which impair the interest of the public in the free flow of such commerce. The elimination of such practices is a necessary condition to the assurance of the rights herein guaranteed.

It is hereby declared to be the policy of the United States to eliminate the causes of certain substantial obstructions to the free flow of commerce and to mitigate and eliminate these obstructions when they have occurred by encouraging the practice and procedure of collective bargaining and by protecting the exercise by workers of full freedom of association, self-organization, and designation of representatives of their own choosing, for the purpose of negotiating the terms and conditions of their employment or other mutual aid or protection.

Definitions

Section 2. When used in this Act—

(1) The term "person" includes one or more individuals, labor organizations, partnerships, associations, corporations, legal representatives, trustees, trustees in bankruptcy, or receivers.

(2) The term "employer" includes any person acting as an agent of an employer, directly or indirectly, but shall not include the United States or any wholly owned Government corporation, or any Federal Reserve Bank, or any State or political subdivision thereof, or any person subject to the Railway Labor Act, as amended from time to time, or any labor organization (other than when acting as an employer), or anyone acting in the capacity of officer or agent of such labor organization.

(3) The term "employee" shall include any employee, and shall not be limited to the employees of a particular employer, unless the Act explicitly states otherwise, and shall include any individual whose work has ceased as a consequence of, or in connection with, any current labor dispute or because of any unfair labor practice, and who has not obtained any other regular and substantially equivalent employment, but shall not include any individual employed as an agricultural laborer, or in the domestic service of any family or person at his home, or any individual employed by his parent or spouse, or any individual having the status of an independent contractor, or any individual employed as a supervisor, or any individual employed by an employer subject to the Railway Labor Act, as amended from time to time, or by any other person who is not an employer as herein defined.

(4) The term "representatives" includes any individual or labor organization.

(5) The term "labor organization" means any organization of any kind, or any agency or employee representation committee or plan, in which employees participate and which exists for the purpose, in whole or in part, of dealing with employers concerning grievances, labor disputes, wages, rates of pay, hours of employment, or conditions of work.

(6) The term "commerce" means trade, traffic, commerce, transportation, or communication among the several States, or between the District of Columbia or any Territory of the United States and any State or Territory, or between any foreign country and any State, Territory, or the District of Columbia, or within the District of Columbia or any Territory, or between points in the same State but through any other State or any Territory or the District of Columbia or any foreign country.

(7) The term "affecting commerce" means in commerce, or burdening or obstructing commerce or the free flow of commerce, or having led or tending to lead to a labor dispute burdening or obstructing commerce or the free flow of commerce.

(8) The term "unfair labor practice" means any unfair labor practice listed in section 8.

(9) The term "labor dispute" includes any controversy concerning terms, tenure or conditions of employment, or concerning the association or representation of persons in negotiating, fixing, maintaining, changing, or seeking to arrange terms or conditions of employment, regardless of whether the disputants stand in the proximate relation of employer and employee.

(10) The term "National Labor Relations Board" means the National Labor Relations Board provided for in section 3 of this Act.

(11) The term "supervisor" means any individual having authority, in the interest of the employer, to hire, transfer, suspend, lay off, recall, promote, discharge, assign, reward, or discipline other employees, or responsibility to direct them, or to adjust their grievances, or effectively to recommend such action, if in connection with the foregoing the exercise of such authority is not of a merely routine or clerical nature, but requires the use of independent judgment.

(12) The term "professional employee" means

(a) any employee engaged in work (i) predominantly intellectual and varied in character as opposed to routine mental, manual, mechanical, or physical work; (ii) involving the consistent exercise of discretion and judgment in its performance; (iii) of such a character that the output produced or the result accomplished cannot be standardized in relation to a given period of time; (iv) requiring knowledge of an advanced type in a field of science or learning customarily acquired by a prolonged course of specialized intellectual instruction and study in an institution of higher learning or a hospital, as distinguished from a general academic education or from an apprenticeship or from training in the performance of routine mental, manual, or physical process; or

(b) any employee, who (i) has completed the courses of specialized intellectual instruction and study described in clause (iv) of paragraph (a), and (ii) is performing related work under the supervision of a professional person to qualify himself to become a professional employee as defined in paragraph (a).

(13) In determining whether any person is acting as an "agent" of another person so as to make such other person responsible for his acts, the question of whether the specific acts performed were actually authorized or subsequently ratified shall not be controlling.

(14) The term "health care institution" shall include any hospital, convalescent hospital, health maintenance organization, health clinic, nursing home, extended care facility, or other institution devoted to the care of the sick, infirm, or aged person.

National Labor Relations Board

Section 3. (a) The National Labor Relations Board (hereinafter called the "Board") . . . as an agency of the United States, shall consist of five . . . members, appointed by the President by and with the advice and consent of the Senate . . . for terms of five years each, excepting that any individual chosen to fill a vacancy shall be appointed only for the unexpired term of the member whom he shall succeed. The President shall designate one member to serve as Chairman of the Board. Any member of the Board may be removed by the President, upon notice and hearing, for neglect of duty or malfeasance in office, but for no other cause.

(b) The Board is authorized to delegate to any group of three or more members any or all of the powers which it may itself exercise. The Board is also authorized to delegate to its regional directors its powers under section 9 to determine the unit appropriate for the purpose of collective bargaining, to investigate and provide for hearings, and determine whether a question of representation exists, and to direct an election or take a secret ballot under subsection (c) or (e) of section 9 and certify the results thereof, except that upon the filing of a request therefor with the Board by any interested person, the Board may review any action of a regional director delegated to him under this paragraph, but such a review shall not, unless specifically ordered by the Board, operate as a stay of any action taken by the regional director. A vacancy in the Board shall not impair the right of the remaining members to exercise all of the powers of the Board, and three members of the Board shall, at all times, constitute a quorum of the Board, except that two members shall constitute a quorum of any group designated pursuant to the first sentence hereof. The Board shall have an official seal which shall be judicially noticed.

(c) The Board shall at the close of each fiscal year make a report in writing to Congress and to the President stating in detail the cases it has heard, the decisions it has rendered, and an account of all moneys it has disbursed.

(d) There shall be a General Counsel of the Board who shall be appointed by the President, by and with the advice and consent of the Senate, for a term of four years. The General Counsel of the Board shall exercise general supervision over all attorneys employed by the Board (other than trial examiners and legal assistants to Board members) and over the officers and employees in the regional offices. He shall have final authority, on behalf of the Board, in respect of the investigation of charges and issuance of complaints under section 10, and in respect of the prosecution of such complaints before the Board, and shall have such other duties as the Board may prescribe or as may be provided by law. In case of a vacancy in the office of the General Counsel the President is authorized to designate the officer or employee who shall act as General Counsel during such vacancy, but no person or persons so designated shall so act (1) for more than 40 days when the Congress is in session unless a nomination to fill such vacancy shall have been submitted to the Senate, or (2) after the adjournment *sine die* of the session of the Senate in which such nomination was submitted.

* * * * *

[Omitted: Sections 4 and 5—Compensation and offices of the NLRB.]

Section 6. The Board shall have authority from time to time to make, amend, and rescind, in the manner prescribed by the Administrative Procedure Act, such rules and regulations as may be necessary to carry out the provisions of this Act.

Rights of Employees

Section 7. Employees shall have the right to self-organization, to form, join, or assist labor organizations, to bargain collectively through representatives of their own choosing, and to engage in other concerted activities for the purpose of collective bargaining or other mutual aid or protection, and shall also have the right to refrain from any or all of such activities except to the extent that such right may be affected by an agreement requiring membership in a labor organization as a condition of employment as authorized in section 8(a) (3).

Unfair Labor Practices

Section 8. (a) It shall be an unfair labor practice for an employer—

(1) to interfere with, restrain, or coerce employees in the exercise of the rights guaranteed in section 7;

(2) to dominate or interfere with the formation or administration of any labor organization or contribute financial or other support to it: *Provided,* that subject to rules and regulations made and published by the Board pursuant to section 6, an employer shall not be prohibited from permitting employees to confer with him during working hours without loss of time or pay;

(3) by discrimination in regard to hire or tenure of employment or any term or condition of employment to encourage or discourage membership in any labor organization: *Provided,* that nothing in this Act, or in any other statute of the United States, shall preclude an employer from making an agreement with a labor organization (not established, or assisted by any action defined in section 8(a) of this Act as an unfair labor practice) to require as a condition of employment membership therein on or after the 30th day following the beginning of such employment or the effective date of such agreement, whichever is the later, (i) if such labor organization is the representative of the employees as provided in section 9(a), in the appropriate collective bargaining unit covered by such agreement when made, and (ii) unless following an election held as provided in section 9(e) within one year preceding the effective date of such agreement, the Board shall have certified that at least a majority of the employees eligible to vote in such election have voted to rescind the authority of such labor organization to make such an agreement: *Provided further,* that no employer shall justify any discrimination against an employee for nonmembership in a labor organization (A) if he has reasonable grounds for believing

that such membership was not available to the employee on the same terms and conditions generally applicable to other members, or (B) if he has reasonable grounds for believing that membership was denied or terminated for reasons other than the failure of the employee to tender the periodic dues and the initiation fees uniformly required as a condition of acquiring or retaining membership;

(4) to discharge or otherwise discriminate against an employee because he has filed charges or given testimony under this Act;

(5) to refuse to bargain collectively with the representatives of his employees, subject to the provisions of section 9(a).

(b) It shall be an unfair labor practice for a labor organization or its agents—

(1) to restrain or coerce (A) employees in the exercise of the rights guaranteed in section 7: *Provided,* that this paragraph shall not impair the right of a labor organization to prescribe its own rules with respect to the acquisition or retention of membership therein; or (B) an employer in the selection of his representatives for the purposes of collective bargaining or the adjustment of grievances;

(2) to cause or attempt to cause an employer to discriminate against an employee in violation of subsection (a) (3) or to discriminate against an employee with respect to whom membership in such organization has been denied or terminated on some ground other than his failure to tender the periodic dues and the initiation fees uniformly required as a condition of acquiring or retaining membership;

(3) to refuse to bargain collectively with an employer, provided it is the representative of his employees subject to the provisions of section 9(a);

(4) (i) to engage in, or to induce or encourage any individual employed by any person engaged in commerce or in any industry affecting commerce to engage in, a strike or a refusal in the course of his employment to use, manufacture, process, transport, or otherwise handle or work on any goods, articles, materials, or commodities or to perform any services; or (ii) to threaten, coerce, or restrain any person engaged in commerce or in an industry affecting commerce, where in either case an object thereof is:

(A) forcing or requiring any employer or self-employed person to join any labor or employer organization or to enter into any agreement which is prohibited by section 8(e);

(B) forcing or requiring any person to cease using, selling, handling, transporting, or otherwise dealing in the products of any other producer, processor, or manufacturer, or to cease doing business with any other person, or forcing or requiring any other employer to recognize or bargain with a labor organization as the representative of his employees unless such labor organization has been certified as the representative of such employees under the provisions of section 9: *Provided,* that nothing contained in this clause (B) shall be construed to make unlawful, where not otherwise unlawful, any primary strike or primary picketing;

(C) forcing or requiring any employer to recognize or bargain with a particular labor organization as the representative of his employees if another labor organization has been certified as the representative of such employees under the provisions of section 9;

(D) forcing or requiring any employer to assign particular work to employees in a particular labor organization or in a particular trade, craft, or class rather than to employees in another labor organization or in another trade, craft, or class, unless such employer is failing to conform to an order or certification of the Board determining the bargaining representative for employees performing such work:

Provided, that nothing contained in this subsection (b) shall be construed to make unlawful a refusal by any person to enter upon the premises of any employer (other than his own employer), if the employees of such employer are engaged in a strike ratified or approved by a representative of such employees whom such employer is required to recognize under this Act: *Provided further,* that for the purposes of this paragraph (4) only, nothing contained in such paragraph shall be construed to prohibit publicity, other than picketing, for the purpose of truthfully advising the public, including consumers and members of a labor organization, that a product or products are produced by an employer with whom the labor organization has a primary dispute and are distributed by another employer, as long as such publicity does not have an effect of inducing any individual employed by any person other than the primary employer in the course of his employment to refuse to pick up, deliver, or transport any goods, or not to perform any services, at the establishment of the employer engaged in such distribution;

(5) to require of employees covered by an agreement authorized under subsection (a) (3) the payment, as a condition precedent to becoming a member of such organization, of a fee in an amount which the Board finds excessive or discriminatory under all the circumstances. In making such a finding, the Board shall consider,

among other relevant factors, the practices and customs of labor organizations in the particular industry, and the wages currently paid to the employees affected;

(6) to cause or attempt to cause an employer to pay or deliver or agree to pay or deliver any money or other thing of value, in the nature of an exaction, for services which are not performed or not to be performed; and

(7) to picket or cause to be picketed, or threaten to picket or cause to be picketed, any employer where an object thereof is forcing or requiring an employer to recognize or bargain with a labor organization as the representative of his employees, or forcing or requiring the employees of an employer to accept or select such labor organization as their collective bargaining representative, unless such labor organization is currently certified as the representative of such employees:

(A) where the employer has lawfully recognized in accordance with this Act any other labor organization and a question concerning representation may not appropriately be raised under section 9(c) of this Act;

(B) where within the preceding 12 months a valid election under section 9(c) of this Act has been conducted; or

(C) where such picketing has been conducted without a petition under section 9(c) being filed within a reasonable period of time not to exceed 30 days from the commencement of such picketing: *Provided,* that when such a petition has been filed the Board shall forthwith, without regard to the provisions of section 9(c) (1) or the absence of a showing of a substantial interest on the part of the labor organization, direct an election in such unit as the Board finds to be appropriate and shall certify the results thereof: *Provided further,* that nothing in this subparagraph (C) shall be construed to prohibit any picketing or other publicity for the purpose of truthfully advising the public (including consumers) that an employer does not employ members of, or have a contract with, a labor organization, unless an effect of such picketing is to induce any individual employed by any other person in the course of his employment, not to pick up, deliver or transport any goods or not to perform any services.

Nothing in this paragraph (7) shall be construed to permit any act which would otherwise be an unfair labor practice under this section 8(b).

(c) The expressing of any views, argument, or opinion, or the dissemination thereof, whether in written, printed, graphic, or visual form, shall not constitute or be evidence of an unfair labor practice under any of the provisions of this Act, if such expression contains no threat of reprisal or force or promise of benefit.

(d) For the purposes of this section, to bargain collectively is the performance of the mutual obligation of the employer and the representative of the employees to meet at reasonable times and confer in good faith with respect to wages, hours, and other terms and conditions of employment, or the negotiation of an agreement, or any question arising thereunder, and the execution of a written contract incorporating any agreement reached if requested by either party, but such obligation does not compel either party to agree to a proposal or require the making of a concession:

Provided, that where there is in effect a collective bargaining contract covering employees in an industry affecting commerce, the duty to bargain collectively shall also mean that no party to such contract shall terminate or modify such contract, unless the party desiring such termination or modification—

(1) serves a written notice upon the other party to the contract of the proposed termination or modification 60 days prior to the expiration date thereof, or in the event such contract contains no expiration date, 60 days prior to the time it is proposed to make such termination or modification;

(2) offers to meet and confer with the other party for the purpose of negotiating a new contract or a contract containing the proposed modifications;

(3) notifies the Federal Mediation and Conciliation Service within 30 days after such notice of the existence of a dispute, and simultaneously therewith notifies any State or Territorial agency established to mediate and conciliate disputes within the State or Territory where the dispute occurred, provided no agreement has been reached by that time; and

(4) continues in full force and effect, without resorting to strike or lockout, all the terms and conditions of the existing contract for a period of 60 days after such notice is given or until the expiration date of such contract, whichever occurs later.

The duties imposed upon employers, employees, and labor organizations by paragraphs (2), (3), and (4) shall become inapplicable upon an intervening certification of the Board, under which the labor organization or individual, which is a party to the contract, has been superseded as or ceased to be the representative of the employees subject to the provisions of section 9(a), and the duties so imposed shall not be construed as requiring either party to discuss or agree to any modification of the terms and conditions contained in a contract for a fixed period, if such modification is to become effective before such terms and conditions can be reopened under the provisions of the contract. Any employee who engages in a strike within any notice period specified in this subsection, or who engages in any strike within the appropriate period specified in subsection (g) of this section shall lose his status as an employee of the employer engaged in the particular labor dispute, for the purposes of sections 8, 9, and 10 of this Act, as amended, but such loss of status for such employee shall terminate if and when he is reemployed by such employer. Whenever the collective bargaining involves employees of a health care institution, the provisions of this section 8(d) shall be modified as follows:

(A) The notice of section 8(d) (1) shall be 90 days; the notice of section 8(d) (3) shall be 60 days; and the contract period of section 8(d) (4) shall be 90 days.

(B) Where the bargaining is for an initial agreement following certification or recognition, at least 30 days' notice of the existence of a dispute shall be given by the labor organization to the agencies set forth in section 8(d) (3).

(C) After notice is given to the Federal Mediation and Conciliation Service under either clause (A) or (B) of this sentence, the Service shall promptly communicate with the parties and use its best efforts, by mediation and conciliation, to bring them to agreement. The parties shall participate fully and promptly in such meetings as may be undertaken by the Service for the purpose of aiding in a settlement of the dispute.

(e) It shall be an unfair labor practice for any labor organization and any employer to enter into any contract or agreement, express or implied, whereby such employer ceases or refrains or agrees to cease or refrain from handling, using, selling, transporting, or otherwise dealing in any of the products of any other employer, or to cease doing business with any other person, and any contract or agreement entered into heretofore or hereafter containing such an agreement shall be to such extent unenforceable and void: *Provided,* that nothing in this subsection (e) shall apply to an agreement between a labor organization and an employer in the construction industry relating to the contracting or subcontracting of work to be done at the site of the construction, alteration, painting, or repair of a building, structure, or other work: *Provided further,* that for the purposes of this subsection (e) and section 8(b) (4) (B) the terms "any employer," "any person engaged in commerce or in industry affecting commerce," and "any person" when used in relation to the terms "any other producer, processor, or manufacturer," "any other employer," or "any other person" shall not include persons in the relation of a jobber, manufacturer, contractor, or subcontractor working on the goods or premises of the jobber or manufacturer or performing parts of an integrated process of production in the apparel and clothing industry: *Provided further,* that nothing in this Act shall prohibit the enforcement of any agreement which is within the foregoing exception.

(f) It shall not be an unfair labor practice under subsections (a) and (b) of this section for an employer engaged primarily in the building and construction industry to make an agreement covering employees engaged (or who, upon their employment, will be engaged) in the building and construction industry with a labor organization of which building and construction employees are members (not established, maintained, or assisted by any action defined in section 8(a) of this Act as an unfair labor practice) because (1) the majority status of such labor organization has not been established under the provisions of section 9 of this Act prior to the making of such agreement, or (2) such agreement requires as a condition of employment, membership in such labor organization after the seventh day following the beginning of such employment or the effective date of the agreement, whichever is later, or (3) such agreement requires the employer to notify such labor organization of opportunities for employment with such employer, or gives such labor organization an opportunity to refer qualified applicants for such employment, or (4) such agreement specifies minimum training or experience qualifications for employment or provides for priority in opportunities for employment based upon length of service with such employer, in the industry or in the particular geographical area: *Provided,* that nothing in this subsection shall set aside the final proviso to section 8(a) (3) of this Act: *Provided further,* that any agreement which would be invalid, but for clause (1) of this subsection, shall not be a bar to a petition filed pursuant to section 9(c) or 9(e).

(g) A labor organization before engaging in any strike, picketing, or other concerted refusal to work at any health care institution shall, not less than 10 days prior to such action, notify the institution in writing and the Federal Mediation and Conciliation Service of that intention, except that in the case of bargaining for an initial agreement following certification or recognition the notice required by this subsection shall not be given until the expiration of the period specified in clause (B) of the last sentence of section 8(d) of this Act. The notice shall state the date and time that such action will commence. The notice, once given, may be extended by the written agreement of both parties.

Representatives and Elections

Section 9. (a) Representatives designated or selected for the purposes of collective bargaining by the majority of the employees in a unit appropriate for such purposes shall be the exclusive representatives of all the employees in such unit for the purposes of collective bargaining in respect to rates of pay, wages, hours of employment, or other conditions of employment: *Provided,* that any individual employee or a group of employees shall have the right at any time to present grievances to their employer and to have such grievances adjusted, without the intervention of the bargaining representative, as long as the adjustment is not inconsistent with the terms of a collective bargaining contract or agreement then in effect: *Provided further,* that the bargaining representative has been given opportunity to be present at such adjustment.

(b) The Board shall decide in each case whether, in order to assure to employees the fullest freedom in exercising the rights guaranteed by this Act, the unit appropriate for the purposes of collective bargaining shall be the employer unit, craft unit, plant unit, or subdivision thereof: *Provided,* that the Board shall not (1) decide that any unit is appropriate for such purposes if such unit includes both professional employees and employees who are not professional employees unless a majority of such professional employees vote for inclusion in such unit; or (2) decide that any craft unit is inappropriate for such purposes on the ground that a different unit has been established by a prior Board determination, unless a majority of the employees in the proposed craft unit vote against separate representation; or (3) decide that any unit is appropriate for such purposes, if it includes, together with other employees, any individual employed as a guard to enforce against employees and other persons rules to protect property of the employer or to protect the safety of persons on the employers' premises; but no labor organization shall be certified as the representative of employees in a bargaining unit of guards if such organization admits to membership, or is affiliated directly or indirectly with an organization which admits to membership, employees other than guards.

(c) (1) Wherever a petition shall have been filed, in accordance with such regulations as may be prescribed by the Board—

(A) by an employee or group of employees or any individual or labor organization acting in their behalf alleging that a substantial number of employees (i) wish to be represented for collective bargaining and that their employer declines to recognize their representative as the representative defined in section 9(a), or (ii) assert that the individual or labor organization, which has been certified or is being currently recognized by their employer as the bargaining representative, is no longer a representative as defined in section 9(a); or

(B) by an employer, alleging that one or more individuals or labor organizations have presented to him a claim to be recognized as the representative defined in section 9(a),

the Board shall investigate such petition and if it has reasonable cause to believe that a question of representation affecting commerce exists shall provide for an appropriate hearing upon due notice. Such hearing may be conducted by an officer or employee of the regional office, who shall not make any recommendations with respect thereto. If the Board finds upon the record of such hearing that such a question of representation exists, it shall direct an election by secret ballot and shall certify the results thereof.

(2) In determining whether or not a question of representation affecting commerce exists, the same regulations and rules of decision shall apply irrespective of the identity of the persons filing the petition or the kind of relief sought and in no case shall the Board deny a labor organization a place on the ballot by reason of an order with respect to such labor organization or its predecessor not issued in conformity with section 10(c).

(3) No election shall be directed in any bargaining unit or any subdivision within which, in the preceding 12-month period, a valid election shall have been held. Employees engaged in an economic strike who are not entitled to reinstatement shall be eligible to vote under such regulations as the Board shall find are consistent with the purposes and provisions of this Act in any election conducted within 12 months after the commencement of the strike. In any election where none of the choices on the ballot receives a majority, a runoff shall be conducted, the ballot providing for a selection between the two choices receiving the largest and second largest number of valid votes cast in the election.

(4) Nothing in this section shall be construed to prohibit the waiving of hearings by stipulation for the purposes of a consent election in conformity with regulations and rules of decision of the Board.

(5) In determining whether a unit is appropriate for the purposes specified in subsection (b) the extent to which the employees have organized shall not be controlling.

(d) Whenever an order of the Board made pursuant to section 10(c) is based in whole or in part upon facts certified following an investigation pursuant to subsection (c) of this section and there is a petition for the enforcement or review of such order, such certification and the record of such investigation shall be included in the transcript of the entire record required to be filed under section 10(e) or 10(f), and thereupon the decree of the court enforcing, modifying, or setting aside in whole or in part the order of the Board shall be made and entered upon the pleadings, testimony, and proceedings set forth in such transcript.

(e) (1) Upon the filing with the Board, by 30 per centum or more of the employees in a bargaining unit covered by an agreement between their employer and a labor organization made pursuant to section 8(a) (3), of a petition alleging they desire that such authority be rescinded, the Board shall take a secret ballot of the employees in such unit and certify the results thereof to such labor organization and to the employer.

(2) No election shall be conducted pursuant to this subsection in any bargaining unit or any subdivision within which, in the preceding 12-month period, a valid election shall have been held.

Prevention of Unfair Labor Practices

Section 10. (a) The Board is empowered, as hereinafter provided, to prevent any person from engaging in any unfair labor practice (listed in section 8) affecting commerce. This power shall not be affected by any other means of adjustment or prevention that has been or may be established by agreement, law, or otherwise: *Provided,* that the Board is empowered by agreement with any agency of any State or Territory to cede to such agency jurisdiction over any cases in any industry (other than mining, manufacturing, communications, and transportation except where predominantly local in character) even though such cases may involve labor disputes affecting commerce, unless the provision of the State or Territorial statute applicable to the determination of such cases by such agency is inconsistent with the corresponding provision of this Act or has received a construction inconsistent therewith.

(b) Whenever it is charged that any person has engaged in or is engaging in any such unfair labor practice, the Board, or any agent or agency designated by the Board for such purposes, shall have power to issue and cause to be served upon such person a complaint stating the charges in that respect, and containing a notice of hearing before the Board or a member thereof, or before a designated agent or agency, at a place therein fixed, not less than five days after the serving of said complaint: *Provided,* that no complaint shall issue based upon any unfair labor practice occurring more than six months prior to the filing of the charge with the Board and the service of a copy thereof upon the person against whom such a charge is made, unless the person aggrieved thereby was prevented from filing such charge by reason of service in the armed forces, in which event the six-month period shall be computed from the day of his discharge. Any such complaint may be amended by the member, agent, or agency conducting the hearing or the Board in its discretion at any time prior to the issuance of an order based thereon. The person so complained of shall have the right to file an answer to the original or amended complaint and to appear in person or otherwise and give testimony at the place and time fixed in the complaint. In the discretion of the member, agent, or agency conducting the hearing or the Board, any other person may be allowed to intervene in the said proceeding and to present testimony. Any such proceeding shall, so far as practicable, be conducted in accordance with the rules of evidence applicable in the district courts of the United States under the rules of civil procedure for the district courts of the United States, adopted by the Supreme Court of the United States pursuant to the Act of June 19, 1934 (U.S.C., title 28, secs. 723-B, 723-C).

(c) The testimony taken by such member, agent, or agency or the Board shall be reduced to writing and filed with the Board. Thereafter, in its discretion, the Board upon notice may take further testimony or hear argument. If upon the preponderance of the testimony taken the Board shall be of the opinion that any person named in the complaint has engaged in or is engaging in any such unfair labor practice, then the Board shall state its findings of fact and shall issue and cause to be served on such person an order requiring such person to cease and desist from such unfair labor practice, and to take such affirmative action including reinstatement of employees with or without back pay, as will effectuate the policies of this Act: *Provided,* that where an order directs reinstatement of an employee, back pay may be required of the employer or labor organization, as the case may be, responsible for the discrimination suffered by him: *And provided further,* that in determining whether a complaint shall issue alleging a violation of section 8(a) (1) or section 8(a) (2), and in deciding such cases, the same regulations and rules of decision shall apply irrespective of whether or not the labor organization affected is affiliated with a labor organization national or international in scope. Such order may further require such person to make reports from time to time showing the extent to which it has complied with the order. If upon the preponderance of the testimony taken the Board shall not be of the opinion that the person named in the complaint has engaged in or is engaging in any such unfair labor practice, then the Board shall state its findings of fact and shall issue an order dismissing the said complaint.

No order of the Board shall require the reinstatement of any individual as an employee who has been suspended or discharged, or the payment to him of any back pay, if such individual was suspended or discharged for cause. In case the evidence is presented before a member of the Board, or before an examiner or examiners thereof, such member, or such examiner or examiners, as the case may be, shall issue and cause to be served on the parties to the proceeding a proposed report, together with a recommended order, which shall be filed with the Board and if no exceptions are filed within 20 days after service thereof upon such parties, or within such further period as the Board may authorize, such recommended order shall become the order of the Board and become effective as therein prescribed.

(d) Until the record in a case shall have been filed in a court, as hereinafter provided, the Board may at any time, upon reasonable notice and in such manner as it shall deem proper, modify or set aside, in whole or in part, any finding or order made or issued by it.

(e) The Board shall have power to petition any court of appeals of the United States, or if all the courts of appeals to which application may be made are in vacation, any district court of the United States, within any circuit or district, respectively, wherein the unfair labor practice in question occurred or wherein such person resides or transacts business, for the enforcement of such order and for appropriate temporary relief or restraining order, and shall file in the court the record in the proceedings, as provided in section 2112 of title 28, United States Code. Upon the filing of such petition, the court shall cause notice thereof to be served upon such person, and thereupon shall have jurisdiction of the proceeding and of the question determined therein, and shall have power to grant such temporary relief or restraining order as it deems just and proper, and to make and enter a decree enforcing, modifying, and enforcing as so modified, or setting aside in whole or in part the order of the Board. No objection that has not been urged before the Board, its member, agent, or agency, shall be considered by the court, unless the failure or neglect to urge such objection shall be excused because of extraordinary circumstances. The findings of the Board with respect to questions of fact if supported by substantial evidence on the record considered as a whole shall be conclusive. If either party shall apply to the court for leave to adduce additional evidence and shall show to the satisfaction of the court that such additional evidence is material and that there were reasonable grounds for the failure to adduce such evidence in the hearing before the Board, its member, agent, or agency, the court may order such additional evidence to be taken before the Board, its member, agent, or agency, and to be made a part of the record. The Board may modify its findings as to the facts, or make new findings, by reason of additional evidence so taken and filed, and it shall file such modified or new findings, which findings with respect to questions of fact if supported by substantial evidence on the record considered as a whole shall be conclusive, and shall file its recommendations, if any, for the modification or setting aside of its original order. Upon the filing of the record with it the jurisdiction of the court shall be exclusive and its judgment and decree shall be final, except that the same shall be subject to review by the appropriate United States court of appeals if application was made to the district court as hereinabove provided, and by the Supreme Court of the United States upon writ of certiorari or certification as provided in section 1254 of title 28.

(f) Any person aggrieved by a final order of the Board granting or denying in whole or in part the relief sought may obtain a review of such order in any circuit court of appeals of the United States in the circuit wherein the unfair labor practice in question was alleged to have been engaged in or wherein such person resides or transacts business, or in the United States Court of Appeals for the District of Columbia, by filing in such court a written petition praying that the order of the Board be modified or set aside. A copy of such petition shall be forthwith transmitted by the clerk of the court to the Board, and thereupon the aggrieved party shall file in the court the record in the proceeding, certified by the Board, as provided in section 2112 of title 28, United States Code. Upon the filing of such petition, the court shall proceed in the same manner as in the case of an application by the Board under subsection (e) of this section, and shall have the same jurisdiction to grant to the Board such temporary relief or restraining order as it deems just and proper, and in like manner to make and enter a decree enforcing, modifying, and enforcing as so modified, or setting aside in whole or in part the order of the Board; the findings of the Board with respect to questions of fact if supported by substantial evidence on the record considered as a whole shall in like manner be conclusive.

(g) The commencement of proceedings under subsection (e) or (f) of this section shall not, unless specifically ordered by the court, operate as a stay of the Board's order.

(h) When granting appropriate temporary relief or a restraining order, or making and entering a decree enforcing, modifying, and enforcing as so modified, or setting aside in whole or in part an order of the Board, as provided in this section, the jurisdiction of courts sitting in equity shall not be limited by the Act entitled "An

Act to amend the Judicial Code and to define and limit the jurisdiction of courts sitting in equity, and for other purposes," approved March 23, 1932 (U.S.C., Supp. VII, title 29, secs. 101–115).

(i) Petitions filed under this Act shall be heard expeditiously, and if possible within 10 days after they have been docketed.

(j) The Board shall have power, upon issuance of a complaint as provided in subsection (b) charging that any person has engaged in or is engaging in an unfair labor practice, to petition any district court of the United States (including the District Court of the United States for the District of Columbia), within any district wherein the unfair labor practice in question is alleged to have occurred or wherein such person resides or transacts business, for appropriate temporary relief or restraining order. Upon the filing of any such petition the court shall cause notice thereof to be served upon such person, and thereupon shall have jurisdiction to grant to the Board such temporary relief or restraining order as it deems just and proper.

(k) Whenever it is charged that any person has engaged in an unfair labor practice within the meaning of paragraph (4) (D) of section 8(b), the Board is empowered and directed to hear and determine the dispute out of which such unfair labor practice shall have arisen, unless, within 10 days after notice that such charge has been filed, the parties to such dispute submit to the Board satisfactory evidence that they have adjusted, or agreed upon methods for the voluntary adjustment of, the dispute. Upon compliance by the parties to the dispute with the decision of the Board or upon such voluntary adjustment of the dispute, such charge shall be dismissed.

(l) Whenever it is charged that any person has engaged in an unfair labor practice within the meaning of paragraph (4) (A), (B), or (C) of section 8(b), or section 8(e) or section 8(b) (7), the preliminary investigation of such charge shall be made forthwith and given priority over all other cases except cases of like character in the office where it is filed or to which it is referred. If, after such investigation, the officer or regional attorney to whom the matter may be referred has reasonable cause to believe such charge is true and that a complaint should issue, he shall, on behalf of the Board, petition any district court of the United States (including the District Court of the United States for the District of Columbia) within any district where the unfair labor practice in question has occurred, is alleged to have occurred, or wherein such person resides or transacts business, for appropriate injunctive relief pending the final adjudication of the Board with respect to such matter. Upon the filing of any such petition the district court shall have jurisdiction to grant such injunctive relief or temporary restraining order as it deems just and proper, notwithstanding any other provision of law: *Provided further,* that no temporary restraining order shall be issued without notice unless a petition alleges that substantial and irreparable injury to the charging party will be unavoidable and such temporary restraining order shall be effective for no longer than five days and will become void at the expiration of such period: *Provided further,* that such officer or regional attorney shall not apply for any restraining order under section 8(b) (7) if a charge against the employer under section 8(a) (2) has been filed and after the preliminary investigation, he has reasonable cause to believe that such charge is true and that a complaint should issue. Upon filing of any such petition the courts shall cause notice thereof to be served upon any person involved in the charge and such person including the charging party, shall be given an opportunity to appear by counsel and present any relevant testimony: *Provided further,* that for the purposes of this subsection district courts shall be deemed to have jurisdiction of a labor organization (1) in the district in which such organization maintains its principal office, or (2) in any district in which its duly authorized officers or agents are engaged in promoting or protecting the interests of employee members. The service of legal process upon such officer or agent shall constitute service upon the labor organization and make such organizations a party to the suit. In situations where such relief is appropriate the procedure specified herein shall apply to charges with respect to section 8(b) (4) (D).

(m) Whenever it is charged that any person has engaged in an unfair labor practice within the meaning of subsection (a) (3) or (b) (2) of section 8, such charge shall be given priority over all other cases except cases of like character in the office where it is filed or to which it is referred and cases given priority under subsection (1).

* * * * *

[Omitted: Sections 11 and 12—Investigatory powers of the NLRB.]

Limitations

Section 13. Nothing in this Act, except as specifically provided for herein, shall be construed so as either to interfere with or impede or diminish in any way the right to strike, or to affect the limitations or qualifications on that right.

Section 14. (a) Nothing herein shall prohibit any individual employed as a supervisor from becoming or remaining a member of a labor organization, but no employer subject to this Act shall be compelled to deem individuals defined herein as supervisors as employees for the purpose of any law, either national or local, relating to collective bargaining.

(b) Nothing in this Act shall be construed as authorizing the execution or application of agreements requiring membership in a labor organization as a condition of employment in any State or Territory in which such execution or application is prohibited by State or Territorial law.

(c) (1) The Board, in its discretion, may, by rule of decision or by published rules adopted pursuant to the Administrative Procedure Act, decline to assert jurisdiction over any labor dispute involving any class or category of employers, where, in the opinion of the Board, the effect of such labor dispute on commerce is not sufficiently substantial to warrant the exercise of its jurisdiction: *Provided,* that the Board shall not decline to assert jurisdiction over any labor dispute over which it would assert jurisdiction under the standards prevailing upon August 1, 1959.

(2) Nothing in this Act shall be deemed to prevent or bar any agency or the courts of any State or Territory (including the Commonwealth of Puerto Rico, Guam, and the Virgin Islands), from assuming and asserting jurisdiction over labor disputes over which the Board declines, pursuant to paragraph (1) of this subsection, to assert jurisdiction.

* * * * *

[Omitted: Sections 15, 16, 17, and 18, relating to limitations.]

Individuals with Religious Conviction

Section 19. Any employee who is a member of and adheres to established and traditional tenets or teachings of a bona fide religion, body, or sect which has historically held conscientious objections to joining or financially supporting labor organizations shall not be required to join or financially support any labor organizations as a condition of employment; except that such employee may be required in a contract between such employees' employer and a labor organization in lieu of periodic dues and initiation fees, to pay sums equal to such dues and initiation fees to a nonreligious, nonlabor organization charitable fund exempt from taxation under section 501(c) (3) of title 26 of the Internal Revenue Code, chosen by such employee from a list of at least three such funds, designated in such contract or if the contract fails to designate such funds, then to any such fund chosen by the employee. If such employee who holds conscientious objections pursuant to this section requests the labor organization to use the grievance-arbitration procedure on the employee's behalf, the labor organization is authorized to charge the employee for the reasonable cost of using such procedure.

* * * * *

[Omitted: Sections 102, 103, and 104, concerning effective dates of certain changes.]

Title II—Conciliation of Labor Disputes in Industries Affecting Commerce; National Emergencies

Section 201. That it is the policy of the United States that—

(a) sound and stable industrial peace and the advancement of the general welfare, health, and safety of the Nation and of the best interest of employers and employees can most satisfactorily be secured by the settlement of issues between employers and employees through the processes of conference and collective bargaining between employers and the representatives of their employees;

(b) the settlement of issues between employers and employees through collective bargaining may be advanced by making available full and adequate governmental facilities for conciliation, mediation, and voluntary arbitration to aid and encourage employers and the representatives of their employees to reach and maintain agreements concerning rates of pay, hours, and working conditions, and to make all reasonable efforts to settle their differences by mutual agreement reached through conferences and collective bargaining or by such methods as may be provided for in any applicable agreement for the settlement of disputes; and

(c) certain controversies which arise between parties to collective bargaining agreements may be avoided or minimized by making available full and adequate governmental facilities for furnishing assistance to employers and the representatives of their employees in formulating for inclusion within such agreements provision for adequate notice of any proposed changes in the terms of such agreements, for the final adjustment of grievances or questions regarding the application or interpretation of such agreements, and other provisions designed to prevent the subsequent arising of such controversies.

Section 202. (a) There is hereby created an independent agency to be known as the Federal Mediation and Conciliation Service (herein referred to as the "Service") . . . The Service shall be under the direction of a Federal Mediation and Conciliation Director (hereinafter referred to as the "Director"), who shall be appointed by the President by and with the advice and consent of the Senate . . .

(b) The Director is authorized, subject to the civil-service laws, to appoint such clerical and other personnel as may be necessary for the execution of the functions of the Service . . .

(c) The principal office of the Service shall be in the District of Columbia, but the Director may establish regional offices convenient to localities in which labor controversies are likely to arise. The Director may by order, subject to revocation at any time, delegate any authority and discretion conferred upon him by this Act to any regional director, or other officer or employee of the Service. The Director may establish suitable procedures for cooperation with State and local mediation agencies. The Director shall make an annual report in writing to Congress at the end of the fiscal year.

* * * * *

[Omitted: Section 202(d), which relates to the original creation of the FMCS.]

Functions of the Service

Section 203. (a) It shall be the duty of the Service, in order to prevent or minimize interruptions of the free flow of commerce growing out of labor disputes, to assist parties to labor disputes in industries affecting commerce to settle such disputes through conciliation and mediation.

(b) The Service may proffer its services in any labor dispute in any industry affecting commerce, either upon its own motion or upon the request of one or more of the parties to the dispute, whenever in its judgment such dispute threatens to cause a substantial interruption of commerce. The Director and the Service are directed to avoid attempting to mediate disputes which would have only a minor effect on interstate commerce if State or other conciliation services are available to the parties. Whenever the Service does proffer its services in any dispute, it shall be the duty of the Service promptly to put itself in communication with the parties and to use its best efforts, by mediation and conciliation, to bring them to agreement.

(c) If the Director is not able to bring the parties to agreement by conciliation within a reasonable time, he shall seek to induce the parties voluntarily to seek other means of settling the dispute without resort to strike, lockout, or other coercion, including submission to the employees in the bargaining unit of the employer's last offer of settlement for approval or rejection in a secret ballot. The failure or refusal of either party to agree to any procedure suggested by the Director shall not be deemed a violation of any duty or obligation imposed by this Act.

(d) Final adjustment by a method agreed upon by the parties is hereby declared to be the desirable method for settlement of grievance disputes arising over the application or interpretation of an existing collective bargaining agreement. The Service is directed to make its conciliation and mediation services available in the settlement of such grievance disputes only as a last resort and in exceptional cases.

Section 204. (a) In order to prevent or minimize interruptions of the free flow of commerce growing out of labor disputes, employers and employees and their representatives, in any industry affecting commerce, shall—

(1) exert every reasonable effort to make and maintain agreements concerning rates of pay, hours, and working conditions, including provision for adequate notice of any proposed change in the terms of such agreements;

(2) whenever a dispute arises over the terms or application of a collective bargaining agreement and a conference is requested by a party or prospective party thereto, arrange promptly for such a conference to be held and endeavor in such conference to settle such dispute expeditiously; and

(3) in case such dispute is not settled by conference, participate fully and promptly in such meetings as may be undertaken by the Service under this Act for the purpose of aiding in a settlement of the dispute.

* * * * *

[Omitted: Section 205, which creates a national labor-management panel to advise the Director of FMCS.]

National Emergencies

Section 206. Whenever in the opinion of the President of the United States, a threatened or actual strike or lockout affecting an entire industry or a substantial part thereof engaged in trade, commerce, transportation, transmission, or communication among the several States or with foreign nations, or engaged in the production of goods for commerce, will, if permitted to occur or to continue, imperil the national health or safety, he may appoint a board of inquiry to inquire into the issues involved in the dispute and to make a written report to him within such time as he shall prescribe. Such report shall include a statement of the facts with respect to the dispute, including each party's statement of its position but shall not contain any recommendations. The President shall file a copy of such report with the Service and shall make its contents available to the public.

Section 207. (a) A board of inquiry shall be composed of a chairman and such other members as the President shall determine, and shall have power to sit and act in any place within the United States and to conduct such hearings either in public or in private, as it may deem necessary or proper, to ascertain the facts with respect to the causes and circumstances of the dispute.

* * * * *

Section 208. (a) Upon receiving a report from a board of inquiry the President may direct the Attorney General to petition any district court of the United States having jurisdiction of the parties to enjoin such strike or lockout or the continuing thereof, and if the court finds that such threatened or actual strike or lockout—

(i) affects an entire industry or a substantial part thereof engaged in trade, commerce, transportation, transmission, or communication among the several States or with foreign nations, or engaged in the production of goods for commerce; and

(ii) if permitted to occur or to continue, will imperil the national health or safety, it shall have jurisdiction to enjoin any such strike or lockout, or the continuing thereof, and to make such other orders as may be appropriate.

* * * * *

Section 209. (a) Whenever a district court has issued an order under section 208 enjoining acts or practices which imperil or threaten to imperil the national health or safety, it shall be the duty of the parties to the labor dispute giving rise to such order to make every effort to adjust and settle their differences, with the assistance of the Service created by this Act. Neither party shall be under any duty to accept, in whole or in part, any proposal of settlement made by the Service.

(b) Upon the issuance of such order, the President shall reconvene the board of inquiry which has previously reported with respect to the dispute. At the end of a 60-day period (unless the dispute has been settled by that time), the board of inquiry shall report to the President the current position of the parties and the efforts which have been made for settlement, and shall include a statement by each party of its position and a statement of the employer's last offer of settlement. The President shall make such report available to the public. The National Labor Relations Board, within the succeeding 15 days, shall take a secret ballot of the employees of each employer involved in the dispute on the question of whether they wish to accept the final offer of settlement made by their employer as stated by him and shall certify the results thereof to the Attorney General within 5 days thereafter.

Section 210. Upon the certification of the results of such a ballot or upon a settlement being reached, whichever happens sooner, the Attorney General shall move the court to discharge the injunction, which motion shall then be granted and the injunction discharged. When such motion is granted, the President shall submit to the Congress a full and comprehensive report of the proceedings, including the findings of the board of inquiry and the ballot taken by the National Labor Relations Board, together with such recommendations as he may see fit to make for consideration and appropriate action.

* * * * *

[Omitted: Section 211, which covers authorization for collection and dissemination of collective bargaining information by federal agencies, and Section 212, which exempts persons covered by provisions of the Railway Labor Act from the provisions of the LMRA.]

Conciliation of Labor Disputes in the Health Care Industry

Section 213. (a) If, in the opinion of the Director of the Federal Mediation and Conciliation Service, a threatened or actual strike or lockout affecting a health care institution will, if permitted to occur or to continue, substantially interrupt the delivery of health care in the locality concerned, the Director may further assist in the resolution of the impasse by establishing within 30 days after the notice to the Federal Mediation and Conciliation Service under clause (A) of the last sentence of section 8(d), which is required by clause (3) of such section 8(d), or within 10 days after the notice under clause (B), an impartial Board of Inquiry to investigate the issues involved in the dispute and to make a written report thereon to the parties within 15 days after the establishment of such a Board. The written report shall contain the findings of fact together with the Board's recommendations for settling the dispute, with the objective of achieving a prompt, peaceful and just settlement of the dispute. Each such Board shall be composed of such number of individuals as the Director may deem desirable. No member appointed under this section shall have any interest or involvement in the health care institutions or the employee organizations involved in the dispute.

* * * * *

[Omitted: Section 213(b), which provides for compensation for members appointed to a Board formed under Section 213(a).]

(c) After the establishment of a board under subsection (a) of this section and for 15 days after any such board has issued its report, no change in the status quo in effect prior to the expiration of the contract in the case of negotiations for a contract renewal, or in effect prior to the time of the impasse in the case of an initial bargaining negotiation, except by agreement, shall be made by the parties to the controversy.

(d) There are authorized to be appropriated such sums as may be necessary to carry out the provisions of this section.

Title III

Suits by and against Labor Organizations

Section 301. (a) Suits for violation of contracts between an employer and a labor organization representing employees in an industry affecting commerce as defined in this Act, or between any such labor organizations, may be brought in any district court of the United States having jurisdiction of the parties, without respect to the amount in controversy or without regard to the citizenship of the parties.

(b) Any labor organization which represents employees in an industry affecting commerce as defined in this Act and any employer whose activities affect commerce as defined in this Act shall be bound by the acts of its agents. Any such labor organization may sue or be sued as an entity and in behalf of the employees whom it represents in the courts of the United States. Any money judgment against a labor organization in a district court of the United States shall be enforceable only against the organization as an entity and against its assets, and shall not be enforceable against any individual member or his assets.

(c) For the purposes of actions and proceedings by or against labor organizations in the district courts of the United States, district courts shall be deemed to have jurisdiction of a labor organization (1) in the district in which such organization maintains its principal offices, or (2) in any district in which its duly authorized officers or agents are engaged in representing or acting for employee members.

(d) The service of summons, subpoena, or other legal process of any court of the United States upon an officer or agent of a labor organization, in his capacity as such, shall constitute service upon the labor organization.

(e) For the purposes of this action, in determining whether any person is acting as an "agent" of another person so as to make such other person responsible for his acts, the question of whether the specific acts performed were actually authorized or subsequently ratified shall not be controlling.

* * * * *

[Omitted: Section 302—Restrictions on payments to employee representatives.]

Boycotts and Other Unlawful Combinations

Section 303. (a) It shall be unlawful, for the purpose of this section only, in an industry or activity affecting commerce, for any labor organization to engage in any activity or conduct defined as an unfair labor practice in section 8(b) (4) of the National Labor Relations Act, as amended.

(b) Whoever shall be injured in his business or property by reason of any violation of subsection (a) may sue therefor in any district court of the United States subject to the limitations and provisions of Section 301 hereof without respect to the amount of the controversy, or in any other court having jurisdiction of the parties, and shall recover the damages sustained by him and the cost of the suit.

* * * * *

[Omitted are the following sections: Section 304—Restrictions on political contributions; Title IV—Creation of a joint committee to study and report on basic problems affecting labor relations and productivity.]

Title V

Definitions

Section 501. When used in this Act—

(1) The term "industry affecting commerce" means any industry or activity in commerce or in which a labor dispute would burden or obstruct commerce or tend to burden or obstruct commerce or the free flow of commerce.

(2) The term "strike" includes any strike or other concerted stoppage of work by employees (including a stoppage by reason of the expiration of a collective bargaining agreement) and any concerted slowdown or other concerted interruption of operations by employees.

(3) The terms "commerce," "labor disputes," "employer," "employee," "labor organization," "representative," "person," and "supervisor" shall have the same meaning as when used in the National Labor Relations Act as amended by this Act.

Saving Provision

Section 502. Nothing in this Act shall be construed to require an individual employee to render labor or service without his consent, nor shall anything in this Act be construed to make the quitting of his labor by an individual employee an illegal act; nor shall any court issue any process to compel the performance by an individual employee of such labor or service, without his consent; nor shall the quitting of labor by an employee or employees in good faith because of abnormally dangerous conditions for work at the place of employment of such employee or employees be deemed a strike under this Act.

Separability

Section 503. If any provision of this Act, or the application of such provision to any person or circumstance, shall be held invalid, the remainder of this Act, or the application of such provision to persons or circumstances other than those as to which it is held invalid, shall not be affected thereby.

Index to Cases for Part One

Case Number and Title	Principal Issues of Case	Principal LMRA Provisions
1. Improper Interference with Union's Freedom of Speech	Company banned handbilling of store in a mall contrary to 8(a) (1) of the Act	Sec. 7, 8(a) (1)
2. Supervisor or Member of Bargaining Unit?	Issues of whether employees are supervisors and whether an employee is part of a community of interest.	2(5), 2(9)
3. Jurisdiction of the NLRB over a Government Contractor	Company's contention that it was not an employer under LMRA because it was subject to requirements of another federal statute.	2(2), 2(6), 2(7), Sec. 6, Sec. 9, 8(a) (5), 8(d)
4. Surveillance of the Employee and Nonemployee Union Organizers	Questioning and observation of union supporters both inside and outside a retail store.	Sec. 7, 8(a) (1)
5. Withholding a Wage Increase Prior to a Representational Election	Employer withholds scheduled pay increase during representational election believing this to be in accordance with NLRB rules.	8(a) (1), 9(c)
6. Independent Contractors or Employees? A Company's Refusal to Bargain	Company claims taxi drivers are not employees, but independent contractors and refuse to bargain.	Sec. 2(3), Sec. 8(a) (1) and (5)
7. On the Dole: A Refusal to Bargain with a Properly Certified Union	Employer contended that a union certification election's results were tainted and therefore it was not obliged to collective bargain with it.	Sec. 8(a) (1) and (5)
8. Racial/Ethnic Prejudice during a Union Representational Election	Union distribution of controversial magazine letter to bargaining unit employees that employer claimed improperly prejudiced election outcome.	9(c)

(continued)

Index to Cases for Part One *(Continued)*

Case Number and Title	Principal Issues of Case	Principal LMRA Provisions
9. Waiver to Arbitrate or Unlawful Refusal?	Union alleges employer's refusal to arbitrate, even though authorized by contract language, is failure to bargain.	Sec. 8(a) (1) and (5)
10. Claim of an Inability to Pay Wage Demands: What is Bargaining in Good Faith?	Union alleges employer claimed inability to pay then refused to provide proof.	8(a) (1) and (5), 8(d)
11. Was the Employee Involvement Committee a Violation of Labor Law?	Company sponsored employee involvement committee during union representational campaign.	2(5), 8(a) (1), 8(a) (2), 8(a) (5), 10(c)
12. A Penny Saved Was a Warning Not Earned	An employee was issued a letter of warning on the pretext of an expanded break, but really for union activities.	8(a) (1), 8(a) (5)
13. Termination for Failure to Report Accident or for Solicitation of Employees	Termination for soliciting bargaining authorization cards.	8(a) (1), 8(a) (3)
14. Causes for Discharge: A Game of Ladders and Questions	Four employees were fired—one for insubordination and three for questioning whether he was fired for union activity.	Sec. 7, 8(a) (1)
15. Discharge for Disruptive Conduct, or for Protected Union Activity?	Discharge of newspaper reporter who wrote article which management claimed violated company rules.	Sec. 7, 9(e) (2), 8(a) (1), 8(a) (3)
16. Was the ESOP Leveraged Buyout Proposal Protected Concerted Activity?	Discipline of employee who proposed an ESOP leveraged buyout of firm by employees.	Sec. 7, 8(a) (1)
17. The Distasteful and Offensive Definition of a "Scab"	Removal of "Scab" memorandum from union bulletin boards by company supervisors.	Sec. 7, 8(a) (1)

18. Deferral to an Existing Arbitration Award: Just Cause or Protected Activity?	Employee discharged for harassment and arbitrator sustained discharge. Union contends award repugnant to the Act.	8(a) (1), Sec. 7
19. Did the Employee Have the Right to Have a Union Representative Present?	Discharge of employee who refused to continue meeting with her supervisor without having union representative present.	Sec. 7, 8(a) (1), 8(a) (3)
20. Was Changing the Christmas Bonus Formula an Unfair Labor Practice?	Company's change of Christmas bonus plan during term of labor agreement.	8(a) (1), 8(a) (5), 8(d)
21. Payment of a Signing Bonus to Nonstriking Employees	Company payment of a contractual signing bonus to employees who crossed picket lines when majority of employees rejected contract and went on strike.	8(a) (1), 8(a) (3), 8(a) (5)
22. Crossing Picket Lines: Union's Right to Discipline?	Employee refused to honor picket line in third-party dispute. Union discipline imposed.	Sec. 7, 8(b) (1)(A)
23. Voluntary Participation Programs and Union Discipline	Union threatened to discipline employee who cooperated in voluntary management program.	Sec. 7, 8(b) (1) (A)
24. Threats and Insubordination, or Performing a Shop Steward's Job?	Discharge of union shop steward who challenged company's assignment of foreman at a construction job site.	2(11), Sec. 7, 8(a) (1), 8(a) (3)
25. Judicial Review of the NLRB's "Punitive" Remedy Concerning the Health Care Plan	Company appeal of order by NLRB to make employees whole for several years' incremental costs of health care plan.	8(a) (1), 8(a) (5), 8(d), 10(c)
26. The Enforcement of No-Solicitation Rules: A Real Whopper	Company rule against solicitation while on the clock, and its enforcement.	Sec. 7, 8(a) (1)
27. Management Teams or Employee Involvement Committees: Authority to Put a Cork in It.	Employer delegated managerial function to employee teams, which were therefore not statutory employee organizations.	Sec. 7, 8(a) (1), 8(a) (2)

(continued)

Index to Cases for Part One ***(Continued)***

Case Number and Title	Principal Issues of Case	Principal LMRA Provisions
28. The Company's Refusal to Provide a List of Disciplinary Work Rules	Union request for a written list of all verbal and written rules that could lead to disciplinary action.	8(a) (1), 8(a) (5), 8(d), 8(b) (3)
29. The Obligation to Reduce the Agreement to a Written Contract	The parties agreed to terms of successor agreement, but employer refused to sign.	8(a)(1), 8(a) (5)
30. Information Requests and the Duty to Bargain Collectively: Not Mickey Mouse	Company's refusal and delay in providing information necessary to the union's policing of the contract.	8(a) (1), 8(a) (5)
31. Default and Paychecks: Concerted Action?	Employee in nonunion setting engaged in concerted action about paycheck errors.	Sec. 7, 8(a) (1)
32. Threatening the Union Dissidents	Union officials directed obscenities and "threats" toward individuals who were former union members.	Sec. 7, 8(b) (1) (A)
33. The Grievance-Processing Fee for Nonmembers in a Right-to-Work State	Union effort to charge nonmembers a fee for processing their grievances.	Sec. 7, 8(b) (1) (A), 14(b), Sec. 19
34. The Union's Letter to Nonmember Employees Who Crossed the Picket Line	Union letter to nonmember bargaining unit employees who crossed picket line to work during strike.	2(13), Sec. 7, 8(b) (1) (A)
35. Resignation from the Union and Checkoff of Dues	Employee resigned from the union, became an agency employee, and the employer stopped checking off her dues.	8(a) (1) and (5)
36. Were the Union's Grievances an Unlawful Secondary Boycott?	Companies party to a master agreement refused to arbitrate union's grievances concerning subcontracting of certain work.	8(b) (4) (ii) (A), 8(e), Sec. 301
37. Whose Work Is It? Case of a Jurisdictional Dispute	Jurisdictional issue involving claims of two unions to perform disputed work.	8(b) (4) (D), 10(k)
38. How Do I Get My Cookies? Information Requests to the Contract	Union requests for information necessary to police contract not honored by employer.	8(a) (1) and (5), 8(d)

Case 1

Improper Interference with Union's Freedom of Speech

Company Sandusky Mall Company

Union United Brotherhood of Carpenters and Joiners of America, AFL-CIO

BACKGROUND

The employer operated a retail mall in which free-standing and independent retail establishments were located. Among these retail establishments was an Attivo store. The union had a dispute with the Attivo stores, which the union claimed were undermining the construction wage and benefit standard in the Sandusky, Ohio, area. Two business agents for the Carpenters Union entered the mall and were passing out handbills at the entrance of the Attivo store, asking potential patrons not to do business with the store because of the dispute the union had with Attivo.

Subsequent to the business agents' beginning their handbilling campaign, a mall security guard asked the union business agents to cease the handbilling and leave the mall. When the business agents refused to leave, the manager of the mall informed them that if they did not cease the handbilling, they would be considered trespassers and dealt with accordingly. The business agents left the mall in accordance with the demand of the mall's manager. Within the week the business agents returned to the mall and again began handbilling the Attivo store. A mall security guard again asked the business agents to cease handbilling and leave the mall. The business agents refused and were then arrested by city police for trespassing.

Upon motion to the court by the union's attorney, the charges of criminal trespass were dropped by the court. The mall did not oppose the dropping of the charges against the union business agents. Further, the mall's management admitted that it had permitted solicitation for charitable, civic, and other reasons on mall property during times when the mall was open to the public for business.

POSITION OF THE UNION

The union contended that the employer had no right to bar informational handbilling while it permitted other organizations to solicit and provide information in the mall during times when the mall was open for business. For a company to discriminate against union handbilling while other (nonlabor) organizations were permitted access to the mall amounted to unlawful discrimination under Section 8(a) (1) of the Act.

The business agents were nonemployee persons simply exercising their rights under the Act to inform customers of a complaint they had with a specific retailer in the mall. The handbills specifically identified the company with whom the union had a difference, and what the nature of that difference was. At no time did the union business agents attempt to block the entrance or exit to the store, and at all times the business agents were polite and peaceful. It was the union's position that the mall's management discriminated against these men for their union activities in clear violation of the law.

POSITION OF THE COMPANY

The company contended that it has both a constitutional and statutory right to deny access to the mall to the union business agents during business hours. The mall property was private property and as such could deny access to nonemployee persons. The mall has long maintained a rule that proscribed informational activities and barred access to the mall by persons who were commercial competitors to the mall retailers or to controversial advocacy groups. Clearly, the company argued, a union with a dispute with one of the mall's retailers falls into the category of persons or organizations barred from access to the mall.

The mall had allowed organizations and persons access to the mall if the purposes were consistent with the requirements of the mall's policies with respect to access. In the case of the union business agents, the purpose for their access was clearly barred, and for good business reasons. The company urged the NLRB to reject the union's claim of an unfair labor practice in this matter.

QUESTIONS

1. Can a private employer, such as a mall in this case, promulgate rules that bar handbilling from areas generally open to the public? If so, under what circumstances can this activity be barred?
2. How can nonemployee persons be subject to rules concerning otherwise peaceful and lawful conduct in a business open to the public? Explain. Would it make a difference if these union business agents were employees? Explain.
3. Does it matter, in this case, that the business agents specifically identified the company with whom they had a dispute? If so, why is this important?
4. Does it make a difference that the allegation against the mall was discrimination for union activity, rather than interference with concerted activity? Explain.

Case 2

Supervisor or Member of Bargaining Unit?

Employer Bredero Shaw, A Division of Shaweor Ltd.

Union Local 653, International Union of Operating Engineers, AFL-CIO

BACKGROUND

This matter involves challenges to five individual employees' ballots in a certification election. The petitioner in this case is the union. The union challenged the ballots of four employees, whom it alleges are supervisors for purposes of the Act and therefore not properly members of the bargaining unit. A fifth person's ballot was challenged because the union alleges that this person does not share a community of interest with the remaining members of the bargaining unit and it was not intended that be included in the bargaining unit.

The four employees that the union alleges are supervisors are Mr. A, Mr. B, Mr. C, and Ms. D. The person the union alleges has no shared interest with the remainder of the bargaining unit is Mr. E.

The record shows that Mr. A and Mr. B are lead men and provided direction and supervision for a crew of seven or eight persons on construction sites. Mr. A on at least one occasion over the past couple of years has sent an employee home because he "got smart on the job." Mr. A also routinely assigned work to the employees. Over the past two years Mr. B sent two employees home for fighting on the job, and on another occasion granted an employee's request for some time off without consulting anyone. Mr. B's title was also lead man.

Mr. C has the title maintenance supervisor, but spends the majority of his time working at his trade, welder. Mr. C routinely assigned other welders to specific tasks, and on at least one occasion in the last two years gave an employee permission to go home. Ms. D's title is electrician-lead person. Ms. D over the past couple of years assigned other electricians to jobs that were identified to her by supervisors that needed to be done. There is no evidence that she ever disciplined an employee. She spends the majority of her time working in her trade.

Mr. E works in a facility of the plant called the GSPU plant. He spends half of his time performing quality control work in that plant, and the remainder of his time performing production work in the bargaining unit.

POSITION OF THE EMPLOYER

It is the position of the employer that all of these employees are members of the bargaining unit. Employees A through D are not supervisors for purposes of the Act, and as such are properly included in the bargaining unit. Each of these employees works at their trade, and each engages in bargaining unit work routinely. Therefore it would be improper under the Act to exclude their ballots in a certification election.

Mr. E is also a member of the bargaining unit. The fact that approximately half of his time is spent doing work in quality control and in a separate area of the production facility does not remove him from a shared community of interest with the remaining members of the bargaining unit. Therefore, this employee's ballot should also be included.

POSITION OF THE UNION

The union challenges employees A through D and claims their ballot ought not count in the certification election. Each of these employees are supervisors by title, each has the ability to direct the work of others routinely, and each has exhibited independent authority by sending employees home or granting them time off. Therefore, these employees are supervisory employees for purposes of the Act.

Mr. E does not have a shared community of interest with the remainder of the bargaining unit. Mr. E works in a separate facility for half of each work day, and while there does primarily quality control work. The fact that the other half of the work day is spent in production work does not serve to overcome the fact that it was not intended for Mr. E to be included in the bargaining unit.

Therefore the union requests that the challenges to these employees' ballots be sustained by the Board.

QUESTIONS

1. What is a supervisor for purposes of the Act? Do any of these four employees qualify as supervisors? Explain.
2. What is meant by a community of interest? Is there a showing in this case that Mr. E does not share a community of interest with the remaining members of the bargaining unit? Explain.
3. If you were the Board in this matter how would you decide? Explain.

Case 3

Jurisdiction of the NLRB over a Government Contractor

Company Dynaelectron Corporation, Aerospace Operations Division, Meridian, Mississippi

Union United Automobile and Aerospace Workers

BACKGROUND

In July 1987, the company was engaged in performing organizational-level maintenance on T-2 aircraft for the U.S. Navy at the Naval Air Station (NAS) in Meridian, Mississippi. Organizational maintenance was performed at the site where aircraft were located, whether shore- or aircraft carrier–based. Such services included inspection, service, lubrication, adjustment or replacement of parts, and other flight line services. The existing contract between the company and the Navy was a one-year fixed-price contract, with an option to renew annually for a total duration not to exceed five years.

The union had filed a petition with the NLRB to conduct a representational election to determine whether the union should represent the production and maintenance employees at the NAS Meridian. The company objected and contended that the petition should be dismissed, because the company was a contractor subject to the terms of the Service Contract Act and thus did not possess the ability to bargain meaningfully with a labor organization. The Service Contract Act, originally passed in 1965 and amended by Congress in 1972, applies to every contract in excess of $2,500 entered into by the federal government where the primary purpose of the contract is to provide services to the federal government. Under the Service Contract Act, the Department of Labor (DOL) issues area wage determinations that set forth the minimum wages and fringe benefits to be provided to service employees in a locality. The DOL wage determination for the Meridian area in 1985 had established the minimum hourly wage rates for 23 job classifications. In addition, the wage determination required that the company must provide fringe benefits with an average contribution of $1.08 an hour. These benefits included life, accident, and health insurance; sick leave; pension and saving plans; personal leave; severance pay; a specified amount of vacation based on length of service; and nine paid holidays each year. As long as it maintained benefits valued at at least the minimum rate, the company could provide these benefits in any form it chose, and the company did not need the approval of the DOL or the Navy to change the benefit package.

POSITION OF THE COMPANY

The company contended that, because it was subject to the requirements of the Service Contract Act, it was not an employer within the meaning of Section 2(2) of LMRA, and that it was not engaged in commerce within the meaning of Sections 2(6) and 2(7) of the Act. Therefore, the NLRB should decline jurisdiction in this case and not hold any representational election pursuant to Section 6 and Section 9 of LMRA.

The company made a number of major arguments in support of its position. First, the company asserted that when the Department of Labor (DOL) established a wage/benefit determination for an area (i.e., Meridian, Mississippi), this in effect had removed the company's control over terms and conditions of employment for its employees. The company's contract with the Navy was based on a compensation package for employees mandated by and consistent with the DOL's determination.

In this context, the company next contended that if the union should gain representational rights for the employees, the company's ability to bargain would be extremely limited and unrealistic. For example, if the company entered into negotiations with a labor organization during the period of the government contract, and a collective bargaining agreement resulted in costs and a contract price higher than that for which the company had bid, the company would not be able to recoup the difference until the next fiscal year, if at all. Therefore, the company would be unlikely to offer the union any additional wages/benefits beyond those specified in the DOL determination. This, in turn, would probably mean that the union would file unfair labor practices alleging that the company was not bargaining in good faith as required under Section 8(a) (5) and 8(d) of the Act.

Finally, the company asserted that it was the U.S. Navy Department which really was the employer, because the Navy exercised control over labor-management relations and the employees. Employees of the company had to adhere to Navy standards of dress and appearance and wear uniforms that identified them as the contractor's employees. The company's employees were subject to Navy regulations and directives, and the Navy's contracting officer could request that the company remove employees from contract work for unethical conduct, violation of Navy regulations, breach of security, or misconduct. Since the Navy really controlled employee relations, it (the Navy) was the true employer, and this, too, meant that the company could not realistically be expected to bargain with a union about wages, hours, and other terms and conditions of employment.

The company urged that the NLRB decline jurisdiction in this case matter and thus refuse to hold a union representational election.

POSITION OF THE UNION

The union argued that the company was using a collection of invalid claims as a pretext for avoiding holding a representational election and eventually having to bargain with the union.

The union contended that the legislative history of the Service Contract Act supported the conclusion that Congress did not intend to exclude employees fulfilling federal government service contracts from the NLRB's jurisdiction. The Service Contract Act was enacted in 1965 to ensure that employees of service contractors received the prevailing wages and fringe benefits paid other employees performing similar work in the same locality. The statute was amended in 1972 to protect employees of successor contractors. These amendments established procedures to permit the Department of Labor to base the prevailing rates on collectively bargained rates, thereby preventing replacement contractors from underbidding incumbent contractors that have collective bargaining relationships with labor organizations.

Nothing in the Service Contract Act excluded an employer from an obligation to enter into a collective bargaining agreement where a union had gained representational rights for the employees. In fact, the Service Contract Act contemplated collective bargaining, since this law expressly provided that collectively bargained wages and benefits could be substituted for the prevailing compensation rates as determined by the DOL.[1] The statute, as amended, requires that every contract to furnish services for the federal government must contain minimum compensation standards based on either (*a*) prevailing wages and benefits; or (*b*) where a collective bargaining agreement exists, on the wages and benefits provided in the collective bargaining agreement.

The union further argued that the company, not the U.S. Navy or the Department of Labor, was indeed the employer and thus subject to the requirements of the Labor Management Relations Act (LMRA). The company was not prohibited from bargaining with a union concerning higher wages or higher fringe benefits. The company also had the ultimate authority to determine the primary terms and conditions of employment, including responsibility for hiring, discipline, and terminations.

The company met the NLRB's standards for asserting jurisdiction under the LMRA. The mere fact that the employer also had to comply with requirements of the Service Contract Act should not bar the NLRB's assertion of jurisdiction over the Dynaelectron company. The union urged that the NLRB should direct that a representational election be held to determine whether the union would represent employees at the company.

QUESTIONS

1. Evaluate the company's contentions in this case. Which are the most persuasive? Least persuasive? Discuss.
2. Evaluate the union's contentions to the effect that the Service Contract Act did not exclude contract employers from also being covered by requirements of the LMRA.
3. Should the NLRB exert jurisdiction in this case? Explain.
4. May the NLRB assert jurisdiction over issues covered by other statutes? If so, under what circumstances? Explain.

---

[1] With respect to employee wage rates, the Service Contract Act provides that each service contract must contain: "A provision specifying the minimum monetary wages to be paid the various classes of service employees . . . as determined by the Secretary . . . in accordance with prevailing rates for such employees in the locality, or, where a collective bargaining agreement covers any such service employees, in accordance with the rates for such employees provided for in such agreement, including prospective wage increases provided for in such agreement as a result of arm's-length negotiations." 41 U.S.C. § 351(a) (1).

With respect to employee fringe benefit levels, the Service Contract Act provides that each contract must contain: "A provision specifying the fringe benefits to be furnished . . . as determined by the Secretary . . . to be prevailing for such employees, in the locality, or where a collective bargaining agreement covers any such service employees, to be provided for in such agreement, including prospective fringe benefit increases provided for in such agreement as a result of arm's-length negotiations." 41 U.S.C. § 351(a) (2).

Case 4

Surveillance of the Employee and Nonemployee Union Organizers

Company Department Store Division of Dayton Hudson Corporation, Detroit, Michigan, area

Union United Automobile Workers

BACKGROUND

These unfair labor practice charges resulted from a meeting of employee and nonemployee union organizers in the company's Westland store on November 24, 1992.

Martha Singer,[1] a Fairlane store employee and a union supporter who was on her day off, went with union organizer Vercille Sargent[2] to the Westland store. The pair had planned a luncheon meeting with Marcia Groza, who was the chairperson of the union's employee organizing committee. Groza worked at the company's Westland store. Singer and Sargent met Jack Niles inside the Westland store. Niles, a union supporter, was on his day off from the company's Briarwood store, and he also had planned to meet with Groza for lunch. Illana Korte, another union organizer, by prearrangement met Sargent, Singer, and Niles. As a group, these four individuals headed to the furniture department where Groza was working. They then "toured" that department while waiting for Groza to take her lunchbreak.

At about the same time, five of the store's managers had been following the group. One manager, Alia Suh, greeted Singer with a hug and some friendly words as the other managers observed this. A second manager, Christie Blumhof, called out to Jack Niles as he went down the escalator; she then spoke to him at the bottom of the escalator, inquiring about why he did not visit with her. As the group "meandered" within the furniture department, still another manager, Jason Cicci, asked them what they were doing. On being told that they were waiting for Marcia Groza for lunch, Cicci said that since the group had no packages, they were not shopping. Cicci then added that all of them should leave, and he would arrange for Groza to meet them. While this was transpiring, Ashley Ponte, the store's manager of human resources, accused Illana Korte of "organizing" and told her to stop "harassing" the Westland employees. Ponte also engaged Korte in a discussion about a Westland employee who previously had been active on behalf of the union but who was not promoted to a management position.

When Marcia Groza was ready for lunch, the union group left for the nearby Coney Island restaurant. The managers followed Groza and her group from the store to the restaurant where both groups ate lunch. Although the managers were too far away to be able to hear the employees' conversation during lunch, the managers could clearly see

[1] The names of all individuals are disguised.

[2] Vercille Sargent and Illana Korte were employed by the International Union as organizers. They frequently worked closely with employees of firms who were interested in forming a union and collective bargaining unit.

where Groza and her party were seated. Not all of the managers remained for the approximately 45-minute lunch.

When the union group led by Marcia Groza left the restaurant and returned to the Westland store, they were followed by three of the managers, Blumhof, Cicci, and Ponte. Upon reentering the store, Jason Cicci asked Martha Singer if she "needed help." When she declined, he indicated that this was "no problem." Ashley Ponte engaged in some bantering with Illana Korte about "old ladies having nothing better to do than walk around the store."

Shortly thereafter, the union filed unfair labor practice charges against the company, claiming that the company by its surveillance of the union's leading supporters had violated Section 8(a) (1) of the Labor Management Relations Act.[3]

POSITION OF THE UNION

The union contended that the company managers had engaged in a course of conduct that demonstrated their intent to monitor the union activities of the employee and nonemployee union supporters. The managers did not simply follow the group. The managers' improper conduct commenced when the managers let the employees know that they were aware of the nonemployee union persons present, and that their associating with the organizers was unwelcome.

The union pointed out that Martha Singer was greeted by a manager as soon as she entered the store, and a group of three or four other managers observed this encounter. Similarly, a manager hailed Jack Niles as he went down the escalator and then engaged him in conversation at the bottom of the escalator. The managers pursued the union group as they "toured" the furniture department and waited for Marcia Groza to commence her lunchbreak. The managers told the union group to leave because they had no packages and were not shopping. When the union group did leave for lunch, the managers followed them through the store and to the nearby Coney Island restaurant.

This was no mere innocent observance of employees Singer, Niles, and Groza that was coincidental with the observance of nonemployees Sargent and Korte on the company's premises. Rather, the group of managers, by their actions and words beginning inside the Westland store and continuing with the return to the store's premises, made it plain that they intended to monitor the union activities of the company's employees. This conduct violated Section 8(a) (1) of the Act.

The union stressed that there was no legitimacy to the company's surveillance when Singer, Sargent, Niles, Korte, and Groza left the Westland store and went to the Coney Island restaurant. The group of employee and nonemployee union organizers no longer were on the store's premises, nor were the employees on working time. Groza was on her lunchbreak, and Singer and Niles were on their days off from other company stores. Yet five managers followed the group to the restaurant, watched them throughout their meal, and then followed them back to the Westland store. Even though the restaurant was often frequented by managers and employees simultaneously—and even acknowledging that the managers could not hear the union group in the restaurant—what was obvious was

[3] The union previously had filed unfair labor practice charges against the company for allegedly prohibiting prounion employees from wearing union buttons, having guests in the employee lunchroom, and talking with co-workers.

that the managers followed and watched employees who chose to associate with union organizers on their free time away from the company's premises. This conduct revealed the company's intention to observe at close range the protected Section 7 activities of Groza, Singer, and Niles; it was intended to be coercive and intimidating.

The union claimed that the employer's unlawful surveillance was an intrusion on the employees' statutory rights and violated Section 8(a) (1) of the Act. The union urged the NLRB to sustain the unfair labor practice charges, to direct the company to cease and desist in these unlawful practices, and to inform employees throughout its area stores that management would not interfere with the employees' protected rights to organize free of the company's unlawful interference.

POSITION OF THE COMPANY

The company vigorously denied that by their actions the managers had engaged in unlawful surveillance and interference with their employees' protected rights. Ashley Ponte, the Westland store's human resources manager, testified that it was the company's long-term policy to give nonemployee union organizers "the utmost customer service and stick right with them and make sure that they do not harass any employees."

In the company's view, the union on November 24, 1992, was engaged in a "show of strength and effort to enlist the support of employees at work by parading through the store during store hours." It was no mere coincidence or happenstance that brought together nonemployee union organizers and employee union supporters inside the Westland store. The company managers addressed most of their remarks to the nonemployee organizers and not the employees. The company lawfully was privileged to engage in surveillance of nonemployee union organizers inside the store. The managers' observance of employees who joined these nonemployee organizers was merely coincidental to this legitimate purpose. The company had the right to observe what this group might do in order to protect the store's other employees and customers from harassment.

The company further contended that the company managers did not intend to monitor the union activities of its employees, either inside or outside of the Westland store. The managers followed the union group into the nearby restaurant pursuant to the company's policy to "stick with" the nonemployee union organizers. This was certainly not intimidating or coercive, especially since managers and employees frequented this restaurant regularly and they often were there together. Further, the managers seated themselves at some distance from Marcia Groza and her party, who were aware that the managers could not hear them.

The company argued that the union's unfair labor practice charges were without merit and were based only upon inference and innuendo, not substantive proof. The company urged that the NLRB should dismiss the union complaint.

QUESTIONS

1. In general, the NLRB has held that an employer does not violate LMRA by prohibiting nonemployee union organizers from attempting to organize employees on company facilities (i.e., in working areas during working hours.) Was the company policy in this regard (as stated by its human resources manager) lawful? Explain.

2. Was the managers' "surveillance" of the union group inside the Westland store lawful? Explain.
3. Was the managers' "surveillance" of the union group outside the Westland store (i.e., the restaurant) lawful? Why, or why not?
4. Why is it sometimes difficult for the NLRB to determine the "dividing line" between lawful and unlawful employer "surveillance" (or monitoring) of union organizing efforts when such efforts involve both employee and nonemployee organizers? Explain.

Case 5

Withholding a Wage Increase Prior to a Representational Election

Employer United Methodist Home of New Jersey, Newark, New Jersey

Union 1115 Nursing Home & Service Employees Union—New Jersey B, Division of 1115 District Council, Hotel and Restaurant Employees Union

BACKGROUND

On June 14, 1993, the union filed a petition with the Regional Office of the NLRB requesting that a representational election be held to determine whether employees in a proposed unit wanted the union to represent them for purposes of collective bargaining with their employer. An NLRB-supervised representational election was held in early August 1993. Forty-seven ballots were cast in favor of the union, and 58 ballots were cast against the union, with 5 challenged ballots. The union immediately filed objections to the election outcome based primarily upon the fact that the employer had withheld pay increases for employees prior to the election.

The union relied upon a number of employee witnesses who gave testimony and affidavits about the employer's pay practices. (The employer did not deny the validity of these witnesses' assertions.) Regarding the employer's practice of granting wage increases prior to 1992, two witnesses stated that they received two annual increases—one on the anniversary date of hire and the other in July. One of the witnesses said that prior to 1992 employees received an increase on their anniversary dates. Three witnesses agreed that in 1992 they received only one increase, in July 1992; however, a fourth witness said she also received a second increase in December of that year.

Regarding pay increases in 1993, the employee witnesses stated that they were told by different representatives of the employer in conversations that occurred from late 1992 until June 1993 that they would receive a wage increase in July 1993. However, no wage increase was given at that time.

There had been at least two occasions when managers explained the decision to withhold a wage increase in July 1993. According to several employees, at a meeting of employees in early July 1993, the employer's top administrator, Frank Hasbrow,[1] stated that according to the NLRB's rules, the employer could not give raises during the pendency of a representation election in order to avoid the appearance of offering employees bribes for their votes. Hasbrow then added that if the union was voted in, all raises would be negotiable, and that if the union wasn't voted in, employees would get their raises as due them. Subsequently, the employer's human resource director issued to employees a memorandum, dated July 14, 1993, which stated that employees would not receive wage increases at that time due to the employer's understanding of NLRB rules. The memorandum stated

[1] Name is disguised.

that the NLRB rules "prohibit management from making any changes in working conditions during the time before the election." The memorandum also added:

> Should the election result in a decision by the employees to have Local 1115 represent them, the issue of a raise and other economic items will be considered at the bargaining table. Should the result be no union, management will act promptly after the election.

POSITION OF THE UNION

The union cited previous NLRB rulings to the effect that it was settled labor law that during a union representational campaign period, an employer is required to proceed with an expected wage or benefit adjustment as if the union were not on the scene.[2]

In this case, the union pointed out that Mr. Hasbrow, the top administrator, only told employees that pay raises would be negotiable if the union got in, and that raises would be given if the union did not get in. Similarly, the employer's memorandum of July 14, 1993, gave no specific assurances concerning when and in what specific amounts wages would be increased after the representational election was over.

In essence, the employer had "placed the blame" upon the union and its efforts to organize the employees for withholding wage increases that the employees were entitled to and otherwise would have received. In the union's view, this was objectionable interference under Section 9(c) of the LMRA and was a violation of Section 8(a) (1). As a remedy, the union requested that the NLRB should order another representational election that was devoid of employer interference in the employees' protected rights under the Act.

POSITION OF THE EMPLOYER

The employer contended that the union's charges of improper interference in the union representational election were without merit and simply a ploy by the union to seek another election. The employer was attempting to comply with the NLRB's requirements about wage increases during a representational campaign period. In his July meeting with employees, administrator Frank Hasbrow had explained the employer's position. This was followed by a July 14, 1993, memorandum which explained that employee raises would be given following the representational election if the union was rejected by the employees; if the union was voted in, the employee raises would become negotiable. Hasbrow's statement and the memorandum of July 14, 1993, were reasonable, accurate, and designed to comply with the NLRB's requirements about changing (or not changing) employee wages and other working conditions during a union representational campaign period. The employer urged that the NLRB should dismiss the union's complaint and certify the results of the representational election.

QUESTIONS

1. Why is the area of contention in this case a legal "minefield" for employers to be scrupulously careful about before deciding what to do during a union representational campaign period?

[2] *Atlantic Forest Products,* 282 NLRB 855, 858 (124 LRRM 1127), and cases cited there.

2. Was the intent of the employer to "place the blame" on the union and its efforts for postponing the wage increases, or was it a good faith effort by the employer to comply with NLRB requirements? Explain.
3. If the NLRB should decide that the employer's conduct in this case was improper interference, should this be sufficient to order another representational election? Critically evaluate.
4. Are the remedies used by the NLRB for misconduct during a certification election sufficient to assure laboratory conditions in which to conduct such elections? Critically evaluate.

Case 6

Independent Contractors or Employees? A Company's Refusal to Bargain

Employer Friendly Cab Company, Inc., Metro-Taxicab Company, Inc., California Cab Company, GRKWSS Enterprise, Inc. Metro-Yellow Taxicab Company and Greyline Cab Co.

Union East Bay Taxi Drivers Association and Brotherhood of Teamsters, Auto Truck Drivers, Line Drivers, Car Haulers and Helpers, Local No. 70, Intervenor.

BACKGROUND

In May 2004 the union was certified as the exclusive bargaining representative of the respondent's full-time and regular part-time taxicab drivers at its 48–49 East 12th Street facility in Oakland, California. This certification was based upon the union having received a majority of the votes cast in a certification election held in August 2002. The delay in the certification was due to the respondent filing a timely request for review contending that the drivers were independent contractors and not employees under Section 2 of the Act. The Board found that the drivers were employees for purposes of the Act and certified the union as the exclusive bargaining representative.

In May 2004 the union's attorney wrote the company requesting that the parties meet for purposes of negotiating concerning the bargaining unit's terms and conditions of employment. The respondent's attorney refused the union's request for a meeting and stated that the company "will not participate in this collective bargaining process." The respondent's attorney also informed the union of its intent to seek judicial review of the Board's finding that the drivers were employees for purposes of the Act.

The union then filed charges of a violation of Section 8(a) (5) and (1) of the Act claiming the respondent failed and refused to meet and bargain with the union as the exclusive bargaining representative of the drivers comprising the certified bargaining unit.

POSITION OF THE EMPLOYER

The respondent employer's position in this matter is straightforward and simple. The drivers who comprise the bargaining unit certified by the National Labor Relations Board are not employees as defined by Section 2 (3) of the Act. The employer contends that the drivers were erroneously classified as employees by the NLRB when determining the propriety of the bargaining unit. The employer therefore intends to seek judicial review of this erroneous Board decision, and it is improper for the Board to order collective bargaining until such time as the issue of independent contractor is settled in the courts.

Therefore, the respondent denies any wrongdoing under the Act and prays that the Board will take no action concerning the allegation that it refused to bargain until the courts decide whether the drivers are employees or independent contractors.

POSITION OF THE UNION

The office of the general counsel and union take the position that the respondent has violated Section 8(a) (5) and (1) by refusing to bargain. Section 102.67 (f) of the Board's Rules and Regulations precludes relitigating "in any related subsequent unfair labor practice proceeding, any issue which was, or could have been, raised in the representation proceeding." In this case, the respondent argued in the determination of the appropriate bargaining unit that the drivers were independent contractors and not employees under Section 2 of the Act. That issue was properly determined at the time of the certification proceeding in this matter. The employer, if then dissatisfied with the decision of the Board, had the option to appeal the certification to the judiciary. This the respondent did not do but, rather, waited until the certification election was held, and the union certified to again raise the issue of independent contractor when the union demanded negotiations.

It is the union's position that the drivers are employees for purposes of the Act, and that they are not independent contractors. Further, it is the union's position that the respondent violated the Act by failing and/or refusing to collectively bargain when requested to do. The respondent should have appealed the Board's findings that the drivers were employees in a timely fashion, rather than wait and refuse to bargain while appealing the determinations of the Board in the certification processes.

QUESTIONS

1. What is the difference between an independent contractor and an employee for purposes of the Act? If the drivers were independent contractors, does this make a difference in the certification proceedings? Does it make a difference after the certification proceedings? Why?
2. Does the respondent have to bargain with the union during the pendency of litigation of certification issues? Is there a certification issue in this case?
3. If you were the administrative law judge how would you rule? Explain your decision.

Case 7

On the Dole: A Refusal to Bargain with a Properly Certified Union

Company Dole Fresh Vegetables, Inc.

Union International Union of Operating Engineers, Local 20, AFL-CIO.

BACKGROUND

On October 31, 2000, the NLRB conducted a certification election for the employer's bargaining unit. On November 21, 2000, the union was certified as the exclusive bargaining representative for this bargaining unit, having demonstrated its majority status by winning the certification election.

The company admitted its refusal to collectively bargain with the union. The company attacked the validity of the election because it believed that supervisors had been placed in the bargaining unit. It was because the company did not recognize the validity of the election that it believed it was under no obligation to collectively bargain with the union. When the company refused to bargain, the union then filed unfair labor practice charges.

The bargaining unit certified by the NLRB was:

> All maintenance employees, including maintenance technicians, maintenance packaging technicians, maintenance parts clerks, and maintenance leads, employed by the Respondent at its 600 Benjamin Drive, Springfield, Ohio, facility, excluding all production employees, quality assurance employees, raw materials employees, sanitation employees, shipping and receiving employees, office clerical employees, and other employees and all professional employees, guards, and supervisors as defined by the Act.

There was no dispute that the employer was an employer for purposes of the Act and was engaged in interstate commerce for purposes of the Act. Therefore, the NLRB had jurisdiction over the parties' dispute.

POSITION OF THE UNION

The union's position was that since the certification election results were made known by the NLRB, the employer was obliged by the Act to collectively bargain with the union. There was no doubt of the union's majority status, and the employer simply refused to be bound by the law.

The union rejected the employer's claim that the maintenance leadpersons were managerial employees and were not properly included in the bargaining unit. The union claimed that the certification election was proper, and that no issues of propriety of the bargaining unit were raised once it was identified. It was the union's position that the employer argued the managerial nature of maintenance leadpersons' positions simply because the employer did not like the results of the certification election. Therefore the union requested the NLRB to order the employer to collective bargain with the duly elected exclusive representative of the bargaining unit.

POSITION OF THE EMPLOYER

The employer (respondent) in this matter admitted its refusal to collectively bargain with the union. The employer claimed that the lead mechanics included in the bargaining unit were statutory supervisory personnel for purposes of the Act. The participation of these lead mechanics in the certification election process, according to the company, tainted the certification election campaign and hence the certification election results. Therefore, the employer contended that the union was not properly the certified exclusive bargaining representative of the bargaining unit.

The employer admitted it had no new evidence to offer concerning the propriety of the certified bargaining unit. The employer also admitted that it did not contest the bargaining unit as determined by the NLRB prior to the certification election.

The employer argued that it was only obliged to collectively bargain with a properly certified bargaining representative, and since this union was not properly certified, the employer believed it had no obligation to bargain with the union.

QUESTIONS

1. Once the NLRB determines what a proper bargaining unit is, can either the employer or union contest that determination? If so, when should such a contest be filed—before or after a certification election is conducted? Why?
2. Are supervisory personnel properly included in a bargaining unit? Is there a difference between supervisory and managerial personnel? Explain.
3. If a union wins a certification election and the NLRB certifies the union as the exclusive bargaining representative, can an employer lawfully refuse to bargain with that union? Explain.
4. Did the employer violate either Section 8(a) (1) or (5) in this case? Explain.

Case 8

Racial/Ethnic Prejudice During a Union Representational Election

Company KI (USA) Corporation, Berea, Kentucky

Union United Automobile Workers of America (UAW)

BACKGROUND

The company was a subsidiary of a Japanese corporation, adhered to certain Japanese management programs, and provided training in Japan for its American managers. The company employed both Japanese nationals and Americans in its management ranks, with Japanese nationals predominant in the higher ranks. At the Berea, Kentucky, manufacturing facility, onsite supervisory management was composed mainly of Americans, whose assigned role was to use a blend of American and Japanese management concepts. The Berea facility was the focus of a union organizing campaign in 1991 and early 1992.

In March 1992, on the day before the representational election, the union held a meeting attended by a number of employees and several union (UAW) representatives. At the end of the meeting, one of the union representatives made available to the employees various printed materials, including a copy of a letter that had first appeared as a "letter to the editor" in the January 1991 issue of *Easy Rider* magazine, a publication directed to Harley-Davidson owners, operators, and fans:

You Should Know
Voice from Japan

> In regard to your article "Bubba's 5th Annual Honda Drop" in the October issue, if you want to destroy Japanese products, you should start with your Harley-Davidson motorcycles. I recently toured a Harley-Davidson dealership and was given the opportunity to examine the 1991 models and "genuine" parts. I saw more made-in-Japan, -Korea, and -Taiwan labels than you could even find in a Japanese company. Perhaps that is why Harley-Davidsons are finally being praised as quality products—because of the excellent Japanese parts on them.
>
> As a Japanese businessman and investor, I am appalled at the typical lazy, uneducated American worker I have had to deal with in your country. The Japanese work force and management philosophy are proven superior, and your half-witted American managers are constantly studying our techniques. In America it is your political leaders who are doing you the most harm, not the Japanese. The fact that Americans believe in such false patriotism and political lies shows how ignorant and weak you have become.
>
> I suggest the Americans start developing a healthy respect for Japan because one of my colleagues will eventually become your boss and/or own your company. In Japan we have a very rich tradition and long history of patience, but we will not show patience with your disrespect and racism toward our proud and growing empire.

Toshito Nakamura
Osaka, Japan

The contents of the letter clearly indicated that it was written in response to an article in the *Easy Rider* publication. The union's sole addition to the letter was the "You Should Know" banner, and underlining some of the text of the letter. The union did not refer to the letter in any of its other campaign materials. The letter was reproduced and widely disseminated among the proposed bargaining unit employees, a majority of whom voted in favor of having the United Automobile Workers Union represent them. Shortly after the election, the company filed exceptions to the representational election under Section 9(c) of LMRA, urging that the results be set aside.

POSITION OF THE COMPANY

The company position relied on a previous NLRB decision[1] in which the Board held that it would set aside elections "when a party engages in a campaign which seeks to overstress and exacerbate racial feeling by irrelevant, inflammatory appeals." The company pointed out that apparently some employees did believe that Japanese employers had very negative attitudes about American workers. These employees were concerned that their own employer shared these views. The union had sought to appeal to these concerns by distributing copies of the letter written by a Japanese businessman, Toshito Nakamura, who had written that American workers were lazy and uneducated, and that Americans were ignorant and weak. However, there was no evidence whatsoever that Mr. Nakamura had any relationship to the company, nor was there any evidence that the company in any way shared his views.

By distributing the letter to the employees the day before the election, the union had sought to capitalize on the employees' concerns that all Japanese, including company management, held negative views of American workers. Thus, the union had sought to lump top company management together with Mr. Nakamura solely on the basis that they were both Japanese, and to ascribe to the company the offensive, biased views of Mr. Nakamura. This was a gross and untruthful distortion, and had no place in a representational election conducted by the NLRB. In the company's view, the high Board standards and "laboratory conditions" required for conducting a representational election had been seriously compromised by the union's appeal to racial and ethnic prejudice. It was logical to conclude that numerous employees had been influenced to vote according to their prejudices rather than according to their real preferences about the UAW's representing them. The company urged the NLRB to set aside the results of the election and to order that another representational election be held that would be untainted by this improper union conduct.

POSITION OF THE UNION

The union position relied to some extent on the same NLRB decision that was cited by the company. In that decision, the Board had distinguished unacceptable racial, inflammatory

[1] This case was *Sewell Manufacturing Company,* 138 NLRB 66, 50 LRRM 1532 (1962).

appeals from "isolated, casual, prejudicial remarks." The Board had stated in this case that it would not set aside a representational election or "condemn relevant campaign statements merely because they may have racial overtones."

The union noted that before the election campaign employees had expressed concern among themselves about the company's Japanese owners and managers not appreciating the American employees and the American supervisors, and although the employees had expressed such concerns during the election campaign, there was no evidence that the union had created or directly contributed to these concerns. The union had not provided any commentary to the employees about how the letter written by a Japanese businessman and investor might relate to the company's attitudes toward its employees. By making available a copy of Mr. Nakamura's letter to the employees without comment, the union was not making an inflammatory, emotional appeal to prejudice. Rather, the union was merely urging the employees to vote for the union to prevent the discrimination or lack of appreciation they perceived might or did exist. Providing the employees with the text of the offensive letter did not lower or dilute the election standards to such a degree that employees could not make up their own minds about union representation.

In the union's view, the company was grossly exaggerating the importance of the letter merely in order to overturn the election outcome. The union urged the NLRB to dismiss the company's complaint, to certify the union as the representative of bargaining unit employees, and to direct the company to recognize and engage in collective bargaining with the union.

QUESTIONS

1. Both the company and the union utilized aspects of the NLRB's *Sewell Manufacturing Company* case decision in support of their respective positions. Why is this type of case precedent one that can be manipulated to justify either side's position?
2. What inferences, if any, can be drawn from the facts that (*a*) the American employees had previously expressed concerns about their company's Japanese owners and (*b*) the union provided the employees with a copy of the Nakamura letter without commentary?
3. Should the NLRB set aside the results of the representational election because its standards for proper election atmosphere/conduct had been compromised? Explain.
4. What are the proper conditions necessary for an appropriate certification election? Critically evaluate this standard.

Case 9

Waiver to Arbitrate or Unlawful Refusal?

Union United Food and Commercial Workers International Union, Local 1096

Employer ACS, LLC

BACKGROUND

The parties to this matter have a collective bargaining agreement, and in that collective bargaining agreement is a grievance procedure which ends in final and binding arbitration. The arbitration clause is as follows:

> 1. Disputes concerning contract interpretation, the disposition of assets, the right of sale, the right to control the number of hours that the plant be open or closed down either for lack of business or for economic reasons, or matters which involve management decision or business judgment shall not be subject to arbitration. Procedural questions of compliance with the contract shall be subject to judicial determination and not arbitration. Either party may seek judicial relief with regard to any of the foregoing.

The union filed six grievances in this matter, concerning: (1) Performance Memorandum and Suspension of an Employee, (2) Work Assignment of an Employee, (3) Notice of Posting concerning Working Conditions, (4) Improper Piecework Pay Assignments, (5) Written Warning concerning Performance and Attitude of an Entire Crew, and (6) Drug Testing Program being Implemented by Employer.

The union processed the grievances through the steps of the grievance procedure, and none of the grievances were resolved. The union then sought a panel of arbitrators from an administrative agency. When the union met with the employer to strike arbitrators, the employer notified the union that the grievances were not arbitrable and that it had no intention of submitting to arbitration. The union then filed a charge with the Board alleging that the employer violated Section 8(a) (1) and (5) of the Act by failing to bargain collectively by submitting to arbitration and unilaterally amending the parties' collective bargaining agreement.

POSITION OF THE UNION

The union claims that each of the six grievances are arbitrable under the parties' collective bargaining agreement. It is the union's position that the employer's position is one of wholesale repudiation of the parties' grievance/arbitration procedure in direct contravention to Section 8(a) (1) and (5) of the Act.

Further, even if the employer's position had merit, which it does not, it is for the arbitrator to decide what grievances are substantively arbitrable. For the arbitrator to make such a determination the grievances must be put before an arbitrator. It is therefore clear that the employer has violated the Act and the Board should find that the employer must submit these matters for arbitration.

POSITION OF THE EMPLOYER

The employer stands on the clear and unambiguous language of the parties' collective bargaining agreement. The contract between the parties makes clear that contract interpretation matters (grievances 1, 2, and 4) are specifically excluded from the arbitration provisions. The contract also makes clear that matters involving management decisions or business judgment (grievances 3, 5, and 6) are also specifically excluded from the arbitration provisions of the contract.

The union's contentions that an arbitrator must decide what is arbitrable and what is not is also without merit. The parties' contract specifically states that "questions of compliance with the contract shall be subject to judicial determination and not arbitration." What the union requests from the Board is a rewriting of the parties' agreement. The employer has simply complied with the expressed terms of the contract, and the grievances are not subject to arbitration and any compliance issue is to be resolved in the courts and not arbitration. Therefore, the employer asks that the charge be dismissed.

QUESTIONS

1. What matters are specifically excluded from arbitration by the language of the parties' collective bargaining agreement? Does this leave anything that can be arbitrated? Explain.
2. Has the employer modified its contract by refusing to arbitrate? Explain.
3. Does the Board have jurisdiction over this case or should an arbitrator decide whether the matters are substantively arbitrable? Explain.
4. If you were the Board how would you rule in this case? What is the basis for your decision? Explain.

Case 10

Claim of an Inability to Pay Wage Demands: What Is Bargaining in Good Faith?

Employer American Polystyrene Corporation

Union International Chemical Workers Union Council of the United Food and Commercial Workers International Union, Local 1C

BACKGROUND

An administrative law judge ruled that the respondent had failed to provide information necessary to discharge its obligation to bargain in good faith with the union. The respondent company has appealed the judge's decision to the National Labor Relations Board.

The respondent company in a negotiation session with the union claimed an inability to pay for the wage demands made by the union in bargaining. When the union requested proof of the financial inability to pay the wage demands, the company refused to provide any such evidence on April 29, 2002. Negotiations continued and subsequently on April 30, management negotiators delivered to the union a note that stated:

> I am rejecting this request. While I have told you that we are a small company and times are tough, at no time have I ever told you we cannot afford your proposals. Rather, in these uncertain economic times, we believe that we need to take a more cautious approach than what you propose.

Throughout subsequent negotiations the parties argued concerning whether the company made the claim of an inability to pay, and the union reiterated demands to see the company's financial records in order to determine if an ability to pay exists.

POSITION OF THE UNION

It is the union's position that the employer clearly and unambiguously claimed that it had an inability to pay for the union's proposals concerning wages and retirement plans on April 29, 2002. During the April 29 negotiations, the company's owner responded to the union proposals by stating: "No, I can't. I'd go broke." Clearly, this was a denial of an ability to pay requiring proof of the financial deficiencies.

The company simply changed the words it used to make its inability to pay claims more ambiguous when it delivered the note on April 30 alleging times are hard and the company must be more cautious than what the union proposes. It is the union's position that the administrative law judge was correct, and the company's position was it had no ability to pay.

When a claim of an inability to pay is made, the company is obliged to provide evidence of that inability to pay. The Board has consistently ruled when such a claim is made, and the company then fails to provide proof of the claim, that conduct is a failure to bargain in good faith, in violation of Section 8(a) (5) and (1), *Truitt Mfg. Co.,* 351 U.S. 153–54.

It is the union's contention that the company has violated Section 8 (a) (5) and (1) by not providing the requested proof of their claimed inability to pay for the union's economic proposals in negotiations.

POSITION OF THE EMPLOYER

The employer contends that the administrative law judge made substantial errors in his findings of fact. The employer admits to the "I'd go broke" comment across the bargaining table. However, the record clearly shows that when the union requested proof of the claim the Company recanted and told the Union it could fund its requests, but rather thought it imprudent to do so. The handwritten note passed to the union across the bargaining table on April 30 clearly shows the change in position by the company.

The company urges the Board may not find that there was a failure to bargain in good faith when the company almost immediately corrects the record and admits an ability to pay, but simply finds the union proposals financially imprudent. It is therefore the company's position that there was no violation of the Act, and that the Board should dismiss the union's petition as being without merit.

QUESTIONS

1. What proof is necessary to show an inability to pay an economic demand made across the bargaining table? Explain.
2. What is a claim of an inability to pay? Is "I'd go broke" a claim of an inability to pay? Did the April 30 note change the company's position on the matter of ability to pay? Explain.
3. If you were the Board would you affirm the administrative law judge's decision in this matter? Explain.

Case 11

Was the Employee Involvement Committee a Violation of Labor Law?

Company Research Federal Credit Union, Warren, Milford, and Detroit, Michigan

Union Food and Commercial Workers, Local Union No. 876

BACKGROUND

The Union Organizing Campaign

The employer was a credit union with its main office in Warren, Michigan, and branches located in Milford and Detroit, Michigan. In early March 1990, several employees met with representatives of the union. The union then actively began an organizational campaign and solicited signed union authorization cards from a number of employees. Shortly thereafter, the union filed a petition with the regional office of the National Labor Relations Board requesting that a representational election be held. The union claimed that it had obtained signed representation authorization cards from a majority of the some 20 to 25 employees in a proposed bargaining unit. The NLRB subsequently directed that a representational election take place on May 21, 1990.

The Employment Involvement Committee (EIC)—Preelection

On April 4, 1990, management advised all its employees that it had retained a management consultant, Walter Meckfuss.[1] On April 30, management called for all employees from its several locations to attend an employee meeting. Walter Meckfuss, the company's new management consultant, was present at this meeting.

Meckfuss announced at the April 30 meeting that the company had decided to form an "employee involvement committee," or EIC, to consist of an employee and a supervisory representative from each of the three offices. Supervisory representatives were to be appointed by management, and employee representatives were to be elected by employees in their respective offices. Meckfuss stated that the purpose of the EIC was to improve communication and morale in the firm and to enable the employees to have an important say in improving work operations and other aspects of their jobs.

Because the first EIC meeting was scheduled for the next day, May 1, representatives and their alternates were selected almost immediately. For example, the Milford branch employees elected Carla Lee and Teresa Coleman as their representative and alternate, respectively, in a restaurant on the way home from the meeting. The Milford branch supervisor, Martin Post, was present during this election process.

EIC meetings were held on May 1, 7, and 16, 1990. All meetings were held at the Warren facility or elsewhere in Warren. The meeting of May 16 was held in the evening; the other meetings were held during working hours. The May 16 meeting was for all

[1] The names of all individuals and certain data are disguised.

representatives and alternates; the other meetings were just for representatives, although an alternate could attend in the absence of the representative. In her representative capacity, Carla Lee received her normal pay for the daytime meetings she attended as well as mileage between her branch in Milford and the meeting site in Warren. Dinner was supplied by the company at the May 16 evening meeting.

The May 1 meeting was attended by the three employee representatives, and Jane Havis, branch manager at Warren, Martin Post, branch manager at Milford, and Walter Meckfuss. Meckfuss explained what the EIC was supposed to do, saying that the employee members were to be the "unbiased eyes and ears" of the employees they represented. They should try to get the employees in their respective departments to talk with them regarding any problems they felt needed attention. The representatives were then to bring these problems and suggestions to the EIC meetings. At the meetings, if solutions to such problems were found, they would be presented to top management or the board of directors. Some possible topics for action by the EIC discussed at the May 1 meeting were smoking policies, part-time benefits, and annual reviews. The meeting lasted about an hour and a half, during which an EIC chairperson and secretary were selected.

At the May 7 meeting, a smoking policy was discussed; Meckfuss suggested that the EIC might come up with ideas to solve the smoking problem if representatives would discuss the matter with the employees they represented and ask for their opinions. The question of a constantly changing sick-time policy was also brought up. Meckfuss responded that it was a difficult subject, and that management had been studying the benefit package and comparing it with similar businesses in the area. On the subject of educational reimbursement, Meckfuss advised the representatives to ask their fellow employees how they wanted it handled, and then a written policy would be developed. Personal leave days, employee reviews, and Christmas bonuses were also discussed.

The May 16 evening meeting of all representatives and alternates took place in Warren at a local restaurant. Two members of the board of directors were also present, Nepah Rentul and Sam Barrow. An outline for discussion was presented, which included such topics as a smoking policy, wage and salary review, and sick-time benefits. Carla Lee asked whether employees were to get an ample pay raise. Meckfuss responded that management was checking with similar-sized credit unions within the area to determine an appropriate salary scale. With respect to sick time, Meckfuss said that he felt the employees would again be allowed seven sick days annually (the number of days of annual paid sick leave had been reduced from seven to five in 1989). However, Meckfuss stated that nothing could be done in these areas until after the union representational election. With respect to the matter of vacation benefits for part-time employees, Meckfuss suggested that the representatives solicit input from the employees and come up with a formula. There was also a discussion about credibility between the employees and the board of directors. Sam Barrow stated that he would meet with the EIC members occasionally, and that he wanted to have more open communication between the Board and all of the staff. Walter Meckfuss stated that he knew that annual reviews were a problem and something had to be done about them. He added that it was possible that a special committee could be established to conduct annual reviews for employees.

The Representational Election

On May 21, 1990, the NLRB conducted a union representational election for the proposed bargaining unit. By a vote of 12 to 9, a majority voted against having the union certified as their bargaining representative.

The Employee Involvement Committee (EIC)—Postelection

Two EIC meetings were held on May 30 and June 20, 1990, after the election. The May 30 meeting was a predinner meeting at a local restaurant. At this meeting, the EIC developed a memo for employees listing and describing six issues that the EIC would be presenting at the next board of directors meeting, scheduled for June 21. Those issues were wage and salary pay scales, including the area wage survey and part-time employee benefits; cleaning out the ventilation system at Warren; smoking areas; sick time; employee transactions; and memos. The latter two issues involved setting a specific time during the day to see supervisors for access to money and slowing down the number of memos that were being issued. By memo to the EIC dated May 31, Sam Barrow responded to some of the issues raised in the EIC's May 30 memo, informing the EIC that the firm was getting bids regarding ventilation system maintenance, that sick-time policy and cash incentive awards would be announced at the June board meeting, and that new procedures were in place to ensure more consistency in policies.

At the June 20 meeting of the EIC, Meckfuss stated with respect to sick-time policy proposals that he did not think there would be any problem with them, and that the employees should have gotten what they had asked for a long time ago. He commented that proposals dealing with part-time benefits would be more difficult because of the costs. With respect to smoking areas, the Warren EIC employee representative had a suggestion for a location in the Warren offices where a smoking area might be designated. Meckfuss said that he would ask management to check with the fire marshal for approval. During the meeting, Meckfuss stated that wages would not be discussed because the wage survey was not complete.

The Union's Unfair Labor Practice Charges

Shortly after the representational election, the union filed unfair labor practice charges against the company claiming that the company had violated Sections 8(a) (1), 8(a) (2), and 8(a) (5) of the Labor Management Relations Act. The union claimed that the employee involvement committee (EIC) was a labor organization within the meaning of Section 2(5) of LMRA, and that it had been created by management to deny the employees their own union representation.

POSITION OF THE UNION

The union claimed that the purpose of the employee involvement committee was to undercut the employees' desire for a union. The EIC had been created by the company without any employee request for such an entity shortly after the union had begun its representational campaign. The nature of the EIC had been determined by management, and employees had been directed to select representatives and alternates. Meetings were called by management, some on company time with the employee representatives paid for attendance. Although the meetings were led by a management consultant, it was clear that Meckfuss was serving as an agent of management and the board of directors. Virtually every topic discussed at the EIC meetings dealt in some way with wages, hours of employment, and working conditions. In the union's view, the EIC was designed to create in the employees' minds the sentiment that there was no need for a labor union. This was particularly evident in the efforts of Meckfuss and members of the board of directors to solicit employee grievances and promise to remedy them.

The union argued that the EIC was a labor organization created and dominated by the company in violation of Sections 8(a) (2) and 8(a) (1) of the Labor Management Relations Act. By soliciting employee grievances and promising to improve various working conditions, the employer further violated Section 8(a) (1) since these matters were contingent upon the outcome of the union election.

The union argued that it had attained a valid majority of employees who had signed union authorization cards. The company had refused to recognize these cards and had insisted on a formal NLRB election. By refusing to recognize and bargain with the union when it had obtained signed authorization cards from a majority of employees, and by having unlawfully interfered with the union, the employer had violated Section 8(a) (5) of LMRA. The union requested as a remedy that the NLRB under Section 10(c) of the Act direct that the EIC be disestablished and that the company recognize and bargain with the union because of the company's significant unfair labor practices that destroyed a valid union majority.

POSITION OF THE COMPANY

The company claimed that it had not violated any provisions of the Labor Management Relations Act by organizing an employee involvement committee (EIC). The purpose of the EIC was to provide a means for employees to address various concerns and to present recommendations for solutions to management and/or the board of directors. The company had contemplated the formation of the EIC for several months prior to the union representational election. No employees were forced to participate in the EIC. The employees and their representatives had found the EIC to be an appropriate forum in which to express their concerns. The EIC was not dominated by management; the management consultant, Mr. Meckfuss, was merely a conduit between management and the employee representatives. No employee was disciplined or reprimanded for anything that was said or brought up within the EIC.

The company contested the allegation that the EIC was a labor organization within the meaning of Section 2(5) of LMRA. The EIC was a venue for presenting employees' concerns to management, such as is widespread in American industry. Quality circles, quality-of-work-life programs, and the like, provide a cooperative means by which employees and management can discuss and solve mutual problems. These nonadversarial programs should be fostered and not condemned by labor laws. The fact that the employees rejected the union was an indication that they considered the EIC to be a viable mechanism for addressing their concerns.

Although the company denied that the EIC violated Sections 8(a) (1) and 8(a) (2), it argued that in the event the NLRB should rule that some technical violation had occurred, an order to recognize and bargain with the union would be totally improper. A majority of employees had voted against the union. If the NLRB should find that the company had inadvertently violated the Act, the appropriate remedy would be to direct that a new representational election be held to determine the employees' wishes concerning union representation.

QUESTIONS

1. Does it make a difference in this case that the employee involvement committee (EIC) was organized during thc union rcpresentational campaign?
2. Even though employee representatives were not forced to serve on the EIC, did the employees have any real alternative to agreeing to participate? Discuss.
3. Was the EIC a labor organization within the meaning of LMRA, or was it rather a means by which employees and management could communicate about employee concerns? Discuss why various types of participative management efforts throughout business and industry often operate in a "gray area" of labor law.
4. If the NLRB finds a violation of the Act because of the EIC, what should be the appropriate remedy directed by the Board?

---

* At the time of writing of this text, proposed legislation was still pending in the Congress called the Teamwork for Employees and Managers (TEAM) Act. The TEAM Act (as reported in the December 1997 issue of *HR News,* published by the Society for Human Resource Management, p. 10) would amend the Labor Management Relations Act to allow employers to "establish, assist and participate in programs that address matters of mutual interest" to employers and employees, provided that workers participated in the program "to at least the same extent practicable" as their managers. Another congressional legislative proposal would prohibit the use of employee involvement committees to thwart union organizing activity undertaken to achieve union recognition. Employers would be barred from forming such committees if 30 percent of their workers had petitioned for a union representational election.

Instructors and students should monitor the outcome of this and any other proposed legislation which could have a major impact upon employee involvement and participative management programs.

Case 12

A Penny Saved Was a Warning Not Earned

Employer California Pie Company

Union Bakery, Confectionery, and Tobacco Workers International Union, AFL-CIO, Local 125, and Charles Penny[1]

BACKGROUND

Charles Penny, who was a second-shift utility man at the company's pie factory had filed a grievance because two junior employees had received an overtime assignment and he had not. Subsequent to the filing of this grievance, Mr. Penny was walking toward the employee breakroom when he saw his union steward. Mr. Penny motioned to the steward who then walked over to Mr. Penny. The two men walked into the breakroom, and Mr. Penny began to quiz the steward concerning the status of his grievance. Mr. Penny's break began at 2:45 P.M.

The union steward's shift had just ended, and he had made arrangements to discuss several matters with Mr. Penny's supervisor, Ms. Hasty. Ms. Hasty had walked past the breakroom and inquired of the steward whether he could meet with her, and he asked for just a minute or so. The supervisor agreed, and the steward then parted company with Mr. Penny, who started back to his work station at about 2:58 according to the breakroom clock. The union steward walked to the office of the supervisor, who then arrived shortly after the steward.

The supervisor inquired of the steward whether Penny was on break and the steward told Hasty that he did not know. A short discussion occurred between the steward and Hasty concerning Mr. Penny's grievance, and the steward left the office and went home. Within a matter of minutes after the steward left, Ms. Hasty called Mr. Penny to her office and interrogated him concerning the time of his break. She told Mr. Penny she observed him leaving the breakroom at 3:10 and he responded that he left at 2:58. Subsequently, Ms. Hasty issued Mr. Penny a letter of warning for expanding his breaktime. The charge noted that Mr. Penny was observed in the breakroom from 2:43 P.M. to 3:10 P.M.

POSITION OF THE UNION

The union alleged that the supervisor, Ms. Hasty, manufactured the charges against Mr. Penny. The union claimed that Ms. Hasty had no idea of when Mr. Penny left for his break, and that she was never told that the steward left the breakroom at 3:10; in fact, the steward denied that he was ever asked anything about his contact with Mr. Penny in the breakroom. In testimony before the administrative law judge the supervisor was inconsistent concerning the exact events that gave rise to the disciplinary warning issued to Mr. Penny.

[1] The individuals' names are disguised in this case.

The union stewards routinely remained after their shifts ended to take care of union business. The company had a rule that permitted access to employees by union officials on company property, but during time when they had no duties (i.e., breaktime, arriving at work, and lunchtime, etc.).

The union claimed that Ms. Hasty was out to "get" Mr. Penny because he was a union activist and had filed a grievance, to which she took offense. Further, the interrogation of Mr. Penny by his supervisor prior to issuing discipline was coercive in the union's view. Further, the union pointed out that no other employee had been disciplined for expanding their breaks during the entire year that this occurred. Therefore, the union believed that Mr. Penny was discriminated against for his union activity and urged the NLRB to find that the company committed an unfair labor practice.

POSITION OF THE COMPANY

It was the company's position that the discipline was issued for just cause and had absolutely nothing to do with any union or concerted activity by Mr. Penny. It was also the company's position that the "access" rule to union stewards was that employees were limited to discuss grievance and other union matters to times when they were not working. Breaks, lunchtime, and before and after their shifts, employees were free to discuss union business, but were to refrain from using working time for such activities. It was clear that Mr. Penny expanded his breaktime, and if he was conducting union business with this stolen time, it clearly was not protected activity.

It was the company's view that the discipline issued was for expansion of breaktime, and if union business was conducted on that expanded breaktime, it was irrelevant to the issue of just cause for the discipline. The company urged the NLRB to find that no unfair labor practices were committed in this matter.

QUESTIONS

1. Is concerted action or union action protected regardless of any other circumstances involved in the case? Explain.
2. Is the fact that the supervisor's testimony was lacking in consistency important in determining the facts in this matter? Explain.
3. How does the fact that no other employees were disciplined for expanding their breaks weigh in this case's decision? Explain.
4. Did the employer violate the Act? Explain.

Case 13

Termination for Failure to Report Accident or for Solicitation of Employees

Employer J. B. Hunt Transport, Inc., Philadelphia, Pennsylvania

Union International Brotherhood of Teamsters, AFL-CIO, Local 17

BACKGROUND

Mr. John Gregory,[1] a truck driver employed by J. B. Hunt Transport in Philadelphia, Pennsylvania, was discharged on March 1, 2000. The reasons cited by the employer for the discharge of Mr. Gregory were that he had a vehicular accident and he failed to report the accident pursuant to company rules and regulations.

The company routinely conducted roundtable meetings in which employees could make suggestions and bring problems to management's attention. Issues concerning the terms and conditions of employment were raised and the employees suggested that a committee represent them in attempting to resolve issues concerning, in particular, compensation. Mr. Gregory was elected chairperson of this committee and engaged in several discussions with management in attempt to raise the employees' compensation levels, all to no avail. Thereafter, Mr. Gregory had been involved in solicitation of union bargaining authorization cards on behalf of Local 17 of the International Brotherhood of Teamsters. By February 18, 2000, Mr. Gregory had obtained 13 signed authorization cards from fellow truck drivers assigned to the company's Philadelphia facility. Frequently, management observed Mr. Gregory speaking while surrounded by as many as four or five truck drivers.

On February 14, 2000, Mr. Gregory took his truck from work to visit his brother in the Philadelphia House of Corrections. Mr. Gregory asserted that he had sought and received permission from Supervisor Terry to drive this vehicle to the House of Corrections. He had parked his vehicle in the parking lot of the prison and, when he returned from his visit, discovered that his vehicle was blocked in by an automobile. At the suggestion of a guard he pulled off the paved lot and attempted to cross a grassy area, and his truck became stuck. Mr. Gregory believed his situation was a "road service" situation and called the company's towing service. The vehicle was towed back to the company's Philadelphia facility, where it was noted to have some minor damage to a mud flap and a light. The company's facility manager Mr. Sosa had made written notations that Mr. Gregory's truck had damage to the mud flap and a light on February 25, 2000. However, the record also showed that Mr. Sosa had not spoken to the tow-truck driver or to Mr. Gregory, nor had Sosa seen the truck until February 26, 2000. Mr. Sosa had noted what the mechanic discovered and assumed the damage was the result of Mr. Gregory's getting the truck stuck at the House of Corrections.

On February 23, 2000, the company received an election petition from Local 17 of the International Brotherhood of Teamsters. The following day a law firm was hired by

[1] Names of the individuals involved are disguised.

the company to represent it with respect to election proceedings, and the company instituted a vigorous antiunion campaign. This campaign included letters warning that the Teamsters thrived on "fear and intimidation."

The tow-truck driver subsequently stated that there was no damage to the truck he had towed back to the company's facility and that the truck was not deeply mired in the grassy area. In fact, there was no damage to the grassy area that could be attributed to the company's truck in the view of the tow-truck driver. No claim was made against the company by the City of Philadelphia for alleged damage at the House of Corrections. Rather than interview Mr. Gregory, Mr. Sosa informed Mr. Gregory over the telephone that he was being terminated. At no time did management give Mr. Gregory an opportunity to tell his side of the story.

POSITION OF THE UNION

The union urged that the cause for Mr. Gregory's termination was not for the incident involving his vehicle on February 14, 2000, but rather Mr. Gregory was discharged for having engaged in solicitation of union bargaining authorization cards in violation of Section 8 (a) (1) and (3) of the National Labor Relations Act.

The company asserted damage to Mr. Gregory's truck, yet Mr. Gregory was not discharged for damaging his truck. He was discharged for failing to report an accident and for using the truck for personal purposes. In fact, Mr. Gregory followed, to the letter, the procedures for road service and called the company's towing service. Under company policy nothing else was required for road service incidents.

Mr. Gregory sought and obtained permission to take his truck to visit his brother on February 14, 2000. Mr. Terry did not remember having interaction with his employee on February 14, 2000, and his claim not to have given Mr. Gregory permission to take his truck for personal use was simply not credible. This type of personal use of company trucks was commonplace.

The union's view of this case was very simple. Management noticed that its employees seemed to have been paying a great deal of attention to Mr. Gregory during the week of February 11, 2000. Subsequently, about February 23, 2000, the company received a certification election petition, and several of these authorization cards were purportedly solicited by Mr. Gregory. The following day, management revisited the towing of Mr. Gregory's truck and decided to use this incident as a pretext to discharge Gregory, which it finally did on March 1, 2000. Clearly, according to the union, this discharge was for concerted action in support of the union and therefore illegal. The union urged the NLRB to reinstate Mr. Gregory, to make him whole for lost wages and benefits, and to order the company to abide by the requirements of the National Labor Relations Act.

POSITION OF THE EMPLOYER

The employer's position was that Mr. Gregory violated its rules concerning reporting accidents and personal use of its vehicles. The company believed that it had just cause to dismiss Mr. Gregory and that Mr. Gregory's discharge had nothing whatsoever to do with his union sympathies or activities.

The company had a practice of permitting drivers to use trucks for short personal trips; however, drivers had to seek and receive permission from their supervisors to use their trucks for these purposes. On February 14, 2000, Mr. Gregory neither sought nor received permission from Mr. Terry to use his truck to visit his brother in prison. Mr. Terry's testimony was clear and unequivocal: He did not have any recall of having given Mr. Gregory permission to take the truck. Mr. Gregory, on the other hand, gave self-serving testimony without the slightest corroboration that he had gotten permission to use his truck for personal reasons.

Worse still, according to the company, was the fact that the truck was damaged and, rather than immediately reporting the damage to his supervisor, Mr. Gregory simply called the towing service. Any incident involving property damage was supposed to be reported to supervision by the driver at the first opportunity. Clearly, Mr. Gregory did not report this damage.

The company therefore urged the National Labor Relations Board to dismiss the union's claims. The union activities of Mr. Gregory were not a consideration in the decision to discharge him for his misconduct of February 14, 2000.

QUESTIONS

1. Are the company rules clear about reporting accidents and obtaining permission to use company vehicles for personal reasons? If so, what are those rules, and how do road service incidents differ from accidents?
2. Does the timing of the events, solicitation, the vehicle incident, the petition transmitted to management, and the discharge of Mr. Gregory seem suspect in this case? If so, how?
3. Is there an issue of credibility in this case? Is Mr. Terry believable in this matter? Is Mr. Gregory believable?
4. Was the vigorous antiunion campaign relevant in determining whether the company may have discharged Mr. Gregory for his union activities? If so, why?

Case 14

Causes for Discharge: A Game of Ladders and Questions

Company Budget Heating and Air Conditioning, Inc.

Union Sheet Metal Workers' International Association, Local Union 15

BACKGROUND

The company in this matter was a construction company engaged in the installation of heating and cooling systems in the state of Florida. Florida is a right-to-work law state in which union members work side-by-side with nonunion employees. The employees involved in this matter were sheet metal workers, one of which was union; the remaining three were nonunion.

Mr. Perry[1] was a union member and activist hired by the company with full knowledge of Mr. Perry's sympathies. Mr. Lawson, Mr. Perry's supervisor, informed Mr. Perry in July of 1999 that the company would need him to purchase his own ladder to do work for the company. Mr. Perry was informed of this in a telephone call. Mr. Perry refused to buy a ladder or to authorize deductions from his pay for the company to supply him with a ladder to be used in his work for the company. After Mr. Perry's repeated refusal of the order to buy the ladder, Mr. Lawson informed Mr. Perry that he was discharged for insubordination for refusing to supply himself with the proper tools to practice his trade. Subsequently, Mr. Lawson went to the worksite where Mr. Perry was and ordered him off the site.

Other workers were present at the site. Mr. Black, Mr. Carpenter, and Mr. Garcia were sheet metal workers who knew that Mr. Perry was a union member and supporter. While Mr. Perry and Mr. Lawson were in discussions concerning the issue of Mr. Perry's discharge and his leaving the construction site, the general supervisor Mr. Clark arrived. Mr. Clark repeated the fact that Mr. Perry was discharged and again ordered Mr. Perry to leave the site.

During the period of time between the telephone conversation with Mr. Lawson and Mr. Lawson's arrival at the construction site, Mr. Perry had been discussing the benefits of unionization with his co-workers. Hearing that Mr. Perry was being discharged, Black, Carpenter, and Garcia gathered around the supervisory personnel and asked whether Perry was being fired and if the reason was for his union activities. Questioned by these three employees, Mr. Clark turned to the three employees and said: "Well, you're fired, too, and, anyone else who wants to organize, you're out of here." Mr. Clark then proceeded to call local law enforcement to have all four employees removed from the construction site.

POSITION OF THE UNION

The union's contentions were that all four employees were discharged for their concerted actions, which are Section 7 rights. The union acknowledged that the circumstances differed between Mr. Perry's discharge and that of the other three employees.

[1] Names are disguised.

In Mr. Perry's case, he was a member of the union and was known to management as a member and activist. Mr. Perry routinely talked to his fellow workers about the benefits of joining the union and urged them to become members. When Mr. Perry was discharged for refusal to buy a ladder, the union contended that it was a pretext and that the real cause of Mr. Perry's discharge was his union activism.

In the cases of Black, Carpenter, and Garcia, they had observed the conduct of Lawson and Clark at the construction site and were fearful that Mr. Perry was being discharged because of his union activities. Naturally, Mr. Perry's co-workers, concerned for their union activist friend, inquired about the situation they were observing. For their concerted action they were rewarded with discharge themselves, after being branded as union organizers by Mr. Clark. Clearly, to the union, the actions of these three employees were concerted actions under the meaning of the Act and thus protected activities under Section 7.

The union urged the NLRB to find that all four employees were unlawfully discharged and should be reinstated and made whole as remedy for the employer's unlawful acts.

POSITION OF THE COMPANY

The company claimed that it did not violate any of the employees' Section 7 rights and that the NLRB should dismiss the charges as being without merit.

In the case of Mr. Perry, it was clear that he needed to have a ladder to be able to practice his trade. The company's ladders were unavailable because of a project that required all equipment of that sort owned by the company. When Mr. Perry was ordered, by telephone, to purchase a ladder, he became argumentative and twice refused the legitimate order of his supervisor. Over the telephone, and before Mr. Lawson went to the construction site, Mr. Perry was notified that he was being discharged for insubordination. At no time was there any reason for Mr. Perry's discharge except his own insubordination.

In the case of the other three employees, they had stopped working and had become an unruly collection of observers to the scene created by Mr. Perry. The inquiry about the cause of Mr. Perry's discharge was meddling in company business and cause for discipline. Because of their own failure to work and for questioning company authority, the company had just cause to discharge these employees. The company claimed there was no concerted or union activity protected by the Act.

QUESTIONS

1. Would Perry have been discharged, except for his union activities? Is this the standard to be applied to determine whether he was discharged for cause or for union activities?
2. Was Perry engaged in union activity when he refused to purchase a ladder? If so, why is this union activity?
3. Is there a difference between union activity and concerted activity? Is that difference in evidence in this matter? Explain.
4. Did it make a difference in this case that Black, Carpenter, and Garcia inquired about whether Perry was being discharged for union activity? If they had simply asked the reason for Perry's discharge, would this have changed the result in this case? Explain.

Case 15

Discharge for Disruptive Conduct, or for Protected Union Activity?

Company Cincinnati Suburban Press, Inc., a Subsidiary of Suburban Communications Corporation, Cincinnati, Ohio

Union The Newspaper Guild

Individual George Fuller[1]

BACKGROUND

The company published and distributed a chain of weekly newspapers in the Cincinnati metropolitan area. The individual who filed charges in this case, George Fuller, was employed as a reporter in the editorial department from November 1984 until his discharge on February 2, 1987.

In October 1985, Fuller helped to initiate a union organizing campaign among employees in the editorial department. The Newspaper Guild union organizing campaign culminated in an NLRB election in April 1986, in which the editorial department employees voted against union representation by a vote of 24 to 19. Efforts to organize the editorial department employees, however, did not end with the April 1986 election. Fuller and other employees formed a committee called "The April 87 Committee," which immediately began efforts to organize the employees, with a view to an April 1987 election. In June 1986 Fuller and others mailed an "opinion survey" to the employees. In July 1986 the results of this survey were mailed to employees and certain members of management. Fuller also passed out prounion "business cards" at the July company picnic, which was attended by both employees and management personnel.

Management was aware of Fuller's continuing efforts to organize its employees. In August 1986, when some literature that had been posted on the employee bulletin board was taken down, Derrick Collins, the company's vice president, spoke with Fuller and asked him how long the union "agitating" was going to continue. Fuller responded that it would continue until April 1987, when another election could be held.[2]

In October 1986, Fuller posted on the employee bulletin board a handwritten "Six Month Update," which urged employees to vote for union representation in April 1987. On October 16, 1986, Duane Silverman, the company's executive editor, asked Fuller if he had posted the document. Fuller admitted to Silverman that he had. In December 1986, an article that Fuller wrote entitled, "Dirty Tricks in the Newsroom," was published in *The Cincinnati Review of Politics and the Arts.* This publication was available for purchase at bookstores throughout the metropolitan area, as well as being a subscription publication that was mailed to regular subscribers. Fuller's article reviewed the

[1] The names of all individuals are disguised.

[2] This response was consistent with Section 9(e) (2) of LMRA.

April 1986 union campaign and the opposition encountered during the drive. As an analytical and historical review of the union's organizing efforts, the article discussed the antiunion acts of certain of the company's managers, supervisors, and employees. Fuller gave copies of the published article to fellow employees, and he talked about using the article as part of the continuing union campaign.

Management first became aware of the article in January 1987. Managing Editor Oscar Willow telephoned Silverman on January 9, 1987, and told him about the article. Although he personally had not yet read the article, Willow told Silverman that he considered it libelous. Willow later obtained a copy of the article and gave it to Silverman. In turn, Silverman contacted Mildred Hawthorne, the vice president of personnel for Suburban Communications Corporation. On January 12, 1987, Hawthorne began an investigation into the circumstances surrounding the article; on January 22, 1987, she suspended Fuller without pay pending completion of the investigation. Although Hawthorne interviewed some of the employees named in the article and others during her investigation, neither she nor Silverman interviewed or questioned Fuller about the article. Acting on Hawthorne's recommendation, management decided to discharge Fuller. On February 2, 1987, Fuller was given a discharge letter signed by Hawthorne, the relevant portions of which follow:

> The Company has completed its investigation of your violation of Company Rules 18 and 29:
>
> 18. Making false, vicious, or malicious statements concerning any employee, supervisor, the Company, or its product.
>
> 29. Unlawful, improper, or unseemly conduct on or off the Company premises or during nonworking hours which affects the employee's relationship to his/her job, to his/her fellow employees, or to his/her supervisors, or affecting the Company's product, reputation, or goodwill in the community.
>
> Our investigation has revealed that you did, indeed, violate these rules. The seriousness of these violations warrants your immediate discharge. Your suspension of January 22, 1987, is converted to an immediate discharge. Your discharge under Rules 18 and 29 is based on the following: Your conduct and the article you authored in the *Cincinnati Review* injured the reputation, image, integrity, and truthfulness of Cincinnati Suburban Press newspapers and its management, and has embarrassed, humiliated, and ridiculed your fellow employees.
>
> Your disruptive conduct has impaired employee relationships with fellow employees and our supervisors.

Shortly thereafter, George Fuller filed unfair labor practice charges with the NLRB claiming that he had been discriminatorily interfered with, suspended, and discharged in violation of Sections 7, 8(a) (1), and 8(a) (3) of the LMRA.[3]

POSITION OF THE INDIVIDUAL

Counsel for George Fuller claimed, first of all, that the two company rules Fuller was accused of violating were themselves in violation of Section 8(a) (1) of LMRA. These

[3] Fuller's unfair labor practice charges were filed on an individual basis. Fuller received financial support from the union in retaining legal counsel to assist him in pursuing these charges.

company rules had been included in Mildred Hawthorne's termination letter to Fuller, and were Company Rules 18 and 29, respectively.

Counsel for Fuller argued that these rules were so overly broad and coercive that, in and of themselves, they would restrict almost any activity or statements by an employee the company considered offensive. The company used these rules as pretext for discharging Fuller, who had been suspended and terminated because of his continual efforts to organize the editorial department employees. Company management was well aware of Fuller's prounion sympathies and efforts. The article Fuller wrote for another publication contained facts and opinions about what had occurred at the company during the union organizing campaign. Even though management found it to be offensive, this does not mean that the article was slanderous or libelous.

Finally, counsel for Fuller claimed that even though Fuller had acted alone when he wrote the article in question, the writing and publication of the article were "inextricably intertwined" with his ongoing union organizing efforts. Such activity is protected by Section 7 of LMRA, and thus the company violated Sections 8(a) (3) and 8(a) (1) by suspending and discharging him. The company should be ordered to reinstate Fuller to his former position and to make him whole for all lost earnings and benefits to which he would be entitled. Further, the company should be directed to cease and desist in its unlawful maintenance of those rules that violated employees' protected rights under the LMRA.

POSITION OF THE COMPANY

The company claimed that its rules No. 18 and 29 were both proper and lawful. These rules were absolutely necessary for maintenance of internal discipline, and were applicable to all company personnel, including certain managers and supervisors. It was essential for the company to have public confidence in its integrity, and these company rules had nothing to do with external employment laws, such as the LMRA.

George Fuller, acting on his own, had chosen to violate these company rules when he wrote the article, which was published in another journal. Fuller's article contained exaggerations, misrepresentations, insults, and distortions of facts. For example, Fuller had reported inaccurately the number and purpose of "merit pay increases" that were granted to company employees during 1985. Most serious, however, was that Fuller had publicly damaged the integrity of Executive Editor Duane Silverman by writing, "One effort at persuasion by executive editor Duane Silverman would have been laughable had it not indicated an insidious disregard for the truth." This sentence alone showed that Fuller had publicly damaged the integrity of Silverman and the truthfulness of the newspapers Silverman published.

The company claimed that Fuller's behavior was not "protected concerted activity" under Section 7 of LMRA. Rather, Fuller had acted on his own in violation of long-standing and appropriate company rules. As an "at-will" employee, Fuller was properly discharged by the company. All the unfair labor practice charges should be dismissed.

QUESTIONS

1. Were company rules No. 18 and 29 in violation of LMRA? Explain.
2. Employees at times write articles or letters for newspapers openly critical of their employers. Should it make any difference in this case that Fuller himself was an editorial employee of a newspaper? Discuss.
3. Although Fuller wrote and published the "offensive" article on his own volition, was his conduct protected under Section 7 of LMRA? Discuss.
4. Was Fuller's discharge for rules' violations a pretext for terminating him because of his prounion activities? Discuss.

Case 16

Was the ESOP Leveraged Buyout Proposal Protected Concerted Activity?

Company Harrah's Lake Tahoe Resort Casino, Stateline, Nevada

Individual Leroy Gastoni[1]

BACKGROUND

In early 1991, the company was a nonunionized employer. The company had a savings and retirement plan for its employees that consisted of a qualified 401(k) plan and an employee stock ownership plan (ESOP).[2] Under the existing ESOP, qualified employees on an annual basis received one share of stock in the firm's parent company, the Promus Corporation. Promus stock was publicly traded, and 1 percent of the stock was dedicated to the company's ESOP. The company's 401(k) plan allowed employees to make their fund contributions from several sources, including Promus stock.

Employee Leroy Gastoni had studied financial analysis at a university business school, and he was convinced that a leveraged buyout of the Promus Corporation by the ESOP would be in the employees' best interests. In essence, Gastoni's idea was that the ESOP borrow $335 million to purchase 50 percent of the outstanding Promus stock and assume $450 million of Promus' corporate debt. Gastoni's plan envisioned that the debt would be serviced by operating income. He prepared and sent to the chairman of the board of the Promus Corporation a written proposal outlining his ideas for a leveraged buyout of Promus Corporation by the ESOP, and distributed copies of this proposal to company employees.

Gastoni also prepared a three-page summary of his proposal, as well as a petition for employees to sign, which he used to solicit employee support. After receiving some complaints from employees that his proposal was still too technical, he wrote a leaflet entitled

[1] Name is disguised.

[2] A 401(k) plan derives its name from Section 401(k) of the Internal Revenue Code that enables employers to establish retirement savings plans in which employees can contribute through a payroll deduction program. An employee's contribution reduces that employee's taxable income, meaning that the employee does not pay income taxes on the contribution amounts until he or she begins drawing from the plan fund after retiring. Many companies match employee contributions in some way, and employees may be permitted to choose in which types of investments they wish to have their money placed, including company stock purchase plans. An employee stock ownership plan, or ESOP, typically is one in which employees purchase company stock through some type of payroll deduction or installment plan. Here, too, employees usually can sell the stock or withdraw dividends only upon retirement or termination of their employment, at which time the proceeds become taxable income. See Arthur W. Sherman, Jr., George W. Bohlander, and Scott Snell, *Managing Human Resources,* 11th ed. (Cincinnati: South-Western, 1998), pp. 447–49 and 459; or Wendell L. French, *Human Resources Management,* 3rd ed. (Boston: Houghton Mifflin, 1994), pp. 427–28.

"Money for Nothin" for distribution among the employees. The "Money for Nothin" leaflet stated in pertinent part:

> Our ESOP Trust borrows money from a commercial bank to buy 50% of Promus stock for the employees.
>
> Since the employees then own 50% of the stock, we get 50% of the operating income ("profits").
>
> For the following 10 to 15 years, we use our share of the profits to pay off the bank loan.
>
> At the end of 10 years, each employee owns stock which could be worth as much as 3 times his annual earnings (salary plus tips). If we leave sooner, we get less. If we stay longer, we get more.

The remainder of the leaflet explained, in Gastoni's words, why "the stock costs us nothin!" The leaflet suggested that by implementing this proposal, the employees could promise to management and the company as a whole "one of the most dynamic and profitable service companies in America." Gastoni claimed in the leaflet that current employees would benefit from his proposal through increased job stability, pay, and pension funding, and from enhanced morale, productivity, and profitability through "participative management." Gastoni distributed the leaflet primarily to employees in the company cafeteria.

Gastoni's leaflet, petition, and proposal became known in due course to company managers, who discussed them at a staff meeting. The managers concluded that Gastoni's activities were an embarrassment to company management, and they were disturbed that Gastoni had perhaps even implied that current management was sympathetic to and even endorsing the leveraged buyout proposal. Leroy Gastoni was summoned to his supervisor's office and terminated.

Subsequently, Leroy Gastoni through his personal attorney filed unfair labor practice charges against the company. Specifically, Gastoni charged that the company had violated Section 8(a) (1) of the Labor Management Relations Act by unlawfully interfering with his Section 7 rights to pursue "concerted activities for the purpose of . . . mutual aid or protection." Although later he was reinstated, and his termination was converted to a month's suspension without pay, nevertheless Gastoni through his attorney persisted in his unfair labor practice charges against the company.

POSITION OF THE COMPANY

The company contended that employee Leroy Gastoni had operated on his own in an improper manner that deserved summary termination. His proposal and the accompanying literature were his own ideas and creations. Section 7 of the LMRA protects concerted activities, not individual actions by an employee acting on his own volition. Gastoni was an at-will employee; therefore, the company had the right to terminate him for his proposals and leaflets that were embarrassing to corporate management and that even implied that management had in some way approved or endorsed the leveraged buyout proposal.

Alternatively, the company argued, if the NLRB should determine that Gastoni's actions were concerted in nature, nevertheless these were not protected by Section 7 of the Act. Counsel for the company pointed to a previous NLRB and court decision, which found that individual actions such as those of Leroy Gastoni were protected by Section 7 of the Act only if the action or proposals related "to employees' interests as employees."[3]

In the company's view, Gastoni's proposal aimed primarily at having employees assume the role of owners with ultimate corporate control, that is, the proposal sought fundamentally to change how and by whom the corporation would be managed. Thus, Gastoni's proposal favoring a leveraged buyout by the ESOP had little or nothing to do with improving the employees' interests as employees, the necessary precondition for protection by Section 7 of LMRA. Counsel for the company pointed out that Gastoni's proposal contemplated the employees themselves controlling the corporation. Gastoni had even used the term "participative management" in a way that anticipated changes by which the employees would take over the running of the corporation.

In summary, the company argued that Gastoni had operated on his own, and that his proposal and related handouts and materials were not directed toward improving the employees' situation as employees but rather toward their taking over ownership and control. This was beyond any construction as "concerted activities for . . . mutual aid or protection" as in Section 7 had been constituted and interpreted. The company urged that the unfair labor practice charges be dismissed.

POSITION OF THE INDIVIDUAL

Gastoni maintained that his activities fell within the interpretation of "concerted activities" under Section 7 of the Act. His proposal and the accompanying literature he'd handed out were designed not just for his own benefit, but for the benefit of his fellow employees. If activities such as his were not concerted in nature, even if initiated by an individual, how could anyone acting on his own do anything in a nonunion setting without fear of being disciplined or terminated?

Through his counsel, Gastoni argued that his proposal and his accompanying leaflet were not aimed at changing corporate management control, but rather at accruing benefits to the employees as employees. His ESOP proposal was not really designed to produce changes in management. At the time of his proposal, employees were able to own Promus stock through the existing ESOP and the 401(k) plan, economic benefits granted and maintained by the company and clearly terms and conditions of employment. It was evident from the language of his proposal and leaflet that his primary objective was to increase employee monetary benefits by enhancing the existing retirement benefit programs. Significantly, his leaflet had not referred to any major increased managerial role by the employees who might become part owners of the company. Rather, the message had focused on the profits that would accrue to employees if they were to own 50 percent of the stock. Although his leaflet mentioned "participative management" in terms of "enhanced morale, productivity, and profitability," this was just a tangential reference to a more cooperative and profitable enterprise that could result, thus improving the savings and retirement benefits of employees.

In summary, Gastoni through his attorney contended that the focus of his ESOP activities was on the improvement of an existing benefit of employment, a matter of immediate

[3] *Eastex, Inc. v. NLRB,* 437 U.S. 556, 567, 98 LRRM 2717 (1978).

concern to employees. Therefore, his activities on behalf of the ESOP proposal were concerted activities protected by the mutual aid or protection clause of Section 7 of the Act. The NLRB should find that the company violated Section 8(a) (1) of the Act by suspending (after first discharging) Gastoni for his activities and by interfering with his right to engage in protected activities. Gastoni should be made whole for all lost pay and benefits.

QUESTIONS

1. Were Leroy Gastoni's essentially individual activities pursued on his own as an at-will employee, or could they be considered "concerted" and thus within the protection of Section 7 of the Act? Discuss.
2. Assuming Gastoni's actions could be considered concerted, were they primarily related to the employees' interests as employees, or were they aimed primarily at changing the management and gaining managerial control of the company? Discuss.
3. Evaluate the primary contentions of Gastoni and of the company. Which do you find the most and which the least persuasive?
4. Compare the issues in this case with those in Case 15, "Discharge for Disruptive Conduct, or for Protected Union Activity?" What are the similarities and differences?

Case 17

The Distasteful and Offensive Definition of a "Scab"

Company Southwestern Bell Telephone Company, Houston, Texas

Union Communications Workers of America, Local No. 12222

BACKGROUND

On a Monday morning in early September 1984, Jan Betheda,[1] an equipment technician, reported to two of her supervisors that there was a "distasteful and offensive" memorandum on two union bulletin boards in the plant and office complex of the company. The supervisors, Art Laclede and Debbie Lynkirk, investigated and discovered on both union bulletin boards a printed memorandum entitled, "Jack London's Definition of a Scab."[2] In pertinent part, the memorandum included the following:

Jack London's Definition of A SCAB

> After God had finished the rattlesnake, the toad, and the vampire, he had some awful substance left with which he made a SCAB. A SCAB is a two-legged animal with a corkscrew soul, a water-logged brain, and a combination backbone made of jelly and glue. Where others have hearts, he carries a tumor of rotten principles.
>
> When a SCAB comes down the street, men turn their backs and angels weep in Heaven, and the devil shuts the gates of Hell to keep him out. No man has the right to SCAB, so long as there is a pool of water deep enough to drown his body in, or a rope long enough to hang his carcass with. Judas Iscariot was a gentleman . . . compared with a SCAB; for betraying his master, he had the character to hang himself—a SCAB hasn't.
>
> Esau sold his birthright for a mess of pottage. Judas Iscariot sold his Savior for thirty pieces of silver. Benedict Arnold sold his country for a promise of a commission in the British Army. The modern strikebreaker sells his birthright, his country, his wife, his children and his fellow men for an unfulfilled promise from his employer, trust, or corporation.
>
> Esau was a traitor to himself. Judas Iscariot was a traitor to his God. Benedict Arnold was a traitor to his country.
>
> A strikebreaker is a traitor to himself, a traitor to his God, a traitor to his country, a traitor to his family, and a traitor to his class.
>
> THERE IS NOTHING LOWER THAN A SCAB.

After discussing their finding with the company's director of human resources management, Laclede and Lynkirk removed the two identical memoranda from the union's bulletin boards. They then informed all employees in several meetings of their actions. They further told employees that any reposting of this "Definition of a Scab" memorandum

[1] The names of all individuals are disguised.

[2] Jack London (1876–1916) was an American writer and adventurer. He wrote a number of novels and adventure books and also wrote several books that dealt with poverty and social injustice. The source of the "Definition of a Scab" attributed to Jack London was not identified on the posted memorandum.

was prohibited, and that any individuals found doing so would be subject to discipline, including suspension.

Shortly thereafter, the union filed unfair labor practice charges with the NLRB, alleging that the company had violated Section 7 and Section 8(a) (1) of the LMRA by removing the memorandum from the union's bulletin boards and by threatening disciplinary action against the employees.

POSITION OF THE UNION

The union claimed that there had never been any company rules concerning what could or could not be posted on union bulletin boards located on company premises. The union had negotiated with the company for the right to have these bulletin boards, and there were no specific negotiated restrictions placed on this privilege.

In the union's view, the "Definition of a Scab" memorandum was an expression of opinion that was not disruptive to employee work performance or discipline. Just because someone considered it distasteful or offensive did not justify the company's actions and threats to discipline employees. There had been no work disruption; even though employees were observed in groups discussing the memorandum, this was not unusual or threatening to anyone. Therefore, the company had violated Sections 7 and 8(a) (1) of the Act by interfering with the union's protected rights and by attempting to coerce and restrain the union and the employees in their expression of those rights. The union requested that the company be ordered to cease and desist in this and any other actions that would tend to interfere with the union's statutory rights and negotiated privileges.

POSITION OF THE COMPANY

The company pointed out that the posting of the "Definition of a Scab" memorandum had occurred only several days following the end of a several weeks' strike during which some one-third to one-half of the employees had crossed the union's picket lines in order to work. In the company's view, the memorandum was aimed primarily at these employees, who had exercised their personal freedom of choice in a difficult situation. Not only was the memorandum offensive to them, but it was likely to contribute to further animosity, internal dissension, and strife that could lead to wholesale disruptions in employee discipline and work performance. An employer cannot afford simply to wait until a breakdown in discipline occurs. In this situation, company management had decided that, for the sake of avoiding further deterioration in workplace harmony and employee morale, the "provocative and inflammatory" memorandum should be removed. The company did not interfere with any of the union's protected rights in this matter when it removed this offensive and "sacrilegious" memorandum.

In support of its position, the company cited a Supreme Court decision that employers have an "undisputed right . . . to maintain discipline in their establishments," which under some circumstances may limit the exercise of employee rights guaranteed by Section 7 [*Republic Aviation Corp. v. NLRB,* 324 U.S. 793, 797–798, 16 LRRM 620 (1945)].

Similarly, the NLRB has found "special circumstances" can exist that would justify an employer's ban on otherwise protected activity in the workplace if "objective evidence supports the employer's belief that the ban was necessary to maintain decorum and discipline among its employees" [*Midstate Telephone Corp.,* 262 NLRB 1291–1292, 110 LRRM 1533 (1982)]. In the company's view, this was a "special circumstance" that fully justified the company's position. The unfair labor practice charges should be dismissed.

QUESTIONS

1. Was the "Definition of a Scab" memorandum a real threat to maintenance of employee decorum and discipline? Explain.
2. Does it make any difference in this case that the company and union had not negotiated any specific limits or rules concerning what could be posted on the union bulletin boards? Discuss.
3. Why does a situation of this type pose a major dilemma for company management? Were there other alternatives that the company might have pursued? Discuss.
4. Was this situation a "special circumstance" under the NLRB's rulings that would justify the company's position? Explain.

Case 18

Deferral to an Existing Arbitration Award: Just Cause or Protected Activity?

Employer Aramark Services, Inc.

Union Linda Canter, represented by Local 1064 of the United Catering, Restaurant, Bar, and Hotel Workers Union.

BACKGROUND

Ms. Canter, a 13-year employee of the respondent, was employed as a cashier by the company. The company and the United Catering, Restaurant, Bar, and Hotel Workers Union, Local 1064, represented the respondent's nonmanagerial employees. The union and respondent were in the process of negotiating a new collective bargaining agreement at the time of the events giving rise to Ms. Canter's discharge.

During negotiations, two employees, Ms. Richards and Ms. Lawson, circulated a petition to conduct a steward election. Ms. Richards and Ms. Lawson were dissatisfied with the performance of the current union steward, and perceived her to be biased and ineffective. In response, Ms. Canter circulated a counterpetition. The counterpetition stated that "I am against a steward's election during the contract negotiations."

Among the employees Ms. Canter approached with her counterpetition were Ms. Lawson and Ms. Richards. Ms. Lawson and Ms. Richards complained to management that Ms. Canter "harassed and intimidated them and tried to coerce them into signing a petition concerning union steward representation." The employees also accused Ms. Canter of "physically poking, swearing at one of the employees, and being verbally abusive to both." The complaints of Ms. Lawson and Ms. Richards were corroborated by two independent and credible witnesses.

This matter went to arbitration under the provisions of the parties' collective bargaining agreement. The arbitrator found that there was cause to discharge the grievant, and that her conduct was not protected by National Labor Relations Act. The arbitrator was convinced that Ms. Canter harassed her fellow employees and prevented them from working, which was just cause for discipline. However, the arbitrator found that in recognition of the grievant's long service and other mitigating factors discharge was too harsh a penalty for her conduct. The arbitrator reinstated Ms. Canter, but without back pay or benefits.

The administrative law judge decided that the arbitrator's decision was "repugnant to the Act" within the meaning of the *Speilberg* and *Olin* decision, and therefore deferral to the arbitrator's award would be inappropriate. The finding of fact by the administrative law judge was "[t]he record here, as well as the opinion of the arbitrator, is devoid of any suggestion that Canter made threat, used intimidating motions or gestures or repeatedly pestered anyone else." The judge cited *Consolidated Diesel* in stating the standard for aggressive solicitation is an objective one, and solicitation does not become unprotected simply because employees who are solicited feel "annoyed or upset" by the efforts to persuade them.

The judge found that the activities of Ms. Canter were protected by the Act, and ordered that she be reinstated to her former position with full back pay and benefits.

POSITION OF THE COMPANY

The arbitrator found that Ms. Canter violated the employer's written policy on harassment. The employer's policy bars "any unwelcome verbal or physical conduct, which denigrates or shows hostility or aversion toward an individual's gender, race, nationality, religion, age, disability, sexual orientation, or other personal characteristic protected by federal, state, or local law. . . ." Ms. Canter's conduct violated this policy and she was discharged for cause under this policy. The arbitrator found that Canter's conduct was in contravention to the company's policy. It was only a matter of mitigation of penalty with respect to the long service and mitigating factors present in this case that Ms. Canter was reinstated without back pay or benefits.

It is the employer's position that there was no violation of the Act by discharging Ms. Canter and that her actions were not protected concerted action under the Act. Ms. Canter was abusive, and that abusive conduct was of such a degree as to not be protected by the Act. Therefore, the arbitrator was correct in finding there was no violation of the Act. However, the arbitrator's finding that mitigating circumstances existed in this matter is inconsistent with the employer's view of the fact.

POSITION OF THE UNION

The position of the union is that Ms. Canter's conduct is protected by the Act. Simply because there is a parallel between the just cause standards and the protection of concerted activity under Section 7 of the Act does not give the employer license to apply just cause standards and ignore Ms. Canter's rights to concerted action. The arbitrator's decision is repugnant to the requirements of the Act and therefore cannot be permitted to stand in this case. Ms. Canter is entitled to reinstatement with full back pay and benefits.

In this case Ms. Canter's actions were offensive. However, it is clear that her actions were not so abusive as to lose for her the protections of the Act. It is a matter of degree that determines whether offensive behavior can be so extreme as to lose the protections of the Act. The arbitrator's finding that the actions of Ms. Canter met that test for losing the protections of the Act were repugnant to the law. Therefore, Ms. Canter's conduct must be found to be protected under Section 7 of the Act.

QUESTIONS

1. For the Board to not defer to an arbitrator's award the arbitrator's finding and award must not be susceptible to an interpretation consistent with the Act. What does this mean? Does this mean the Board would have ruled the same way as the arbitrator? Explain.
2. Can union solicitation be offensive or abusive? What standard applies in determining how far this aggressive solicitation can go?
3. Why would the NLRB defer to arbitrators' awards as a matter of policy?
4. How do you suppose the Board ruled in this case? Support your conclusion with the facts in this record, and the law.

Case 19

Did the Employee Have the Right to Have a Union Representative Present?

Company Eagle Discount Supermarkets, Midwestern Food Division of Lucky Stores, Inc., Glen Ellyn, Illinois

Union Food and Commercial Workers, Local No. 1540

BACKGROUND

On May 1, 1982, the company acquired several grocery stores from another retail chain, Kohl's. The employees working at Kohl's were represented by the Food and Commercial Workers Union. As part of the transfer-of-ownership agreement, the company and the union agreed to continue in effect most terms of the collective bargaining agreement. One major change, however, was the elimination of a provision concerning "just cause" for discharge during a 30-day probationary period for store personnel. Under the transfer-of-ownership agreement, an employee could be terminated during the 30-day probationary period at the sole discretion of the company. Of approximately 450 employees affected by this transfer of ownership, about 40 were terminated under the new probationary provision.

Pamela Golden[1] first began working for Kohl's in 1977. By March 1979 she had attained the position of deli manager of the Hanover Park store. Despite the title of "deli manager," this was a bargaining unit position and Golden was included within the unit represented by the union. She held this position until the Hanover Park store closed late in 1981. Following the closing of that store, her next job placement became the subject of dispute. Her permanent assignment remained unsettled until February 1982, when certain grievances were resolved on her behalf. Golden was on maternity leave from mid-February until August 1982. During her leave, Eagle Discount Stores had acquired ownership of the stores in which Golden had worked, and her assignment upon her return to work again became the subject of controversy. She once more grieved the issue. On August 11, 1982, Golden began working at the Glen Ellyn store under Manager Elmer Ellis. Golden was subject to a 30-day probationary period at this time.

A scheduling problem arose almost immediately. Golden told Ellis that her child care responsibilities made it inconvenient for her to have to open the deli in the mornings. Ellis agreed to keep her situation in mind when arranging the schedule. Golden was not scheduled to work on August 12, and she was out sick on both August 13 and 14. When she returned to work and saw the posted schedule, she objected to the number of successive workdays she had been given. The schedule was then revised. On August 19, she again raised objections to the following week's schedule. This led Ellis to respond that she would have to abide by the schedule. Golden in turn responded that she probably would have to "take my problem to the union."

[1] The names of all individuals are disguised.

On August 20, 1982, Pamela Golden worked until 9:30 P.M., one-half hour past her scheduled quitting time, because she had to serve a late customer. She did not put the deli in good order before she left. When Elmer Ellis arrived the next morning, he discovered that the deli case was in disarray, some unwrapped cheese had been left out on the counter, and the refrigerator door was ajar. When Golden came in to work, Ellis gave her a written reprimand about the condition of the deli. The writeup contained admonishments about Golden's "poor attitude and work habits."

On August 24, Golden was scheduled to begin work at 1 P.M. At noon she called Ellis and told him that she had been unable to get a babysitter. She asked if it would be all right not to report as scheduled. Ellis replied that it was not all right in view of the difficulty he would have trying to find a replacement, but he also said, "If you cannot come in, you cannot come in."

Midway through her shift on August 26, Golden was called to Ellis's office. He told her he wanted to discuss her attendance with her. Assistant Manager Christine Kuroski was present in Ellis's office. When Golden arrived, she asked that she be permitted to have a union representative present as her witness. Ellis, however, handed her a written warning concerning her absences on August 13 and 14 and her having called off work on short notice on August 24. Golden looked at the writeup and said that she refused to sign it. Ellis stated he would read the warning to her, whereupon Golden began to leave the room, stating that she wanted her union representative present. At that point Ellis pointed to the telephone on his desk and said, "Here, call and we can set up a meeting whenever you want to talk." Golden did nothing. Ellis then attempted to read the warning aloud, and Golden left the office and walked down the hall. Ellis followed her, reminding her that he was her boss and that it was important that they talk. He told her she could either return to his office or punch out and leave. Golden followed Ellis back into his office. Ellis again attempted unsuccessfully to have her read the warning or to listen to him read it to her. At that point Ellis told her to punch out and that she was suspended. Ellis then called District Manager Tony Carbo to inform him what had happened. Upon Carbo's instructions, Ellis telephoned Golden later that day and told her she was fired.

Shortly thereafter, the union filed unfair labor practice charges against the company, claiming that the company had violated Sections 7, 8(a) (1), and 8(a) (3) of LMRA by denying Pamela Golden her right to have a union representative present at the meeting of August 26, 1982, and by discriminatorily reprimanding and later discharging her in retaliation for asserting her protected rights. The union requested that Pamela Golden should be reinstated to her job position and made whole for all lost pay and benefits.

POSITION OF THE UNION

The union claimed that the first written reprimand given to Pamela Golden on August 20 was in major part a retaliation for her statement that she would probably seek the union's assistance in her scheduling dispute with Manager Elmer Ellis.

The union's primary charges, however, focused on the incidents of August 26, 1982, during which Pamela Golden requested that a union representative be present during her meeting with two company managers. The union claimed that the company had clearly violated Golden's statutory right under the well-known NLRB *Weingarten*[2]

[2] *NLRB v. J. Weingarten,* 420 U.S. 251, 88 LRRM 2689 (1975).

decision, which was upheld by the U.S. Supreme Court. This right, which is well-established law, required the company to permit Golden to have a union representative present at an investigatory interview that she reasonably believed could result in disciplinary action.

The company's illegal refusal to permit her to have her union representative present was the primary cause for the subsequent behavior of Pamela Golden in her refusal to listen to Ellis read a warning to her. Golden was not being insubordinate to Ellis; rather, she was asserting her rights under LMRA to have a representative present in a meeting that she believed was disciplinary in nature. The union concluded that Golden was suspended and discharged because she insisted upon her right to a representative and also because she had filed grievances during the summer of 1982 concerning her assignment dispute. The union urged that the unfair labor practice charges be upheld, and that the company be ordered to comply with the reinstatement remedy requested by the union.

POSITION OF THE COMPANY

Concerning the first written reprimand issued by Manager Ellis on August 20, the company argued that this reprimand had nothing to do whatsoever with any retaliation against Golden for her seeking help from the union with her work schedule. Ellis issued the reprimand solely because of the unsatisfactory condition in which Golden had left the deli area the evening before.

The company contended strongly that it had not violated Golden's statutory (i.e., *Weingarten*) rights. Elmer Ellis had called Pamela Golden into his office on August 26 for the purpose of delivering to her a disciplinary writeup concerning her poor attendance and of advising her orally of the necessity of improving her attendance. He was taking a firm disciplinary step based on what he had concluded was an unacceptable record. In this type of meeting, an employee does not have a statutory right to have a union representative present. The company stressed that the NLRB had held that when an employer has reached a decision to levy certain discipline upon an employee, no Section 7 right to union representation arises if the meeting is held simply to inform or to impose that discipline upon the employee.[3]

Pamela Golden refused in this meeting to permit her manager to administer that discipline to her. She became totally insubordinate and therefore was suspended. After review of her entire work and attendance record, she then was discharged as an unsatisfactory probationary employee, as the company contractually had the right to do.

In summary, the company claimed that the unfair labor practice charges should be dismissed, since they primarily were an effort by Golden and the union to obtain reinstatement for her to which she was not entitled under either LMRA or the labor agreement.

QUESTIONS

1. Why is a decision in this type of case a "close call," which causes difficulties for all parties concerned?
2. Distinguish between the *Weingarten* case cited by the union and the *Baton Rouge Water Works* case cited by the company. Is there a clear demarcation between the major considerations in these cases? Discuss.

[3] The key NLRB case cited here was *Baton Rouge Water Works,* 246 NLRB 995, 103 LRRM 1056 (1979).

3. Should an employer permit an employee to have a union representative present in a meeting whenever an employee requests this? Explain.
4. Under Section 7 of LMRA, which speaks of protected "concerted activities" and "mutual aid or protection," the NLRB in 1982 held that an unrepresented employee had the right to have a co-worker present during an investigatory interview that the employee reasonably believed could lead to disciplinary action. In 1985, the NLRB reversed itself and held that only employees represented by a labor union had the (*Weingarten*) right to representation during an investigatory interview. However, in 2000, a different NLRB ruled that nonunion workers did have the (*Weingarten*) right to request that a co-worker accompany them to investigatory interviews that could have disciplinary action as an outcome. Why is this area of "unsettled" labor law apt to become a major judicial issue at some time in the future? Discuss.

Case 20

Was Changing the Christmas Bonus Formula an Unfair Labor Practice?

Company Bonnell/Tredegar Industries, Inc., Newman, Georgia

Union United Steelworkers of America, Local Union No. 14102

BACKGROUND

At the time of this case, the union had represented the company's production and maintenance employees for some 18 years. The parties' most recent collective bargaining agreement was effective from January 20, 1990, to January 19, 1993. For many years prior to December 1991, the company paid employees a Christmas bonus and calculated the bonus on the basis of a formula of 1 hour's pay for each week of the year that an employee had worked at least 32 hours, up to a total of 40 hours. Under this formula, each employee typically received an annual Christmas bonus of approximately $300 to $400. The company's obligation to pay employees a Christmas bonus was stipulated in Article XVI of the collective bargaining agreement, in conjunction with the firm's other "Industrial Relations Plans," as follows:

Article XVI
INDUSTRIAL RELATIONS PLANS

All employees in the plant are entitled to such service credit as accrued under the COMPANY's continuity of service rules and the COMPANY will recognize such service for participation in the following COMPANY Industrial Relations Plans:

1. Group Insurance Plan (Exhibit B)
2. Vacation Plan (Article XII)
3. Military Leave Plan (Article XI and Article XV)
4. Leave of Absence Plan (Article XV)
5. Pension Plan (Exhibit C)
6. Continuity of Service Rules (Exhibit C)
7. Jury Duty Plan (Article XI)
8. Funeral Leave Plan (Article XI)
9. Christmas Bonus
10. Thanksgiving Turkey

All of these plans shall remain in full force and effect during the term of this Agreement. However, the COMPANY may, on notice to the UNION, make any changes in such plans as necessary to keep such plans in compliance with the regulations of the Treasury Department or other governmental agencies so that COMPANY contributions to such plans shall be proper tax deductions and all not be considered wages for any purpose. The COMPANY may make such changes as may be required or desirable in the contracts between the COMPANY and Insurance Underwriters to make the plans conform to any subsequent statutory enactments or judicial or administrative interpretation of any law relating to such plans, or changes to conform to actuarial experience from time to time, or changes of wording for clarity of any plan.

> With respect to life insurance, dependent life insurance, accidental death and dismemberment insurance and weekly disability coverage under the Group Insurance Plan, the COMPANY will continue to pay the full cost of these plans for employee coverage and reserves the right to change employee contributions to the extent required by reason of adjusted premium rates assessed by the carrier.

In December 1990, the initial Christmas holiday period arising under the 1990–1993 bargaining agreement, the company paid employees a Christmas bonus that was calculated according to the established formula of 1 hour's pay for each 32-hour week worked, up to a total of 40 hours. Consistent with its December 1990 Christmas bonus payment, the company in early 1990 had distributed to employees a booklet summarizing employee benefits. Item VI of this booklet provided as follows:

VI. CHRISTMAS BONUSES

> Employee will receive one (1) hour's pay for each week in which he worked thirty-two (32) hours up to a maximum of forty (40) hours.

However, on November 13, 1991, the company notified employees by letter that "the decision has been made to reduce the Christmas bonus this year to $100 per employee." By a letter dated November 15, 1991, the union advised company management that it "strongly objected" to the reduction of the Christmas bonus. Nevertheless, in late December 1991, after having met with union representatives, the company paid each eligible employee a Christmas bonus of $100 for Christmas 1991. The union filed a grievance over the reduced Christmas bonus payment. On January 28, 1992, the company denied the grievance and refused to arbitrate the dispute. The company relied upon Article VIII, Section 1, of the collective bargaining agreement with respect to grievances and arbitration which included the following:

Article VIII
GRIEVANCES AND ARBITRATION

> Section 1
> It is further understood and agreed that the provisions of this article shall not apply to matters affecting the change in wages and rates of pay as set forth in Exhibit "A" attached hereto, nor shall the provisions of this article apply to the administration and contents of the COMPANY benefits plans listed in article XVI hereof, except that specific cases affecting administration of the benefits received under the following plans (Vacation, Leave of Absence, Jury Duty, Funeral Leave and Military Leave) shall be subject to the grievance and arbitration provisions of this Agreement. It is understood and agreed that this provision will not alter or change any part of this Agreement.

The same 1990–1993 collective bargaining agreement also contained the following provisions:

Article IV
MANAGEMENT OF PLANT

> Except as abridged by a specific provision of this Agreement, the management of the plant and the direction of the working force, including the right to plan, direct and control plant operations; to contract for work and services; to schedule and assign work to employees; to determine the means, methods, processes, materials and schedules of

production; to determine the products to be manufactured, the location of its plant and the continuance of its departments; to establish production standards and to maintain the efficiency of employees; to establish and require employees to observe COMPANY rules and regulations; to hire, terminate or relieve employees from duties; to maintain order and to suspend, demote, discipline and discharge employees for just cause are rights solely vested in the COMPANY.

The foregoing enumeration of Management's rights shall not be deemed to exclude other rights of Management not specifically inconsistent with this Agreement.

Article XXIV
ENTIRE AGREEMENT

This Agreement constitutes the sole and entire existing agreement between the Parties and supersedes all prior agreements, commitments and practices, whether oral or written, between the COMPANY and the UNION or the COMPANY and any of the covered employees, and expresses all obligations of, and restrictions imposed on, the COMPANY.

Subsequently, the company and union had several meetings to discuss the Christmas bonus for 1992. However, in December 1992, the company again paid each employee a \$100 bonus as in 1991. Thereafter, the union filed unfair labor practice charges against the company, claiming that by changing the Christmas bonus formula and reducing the amount of the Christmas bonus in 1991 and 1992, the company had violated Sections 8(a) (5) and 8(a) (1) as further related to Section 8(d) of the Labor Management Relations Act.

In processing this complaint, the company and union agreed to several stipulations. First of all, they stipulated that the company's decision to limit Christmas bonuses to \$100 per employee in 1991 was done unilaterally and without prior consultation with the union. Secondly, the parties stipulated that the company and union had negotiated to impasse over the amount of the Christmas bonus for 1992, and that the company thereafter implemented its last offer which was again a \$100 bonus for each employee. The parties further stipulated that the 1991 Christmas bonus was approximately 29 percent, and the 1992 Christmas bonus was approximately 30 percent, of the average Christmas bonus paid in 1990.

POSITION OF THE UNION

The union cited case law decisions as settled labor law that an employer violates Sections 8(a) (5) and (1) of LMRA, as further described in Section 8(d) of the Act, by modifying a term of a collective bargaining agreement while the contract is in effect without the consent of the other party.[1] In this case the company did not, either in 1991 or 1992, obtain the union's consent to payment of a Christmas bonus in an amount less than those that would result from application of the long-followed workweek-based formula.

The company's obligation to pay employees a Christmas bonus benefit was mandated by the terms of the parties' 1990–1993 collective bargaining agreement. Article XVI provided that employees "are entitled" to accrued service credit for a variety of "Industrial Relations Plans," including a "Christmas Bonus." Article XVI also provided with respect to "all of these plans" that they "shall remain in full force and effect during the term of this Agreement."

[1] *Manley Truck Line*, 271 NLRB 679, 681 [117 LRRM 1151] (1984), enfd. 779 F.2d 1327 [121 LRRM 2289] (7th Cir. 1985), and cases there cited.

When the 1990–1993 agreement was negotiated, the company for many years had maintained the Christmas bonus plan by payments to each employee of 1 hour's pay for each 32-hour week worked during the year, up to a maximum of 40 hours. That formula was the Christmas bonus plan as it existed during negotiations for the 1990–1993 bargaining agreement. It similarly existed through the initial year of that agreement when the company paid employees their Christmas bonuses in 1990 using the above-described formula. Further, when the company distributed a booklet to employees in 1990, it advised them what it understood to be the Christmas bonus plan, namely, 1 hour's pay for each week worked, up to a maximum of 40 hours.

Article XVI was clear as to what the company was contractually obligated to do. It was contractually required to maintain the Christmas bonus plan "*in full force and effect during the term of this Agreement*" (emphasis added).

The union contended that the company's various reasons for unilaterally changing the Christmas bonus formula and reducing the Christmas bonus payments were misplaced and inapplicable. Under LMRA, the company could not lawfully change the terms of its collective bargaining agreement without consent of the union. By its actions, the company had committed unfair labor practices under the Act. The union urged that the company should be required to make all employees whole for the full amount of the Christmas bonuses to which they were entitled for 1991 and 1992 using the previously established formula for calculation of those bonuses.

POSITION OF THE COMPANY

The company claimed that the union's unfair labor practice charges were without merit, because the calculation of the Christmas bonus and its payment were contractually reserved to the company under the parties' collective bargaining agreement. Among the company's major contentions were the following:

1. The methods for calculating other contractually required "nonwage benefits" were explicitly set forth in the collective bargaining agreement while the formula for calculating the Christmas bonus was not. The Christmas bonus formula was included in the company's employee benefits booklet; this had not been negotiated with the union and was within the company's discretion to change.
2. Article VIII, the contractually established arbitration provision of the collective bargaining agreement, specifically excluded bonus disputes. This supported the company position that the calculation of the Christmas bonus was within the company's reserved rights and beyond the union's challenge through the grievance-arbitration mechanism.
3. Article XXIV, the contract's Entire Agreement "zipper clause," specifically excluded past practices not expressly incorporated into the agreement from being an obligation upon the company.
4. Similarly, Article IV, the management rights provision of the collective bargaining agreement, stated that the company retained all rights not "specifically inconsistent" with the agreement. This, too, preserved for the company its discretion to determine the amount of the Christmas bonus to be paid to employees.

In summary, the company maintained that these various provisions of the collective bargaining agreement showed that the union had waived any rights the union might have had to bargain about the formula for calculating the Christmas bonus. The company acted within its contractually determined and reserved rights when it decided in 1991 and 1992 to change the basis and amount of the Christmas bonuses. The union's unfair labor practice charges should be dismissed.

QUESTIONS

1. Evaluate each of the company's contentions that the parties' collective bargaining agreement supported its decisions and actions regarding the 1991 and 1992 Christmas bonuses. Which do you find to be the most persuasive? Least persuasive?
2. Evaluate the union's primary contention that Article XVI of the bargaining agreement mandated the company to maintain the prior Christmas bonus plan "in full force and effect during the term of this agreement."
3. Does Article XVI outweigh the various contractual provisions cited by the company? Explain.
4. Should the NLRB direct the company to submit this dispute to arbitration? Discuss.

Case 21

Payment of a Signing Bonus to Nonstriking Employees

Company Kimtruss Corporation, Madera, California

Union Woodworkers, Local Union No. 3-533

BACKGROUND

The company was engaged in the manufacture and nonretail sale of wooden trusses, with an office and place of business in Madera, California. About two and one-half years earlier, the company had purchased the business, recognized the union, and adopted the existing collective bargaining agreement that would expire on May 31, 1990. The parties had agreed to meet and negotiate a new collective bargaining agreement on May 23, 24, and 25, 1990. The union's negotiating team was headed by business representative Adam Bullock, assisted by business agent Tony Bailey. The company's chief negotiator was attorney Celia Parsons, aided by plant manager Arthur Jerome.[1]

On May 25, 1990, the parties reached a tentative agreement for a new three-year labor-management contract that would expire on May 31, 1993. Wage rates during the first year of the new agreement would not change; however, all employees who were working the week ending June 8, 1990, would receive a bonus based on their length of service with the company as follows:

30 days to six months—$125 bonus.

Over six months—$300 bonus.

Effective June 1, 1991, all employees would receive an across-the-board increase of 15 cents/hour. A similar across-the-board increase of 15 cents/hour would become effective on June 1, 1992.

The bonus was referred to as a "signing bonus" to be paid in lieu of an hourly wage rate increase during the first year of the contract. On May 25, 1990, Bullock and Bailey and other members of the union bargaining committee said that they would recommend the agreement subject to ratification by union members.

However, on May 25, too many employees were absent and could not vote; consequently the union ratification vote was rescheduled for May 31. On that date, business agent Tony Bailey, discussing the tentative agreement with union employees prior to the vote, stated that those employees who voted "no" on the tentative agreement would be voting to strike. A majority of the employees voted to reject the tentative agreement.

Bailey reported the contract rejection to the union's chief negotiator, Adam Bullock. Bullock then telephoned plant manager Jerome; upon hearing that the employees had rejected the contract, Jerome expressed surprise. Bullock indicated that he, too, was surprised. Next, Bullock reported the contract rejection to the company's attorney, Celia

[1] The names of all individuals are disguised.

Parsons. Parsons stated that the company would implement its last offer the next day. Bullock responded, "Okay, and we know what we have to do." Both the company and the union spent the remainder of the day preparing for a strike, which was to begin the next day, June 1.

Parsons, after learning about the employees' vote to reject the contract, advised plant manager Jerome:

> We ought to put up a notice to the employees telling them that we are going to implement our last offer and get it out to them this afternoon if at all possible.

After talking with attorney Parsons, Jerome called the plant and dictated a statement to his secretary, Karen Hardy. After Hardy typed the statement, she faxed it to Jerome for his review. Jerome reviewed it, made no changes, and telephoned Hardy with instructions to mail a copy to every bargaining unit employee and to post the notice at various places around the plant. The notice stated, in relevant part:

> Kimtruss Corporation will implement its last contract offer as of June 1, 1990. Current wages, hours, and conditions plus bargaining agreements . . .
>
> All employees not working June 1, 1990, through June 8, 1990, will not be paid the signing bonus.

By late afternoon of May 31, the notice had been posted at the plant. It was seen by swing-shift employees, who reported the notice to business agent Tony Bailey, who had come to the plant to begin strike preparations for the next day. Bailey telephoned Howard Mackey, a vice president of the International Union, and informed Mackey of the exact wording of the notice. Mackey told Bailey that the notice did not reflect the company's final offer and, in his opinion, the company had committed an unfair labor practice. Following Mackey's instructions, Bailey wrote "Unfair Labor Practice" on the union's picket signs and informed the employees of the alleged unfair labor practice.

On June 1, the employees began the strike. On June 8, the company paid the bonuses only to nonstriking employees who had crossed the picket lines to report to work. On June 14, the company began to hire permanent replacements to fill the jobs left open by striking employees.[2]

The union immediately filed unfair labor practice charges against the company, claiming that by its actions the company had violated Sections 8(a) (1), 8(a) (3), and 8(a) (5) of the Labor Management Relations Act.

POSITION OF THE UNION

The union contended that the company had violated Section 8(a) (1) of the Act, when on May 31, 1990, in anticipation of a strike by employees to begin the next day, management announced that a bonus would not be paid to employees who were not working June 1 through 8, 1990. The company further violated Section 8(a) (3) by paying the bonuses to otherwise eligible nonstriking employees and denying the bonuses to otherwise eligible striking employees.

[2] The bargaining unit consisted of some 40 employees; about a third of these employees did not strike and were paid the bonuses.

After committing these unfair labor practices, the company subsequently fired striking employees. What had begun as an economic strike then became an unfair labor practice strike in violation of Section 8(a) (5).

The union argued that the company notice concerning the bonus payments as written by plant manager Arthur Jerome was blatant interference intended to deter the employees from their protected right to strike. The notice requiring employees to be working June 1–8, 1990, was not consistent with what the parties had agreed upon, namely, a signing bonus in lieu of a wage increase during the first year of the contract. Further, the timing of the company notice was obviously an inducement to discourage employees from striking. By paying the bonuses only to nonstriking employees and subsequently replacing striking employees, the company was discriminating against employees who had exercised their protected right to strike. Thus, what began as an economic strike became an unfair labor practice strike, and the company had engaged in bad faith bargaining prohibited by Section 8(a) (5) of the Act.

The union urged that the company be held in multiple violations of the Act. The union requested that all permanently replaced employees be reinstated to their job positions and be made whole in every way, including payment of the bonus and all lost wages and benefits.

POSITION OF THE COMPANY

The company claimed that there was no evidence whatsoever that it had timed the contested notice in order to deter the employees from a strike. The ratification vote took place on the afternoon of May 31, 1990, the day the collective bargaining agreement expired. It was necessary for the company, once it learned that the employees had rejected the tentative agreement, to issue a notice of its decision to implement its final offer and to inform employees of the terms and conditions under which employees would be working on June 1. That the union had planned a strike for June 1 should not in any way warrant a conclusion that the notice was a response to the planned strike. Nor by posting the notice on May 31 had the company interfered with the employees' protected rights or violated the LMRA.

The company reiterated its position that its May 31 notice that the signing bonus contained in its last contract offer would be withheld from employees not working between June 1 and 8 was proper and lawful. When the company paid the bonuses only to employees who worked after the strike began, this payment constituted an implementation of a wage increase bargained in good faith. The bonuses were based on employee service and were in lieu of a wage increase; thus, each bonus was an accelerated wage increase and compensation for services to be performed during the coming year.

The company pointed out that the NLRB had long established that an employer who had bargained in good faith to impasse with a union could implement its final offer and pay wage increases contained within the final offer to nonstriking employees and any replacements. The company claimed that it had not committed any unfair labor practices. The union strike was clearly an economic one. The company had bargained in good faith with the union. The employees rejected the tentative agreement and some of them went out on strike. Thus it was an economic strike, since it was neither caused nor prolonged by any unfair labor practices on the part of the company. Those employees who continued to be on strike after June 14, 1990, were replaced; this, too, was lawful.

The company contended that all the unfair labor practice charges were without merit and should be dismissed by the NLRB.

QUESTIONS

1. Evaluate the major contentions of both parties. Which of these do you find to be the most and which the least persuasive?
2. Was the company notice issued by plant manager Jerome consistent with the parties' contractual agreement? Explain.
3. Did the company commit unfair labor practices by: *(a)* making the contested announcement? *(b)* paying the signing bonuses to nonstriking employees? *(c)* hiring replacements for striking employees? If so, what should be the remedy ordered by the NLRB?
4. Why is it difficult at times for the Board to determine whether a strike of this nature is economic, or whether it is the result of an employer's (alleged) unfair labor practices?

Case 22

Crossing Picket Lines: Union's Right to Discipline?

Union International Brotherhood of Teamsters, Local 688

Employer Frito-Lay Inc.

RELEVANT CONTRACT LANGUAGE

Article 17—Picket Line

It shall not be a violation of this agreement, and it shall not be cause for discharge or disciplinary action in the event an employee refuses to enter upon any property involved in a lawful primary labor dispute, or refuses to through or work behind any lawful picket line of any Union party to this agreement, and including lawful primary picket lines at the Employer's places of business.

Article 18—Unauthorized Activity

Section 4. For the duration of this Agreement, the Union will not authorize *any strikes, work stoppages,* or interference with the activities required of employees under this Agreement. In the event that the Employer refuses to comply with a valid arbitration award pursuant to the Grievance Procedure, this provision shall be of no force or effect for so long as the refusal continues. The only exception to this Section could be the economic action as called for in Articles 13 [Subcontracting] and 24 [How Paid].

BACKGROUND

The facts in this matter were not in substantial dispute. The union represents sales route representatives at Frito-Lay (complaining party) distribution centers in the St. Louis, Missouri, area. A separate union, the United Food and Commercial Workers (UFCW), disputes with three retail outlets in the St. Louis area and had set up picket lines at those retailers. Three Frito-Lay sales representatives, Mr. Clark, Mr. Smith, and Ms. James, regularly serviced retailers that the UFCW was picketing. The union told its members not to cross the UFCW picket lines because it violated the union's bylaws, and if they did they could be fined for doing so.

In October 2003, the three sales representatives, Mr. Clark, Mr. Smith, and Ms. James, crossed the UFCW picket lines and performed their normal duties. Upon discovering what these three union members had done, the union conducted a trial, found the three employees guilty of violating the union's bylaws, and fined them each $1,000. The employer alleges the union violated the Act.

POSITION OF THE EMPLOYER

The employer is the complaining party in this matter. The employer charges that union violated Section 8 (b) (1) A of the Act by disciplining the three sales representatives who crossed the UFCW picket lines. The employer has an interest to service its customers, the retailers who had a dispute with the UFCW. In order to service its customers, the employer relied upon employees to cross that picket line—a right guaranteed to the employees by Section 7 of the Act.

The specific language of Article 18 of the parties' collective bargaining agreement provides that the union will not authorize any strikes or work stoppages or interfere with activities required of employees. Article 18 provides for only three exceptions, those being violations of arbitration awards, and as provided for in Articles 13 and 25, which the parties stipulate do not apply in this case. For the union to fine employees for crossing a picket line to perform their normal duties violates Article 18, and the employees' rights under Section 7 of the Act to refrain from such conduct.

The employer also argues that Article 17 protects employees from disciplinary action if they decline to cross a third-party picket line. This contract provision protects an employee only in the event they wish not to cross the picket line, and provides an employee discretion to not cross a picket line. To find otherwise would be to eliminate the voluntary aspect of the employee's discretion concerning third-party picket lines. Therefore, the employer urges a finding against the union for violating the Act, that the union be ordered to cease and desist its conduct, and that the three sales representatives be made whole.

POSITION OF THE UNION

There is no doubt that the union's bylaws bar crossing picket lines. To cross a picket line and fail to honor the requests of fellow union members is unacceptable conduct to the union. Because this is a sympathy strike, the employer party to this collective bargaining agreement has no legitimate interest in the union enforcing its bylaws with respect to crossing a picket line with third-party employers.

The union contends that Article 18 applies only to strikes against this employer, Frito-Lay, and does not provide a bar to sympathy strikes against third parties. Further, the union contends that Article 17 provides for an exception to the no-strike language of Article 18. Because of the discretion granted employees in Article 17, the union's bylaws apply and it is perfectly permissible to fine a member for violating those union bylaws.

The union believes it has done nothing wrong, and it was well within its rights to discipline members who crossed the subject picket lines. Therefore the charges of violations of Section 8 (b) (1) of the Act are without merit and should be dismissed.

QUESTIONS

1. Does Section 7 of the Act provide employees with the right to refrain from honoring a picket line established against a third party? If so, under what circumstances?
2. May a union fine members who violate its bylaws? If so, can a collective bargaining agreement limit the union's right to discipline its members? Does the collective bargaining agreement here limit that right? Explain.
3. Does the employer really have an interest in this dispute? If so, what is that interest? Is it a monetary interest?
4. How would you rule in this matter if you were the judge? Defend your decision.

Case 23

Voluntary Participation Programs and Union Discipline

Individual Mr. Lincoln, an individual member of the bargaining unit

Union Communications Workers of America, Local 13000, AFL-CIO (Verizon Communications Inc.)

BACKGROUND

Verizon Communications began a voluntary program whereby members of the bargaining unit could report to work at company facilities closer to their homes. Desks, telephones, and computer terminals were installed at switching offices and other locations where employees could park their company-owned vehicles and obtain work assignments. This permitted employees to report to work at places closer to home, and saved the company time and money by have employees report to work closer to where they were needed to perform repairs and do other work.

The company had laid off employees immediately prior to implementing this program. The union disagreed with the company's assertion that the lay-offs were financially prudent, and as a result adopted a position that employees were not to participate in these voluntary company programs.

Four employees were observed parking their vehicles at various remote locations in participation in the voluntary parking program after they had been personally warned not to participate in this program. This voluntary participation in the company program was in violation of union directives to the four employees not to participate. Charges were filed with the union against these four employees. Three of the employees got their supervisors to write memoranda ordering them to park at the remote locations; the fourth employee, Mr. Lincoln, filed an unfair labor practice charge with the Board alleging violation of Section 8(b) (1)(A) of the Act. Eventually the charges against the employees were dropped and the union did not discipline any of the employees who participated in the company's program.

POSITION OF THE INDIVIDUAL EMPLOYEE

Mr. Lincoln claims that the union violated his Section 7 rights with respect to his participation in the voluntary remote parking program. Mr. Lincoln believes he has the right to participate in this program because it is to his advantage and does the union no harm whatsoever. It is therefore clear that his participation is protected by Section 7 of the Act.

The individual employee also claims that when the union engaged in its conduct toward employees who voluntarily participated, the company began ordering employees to park at remote locations. Again, the union's threatened disciplinary action violates Mr. Lincoln's Section 7 rights under these facts and circumstances. The individual employee asks the Board to find the union violated his rights, and requests an appropriate remedy.

POSITION OF THE UNION

In response to Verizon's having laid off several employees in December 2002, the union's executive board informed its members that:

> Local 13000 member will not voluntarily participate in any company sponsored initiative, committee, or program of any kind.
>
> This means that you come into work, do your job, go home at the end of your respective workday. Once a week you accept, sign, and cash your paycheck.
>
> There are no exceptions.
>
> Any member violating this Executive Board policy will be subject to charges under the CWA Constitution and Local 13000 Bylaws and Rules.

The company initiated a purely voluntary program of permitting employees to remotely garage their company vehicles. That means employees could park their vehicles at switching offices and other company facilities other than the main garage. This permits the company to assign work close to those facilities and save time and money. Further, it often benefited employees who could report to work at a location closer to their home. Such a voluntary program is not required of employees, and employees had discretion in these matters. The Union Executive Board, in response to layoffs, decided that such cooperation with management was inappropriate when management was laying off bargaining unit members when other cost savings activities were available to it. Therefore, it is proper and appropriate for the union to take the position it has with respect to voluntary programs, and it is well within the union's rights to discipline members of the bargaining unit who ignore the union's directives concerning these voluntary programs.

QUESTIONS

1. Does the evidence show that the employees were ordered to participate in the remote parking program, or was this voluntary?
2. Does the union have the right to discipline employees who violate Executive Board directives made pursuant to rules and bylaws? Explain.
3. If you were the Board, in this case, how would you rule? Explain.

Case 24

Threats and Insubordination, or Performing a Shop Steward's Job?

Company Tillford Contractors, Murray, Kentucky

Union Plumbers and Pipefitters, Local Union No. 184

BACKGROUND

The facts in this case for the most part were undisputed. On February 2, 1994, Dirk Behrens[1] and Kent Murphy were referred to one of the company's job sites (a major building project) by Plumbers and Pipefitters Local No. 184. The union had designated Behrens to be the job site shop steward. The company had made Murphy the working foreman[2] at the job site for the duration of the project. Behrens and Murphy were initially supervised by Lyle Souter, an area foreman.[3] Souter informed Murphy that he would be bringing Dick Bacon to the site to act as a materials expediter. Murphy initially believed that he would be supervising Bacon. However, when Bacon arrived on February 14, 1994, Murphy observed that his actions were more consistent with those of an area foreman than a materials expediter. That afternoon, Kent Murphy asked Bacon if he was replacing Souter as area foreman. Bacon responded that he was just told to be at the site. Murphy repeated the question later that day and the following morning. Each time, he received the same response from Dick Bacon.

On February 15, Murphy told Bacon that he thought the collective bargaining agreement governing the parties prohibited the company from assigning an employee to be area foreman over more than one job. If correct, that would mean the company's assignment of Bacon as area foreman on this job might be in violation of the collective agreement since Bacon was already serving as an area foreman at another job (or jobs). Murphy also told his shop steward, Dirk Behrens, that he had asked Bacon three times about his position, and Bacon had refused to respond.

Dirk Behrens then attempted to determine Bacon's job status. Behrens asked Dick Bacon if he was the area foreman on the Tillford project, to which Bacon merely replied, "Tillford sent me to the job." Behrens then told Bacon, "If you're our area foreman, ain't you area foreman on two more different jobs? I believe that in our agreement, you can't be area foreman on two or three jobs." Behrens then threatened to bring internal union charges against Bacon for violating the parties' collective bargaining agreement.[4]

[1] The names of all individuals are disguised.

[2] The "working foreman" position (i.e., Kent Murphy) was not a supervisor within the meaning of Section 2 (11) of LMRA.

[3] The area foreman position was a supervisory (managerial) one, although individuals (i.e., Dick Bacon) were typically members of the union, since they also could be assigned to nonsupervisory positions depending on the work project.

[4] The Tillford company was a signatory to a multiemployer agreement between the union and a number of other contractors.

Behrens also said, "You've got no goddamn business being here. The best thing you could do is get the hell away from us!"

Following this conversation, Dick Bacon attempted to contact his union business agent, Barton Blake, to determine whether the union contract prohibited his being area foreman on the Tillford project. After he was unable to reach Blake, Bacon went to the company's main office and asked to review a copy of the collective bargaining agreement. The company president, Vic Todd, and Bacon together examined the contract, and they determined that it did permit the company to place Bacon at the job site as an area foreman.

At this point, Todd decided to fire Dirk Behrens since Bacon had told him that Behrens had said he had "no goddamn business" being on the job. Todd decided to contact Barton Blake, the union business agent, to inform Blake about his decision. Todd learned for the first time from Blake that Behrens was a union job site steward. Nevertheless, Todd remained firm in his decision to discharge Behrens, because as he told Blake, he could not abide an employee "talking back" and "sticking his nose where he had no business," and "trying to intimidate and threaten one of our people."

On the next day, Dirk Behrens was terminated by the company; that is, he was told to leave the company's construction project job site. Further, the company president, Vic Todd, wrote the union a letter informing the union that Dirk Behrens was not ever to be referred by the union to perform work at any future job site of the Tillford company.

Shortly thereafter, the union filed unfair labor practice charges, protesting Behrens's termination as being a violation of Sections 8(a) (3) and 8(a) (1) of the Labor Management Relations Act.

POSITION OF THE UNION

The union argued that when Dirk Behrens queried Dick Bacon concerning whether or not Bacon was a job site area foreman, Behrens was engaged in "protected concerted activity" within the meaning of Section 7 of LMRA. As a union steward, Behrens was acting in regard to his understanding of the application and interpretation of the parties' collective bargaining agreement. Even though Behrens may have been incorrect or in error concerning any alleged violation, he nevertheless had the right to pursue what he thought was the union's contractually guaranteed rights under the agreement.

The termination of Dirk Behrens by the company was obviously discrimination and interference with a union shop steward who was trying to carry out his appropriate union representational duties. Even though the company president, Vic Todd, made his decision before learning of Behrens's shop steward status, nevertheless Todd refused to rescind Behrens's termination. This was flagrant unlawful discrimination. The allegation that the shop steward's statements to Dick Bacon constituted insubordination, intimidation, and threats was a pretext in order to find a basis for terminating Behrens. At most, Behrens's conduct included profanity and was inappropriate, but such statements are widely used in the workplace and were not so severe as to justify his termination.

The union urged that the company's termination of Dirk Behrens violated Section 8(a) (3) and 8(a) (1) of the Labor Management Relations Act. The union requested that Dirk Behrens should be made whole for all lost income and benefits that he had lost from the company's action removing him from the company's construction project. Further, the union urged that the NLRB fashion a remedy that would negate the company's letter that had instructed the union that Behrens should never be assigned to any other work projects involving the Tillford company.

POSITION OF THE COMPANY

The company position was that Dirk Behrens had been terminated because of gross insubordination, which included his threatening and intimidating an employee, Dick Bacon. The company in the person of its president, Vic Todd, believed that Behrens was improperly attempting to usurp management rights under the guise of trying to interpret a collective bargaining agreement. Behrens was clearly wrong, and his insubordinate and threatening comments to Dick Bacon justified his termination.

The company noted that the company president had made his decision to terminate Behrens before learning about any role that Behrens may have been assigned as the union's job site steward. Being a union steward does not give an individual the right to threaten and intimidate other employees, or to attempt to usurp management's contractual rights. Behrens justly was terminated for his misconduct, and the company did not want someone of his character working on any of its future projects.

The company urged that the unfair labor practice charges were without merit and should be dismissed.

QUESTIONS

1. Were the comments of Dirk Behrens to Dick Bacon of such an egregious nature as to justify his termination, irrespective of any role he may have had as the job site union steward? Discuss.
2. Does it make any difference in the determination of this case that the company president decided to terminate Dirk Behrens before learning of his position as the job site union steward? Explain.
3. What should be the NLRB's decision? Explain.
4. If you decide for the union position and find that the company violated LMRA, what type of remedy would be appropriate, given the fact that Dirk Behrens was not a direct employee of the company?

Case 25

Judicial Review of the NLRB's "Punitive" Remedy Concerning the Health Care Plan

Company North Star Steel Company, St. Paul, Minnesota

Union United Steelworkers of America

BACKGROUND

On July 30, 1987, the United Steelworkers of America was certified by the NLRB as the recognized bargaining agent for 24 clerical employees of North Star. The company refused to acknowledge this certification; the company would not bargain with the union and filed an exception to the unit certification with the Board. On July 27, 1988, the Board found that the union's certification was valid, and that North Star had violated Sections 8(a) (5) and 8(a) (1) of the LMRA by refusing to recognize and bargain with the union. This ruling was affirmed by the District of Columbia Circuit in December 1989. The company then began bargaining with the union.

Before the union's certification, North Star had maintained a health care insurance plan for its employees. Historically, this plan had required employees to contribute to the payment of premiums. The plan covered the majority of employees at the North Star plant, including the clerical workers, and allowed North Star to make unilateral changes in the amount of money the employees needed to contribute to maintain their coverage. This system was continued after the union was certified to represent the clerical employees, even though North Star was challenging that certification and refusing to bargain.

In early 1990, the union and the company began bargaining. They started with noneconomic issues and moved on, after making no headway, to economic issues. In May 1990, the parties reached a tentative agreement on many of the issues. Included in this agreement was a union proposal for continuation of the employer's health care plan in its current form, allowing the company to continue making unilateral changes in the contribution amounts paid by employees each year. The tentative agreement had as a condition, however, that the parties reach a final, total collective bargaining agreement. The union maintained that its agreement to continue the health care plan represented an effort to stimulate negotiations on other, more pressing issues. Despite this concession, however, no final overall agreement was reached.

After the parties failed to reach a final agreement, the union filed an amended complaint with the NLRB, alleging that North Star had violated Sections 8(a) (5) and 8(a) (1) of the Act by unilaterally raising the employees' contribution amounts to the health care plan during 1988, 1989, and 1990. The case was submitted to an administrative law judge (ALJ) on stipulated facts. North Star conceded that it had committed a technical violation of Section 8(a) (5), but the company argued that imposing a monetary make-whole remedy was inappropriate because the employees were in the same position that they would have been in had the company bargained with the union when it was originally certified.

The ALJ concluded otherwise, however. The ALJ ordered North Star to return the employees to the status quo that had existed in 1987 and to reimburse them for all the incremental health care premium costs they had paid from January 1988 to July 18, 1990, when the negotiations, according to the ALJ, had reached an impasse.

On appeal to the NLRB, the ALJ's decision was affirmed, with the exception of the ALJ's finding that negotiations had reached an impasse in 1990. The Board determined that no impasse had occurred, and that the monetary make-whole remedy should continue to accrue until an agreement was reached or until a negotiating impasse did occur. The Board stated:

> Consequently, we shall order that the status quo ante be restored. That is, the terms and conditions of the unit employees' health insurance program shall be returned to the level in existence before January 1988, the date of the Respondent's initial illegal unilateral action. The Respondent's monetary liability shall also continue until the status quo ante is restored.[1]

The company decided to appeal the NLRB's decision insofar as the Board's make-whole remedy order was concerned. The company claimed that this remedy was "punitive" and beyond the Board's authority as provided in Sections 6 and 10(c) of LMRA.

REASONING OF THE NLRB

In its decision, the NLRB disagreed with the administrative law judge's conclusion that a bargaining impasse had occurred between the parties as of July 18, 1990. The ALJ had concluded that because of the bargaining impasse, the company had lawfully implemented changes in its health care plan as of July 18, 1990. Therefore, the ALJ had only ordered the company to make the employees whole for "any losses they had incurred" as a result of the company's Section 8(a) (5) violation prior to that date, that is, from January 1988 to July 18, 1990.

However, the NLRB determined that a collective bargaining impasse had not occurred as of July 18, 1990. The Board reviewed the history of the parties' attempts beginning January 19, 1990, to negotiate an initial collective bargaining agreement. The first and subsequent sessions during January and February had focused on noneconomic matters. After failing to reach agreement on noneconomic items, the parties had begun, in March 1990, to discuss economic issues.

On March 7, 1990, the union presented its economic proposals. One union proposal was that the company continue its current health care insurance program. The parties met several times between March 7 and May 2, 1990, when they reached tentative agreement on some issues, including the proposal that the clerical bargaining-unit employees should be covered by the health insurance program then in effect. However, all agreed-upon provisions were tentative and conditioned on the terms of a final collective bargaining agreement. The parties subsequently met on May 16 and July 18, 1990. No further collective bargaining sessions were scheduled after July 18, 1990, and no collective bargaining agreement was concluded.

[1] *North Star Steel Company and United Steelworkers,* 305 NLRB No. 7, September 30, 1991, 139 LRRM 1090. The "Respondent" is the company.

The NLRB cited a previous case decision, where it had held:[2]

> Whether a bargaining impasse exists is a matter of judgment. The bargaining history, the good faith of the parties in negotiations, the length of the negotiations, the importance of the issue or issues as to which there is disagreement, the contemporaneous understanding of the parties as to the state of negotiations, are all relevant factors.

In the instant case, the NLRB determined that the company's claim that a bargaining impasse had been reached on July 18, 1990, was not conclusive, and therefore the effect of the company's prior Section 8(a) (5) violation continued beyond that date. The NLRB ordered the company to restore the employees' health care plan to the status quo of January 1988, and to make the clerical employees whole for all the incremental premium costs and losses they had incurred from January 1988 until such time as the parties would reach a binding agreement on the health care plan stipulations, or until a lawful bargaining impasse between the parties on the health care plan had occurred.

POSITION OF THE COMPANY

The North Star Company filed an appeal of the National Labor Relations Board's make-whole remedy arguing that the Board's order was "punitive" and excessive and exceeded the Board's statutory authority under Section 10(c) of the LMRA. The company acknowledged that it technically had violated Section 8(a) (5) of the Act when it did not bargain with the union while it was filing exceptions to the certification of the union in 1987. The company was within its legal right to file exceptions to the NLRB's determination of the election outcome and the company's judicial appeal of that decision. When the court affirmed the certification of the union in December 1989, the company began bargaining for an initial contract with the union.

In the company's view, it had bargained in good faith with the union and attempted to reach an initial collective bargaining agreement. Section 8(d) of the Act does not require the parties to agree on every proposal that may be forthcoming. In 1990 the union itself had proposed a continuation of the health care insurance program for clerical employees then in effect. This program included a provision that the company could make the necessary changes in the employees' contributions to premium costs of the health care plan, and this was reasonable, especially in view of the incredibly rising costs of health care coverage.

The company had implemented various changes in this health care plan during the period of the company's challenge to the certification of the union. The union in fact had agreed to what the company had done, when during the negotiations in early 1990 it proposed the old plan's continuation. Nevertheless, the National Labor Relations Board had ordered that the status quo of January 1988 be returned. This was an excessive and punitive determination by the NLRB because the employees really had suffered no financial loss. The employees would have been subject to the same premium rate changes even if a collective bargaining agreement had been reached as early as 1988. This was apparent because the union had reached the same conclusion during negotiations in 1990.

[2] *Taft Broadcasting Co.*, 163 NLRB 475, 478, 64 LRRM 1386 (1967), enfd. 395 F.2d 622 (67 LRRM 3032) (D.C. Cir. 1968).

In summary, the company contended that its minor technical violation of LMRA did not deserve the punitive remedy ordered by the National Labor Relations Board. The company claimed that the employees had not suffered any financial loss during the period in question, and therefore the NLRB's remedy was beyond its statutory authority, which only permitted make-whole remedies involving real financial loss. The company urged that the court of appeals overturn the National Labor Relations Board's order.

QUESTIONS

1. In a whole line of prior decisions concerning this issue, the courts have generally deferred to the National Labor Relations Board's judgment unless there is a finding that the NLRB exceeded its statutory authority granted under Section 10(c) of the Act. Why is this a "slippery" area of determination, especially for a court of appeals?
2. Evaluate the conclusions reached by the administrative law judge and the National Labor Relations Board concerning whether a bargaining impasse between the parties had occurred as of July 18, 1990. Why is this determination critical in regard to the remedial orders?
3. Is the company position valid that the employees had suffered no monetary loss during the period that the company was challenging the union certification and beyond?
4. Should the court of appeals sustain or set aside the NLRB's remedial order? Discuss.

Case 26

The Enforcement of No-Solicitation Rules: A Real Whopper

Employer Midon Restaurant Corporation, d/b/a Burger King

Union Industrial Workers of the World, Philadelphia General Membership Branch

BACKGROUND

The employer operated Burger King restaurants in the upstate New York area, among which was a store in Albany, New York. The company maintained a broad no-solicitation rule that proscribed soliciting for union activities or membership (or other forms of solicitation) on company property. The employees were otherwise permitted to discuss whatever they pleased during periods of time when no customers were being served.

Mr. Pohr[1] began his employment at the Burger King restaurant in Albany, New York, in June of 1999. He was employed in a shift position where he waited on customers, prepared food, and did general clean-up duties as required. The shift manager under whom he worked was Ms. Johns. The district manager for the company was Mr. Myers.

On July 29, 1999, Mr. Pohr was discussing the benefits of unionization with Ms. Johns and his fellow employees when Mr. Myers walked into the store. Mr. Myers overheard Mr. Pohr stating that if the employees at Burger King were represented by a union they would be paid enough for the work they were required to do. It was also Mr. Pohr's stated opinion that, at the time, the employees were not presently paid a fair wage for the work they were required to do. Mr. Myers then directed Mr. Pohr to cease discussing unions while on the clock or he would be looking for a job elsewhere. This statement was made in the presence of all of the store's employees then at work. Mr. Myers also offered the opinion that the employees were fairly compensated and were obliged to provide quick and efficient service to the restaurant's customers because they received a fair wage to do that work.

Mr. Myers then used the opportunity to engage in a discussion with the store's employees about the importance of service time and that quick, efficient service was very important to the profitability of their operations. Mr. Pohr then stated, "You don't pay me enough to do this job." Then Mr. Pohr made some reference to organizing unions, to which Myers responded that the company's handbook proscribed solicitation in the restaurant regardless of whether the employee was on the clock or not, and that union solicitation was banned, especially during times when the person was on the clock. Mr. Myers remained in the area and Mr. Pohr again returned to the subject of discussion with his fellow employees—specifically that unionization would result in better wages for the employees.

After those comments by Mr. Pohr, Mr. Myers took Mr. Pohr into the employees' breakroom for a short (approximately 10-minute) conversation that was not witnessed. Ms. Johns then overheard Mr. Pohr respond to Mr. Myers that "you can't control my mind" and then Mr. Pohr made an obscene gesture toward Mr. Myers and told Ms. Johns

[1] Names are disguised.

that he quit his job; he then left the restaurant. Mr. Pohr did not return to the restaurant except to pick up his final paycheck.

POSITION OF THE UNION

The union alleges that the employer maintained a no-solicitation rule that violated Section 8(a) (1) of the Act. Further, the union claims that the employer violated Mr. Pohr's rights, through constructive discharge, by unlawfully restricting his rights to solicit union membership and freely discuss the benefits of unionization, thus making his employment with the company sufficiently intolerable that he could not continue.

The employer may maintain a "reasonable" no-solicitation rule to assure that union solicitation does not interfere with servicing customers. However, in this case, alleged the union, the nature of the no-solicitation rule and the enforcement of that rule by Mr. Myers were well beyond the scope of protecting its operations and was therefore illegally broad. Mr. Myers clearly stated that the company would not permit unions in their restaurants. The Act in Section 7 guarantees employees the freedom to engage in union activities, including their exercise of free speech. To attempt to interfere with those rights, according to the union, violates employees' Section 7 rights.

Further, the employer, by restraining Mr. Pohr in the exercise of his rights, created an intolerable work environment that resulted in Mr. Pohr's resigning from employment with the company; this is constructively the same as having discharged Mr. Pohr. Therefore, the union also alleged that, effectively, Mr. Pohr was fired for his union activities, in violation of Sections 8(a) (1) and (3) of the Act. The union requested that the employer be ordered to cease the promulgation of such a broad no-solicitation rule, and that the constructive discharge of Mr. Pohr be ordered rescinded.

POSITION OF THE COMPANY

Although there are differences in the testimony of the various witnesses, it was the company's position that it did not violate the Act either in the enforcement of the no-solicitation rule or by discharging Mr. Pohr.

The company had the right to make and enforce reasonable rules. Mr. Myers denied having made the statement that unions would never be permitted in the company's stores. That allegation was false. Further, the company had the right to restrict employee speech when they were serving customers and on the clock. It was only reasonable that union solicitation and other such business should be reserved to places not open to the public, and not while employees were expected to be engaged in productive work.

The allegation that Mr. Pohr was constructively discharged was also denied. Mr. Pohr quit his job and he did so of his own free will. The employee was not subjected to unreasonable working conditions or threatened in any fashion. Employees must act with prudence and act to preserve their own interests if their rights are to be preserved under the Act. An employee reacting unduly to Mr. Myers's statements and quitting his job was not a violation of that employee's Section 7 rights (hence, constructive discharge), and therefore that charge was also false according to the company.

The employer urged the administrative law judge to deny the complaints on both counts as being without merit.

QUESTIONS

1. What are the appropriate standards for determining whether a no-solicitation rule is appropriate under the Act? Critically evaluate.
2. Why would an employer wish to limit an employee's free speech concerning unions? What interest do unions have in not seeing employees' free speech rights limited with respect to organizing? Explain.
3. What is constructive discharge? What are the standards to be employed in determining whether constructive discharge occurred?
4. What is the relationship between an employer's right to make reasonable rules and the employees' right to free speech under the Act? Are the balancing of these rights difficult for the Board? Critically evaluate.

Case 27

Management Teams or Employee Involvement Committees: Authority to Put a Cork in It

Company Crown Cork and Seal Company, Incorporated

Individual Employee Herman Melville[1]

BACKGROUND

The employer in this case had approximately 150 employees at its aluminum can factory in Texas. The company used an employee-management system referred to as the Socio-Tech System. The expressed purpose of this system was to create and empower teams and committees and to delegate to the company's employees serving on these teams and committees substantial authority over the day-to-day operations of the aluminum can factory. This authority was delegated to committees and teams comprised of employees in the plant, but these groups were chaired by members of management.

The company had no bargaining relationship with a union and, at the time of this case, there were no collective bargaining agreement, organizing activities, or union otherwise involved in representing the company's employees in the Texas facility. There was also no evidence that Mr. Melville was a union member or activist at the time this case was filed with the NLRB, or at any time prior to the filing of this charge.

At the time this case was filed, the company had four production teams and four other committees dealing with various issues in the plant. These committees and teams (both *ad hoc* and standing) had responsibilities for a wide range of activities, including production, quality, training, attendance, maintenance, and discipline. In the case of discipline, the committees had authority to administer corrective action short of suspensions or discharge. If the committee believed that a suspension or discharge was warranted under the specific facts and circumstances, the case was sent to the plant's justice system with appropriate recommendations. Appropriate committees[2] could recommend such severe discipline to an Organizational Review Board.

Mr. Melville's tale of woe began when he was assigned to one of these committees. Every employee in the company's plant was assigned to at least one team or committee. Each team or committee had a chairperson who was a member of management. For a team or committee to take action required a three-quarters majority vote of the members of the committee.

Mr. Melville observed several incidents involving these teams and committees that led him to believe that these teams and committees dealt with management concerning various issues that had to do with activities in the plant, including discipline and work rules that he

[1] Employees names are disguised.

[2] For an employee's failure to meet performance or quality standards or to comply with attendance rules discipline was possible. The production or safety teams had the authority to recommend more severe forms of discipline if their direct counseling efforts or warnings proved ineffective. The same process was true of safety standards and other issues in the plant.

believed fell within the meaning of terms and conditions of employment for the purposes of the Act. Therefore, Mr. Melville believed these committees and teams were employee organizations being dominated by management in violation of the employees' Section 7 rights. He therefore filed charges that the company was dominating labor organizations in violation of the Act.

POSITION OF THE INDIVIDUAL

Mr. Melville was not a union activist at the time of this case, or at any other time during his tenure with the company. Mr. Melville's concern was what the Section 7 rights were with respect to concerted activities of employees in a nonunion environment. He believed that the system at the aluminum can factory was one of employee involvement, hence concerted activity protected by Section 7 of the Act. The company structured the system of employee involvement, charged the groups with their responsibilities, paid the employees for participation in these activities outside of regular working hours, and appointed management personnel as the chairpersons of these groups.

Mr. Melville believed that the management personnel who served as chairs of these teams and committees and had veto power over the committees became suspicious of the intent of these groups. As a result, he carefully observed the operation of these groups and became convinced that these groups were company-dominated unions. Management, in other words, dictated policy to these groups.

The position of this individual employee, as represented by the NLRB's general counsel, was that the company was violating the Section 7 rights of its employees by dominating these employee organizations. Further, it is also charged that the employees were not free from the interference of management in selecting their representatives, in violation of Section 8(a) (2) of the Act.

POSITION OF THE COMPANY

The company contended that there was no violation of the Act associated with its creation and reliance upon its Socio-Tech System. This system, according to the company, was a system of management, not an employee representational group. The company's intentions were to delegate managerial authority to those teams and committees—to provide those groups with authority to decide issues important to the economic welfare of the plant, the company, and the employees.

The company's position was that these groups were managerial in nature and not organizations for employee representational purposes as contemplated by Section 7 of the Act. The issues with which these groups dealt, together with their authority to resolve matters or at least effectively recommend solutions, discipline, and policy made clear these organizations were managerial in nature. Further, there was no give and take associated with collective bargaining, there was no representative attempting to glean from management better terms and conditions of employment, or any other trapping of an employee organization as contemplated under Section 7 of the Act.

The employer's position was that it had in no way violated its employees' Section 7 rights under the Act. The teams and committees operating under the Socio-Tech System were managerial, not representational, and were therefore not employee organizations protected by Section 7. Consequently, the employer urged the NLRB to dismiss these charges as being without merit.

QUESTIONS

1. What are statutorily protected employee organizations under the Act? What standards does the NLRB apply to determine whether a group is an employee organization for purposes of the Act? Explain.
2. What are the standards the NLRB applies to determine if employees are managerial? Critically evaluate these standards.
3. Are the employees in this case managerial? If so, by what standards are they managerial? Explain.
4. Does it make a difference in this case that there is no union complaining about company domination? Does an individual have standing to make such a charge? Explain.

Case 28

The Company's Refusal to Provide a List of Disciplinary Work Rules

Company Praxair, Inc., Knoxville, Tennessee

Union Teamsters Local Union No. 67

BACKGROUND

The company sold and distributed propane gas, and certain of its employees were represented by Teamsters Local Union No. 67.

Because of a number of union grievances involving employee discipline, on May 6, 1993, the union's business agent, Andy Alamo,[1] by letter asked the company plant manager, Gerry Falice, to provide the union with a complete list of the firm's disciplinary rules and/or disciplinary policies. Alamo explained that the union needed this information to facilitate administration of the parties' current collective bargaining agreement. Receiving no response, in late October Alamo called Falice concerning the matter. Falice told Alamo that the company had no fixed disciplinary policies for violations of work rules. In a November 15, 1993, letter to Alamo and the union, Falice stated that some of the company's disciplinary rules/policies appeared in the parties' contract, but other relevant policies and rules were not in writing and were determined case-by-case based on a progressive disciplinary system.

On November 29, Andy Alamo responded for the union with a letter requesting the company's "verbal rules reduced to writing and any written rules which could lead to discipline, and a copy of the progressive steps for each of these rules." On December 3, 1993, in a letter to Alamo prepared for Gerry Falice by the company's attorney, the company refused to "generate a written set of disciplinary rules." The letter advised the union of its rights to attempt to negotiate a contract containing disciplinary rules. Further, the letter mentioned that in previous contract negotiations, the union had unsuccessfully attempted to include disciplinary rules in the parties' labor-management agreement.

Shortly thereafter, the union filed unfair labor practice charges with the NLRB, claiming that the company's refusal to provide the information it had requested was a violation of Sections 8(a) (5) and 8(a) (1) of the Labor Management Relations Act.

POSITION OF THE UNION

The union asserted that the company had in place both written and verbal work rules. Among the company's acknowledged work rules were the following:

Facial hair was not permitted (written).

The presence of two employees in the plant was required during the performance of certain work (written).

[1] The names of all individuals are disguised.

An employee was required to obtain permission to arrive at work before the beginning of a scheduled shift (verbal).

An employee was required to notify the company of an absence before the beginning of a scheduled shift (written).

Excessive tardiness and absenteeism would not be tolerated (verbal).

Additionally, there was a verbal rule regarding employees arriving late for work, and there were a number of work rules dealing with smoking, alcohol, drugs, and firearms on company property. Some of these were written and posted; others were not.

The union claimed that the company had disciplined employees for violating both written and verbal rules. For example, the company admitted that it had disciplined employees for tardiness and absenteeism, even though there were no specific written rules about this. The company had issued a series of reprimands to employees for violating the written rule prohibiting facial hair. In addition, pursuant to a contractual rule, the company had disciplined employees for not reporting to work for three consecutive days without notifying a supervisor. Much more seriously, the company had discharged employee Mary Henley for leaving work before the end of a shift without notifying her supervisor. The rule for which she was discharged was only in verbal form. When the union arbitrated Henley's discharge, the company's attorney contended: "Employees had been verbally informed of the rule that if they were going to leave the plant prior to the end of their scheduled shift, they must notify the plant manager or a supervisor. The grievant's notice to another employee did not suffice to bring her into compliance with this rule."

The union cited several prior NLRB decisions in support of its request for a listing of all of the company's disciplinary work rules.[2] The Board had long established that an employer must furnish information a union requests if there is a probability that the information is relevant and necessary to the union in carrying out its statutory duties as the employees' bargaining representative. This duty to furnish information was derived from Section 8(a) (5) and Section 8(d) of LMRA, which require employers and unions to bargain in good faith with respect to mandatory subjects of bargaining. Work rules that could be grounds for discipline clearly were mandatory subjects of bargaining according to numerous Board rulings. Thus, a union with a statutory duty to represent employees in disciplinary proceedings—Section 8(b) (3) of LMRA—had the right to be informed of the existing work rules that might lead to disciplining of its unit employees.

The union urged that by its refusal to provide the requested information, the company had violated Sections 8(a) (5) and 8(a) (1) of LMRA. The union requested as a remedy that the company should be directed to provide the union with a listing of all of its work rules—both written and verbal—that could lead to a bargaining unit employee being disciplined.

POSITION OF THE COMPANY

The company asserted that it had met its obligations to provide the union with all of the necessary information that was available and needed by the union in order to represent

[2] Among these were the following: *Westinghouse Electric Corp.*, 239 NLRB 106, 107, 99 LRRM 1482 (1978), enfd. as modified 648 F'2d 18, 105 LRRM 3337 (D.C. Cir. 1980); *Cowles Communication,* 172 NLRB 1909, 69 LRRM 1100 (1968); *Laidlaw Waste Systems,* 307 NLRB 1211, 1213–1214, 140 LRRM 1225 (1992).

employees in disciplinary matters. Specific written rules that could lead to discipline were contained in the parties' collective bargaining agreement (e.g., the rule regarding loss of seniority for failing to provide an acceptable excuse for failing to report to work on three consecutive scheduled days). Certain written rules were included in the company's safety manual (e.g., the facial hair rule and the rule regarding loss of seniority for failing to provide an acceptable excuse for failing to report to work on three consecutive scheduled days). Additionally, there were written rules posted at the plant (e.g., rules regarding smoking, alcohol, drugs, and firearms on company property). Beyond these specific written rules, the company maintained a general policy of progressive discipline (e.g., for absenteeism and tardiness), and a general policy that considered the totality of circumstances in any given situation in determining whether certain questionable conduct required discipline. All of the available written rules and these general policy statements had been provided to the union, but the union still was not satisfied by the company's response.

The company argued that just because some employee misconduct not specifically identified in written rules had resulted in discipline, this did not mean that the company maintained some uniform and definite work rules or policies that it unlawfully refused to supply to the union. The verbalized disciplinary situations (e.g., an employee's late arrival at work; notifying the company about leaving work before the end of a scheduled shift; obtaining permission to arrive at work before a scheduled shift begins) were merely factors that might, under the company's "totality-of-the-circumstances" approach, lead to discipline, depending upon all of the attendant factors in a given case situation. These factors did not rise to the level of a "work rule." Moreover, whatever judgments the union had about the company's system of disciplinary management, the fact remained that the union had not been able to gain a better system at the bargaining table. The NLRB had no authority to order the company to rationalize its system by generating another set of written rules.[3]

In summary, the company asserted that by providing the union with (or pointing to) the written rules contained in the parties' collective bargaining agreement, the safety manual, and the posted signs around the plant, as well as informing the union of its general policies, the company had adequately provided the union with the information it requested. The company thus did not violate the Act by failing to generate and provide to the union an all-encompassing set of written work rules that it had requested but which did not exist. The company urged that the unfair labor practice charges were not meritorious and should be dismissed.

QUESTIONS

1. Why would the union press its unfair labor practice charges in this case? Discuss.
2. Why would the company refuse to put its disciplinary rules—both verbal and written—in a written format that would be acceptable to the union? Discuss.
3. Was the company's refusal to provide the requested list of disciplinary work rules an unfair labor practice? Why, or why not?

---

[3] The company cited *H. K. Porter Co. v. NLRB,* 397 U.S. 99, 73 LRRM 2561 (1970).

Case 29

The Obligation to Reduce the Agreement to a Written Contract

Company HCL, Inc. a/k/a A. B. Inc.

Union Laborers International Union of America, AFL-CIO, Local 576

BACKGROUND

The facts of this case are not in substantial dispute. In May or June of 2001, the company, a construction firm, recognized the union as the exclusive bargaining representative of its employees pursuant to Section 8 (f) of the Act. The company, as one of several employers utilizing the Laborers' hiring hall, signed a collective bargaining agreement with the union that expired on June 30, 2002. In June 2002 the parties executed a letter of intent which stated that the parties have agreed to a new collective bargaining agreement that replaces the contract expiring on June 30, 2002. The new agreement was effective from July 1, 2002, to June 30, 2005. Subsequently, a signature page for the new contract was sent to each of the contractors who were signatory to the new contract and all of the employers signed the agreement except the company. In August 2002 the company met with the employees in its bargaining unit and offered them new wages and other benefits.

The union filed complaints with the Board that the company violated Sections 8(a) (5) and (1) of the Act. The administrative law judge dismissed the complaints that the company was obligated to sign the agreement and directly dealt with the bargaining unit members. The union appealed the judge's findings to the National Labor Relations Board, which asserted jurisdiction.

POSITION OF THE UNION

It is the position of the union that once an agreement is reached between the parties, it must be reduced to writing if either party so demands. An agreement was reached for a 2002–2005 collective bargaining agreement. That agreement is evidenced by the letter of intent executed by the parties. The company simply failed to sign the agreement as required, hence violating Section 8 (a) (5) and (1) of the Act.

To make matters worse the company, admittedly, then engaged in direct negotiations with the members of the bargaining unit and negotiated a wage and benefit increase. The union was then the exclusive bargaining representative of those employees with whom the company dealt. Therefore, the company also violated Section 8 (a) (5) and (1) of Act by circumventing the exclusive representative of those employees.

POSITION OF THE COMPANY

The administrative law judge agreed with the company that the letter of intent was not a demonstration of the company's intent to be bound by the successor agreement. The company claimed that it was not part of a multi-employer group and that the multi-employer group was not authorized to negotiate on behalf of the company with the purpose of arriving at a successor collective bargaining agreement.

The company further claimed that since it had not entered into a collective bargaining agreement with the union there was no bar to it negotiating with its own employees concerning wages, hours, or other terms and conditions of employment. Therefore, the company's direct dealing with its employee is not a violation of the Act.

It is the company's position that it did nothing wrong. Therefore, the Board should dismiss the union's complaint and affirm the administrative law judge's decision in this matter.

QUESTIONS

1. Is the letter of intent clear evidence that the company accepted the successor agreement? Did the company ever deny the plain meaning of the letter of intent?
2. In a hiring hall arrangement, does each employer negotiate a separate contract, or does an employer accede to an existing contract or product of a multi-employer negotiation? What is a multi-employer bargaining unit?
3. Did the employer violate the Act by not executing the contract as described in the letter of intent?
4. If the contract is binding can an employer deal directly with its employees concerning wages, hours, or other terms and conditions of employment? Explain.
5. If you were the Board, would you affirm the administrative law judge's decision and order in this case? Why?

Case 30

Information Requests and the Duty to Bargain Collectively: Not Mickey Mouse

Employer Walt Disney World Corporation

Union Actors' Equity Association

BACKGROUND

The employer in this matter was Walt Disney Corporation, which had a collective bargaining relationship with the Actors' Equity Association. The bargaining unit in this matter was the Chorus, Chorus Stepping-out, and Principal Performers at the Walt Disney World Vacation Kingdom, which included, among others, the Magic Kingdom, Epcot Center, and the Disney-MGM Studio. This agreement also covered all Disney employees cast or rehearsed to make appearances anyplace in the United States in which the union had jurisdiction. Both the full-time and casual employees in these classifications were represented by the union.

Beginning in 1996, Disney was going to expand its interests in live entertainment throughout the country. Disney characters would be making live appearances at special events throughout the United States. It was also Disney's intention to subcontract at least some of these live performances to the Renaissance Entertainment Group. However, it was then contemplated by the union that World Vacations was being used as an alter ego company by Disney in an attempt to circumvent the collective bargaining agreement. These intentions were published in newspaper interviews across the United States. Even though the company's intentions were not made clear to the union, audition notices were subsequently received by members of the bargaining unit announcing casting in these expanded operations.

The union subsequently wrote to Disney and asked for detailed and specific information concerning the various entertainment operations of the company outside of the amusement parks. The union also asked for listings of persons employed as performers in these entertainment activities for the past three years, whether they were members of the union, members of a Teamsters' unit, or nonunion employees. The union also requested information concerning the ownership and corporate relationship of World Vacations with the rest of the Walt Disney Corporation holdings.

Disney Corporation, through the offices of the World Vacations entity, denied the union's requests concerning the ownership of the various subsidiaries of Disney involved in this matter as being burdensome. World Vacations then responded that it had no collective bargaining relation with the union, and that the collective bargaining relationship with the theme parks had no bearing with the off-site entertainment activities done by other divisions of the corporation. Disney Corporation then identified to the union two other divisions, which it claimed were the entities responsible for the appearances of Disney characters and performers across the United States.

Subsequently, the company did provide some information about the ownership of subsidiaries of the Disney Corporation, long after the fact of the request. Further, some limited amounts of information concerning performances were finally provided, but only long after the fact of the performances. The union, after another failed request to obtain information concerning the performances, filed unfair labor practice charges, alleging the company failed to collectively bargain by having failed to provide information necessary to the performance of its representational duties on behalf of the bargaining unit.

POSITION OF THE UNION

The union claimed that the work being performed across the United States in special performances was likely within the jurisdiction of the bargaining unit and therefore covered by the parties' collective bargaining agreement. When the union requested specific information concerning performances and performers, the company then claimed that the information was not relevant because the performances and performers were employees of other organizations held by Walt Disney Corporation as wholly owned subsidiaries that did not have bargaining relations with the union. The union then requested information to determine whether these were really alter ego operations designed to undermine the bargaining unit and improperly deny bargaining rights.

The performances and performer information was also necessary to determine whether the work was properly done under the parties' collective bargaining agreement, and if not, what remedies should be sought in any grievance the union may deem appropriate to file. It was clear to the union that the company intended to share nothing with the union and that the union's information came from the company via news releases and reports in the media. The union therefore believed that the company had failed in its obligations under the law to bargain collectively with the union.

The union therefore charged that the employer failed to collective bargain by refusing to supply information that the union requested or by supplying very limited information in an untimely fashion—the information the union claimed was necessary to the proper representation of its bargaining unit. Therefore, the union urged the NLRB to find a failure to bargain and order the company to supply the requested information forthwith and completely.

POSITION OF THE COMPANY

The company claimed that the union's requests concerning the company's organization and owners with respect to the alter ego contentions were subsidiary requests, unrelated to its duties to represent the bargaining unit, and should be rejected. Further, the union had presented no objective facts to support its request and had therefore fallen victim to its own self-induced confusion.

The company also claimed that the requests for information concerning performances and performers, together with their union affiliations, were burdensome and unrelated to any possible interests the bargaining unit might have in these performances. The company responded to requests for information from the union, explaining that the entities that the union identified in those requests were informal references to activities, rather than specific divisions with the corporation, and therefore they were not data available to share with the union.

The company claimed that it bargained in good faith with the union and that there were no violations of the Act by its failure to provide specific documents about things the union seemed to be confused about. Therefore, the company's position was that the charges should be dismissed as being without merit.

QUESTIONS

1. What obligations, if any, exist concerning informational requests? Do these obligations extend to both parties equally? Explain.
2. Why must a company provide proprietary information to unions when requested? Under what circumstances might a company legally refuse such requests?
3. Are alter ego divisions of a company illegal? What are the standards applied to determine the legality of alter ego operations?
4. Why would a company want to create an alter ego and then attempt to withhold information concerning its ownership from a union with which it had a bargaining relation? What role does the law play in such matters?

Case 31

Default and Paychecks: Concerted Action?

Employer FJN Worldnet, Inc.

Individual Joe Winter, an individual employee

BACKGROUND

FJN Worldnet, Inc., Grafton, North Dakota, is a construction company performing work at a site at the Air Force Base in Minot, North Dakota. The company's business has an appreciable effect on interstate commerce, and is therefore covered by the National Labor Relations Act. The employees of the company are not represented by a union and there is no collective bargaining agreement or negotiated grievance procedure.

Sometime during November 2004 the company threatened an employee with discharge if he did not quit complaining to other employees about paycheck errors. Subsequently, Joe Winter, an employee of FJN Worldnet, Inc., employed on the construction site at the Minot, North Dakota, Air Force Base concertedly spoke with several of his fellow employees about wages, hours, and working conditions. Among the issues Mr. Winter discussed with his fellow employees were the numerous paycheck errors experienced by the employees.

On January 6, 2005, the company discharged Mr. Winter because of his complaints about the paychecks and his bringing these matters to the attention of his fellow workers.

POSITION OF THE EMPLOYER

The employer was contacted by the Office of the General Counsel to answer the complaint brought against the company by the individual employee. The general counsel faxed a copy of the complaint on May 3, 2004. The company was given until May 10 to respond. A telephone call was received from the employer indicating an attorney would be representing the company. Nothing was received on May 10, and another fax was sent to the company indicating the general counsel would proceed on May 13 to file a motion for default judgment. The company may have no further contact with the Office of the General Counsel.

POSITION OF THE INDIVIDUAL

The Office General Counsel alleged that the record of evidence demonstrated that Mr. Winter was discharged for having engaged in concerted actions, which included complaining about paycheck errors, conditions of employment, wages, and hours. This, the general counsel argued, is protected concerted exercise of Section 7 rights by these nonunion employees. The general counsel also argued that the employer engaged in this behavior to discourage other of its employees from engaging in the same behavior as Mr. Winter in violation of Section 8(a) (1) of the Act.

The general counsel moved for a default judgment against the company and asked for an order reinstating Mr. Winter, making him whole, and an order that the company cease and desist from violating the Act.

QUESTIONS

1. Are nonunion employees covered by the National Labor Relations Act in matters involving concerted action, such as present in this case?
2. What is a default judgment requested by the Office of the General Counsel in this case? Can the NLRB make a decision and order a remedy when the company has not presented a case? Why?
3. Are there concerted activities present in this case? If so, what are they?
4. How would you rule in this case? Why?

Case 32

Threatening the Union Dissidents

Company Consolidated Edison of New York, New York, NY[1]

Union Local Union No. 1-2, Utility Workers of America

Individuals Milo Cimoli and Wally Morris[2]

BACKGROUND

The company and union had been parties to a number of successive collective bargaining agreements. In August 1990, new Local Union No. 1-2 officers were elected. This new administration included Jackson Walls, president; James Guilfoil, business manager; and Paul Vahey and Parker Vroom, assistant business managers.

A number of union members who had been part of, or active with, the previous local's administration formed a dissident group and published a newsletter called "Members' Voices," which sharply criticized the new administration. Further, the dissidents requested permission to see some of the local's books and records, and they proposed several new bylaws that they wanted to advance and have read and discussed at a local union meeting. When the officers of the local refused to cooperate on these matters, the dissidents filed a suit in district court. Pursuant to a district court judge's temporary restraining order, it was arranged for the dissident group to inspect the requested records at the local union office on March 7, 1991, and for the dissident-supported bylaw proposals to be read at the March 10, 1991, local union meeting.

On March 7, 1991, as dissidents Milo Cimoli and Wally Morris reviewed the requested records in a conference room in the local's office, a dispute arose over the dissidents' request for photocopies of some of the records.[3] James Guilfoil, the local's business manager, confronted Cimoli and Morris. Guilfoil said that he was furious about an article that had been printed in the "Members' Voices" publication, which he felt was totally untrue about him and the union and libelous to him personally. Guilfoil then added: "You sued us; now it will be my turn to sue you!"

Morris then left the room to telephone the dissidents' attorney, Alice Susman, while Cimoli continued to read the records. At this time, Marty Dincks, a union business agent, came into the conference room and began yelling about " such *** democracy" and looking at what was transpiring. When Cimoli remarked that the district judge had ruled in the dissidents' favor, Dincks became very agitated. He cursed the dissidents individually and collectively, including profanities aimed at the dissidents' attorney, Alice Susman.

At this point, Jackson Walls, president of the local union, started to pull Dincks away, telling him to "take it easy." Wally Morris had returned to the conference room, and as

[1] The company was not a party to the unfair labor practice charges in this case.

[2] The names of all individuals are disguised.

[3] Although the judge's order had specified that the local was to permit copying of the records, the local's attorney interpreted this to mean hand copying only.

he walked toward the group, he could hear Dincks shouting obscenities. Morris told Dincks to "calm down" and "knock it off." Morris asserted that he and Cimoli were "there to do a job," and they were not there "to take verbal abuse." Dincks then replied: "I'll give you verbal abuse. I'll give you physical abuse. I'll take you both outside and kick both your asses." Dincks then turned to Cimoli and said: "I'm telling you right here and now that I'm going to kick your ass, too!"

A few minutes later, several other officials of the local, including assistant business manager Parker Vroom, arrived on the scene. They saw to it that Marty Dincks left the area. With Dincks out of the room, Vroom and Walls then talked to Milo Cimoli and Wally Morris. Walls assured them that Dincks wouldn't be bothering them "the rest of the time." Vroom added, "Don't worry about it. We'll take care of Mr. Dincks."

Cimoli and Morris eventually completed their work of copying the union documents. On the same day, they reported what had happened to their attorney, Alice Susman. Shortly thereafter, on their behalf Susman filed unfair labor practice charges against the local union, claiming that the union had engaged in restraint and coercion of these individuals in violation of Section 8(b) (1) (A) of the Labor Management Relations Act.

POSITION OF THE INDIVIDUALS

Counsel for Milo Cimoli and Wally Morris claimed that the threats issued by James Guilfoil, the local union's business manager, and by Marty Dincks, a union business agent, constituted a clear violation of LMRA, because they were designed to restrain and coerce the union dissidents in regard to their lawful activities within the union. Guilfoil's threat to sue Morris and Cimoli for printing an article that was critical of him in the dissidents' newsletter and as retaliation for the court injunction that had been found against the local union were clearly designed to intimidate Morris, Cimoli, and other dissidents from carrying out their "protected activities" guaranteed under Section 7 of the Act. Even though Guilfoil and the local union did not sue Cimoli and Morris in a civil court action, nevertheless the statements made by Guilfoil—and not repudiated by union officers—were made in connection with attempting to intimidate Cimoli and Morris in carrying out their lawful protected activities.

Counsel argued that the physical threats uttered by Marty Dincks toward Cimoli and Morris were representative of the local union's attitude and also designed to coerce and intimidate them from carrying out their protected activities on behalf of the dissident group. Dincks's statements toward Cimoli and Morris threatening physical abuses were made in his capacity as a union business agent, not because of some individual personality conflict or problem that existed between them as individuals.

Counsel for the dissidents urged that the NLRB should find that the local union, primarily in the persons of James Guilfoil and Marty Dincks, had violated Section 8(b) (1) (A) of the Act. The local union should be required to cease and desist in any such threats or activities designed to discourage or intimidate any union members from carrying out their lawful protected activities, and to post a notice and inform all of the union members accordingly.

POSITION OF THE UNION

Counsel for the local union argued that the statements of Guilfoil and Dincks were not designed to intimidate or coerce Milo Cimoli and Wally Morris in carrying out their protected activities under the Act. Rather, these were personal statements made by these men, which reflected their own animosities toward the dissidents; these did not reflect the local union's positions on these matters.

Concerning Guilfoil's statement that he would sue Cimoli and Morris, the union claimed that Guilfoil rightfully was upset about statements in the dissidents' newsletter that he considered to be totally untrue and libelous in nature. Guilfoil never did file any type of lawsuit against these individuals, and the local union never was party to any such action. These isolated statements made by Guilfoil did not constitute a violation of Section 8(b) (1) (A) of the Act.

Similarly, the union claimed that the statements made by Marty Dincks, although crude and not condoned by the union, were statements made by a very agitated and angry individual. Both the president and the assistant business manager of the union had quickly removed Dincks from the conference room where the confrontation had occurred. They assured Cimoli and Morris that these statements were only those of Dincks, and that the local union would not condone or permit physical abuse of Cimoli and Morris. Here, too, the local union should not be held accountable for a violation of the Act, since Dincks's statements were personal in nature and did not in any way reflect the union's official position.

Counsel for the local union urged that the unfair labor practice charges should be dismissed.

QUESTIONS

1. On what basis can the NLRB distinguish between "threatening" remarks that are essentially personal in nature as compared to "threatening" remarks that may be considered a violation of LMRA? Discuss.
2. Were the statements made by James Guilfoil, the local union's business manager, an unfair labor practice? Explain.
3. Were the statements made by Marty Dincks, a union business agent, an unfair labor practice? Explain.
4. Section 8(b) (1) (A) includes a proviso that a labor organization may "prescribe its own rules with respect to the acquisition or retention of membership therein." Regardless of the outcome of the unfair labor practice charges in this case, can you think of ways in which a union could deal with dissidents, such as the ones in this case, as an internal union matter without violating LMRA?

Case 33

The Grievance-Processing Fee for Nonmembers in a Right-to-Work State

Company Davis Company, Memphis, Tennessee

Union Local No. 282, International Union of Electronic, Electrical, Salaried, Machine, and Furniture Workers

BACKGROUND

The union represented the production and maintenance employees at the company's plant located in Memphis, Tennessee. Tennessee is a so-called right-to-work state. Under Tennessee state law, union shop contracts cannot be negotiated; this type of state law is authorized by Section 14(b) of the LMRA.[1]

The parties negotiated a collective bargaining agreement, effective September 12, 1986, through September 11, 1989, which contained a grievance and arbitration procedure. However, this collective bargaining agreement did not contain either a union security or agency shop clause.

On or about September 10, 1987, the union sent or hand-delivered a memorandum to all the bargaining unit employees who were not members of the union. This memorandum included the following statement:

> ATTENTION ALL NONMEMBERS
>
> Effective immediately, all nonmembers will be charged a fee for handling grievances, an equal amount to the cost of representation, or the dues left to be paid under the contract, whichever is less.

Subsequently, on November 20, 1987, the union posted the following notice on the employee bulletin board:

> ATTENTION ALL NONMEMBERS
>
> Effective immediately, all nonmembers will be charged a fee for handling grievances, an equal amount to the cost of representation, or the dues left to be paid under the contract, whichever is less.
>
> The Union will not refuse to process your grievances because of this policy. Should you wish to file a grievance, please follow the normal contract procedures.

Shortly thereafter, the company on behalf of Alexandria Yowell,[2] an employee, filed unfair labor practice charges against the union. These charges alleged that the

[1] Section 14(b), the so-called right-to-work provision, reads as follows: "Nothing in this subchapter shall be construed as authorizing the execution or application of agreements requiring membership in a labor organization as a condition of employment in any State or Territory in which such execution or application is prohibited by State or Territorial Law."

[2] Name is disguised.

union's action was in violation of Section 8(b) (1) (A) and Section 7 of the LMRA as amended.

POSITION OF THE COMPANY

The company contended that in the absence of a valid union security clause, a labor organization breaches its duty of fair representation by charging or threatening to charge nonmembers the costs of processing grievances. The LMRA requires that an exclusive bargaining representative must act fairly and impartially on behalf of all bargaining unit employees, particularly in right-to-work states where union security clauses are prohibited. Both the September 10 and November 20, 1987, notices represented discriminatory treatment of nonmembers, because they indicated that the union would attempt to collect future payments for grievance processing.

The company argued that the union was attempting to coerce nonmember employees to join the union, which was violative of their protected rights under Section 7 of the Act to refrain from joining the union. The company urged that the union's proposed grievance-processing fee be held in violation of the LMRA, and that the union be ordered to cease and desist in any efforts to impose such a discriminatory fee.

POSITION OF THE UNION

The union contended that it had not breached its duty of fair representation, because the proposed grievance-processing fee was reasonable and for services rendered. Failure to charge nonmembers any fee would treat nonmembers and members unequally. The union argued that the November 20, 1987, notice stated that implementation of the grievance-processing charge would not interfere with employees' rights under the collective bargaining agreement. The union further claimed that it had acted in accord with the notice by not refusing to process nonmembers' grievances or threatening to institute suits to compel payment for such services. However, the union asserted that the LMRA did not mandate that unions must provide grievance-processing services free of charge. A union should not be required to provide totally free representation and services to those employees who decided not to be members even though they received all rights and benefits of union membership. This principle is established in Section 19 of LMRA, which provides that even where a union shop is present, a union may charge a grievance-processing fee for an employee who is not in the union because of valid religious conscientious reasons.

Common sense and fundamental fairness should support the concept that a labor organization be able to collect reasonable expenses it incurs on behalf of nonmembers (called free-riders) the union by law must represent. In a right-to-work state, nonmember employees in a bargaining unit benefit directly from union efforts on their behalf. Letting unions recoup the costs of grievance processing does not constitute coerced "membership" within the meaning of Section 14(b) of LMRA.

For all these reasons, the union claimed that it was well within its rights in its effort to charge a grievance-processing fee for nonmembers. The union requested that the unfair labor practice charges filed by the company be dismissed.

QUESTIONS

1. Evaluate the union's arguments concerning the need for grievance-processing fees to cover the union's expenses incurred representing nonmembers in the bargaining unit. Why is this problem at the core of any union's efforts to attain a union shop in those states where union shops are not prohibited by state law?
2. Why would the company be interested in pursuing these unfair labor practice charges when the issue is largely an internal union problem? Discuss.
3. Why was this case an important one in the continuing controversy over union representation and rights in right-to-work states?
4. Discuss the pros and cons of Section 14(b) of LMRA from the standpoint both of this case and of labor relations in general. Why will the application of Section 14(b) likely continue to be a controversial issue?

Case 34

The Union's Letter to Nonmember Employees Who Crossed the Picket Line

Company Unit Distribution of Bloomington, Inc., Normal, Illinois

Union Chicago Truck Drivers, Helpers, and Warehouse Workers (Independent) Union

BACKGROUND

In mid-1990, an election was conducted in which a majority of voting employees in the bargaining unit selected the union as their collective bargaining representative. The bargaining unit had been defined by the NLRB regional office as follows:

> All full-time and regular part-time production, maintenance, shipping and receiving employees, including all fork lift operators, material handling associates, and material expeditors (inventory control specialists) employed by the Employer at its Inbound Logistics Center located in Normal, Illinois, serving the Caterpillar, Inc., customer; but excluding all office clerical employees, guards, professional employees, and supervisors as defined in the Act.

The company filed certain objections to the election. However, the NLRB overruled these objections and certified the union as the exclusive representative of unit employees.

In late 1990, the union called a strike against the company as part of its efforts to secure a favorable collective bargaining agreement. This strike lasted from November 3 through December 12, 1990. However, during the strike, a number of employees who had not joined the union and who had voted against having the union represent them crossed the union picket lines and continued to work.

On November 20, 1990, the union's vice president, Peter Gorman,[1] authored, signed, and distributed a letter to those bargaining unit employees who had crossed the picket line to work for the company. This letter stated in part:

> Once the National Labor Relations Board certifies the Union as the collective bargaining representative, all employees who are members of the bargaining unit—those that were eligible to vote in the election—will be required to become members of the Union under the Union security provision that will be contained in the contract, or seek employment elsewhere. A member of the Union is bound by the Constitution of the Union (Article VI, Section 5.1) and is subject to <u>fines</u> if he/she violates the Constitution of the Union (Article VIII). Violation of a lawfully called strike by crossing an authorized picket line is a violation of the Union's Constitution (Article VI, Section 8; Article VIII). Those unit employees who continue to cross the picket line and work will become members of the Union and will be subject to charges, trial, and fines under the Union's Constitution.
>
> We ask you to reconsider your decision to continue to work and instead <u>Join Us on the Picket Line</u>. Those employees who have crossed the picket line but at this time choose to stop working and join their fellow workers will not be subject to any fines or other disciplinary action by the Union.

[1] Name is disguised.

The bargaining unit employees to whom the November 20 letter was distributed were not members and had paid no dues to the union. Further, there was no signed collective bargaining agreement between the parties covering bargaining unit employees, nor had any union security clause (such as a union shop) been negotiated. The company filed unfair labor practice charges against the union, alleging that the union's letter to the nonmember, nonstriking employees had violated Section 8(b) (1) (A) and Section 7 of the LMRA.

POSITION OF THE COMPANY

The company contended that the union's November 20 letter was unlawful because it was distributed to nonmembers at a time when there was no collective bargaining agreement and no union security clause in effect. Thus, the union violated Section 8(b) (1) (A) by threatening to fine or otherwise discipline the nonmember employees, since these threats were coercive and calculated to deter them from exercising their statutory rights protected by Section 7 of LMRA.

The company claimed that the union was trying to subject the nonmember employees to the requirements of its constitution prior to the existence of a contract between the company and the union. The union was suggesting that fines would be imposed retroactively after the employees were required to become members of the union, assuming that an agreement was reached containing a union shop provision. Allowing a union to discipline members retroactively for premembership conduct would undermine the statutory right of nonmember employees to cross picket lines and to engage in other protected activities without penalty.

The company urged the NLRB to find that the union by the actions of its officer Peter Gorman[2] had violated the Act. The company requested that the union be required to rescind the unlawful letter, and that the union be required to notify all the employees in the bargaining unit accordingly.

POSITION OF THE UNION

The union contended that the unfair labor practice charges filed by the company were nonmeritorious and simply an effort to interfere with the union's right to impose discipline on the nonmember employees it was required by the Act to represent. The union pointed to the proviso within Section 8(b) (1) (A) that enables a union to "prescribe its own rules with respect to the acquisition or retention of membership therein." The NLRB and the courts have long maintained that a union may lawfully fine member employees for crossing a picket line during an authorized strike. Without the right to impose this collective self-discipline, a union would be impotent to exert a unified effort to achieve a better contract. In the instant case, the nonmember employees who crossed the picket line were nevertheless represented by the union. Once a collective bargaining agreement was negotiated with the company, it would have a union shop provision. During negotiations prior to the strike, company management had not expressed objections to the inclusion of a union security provision in the agreement. The union letter of November 20, 1990,

[2] There was no dispute that the union vice president who wrote and sent the letter was an agent of the union under Section 2(13) of LMRA.

was only an effort by the union to maintain the same standards for all the employees it represented, members and nonmembers. It was only a matter of time before all employees would become members of the union.

In summary, the union contended that its November 20 letter was lawful and permitted by LMRA, that the company unfair labor practice charges were without merit and an intrusion into union affairs, and that the NLRB should dismiss the unfair labor practice charges accordingly.

QUESTIONS

1. Section 8(b) (1) (A) of LMRA has long been a controversial section. Why is it difficult to differentiate between protected Section 7 rights and the union's right to prescribe its own rules and regulations?
2. What was the primary purpose of the November 20 letter sent by the union to the nonstriking nonmembers? Was the letter essentially a threat to nonmembers who had crossed the picket line, or was it a realistic notification of a likely outcome of negotiations with the company?
3. Is there a difference between a nonmember who crosses a picket line and an employee who previously was a union member but who resigns from the union during a strike and crosses a picket line? Discuss.
4. To what extent may a Union discipline members of a bargaining unit who are not members of the Union, under any circumstances? Explain.

Case 35

Resignation from the Union and Checkoff of Dues

Company The Hearst Corporation Capital Newspaper Division

Union Newspaper Guild of Albany, Communication Workers of America, AFL-CIO, CLC

BACKGROUND

Section 13 of the parties' collective bargaining agreement provides for the voluntary checkoff of union dues. Section 13 of the contract permits an employee to revoke the checkoff on the first anniversary of its execution. After that date, the employee may revoke the checkoff between 30 and 15 days before the expiration of the annual anniversary of the execution of the checkoff authorization, or upon the expiration of the collective bargaining agreement.

Ms. O'Toole is a permanent employee of the company who has worked in the bargaining unit since 1985. Ms. O'Toole exercised an authorization for the checkoff of union dues shortly after she was employed by the company.

Section 2 of the parties' collective bargaining agreement makes provision for procedures for employees to resign from the union by appealing to the Job Classification and Compensation Committee. The same section of the agreement states that employees could also apply to be relieved of any financial obligations imposed upon them by the contract.

By a letter dated April 14, 1999, Ms. O'Toole informed the union of her desire to resign from the union and willingness to discuss the matter with the appropriate union officials. Ms. O'Toole met with union officials on April 16, 1999. In that discussion Ms. O'Toole indicated that she would resign from the union and become an agency-fee payer to the union.

Subsequently, Ms. O'Toole changed her mind and asked that the union take up her request to resign from the union and cease being obliged to pay dues or agency fees to the union. Subsequently, a meeting was scheduled for the purposes suggested by Ms. O'Toole, but she failed to attend the meeting.

In May 1999, the company ceased checking off Ms. O'Toole's union dues. The union noticed that the last fee accounting that Ms. O'Toole's dues were deducted was in May. In June the union filed a grievance protesting the company's failure to checkoff Ms. O'Toole's dues. At about this time a second bargaining unit employee made the same requests as Ms. O'Toole. The company subsequently ceased deducting this second employee's dues and remitting them to the union.

The union scheduled another meeting for Ms. O'Toole and the second employee to meet with the union and discuss what was necessary to resign from the union and for them to make application to be relieved from financial obligations to the union. Again, neither employee attended the meeting. At no time did either employee revoke their checkoff authorizations as specified by Section 13 of the parties' collective bargaining agreement. Neither employee paid union dues or fees once the company ceased checkoff. The union did not request that either employee be discharged for their failures to tender dues and fees.

POSITION OF THE UNION

It is the position of the union that both employees have resigned from the union, however, both employees are agency employees and must pay the equivalent of dues and fees. Neither employee attended either of the two meetings scheduled with the appropriate committee for them to make application to be relieved of financial obligations to the union. Further, neither employee revoked their dues checkoff authorizations as provided for in Section 13 of the parties' collective bargaining agreement.

The company simply took it upon itself to cease deducting and remitting these two employees' dues in direct contravention to Articles 2 and 13 of the parties' collective bargaining agreement. Clearly this is a violation of Section 8(a) (1) and (5) of the Act, and the Board should order the company to cease and desist its violation of the Act and remit the dues owing.

POSITION OF THE COMPANY

The company denies any wrongdoing in this case. The company relies on Section 2 language in the collective bargaining agreement. Section 2 permits employees to resign from the union and this is what the two subject employees did. Further, the two employees made applications to the union to be relieved from financial obligations to the union.

When the company was informed of the employees' resignation from the union it was clear to the company that they no longer wished to have any relations with the union. It is at that point that the obligation to checkoff dues is no longer binding on the employee, and by implication the company. Therefore, it is the company's position that there is no violation of the Act and these charges should be dismissed.

QUESTIONS

1. Is resignation from the union the same as revocation of the authorization for dues checkoff? Explain.
2. Logically, is the company obliged to deduct and remit to the union the dues of a bargaining unit member who resigned from the union? If not, what is the standard for cessation of checking off union dues? Explain.
3. If you were the Board, how would you rule in this case? Explain.

Case 36

Were the Union's Grievances an Unlawful Secondary Boycott?

Company Stief Company West with locations in the state of California, and "parties in interest": Kasler Corporation, M.C.M. Construction, and Kiewit Pacific Company

Union International Union of Operating Engineers, Local Union No. 12

BACKGROUND

Stief Company West was a construction firm engaged in the construction of concrete barriers on bridge and highway projects in the state of California. In the course of the construction process, the company would use boom trucks and tractors with cranes mounted behind their cabs. Heavy steel forms used in constructing the concrete barriers were transported to the construction site on the trailers and on the boom truck and positioned and removed at the job site using the crane.

The Stief Company had never had a collective bargaining agreement with the International Union of Operating Engineers, Local No. 12. However, the union had a collective bargaining agreement, known as the Master Labor Agreement (MLA), that had been negotiated with the Associated General Contractors of California, Inc. Kasler Corporation, M.C.M. Construction, and Kiewit Pacific Company were construction companies that were members of the Associated General Contractors of California and signatories to the MLA agreement with the union.

Included within the MLA agreement were the following provisions regarding certain work jurisdiction and subcontracting of work:

Article I, Section B, Paragraph 10 Subcontracting, Employee Rights, Union Standards and Work Preservation

(a) The purposes of this Section 10 are to preserve and protect the work opportunities normally available to employees and workmen covered by this Agreement, maintenance and protection of standards and benefits of employees and workmen negotiated over many years and preservation of the right of Union employees, employed hereunder, from being compelled to work with non-Union workmen.

* * *

(c) Neither the Contractor nor any of his Subcontractors shall subcontract any work to be done at the site of the construction, alteration, painting or repair of a building, structure or other work coming within the jurisdiction of the Cement Masons, Laborers, Operating Engineers, Teamsters or Ironworkers except to a person, firm or corporation party to an appropriate labor agreement with the appropriate Local Union or Council of Laborers, Cement Masons, Operating Engineers, the International Brotherhood of Teamsters or Ironworkers.

The MLA also contained grievance-arbitration provisions, including the resolution of jurisdictional disputes.

In late 1991 and continuing into 1992, Kasler, M.C.M., and Kiewit each subcontracted to Stief Company contracts for the construction of permanent concrete walls on freeway bridges for a number of projects, which were as follows: a Kasler project on Interstate 10 in Redlands, California; a Kasler project at Century Freeway and Crenshaw Boulevard in Los Angeles; an M.C.M. project at the Century and 710 freeways in Los Angeles; and a Kiewit project on North Bristol Street in Santa Ana. These projects were estimated to take six months (Kasler-Redlands), two years (Kasler-Crenshaw), two and one-half years (M.C.M.), and four years (Kiewit) to complete.

In response to these subcontracting arrangements, from August 28, 1991, to August 19, 1992, the union filed four grievances against these general contractors, protesting that they subcontracted steel form hoisting, lowering, placing, and removal (that was covered by the MLA agreement) to the Stief Company, a company that was not a party to the MLA. The union claimed that this subcontracting of operating engineers' work was in violation of the subcontracting clause contained in Article I of the MLA.

The Kasler, M.C.M., and Kiewit companies denied the union grievances and refused to arbitrate the disputes. Subsequently, as a test case, the union in December 1991 filed a Section 301 lawsuit under the Labor Management Relations Act against the Kasler Corporation to compel arbitration concerning the grievance over the Interstate 10 project. The United States District Court, Central District of California, granted summary judgment in favor of the union's position.

Thereupon, the Stief Company filed unfair labor practice charges against the union, claiming that the union by its actions had violated Section 8(b) (4) (ii) (A) of LMRA by attempting to coerce an employer to enter into and comply with an agreement that was prohibited by Section 8(e) of the Act.

STIPULATIONS OF THE PARTIES CONCERNING THE WORK INVOLVED IN THE DISPUTE

The parties agreed to certain stipulations concerning the nature of the work involved in the dispute.[1] The following is a summary description of the work processes and associated factors that were relevant to the NLRB's determination.

> Stief Company—to be referred to in these stipulations as *the Employer*—was responsible as general contractor at each project for constructing barrier walls on the decks of the freeway bridges, pursuant to contracts which generally called for the Employer to furnish all necessary materials and labor. The barrier walls were approximately 12 inches thick and 2 feet high, with a front wall facing the deck of the freeway and a back wall facing out over the freeway bridge. The barriers were constructed using 10-foot-long, and 3/4-inch-thick, steel forms weighing approximately 75 pounds each. The Employer generally joined three of these forms together and worked with 30-foot-long sections.
>
> The Employer transported the steel forms using boom trucks and tractors that each had a boom mounted behind the cab. A boom is a steel arm with a large steel hook

[1] At the time the parties entered into these stipulations, the Kasler Interstate 10 project was 100 percent complete, the Kasler project at Century Freeway and Crenshaw Boulevard was 98 percent complete, and the Kiewit project was approximately 13 percent complete.

connected to two chains ending with two smaller hooks. The boom is manipulated vertically and horizontally using levers mounted on a panel behind the cab of the trucks. Each of the boom trucks pulls a 20-foot trailer while each of the tractors pulls a 45-foot trailer.

The barrier wall construction process at each of the projects was substantially the same. The Employer employed drivers represented by the Teamsters to transport the steel forms to and from the project. The forms were initially delivered from the Employer's own yard to the general contractor's storage yard and thereafter moved between the job site and the storage yard as needed. The driver arrived at the project in the morning and drove a load of forms to the place at the construction site where they were used. The driver met the Employer's composite crew at the construction site. The composite crew was typically made up of one foreman, two laborers, one carpenter, and one cement mason. The foreman instructed the crew and driver about where the steel forms were to be set that day. The driver then got into the boom truck and, starting in the place where the first barrier would be constructed, slowly drove along the deck about 300 feet. The composite crew walked behind the boom truck unloading hardware used to fasten the forms to the decking. After the hardware was laid out, the composite crew went back and secured it to the deck.

The driver next returned the boom truck or tractor to the place where the first form would be placed. The driver manipulated the levers on the control panel to raise the boom and to lower it above the first form on the truck or trailer that was to be removed. A laborer from the composite crew attached the small chain hooks into the eye-holes on the lengthwise ends of a steel form. The driver then raised the form from the trailer and moved the form above the location on the concrete deck where it would be placed. Two members of the composite crew stood on either end of the form to guide it to the deck and to prevent swinging. The driver next lowered the form to the deck. The composite crew aligned the form on the deck; a laborer unhooked the chains; and the driver raised the boom and swung it to the next form on the trailer. A laborer connected the chains to the next form; the form was lifted by the driver manipulating the boom; and the form was swung over to the appropriate place on the deck. After the second form was placed, the composite crew started connecting the forms together lengthwise. This process was repeated until 300 feet of front forms were set in place.

After the front forms had been set, all of the back forms were hoisted and placed in their final positions on the deck approximately 12 inches behind the front forms. After each back form was placed, the composite crew attached hardware to the front and back panels to connect them together. Final placement of 300 feet of front and back forms created a mold for the first portion of the barrier wall. Creating the mold took most of a morning. After lunch, the composite crew and driver would go back to the forms that were set earlier and would pour concrete into the barrier molds. At the end of the day, the driver transported any leftover forms to the storage yard.

The next day, the driver picked up the trailer and any needed forms from the storage yard and proceeded to the construction site. The driver drove the truck to the place on the deck where the barrier walls were poured the day before, swung the boom over the first form that was placed, and lowered the chains on the boom down to the form. The composite crew connected the chains on either side of the form, and the driver pulled the form away from the newly made wall. The composite crew then scraped any remaining concrete from the form and sprayed an oil-like substance on the form. The driver raised the boom and swung the form back onto the trailer, and then drove the truck to the place along the wall where the form needed to be placed to create the next mold. The process of stripping the new walls of the forms was repeated until all of the forms were stripped. If a form was not needed again that day, it was set on the trailer and transported back to the storage yard.

When the barrier walls were dry, the exterior and interior of the walls were finished to rid the walls of excess concrete. A driver was involved in the finishing process only for the exterior portions of the walls at one of the Kasler projects. The driver used the control panel levers to hoist a man cage over the exterior walls so that a composite crew member could sandblast them.

Forms were often transported to or from a project, during the course of the project, because they were needed at other projects. When the projects were completed, the forms were taken back to the Employer's yard or delivered to other Employer projects. The forms never became permanent fixtures of a project.

There was no special training program or apprentice program for drivers to train them to operate the boom control panel, or for most of the Employer's other employees who performed work at the Kasler, M.C.M., and Kiewit projects.

CONTENTIONS OF THE PARTIES

The company (Stief Company West) contended that the union violated Section 8(b) (4) (ii) (A) of the Act, which makes it unlawful for a union to coerce an employer to enter into an agreement that is prohibited by Section 8(e). Section 8(e) of the Act makes it an unfair labor practice for an employer and a union to enter into an agreement whereby the employer agrees to refrain from doing business with any other person. The company argued that the union further violated Section 8(b) (4) (ii) (A) by filing grievances against Kasler, M.C.M., and Kiewit, as well as a lawsuit against Kasler, in an effort to force those contractors to comply with the unlawful subcontracting provision of the MLA agreement as applied to the work at issue here, and thereby to enforce an agreement to cease doing business with the Stief Company.

However, the union contended that it had not violated the Act, because the process of hoisting, lowering, placing, and removing the steel forms fell within the construction industry proviso of Section 8(e) of LMRA which states:

> *Provided,* That nothing in this subsection (e) shall apply to an agreement between a labor organization and an employer in the construction industry relating to the contracting or subcontracting of *work to be done at the site* of the construction, alteration, painting, or repair of a building, structure or other work." [Emphasis added.]

In the union's view, the work in question was clearly construction work done at the job sites, and therefore this proviso to Section 8(e) exempted the union in this matter from Section 8(e)'s general provisions. The union pointed out that the purpose of this proviso and of the Article I provisions within the MLA master agreement was to prevent potential labor strife between union and nonunion personnel working at the same job site. This was a legitimate and lawful objective of the union's actions in this matter, and the unfair labor practice charges should be dismissed.

In rebuttal, the company argued that the hoisting, lowering, placing, and removing of the steel forms constituted the "final act of delivery" of the forms. Thus, such work did not fall within the proviso to Section 8(e). The company urged that the 8(b) (4) (ii) (A) unfair labor practice charges should be upheld by the NLRB, and the Board should issue an appropriate cease and desist remedial order.

QUESTIONS

1. What are the standards the NLRB applies in determining whether subcontracting clauses are lawful? What are "hot cargo" agreements? Do these differ from the type of subcontracting clause in this case? Explain.
2. The NLRB has previously held that negotiated contractual subcontracting provisions—such as Article I in this case—are not "facially unlawful." Why is it difficult to define exactly where the application and enforcement of such subcontracting provisions "crosses the line" from being lawful to unlawful?
3. Examine closely the description of the nature of the work involved in this dispute as stipulated by the parties. Why is an evaluation of the technical/procedural aspects of this work crucial to the determination by the NLRB concerning the unfair labor practice charges?
4. Was the hoisting, placing, and so on, of the steel forms construction work at the job sites that was exempted from Section 8(e)'s prohibitions, or was it essentially final delivery work and thus not part of Section 8(e)'s proviso exemption? Discuss.

Case 37

Whose Work Is It? Case of a Jurisdictional Dispute

Union 1 International Union of Operating Engineers, Local 150

Union 2 International Brotherhood of Teamsters, Local 325

Company R&D Thiel, a Division of Carpenter Contractors of America, Inc.

BACKGROUND

The company manufactures and installs wooden building components, that is, roof trusses, floor sections, and walls on residential buildings in the Chicago area. Crane truck drivers employed by the company transport these wood products to the job sites and the drivers lift components off of the trucks and place the components where the customer wants the component—including into place on the building or on scaffolding—as well as simply putting the material on the ground. This work is currently done by the Teamsters.

In the fall of 2004, officials of the Operating Engineers, Local 150, tried to persuade the company to sign a collective bargaining agreement requiring the placement of the components, once delivered, be done by Operating Engineers. The Operating Engineers informed the Teamsters that they disputed the work currently being done on two job sites in Northern Illinois. In November 2004, the Operating Engineers stopped the Teamsters from unloading materials at these two job sites, claiming that the Teamsters were doing work rightfully within the jurisdiction of the Operating Engineers pursuant to an agreement between the Operating Engineers and the Teamsters Joint Council 25 (included in the Appendix). The Operating Engineers informed the Teamsters that if they did not cease doing Operating Engineers' work they would picket those job sites. The Teamsters' response to the Operating Engineers was that if any work was reassigned from the Teamsters to the Operating Engineers they would picket the subject job sites.

The record shows that the unions in this matter have entered into a voluntary arrangement to resolve disputes between them arising out of jurisdictional claims, but the company is not a signatory to this agreement between the unions and is not bound by the unions' agreement by any other contract.

POSITION OF THE OPERATING ENGINEERS

The Operating Engineers claim that the agreement between the Teamsters and the Operating Engineers makes clear that any work that involves using the cranes to put material in place or on scaffolds is exclusively within the jurisdiction of the Operating Engineers. The Operating Engineers have a contract with the company and operate cranes, which are not mounted on flatbed trucks, for the purpose of installing components and hoisting equipment on the job site. It is the position of the Operating Engineers that the agreement between the unions makes clear that the hoisting work identified in that agreement as belonging to the Operating Engineers is their work exclusively and the Teamsters have violated the Operating Engineers' jurisdiction in this matter.

POSITION OF THE TEAMSTERS

The Teamsters claim that the disputed work belongs to the Teamsters because it has a collective bargaining agreement with the company who has consistently assigned this work, as presently performed, to the Teamsters' bargaining unit. This has always been the practice at R&D Thiel worksites, and the Operating Engineers have never before objected. Further, it is an efficient mode of operation to have a single crane perform a single hoist, rather than always set the material on the ground and sometimes cause an inefficient second hoisting of material. Therefore, the company's preference for the Teamsters performing the work as had been customary between the parties has a sound business basis.

In most cases the agreement between the Operating Engineers and the Teamsters has been honored and the unions peacefully coexist; however, in this case there is a well-established company preference, practice between the parties, and a collective bargaining agreement all supporting the Teamsters' contention that this work belongs to their bargaining unit.

POSITION OF THE COMPANY

The company is an innocent third party in this dispute. The company entered into collective bargaining agreements with both unions and has over the years provided work to both bargaining units. The practices of the parties, the company and both unions, are well established and the jurisdiction between the unions has never been a problem in the past. For the Operating Engineers to have interfered in the delivering and hoisting of the subject materials on the job sites in Northern Illinois violates Section 8(b) (4) (D) of the Act. Therefore the company prays that the Board will assert jurisdiction in this matter pursuant to Section 10 (k) of the Act because there is no voluntary settlement process to which the company is signatory. The threatened picketing and interference with the delivery of materials to the company's job sites is proscribed by Section 8(b) (4) (D) of the Act.

Appendix

Agreement Between the Teamsters and the Operating Engineers

The driving of material delivery trucks with hoisting equipment attached is recognized as the jurisdiction of the Teamsters. Drivers of this type of truck shall be permitted to unload materials at any place on the job site as directed by the contractor's supervisors except that he shall not be permitted to (1) hoist materials or equipment onto scaffolds, (2) hoist materials of equipment into place, or (3) lower materials and equipment into place. This work is recognized as the jurisdiction of the Operating Engineers.

QUESTIONS

1. Must an employer be a signatory to a contract between two unions concerning jurisdiction before that contract is binding upon the employer? Explain.
2. What standards does the Board employ to determine the merits of jurisdictional disputes? How are they applied?
3. If you were the Board in this case, to which union would you assign this work? Explain.

Case 38

How Do I Get My Cookies? Information Requests to the Contract

Company Kellogg's Snack Company

Union International Brotherhood of Teamsters, Local 560

BACKGROUND

The union filed a grievance in February 2003 alleging that the company violated Article 16 of their collective bargaining agreement in that goods from the company's distribution center were finding their way to customers without being delivered by Local 560 personnel (relevant contract language is contained in the Appendix). The union also alleged that there was company product at the wholesalers that had not been delivered by Local 560 personnel.

The union and company attempted to resolve the grievance, short of arbitration, through negotiations. During those negotiations the union asserted that it would be able to demonstrate that deliveries were being made to customers and wholesalers by the company's use of common carriers rather than Local 560 personnel. In March 2004, the union wrote a letter to the company stating:

> Consistent with our discussions of February 11, 2004, I have been able to prepare a listing of carriers and dates or violations which are the subject matter of the Union's arbitration. Please note that the Union continues to obtain additional documentation which we believe evidences the violation. It is requested that you please conduct an investigation concerning each of these vendors during the relevant time period as specified in my schedule and provide information in that regard.

The letter contained an attachment with alleged deliveries by specified common carriers during certain months in 2003 and 2004. When the company did not respond, the union again communicated its request that the company provide specific bills of lading for specified dates and common carriers. By April 2004, the union had not received the requested information and again requested the specific information from the company. This time the union stated that without the information requested it would have no choice except to seek remedy from the National Labor Relations Board. The company did not respond.

POSITION OF THE UNION

The union requested a subpoena from the New Jersey courts, and the information requested is a subset of the information sought in that subpoena. The subpoena was sought in conjunction with the arbitration of the merits of the union's grievance concerning the alleged violations of Article 16. The union requested that the Board find that the company had violated Section 8(a) (1) and (5) by its failure to provide the requested information necessary to the union's policing of the parties' collective bargaining agreement. The union asserted that the information is necessary and relevant in determining the amount of work lost to the bargaining unit and any damages should it prevail on the grievance before the arbitrator.

It was therefore the union's position that the company violated its duty to bargain collectively by failing to provide information known to it in the grievance process and that is necessary to the union's prosecution of its grievance. The union, therefore, requested that the company be ordered to provide the information the union had requested and that it believes is necessary to the proper representation of the bargaining unit in the grievance/arbitration process.

POSITION OF THE COMPANY

The company asserted that it did not provide the requested information because it did not believe that the information was relevant to any legitimate grievance the union was prosecuting. The company contended that the deliveries the union asserted were made by common carriers from or to the distribution center were deliveries of products that came directly from the manufacturing facilities to wholesalers such as W. B. Brown. The company's position was that since these deliveries were consistent with the company's practices there is no violation of Article 16 or the memoranda of agreement.

Therefore, unlike past grievances, it was the company's position that the work preservation clause does not apply since the deliveries grieved by the union were never in the union's jurisdiction. The deliveries to the customers and wholesalers were done exclusive of any participation by the distribution center. Therefore, the subject products bypassed the distribution center, the grievance is without merit, and the union's requests for information are frivolous. The company asserted there was no failure to bargain collectively.

Appendix

Relevant Contract Language

The following language from the collective bargaining agreement and memoranda of agreement are applicable in this matter:

Article 16

> The Employer agrees to respect the jurisdiction rules of the Union and shall not direct or permit their employees or persons other than the employee in the bargaining unit here involved to perform work which is recognized as the work of the employees in said unit. Deliveries shall not be made by sales employees except in cases of extreme emergencies . . .

Memorandum of Agreement June 11, 1998

> It is understood that the deliveries to non-DSD customers will be made by the bargaining unit unless under unusual circumstances beyond the control of Kellogg's Snack Company.

Vendors such as Condel or D. W. Brown may make an occasional pickup at the Kellogg's facilities. It is understood that prior agreements not in existence regarding these vendors remain in force. In these limited instances there shall be no violation of the CBA for customer pickups due to these limited circumstances.

Memorandum of Agreement June 12, 2001

The Company agrees that all deliveries to step-van sales mini warehouses in the Long Island Distribution service area will be delivered by bargaining unit employees and step-van sales employees will not be permitted to pick up product from the Distribution Center.

QUESTIONS

1. Does the company have an obligation to bargain collectively during the life of the collective bargaining agreement? If so, does that obligation extend to providing information to the union concerning its business?
2. Are there discovery rules appropriate to the processing of grievances implied by Section 8(a) (1) and (5) of the Act? If so, what might those discovery rules be?
3. Are the merits of the grievance relevant to the determination of the unfair labor practice issues here? Explain?
4. Could this matter have been deferred to the arbitrator in this matter? Should the Board decide the merits of the grievance in this matter? Explain.

Part Two

Case Problems in Union-Management Relations: Cases from Grievance Arbitration

Conflict Resolution, Grievance Procedures, and Arbitration

Selected Bibliography

Index to Cases for Part Two

The Cases

Conflict Resolution, Grievance Procedures, and Arbitration*

The potential for conflict exists within every organization. This is true of families, business organizations, social groups, or government agencies. Conflicts may range from minor differences of opinion to open hostility resulting in physical violence. Yet, humane democratic institutions attempt to resolve intraorganizational and interpersonal conflicts in an orderly manner. While conflict can be destructive, and often is, it need not be. Differences of opinion, when openly confronted and fully aired, often lead to new understandings and subsequent improved relationships.

The resolution of conflict is critical to personal, group, and organizational viability. Conflict creates in both individuals and organizations tensions and diversions that hinder or prevent attainment of goals. Further, striving to attain goals in itself creates tension and conflict. It is imperative that conflicts be resolved in such a manner that attainment of goals of the organization will not be thwarted. It may be hoped that resolution of conflict will produce new understanding and harmony, which will help move the organization toward its goals at an increased pace.

While an organization is concerned with the attainment of its goals and objectives, individuals in the organization are also concerned about the attainment of their own goals and objectives. Hence, the potential for conflict between an organization and the individuals in it arises. A company's need for higher productivity may conflict with an individual's need for security in advancing years. Differences may develop over the relative importance of productivity and of length of service in determining layoffs. Not all individuals in an organization share the same objectives. Young employees place less importance on length of

* This section provides a brief introductory overview of major considerations and issues inherent in the grievance-arbitration process. It does not include, however, a discussion of the sizable body of law that has developed on the subject of labor arbitration. This topic usually is covered fully in major texts with which these cases are normally used. A selected bibliography is included at the end of this section.

service in determining promotions than do older employees. Interpersonal and intergroup conflict in the workforce may develop from such differences.

Ours is a democratic society that places a high value on justice and the protection of individual rights. Democratic ideals are consistent with the concept of participation in organizations. Values attached to protection of human rights have stimulated the development of various mechanisms that aim to promote the administration of laws, policies, rules, and procedures in a humane and equitable manner, giving full consideration to human dignity and welfare.[1]

APPROACHES TO CONFLICT RESOLUTION

Concern for human rights in our society has resulted in the development of various means whereby injured parties may appeal decisions made by those exercising power over them. Almost every type of organization has developed one or more appeal procedures.

Most government agencies have appeal procedures that enable employees to seek redress from acts of agency administrators. Labor unions have internal procedures for the protection of members from harassment within their own ranks. For example, the International Union of United Automobile, Aerospace, and Agricultural Implement Workers of America has expended unusual effort to provide its members a fair opportunity for defense against union decisions concerning them, and has provided well-defined and speedy avenues of recourse in the event of alleged unjust acts by officers and administrators. Religious institutions have developed appeal procedures that provide members with avenues of recourse against the clergy or governing boards. For example, the Roman Catholic Church has formulated internal procedures that members may employ to seek redress.

Many business organizations also have appeal procedures, which exist in both union and nonunion companies. Many nonunion organizations have developed formalized problem-solving or complaint procedures that provide employees the right to appeal decisions made concerning them by their supervisors. In most instances, recourse may be sought all the way up through the organization to the president. Some nonunion employers are even offering opportunities for "juries" of employees to render final decisions in complaints that have gone through a number of steps without resolution.

Formalized appeal procedures seem to become more necessary as organizations become larger and more institutionalized. Further, the more demanding and urgent the goals and objectives of the organization, and the more they press on individuals, the less freedom an individual is able to exercise. The hierarchical and authoritarian nature of some organizations tends to produce dependency of the subordinate on the superior. Dependency, in turn, tends to create frustration in the individual seeking freedom of self-expression on the job. Inability to exercise freedom of self-expression, in turn, may block the individual's search for satisfaction through work.

Thus, appeal procedures provide opportunity for individuals to exercise greater control over their environment and expand the opportunities to achieve personal goals

[1] For an excellent discussion of the historical and legal background of the grievance-arbitration mechanism in labor relations, see Daniel Quinn Mills, *Labor-Management Relations,* 5th ed. (New York: McGraw-Hill, 1994), pp. 582–98.

through work. Such procedures give individuals a chance to contest those decisions or actions of management that employees feel are unfair and that violate their rights and the obligations of the employer.

GRIEVANCE PROCEDURES

Appeal opportunities are generally formalized in unionized organizations in grievance procedures that are included in the collective bargaining agreement. These procedures vary considerably from organization to organization. Typically, however, they provide that, at the first step, the employee take the grievance to either the immediate supervisor or the union steward.[2] The supervisor, the steward, and the employee discuss the issue and, in many circumstances, arrive at an amicable settlement. Most grievances are settled on an informal basis at this first step. If the parties are unable to agree, either because the supervisor disagrees with the request of the employee or because the supervisor lacks authority to make a decision, the grievance is appealed to the second step of the grievance procedure. Typically, the grievance committee of the union and the plant superintendent or office manager attempt to reach a settlement. However, grievances that are not settled at the first step of the grievance procedure may not be settled at the second step either; they are then usually appealed to the third step of the grievance procedure. At this level, the handling of the grievance is quite formalized; the parties involved may include members of top management of the company and members of the national office of the union. An estimated 97 percent of all collective agreements in the private sector provide that, if the parties are unable to arrive at a decision at the third (or fourth) step of the grievance procedure, either party may petition for arbitration of the dispute by a third party.

The following is a typical grievance procedure that shows the various steps to be followed in processing a grievance to final resolution.[3]

Article VI—Grievance Procedure and Arbitration

Section 6.1 If any differences, disputes or complaints arise over the interpretation or application of the contents of this Agreement, there shall be an earnest effort on the part of the parties to settle such promptly through the following steps:

STEP 1. By conference between the aggrieved associate, the shop steward, or both, and the manager of the store within five (5) working days of the occurrence of the grievance.

STEP 2. By conference between the Business Representative, with or without the shop steward of the Union, and the store manager or his/her supervisor within ten (10) working days of the occurrence of the grievance.

STEP 3. By conference between an official or officials of the Union and the Company's designated representative within fifteen (15) working days of the

[2] A distinction customarily is drawn in labor relations between a *complaint* and a *grievance.* A complaint refers to any feeling of injury or injustice, real or imagined, expressed or unexpressed. A grievance is a complaint that has been formally presented to the supervisor, union steward, or some other union official under the provisions of a grievance procedure, alleging a violation of the labor agreement.

[3] From the June 6, 1993, through September 23, 2000, agreement between Schnuck Markets, Inc. (primarily St. Louis, Missouri, area), and Local Union No. 88, United Food and Commercial Workers Union.

occurrence of the grievance. At the conclusion of Step 3, the Company will give the Union their answer in writing within twenty (20) working days. Should a settlement be reached it will be reduced to writing within ten (10) calendar days.

STEP 4. In the event the last step fails to settle the complaint, it may be referred to arbitration within five (5) days. A date for the arbitrator to hear said complaint must be set within one hundred twenty (120) days of the complaint being referred to arbitration or the complaint will be considered to be withdrawn and no further action will be allowed. The one hundred twenty (120) day period may be extended by mutual agreement between the parties. Both parties will act in good faith to comply with the aforementioned time limits.

Section 6.2 The Company and the Union shall mutually agree to an impartial arbitrator to hear said arbitration case; however, if said arbitrator cannot be chosen within three (3) days, then the Federal Mediation and Conciliation Service will be requested to furnish a panel of seven (7) names from which the arbitrator may be chosen. The arbitrator will be selected within seven (7) days after the receipt of the panel by alternately striking names. The party striking first will be determined by the flip of a coin. The decision of the arbitrator shall be binding on both parties. The expenses of the arbitrator shall be paid for jointly.

Such arbitrator shall not be empowered to add to, detract from, or alter the terms of this Agreement.

Section 6.3 No grievance may be presented later than ten (10) calendar days after the occurrence from which such grievance arose. Grievances which progress past Step 2 shall be reduced to writing.

It shall be acceptable to use facsimile transmission ("Fax") in lieu of certified mail for grievance notification. When "Fax" is used, it will be followed by a telephone call to the other party to inform them a "Fax" is being sent. The Company will provide the current "Fax" number to be used for notification purposes.

Section 6.4 At any step in this grievance procedure, the Executive Board of the Local Union shall have the final authority, in respect to any aggrieved associate covered by this Agreement, to decline to process a grievance, a complaint, difficulty or dispute further if, in the judgment of the Executive Board, such grievance or dispute lacks merit or lacks justification under the terms of this Agreement to the satisfaction of the Union Executive Board.

Although used for numerous reasons, the following are among the most important purposes that grievance procedures serve. First, they serve to locate problems that exist in the relationship between the union and the company, and also to locate problems that exist within both organizations. Second, they tend to open the channels of communication between employees and management. They are especially helpful in stimulating communication upward from employees to management, often to the discomfiture of the managers! Third, the grievance procedure is the instrument that enables the parties to initiate action, to interpret provisions of the collective agreement, and to apply the contract to new and changing aspects of daily relations between the employees and management. Finally, it serves as a valuable source of information and data at contract negotiation periods.

ARBITRATION

Arbitration constitutes the final step in most grievance procedures. It begins where the other procedures leave off, since the parties are presumed to have explored alternatives of settlement and compromise before resorting to an arbitrator. When the parties turn to arbitration, they voluntarily agree to refer their dispute to an impartial third person. The arbitrator's determination will be made on the basis of the evidence and arguments presented by the parties, who agree in advance to accept the decision of the arbitrator as final and binding.

In the United States, grievance arbitration is essentially a voluntary system. Federal labor law does not require the parties to include an arbitration clause in their collective agreement. However, the NLRB and the federal courts normally will defer to private arbitration for the settlement of those disputes that occur during the life of a labor agreement, provided that there is no dispute involving a legal statute.[4] Thus, grievance arbitration is considered a voluntary process in the United States, since an arbitration clause is the result of negotiations between management and a labor union.[5]

Arbitration is usually viewed as a judicial process. However, the parties do influence this process by the internal policies that each has adopted with respect to it. For example, either the company or the union may follow a policy of carefully screening disputes that are referred to arbitration. Their objectives may be to present to arbitration only those cases that have merit and that the appealing party believes it has a good chance of winning. On the other hand, one or both parties may operate on a percentage basis. If they adopt this approach to arbitration, they may elect to appeal doubtful cases on the theory that arbitrators will tend to compromise. According to this reasoning, they expect to win certain points that they might otherwise have conceded. Of course, this approach to arbitration can be shortsighted; the theory that arbitrators will split decisions is generally not valid, since most arbitrators try to judge each case on the specific issues involved in the case. Thus, while the arbitration process is essentially a judicial one, in certain respects it is an extension of collective bargaining.

Arbitration has become an important means for the resolution of conflict. First, it has prevented open conflict, which tends to be very costly in terms of income lost to workers and profits lost to companies. Second, arbitration creates a better climate for the resolution of disputes. The parties resolve, as a matter of principle, to settle their disputes amicably. It can promote a spirit of cooperation that tends to pervade the entire grievance-handling process. Third, the parties know in advance that if they do not settle a dispute between themselves, it will ultimately be settled by a third party. While this may, in a few instances, prevent the parties from behaving in a responsible manner, as a

[4] This principle was enunciated in a series of U.S. Supreme Court decisions in 1960, collectively referred to as the Steelworkers Trilogy. This principle was affirmed in a 1987 U.S. Supreme Court decision, *United Paperworkers International Union, AFL-CIO, v. Misco, Inc.* (108 S.Ct. 364, 1987).

[5] Arbitration of a grievance as the final step of a grievance procedure is referred to as "rights arbitration," meaning arbitration of rights already established within a collective bargaining agreement. If an arbitrator is asked to render a decision that specifies contractual language, that is, that in effect establishes new terms of a contract, this is referred to as "interest arbitration."

general rule arbitration helps foster mature dispute settlements. Finally, no-strike and no-lockout provisions in a collective agreement are possible only if an alternative means for final settlement exists. If a union gives up the right to strike and if a company gives up the right to lock out employees over a grievance during the life of the agreement, both must be assured that some other method for settlement of disputes is available.

Many years ago, Harry Shulman, former dean of the Yale School of Law and a distinguished labor arbitrator, summarized the role of arbitration and of the arbitrator in a classic statement:

> The arbitration is an integral part of the system of self-government. And the system is designed to aid management in its quest for efficiency, to assist union leadership in its participation in the enterprise, and to secure justice for the employees. It is a means of making collective bargaining work and thus preserving private enterprise in a free government . . .
>
> The important question is not whether the parties agree with the award but rather whether they accept it, not resentfully, but cordially and willingly. Again, it is not to be expected that each decision will be accepted with the same degree of cordiality. But general acceptance and satisfaction is an attainable ideal. Its attainment depends upon the parties' seriousness of purpose to make their system of self-government work, and their confidence in the arbitrator. That confidence will ensue if the arbitrator's work inspires the feeling that he has integrity, independence, and courage so that he is not susceptible to pressure, blandishment, or threat of economic loss; that he is intelligent enough to comprehend the parties' contentions and empathetic enough to understand their significance to them; that he is not easily hoodwinked by bluff or histrionics; that he makes earnest effort to inform himself fully and does not go off half-cocked; and that his final judgment is the product of deliberation and reason so applied on the basis of the standards and the authority which they entrusted to him.[6]

LIMITS AND OBJECTIONS TO ARBITRATION

Voluntary arbitration is a valuable device for settling disputes during the life of a contract, when the arbitrator's function is primarily that of interpreting the language or intent of the parties. Both management and unions generally reject arbitration as a method for determining the language of the contract. The contract is "law," since it represents critical areas of managerial and union decision making. Matters in dispute often are considered by the parties to involve issues of principle, rights, or prerogatives. Neither management nor unions wish to permit an outside third party to resolve such important issues. Not only do they fear losing control over their destinies, but they also fear that a provision of an agreement determined by arbitration could rarely, if ever, be changed. This apprehension is in contrast to their belief that, if an arbitrator's ruling on a clause of an existing contract indicates to a party that the clause is unsatisfactory, that party can hope to change or eliminate that clause in the next contract negotiation.[7]

Arbitration is most useful when the parties resort to its use sparingly and only as a last resort. Constructive conflict can lead to new insights and understandings by the

[6] Harry Shulman, "Reason, Contract, and Law in Labor Relations," *Harvard Law Review* 68 (1955), p. 999.

[7] See Frank Elkouri and Edna Asper Elkouri, *How Arbitration Works,* 4th ed. (Washington, D.C.: Bureau of National Affairs, 1985), pp. 342–65.

parties. Settlements reached after serious discussion or negotiation also tend to be more acceptable than those imposed from outside. If the parties turn to an arbitrator primarily as a means to avoid a confrontation or to save face, they may be showing a lack of collective bargaining skills and the maturity essential for a satisfactory relationship. In fact, arbitrators often make comments about unsatisfactory grievance handling such as the following: "This case should never have gotten to arbitration," or "The parties should have been able to resolve this case themselves."

ARBITRATION PROCEDURES

Arbitration clauses in collective agreements usually are individually tailored to meet the needs of each union-management relationship. Some contracts specify the services and procedures of the American Arbitration Association, as the provision from the following contract demonstrates.[8]

Article IV—Arbitration

Section 2. In the event that either party hereto, within 60 days after completion of the Formal Grievance procedure aforesaid, elects to submit a matter described in the preceding section to arbitration the parties agree that the matter shall be so submitted, and agree that such submission shall be to one arbitrator. The parties shall endeavor in each instance within a three weeks' period to agree upon the arbitrator, but if unable to so agree, the arbitrator shall be designated by the American Arbitration Association upon the written request of either party. In either such event, the arbitration shall be conducted under the then obtaining rules of the Voluntary Labor Arbitration Tribunal of the American Arbitration Association. Each party shall pay for the time consumed by and the expenses of its representatives, and shall be equally responsible for the compensation, if any, of the arbitrator, and any other general administrative expense that may occur.

However, the majority of arbitration provisions in collective bargaining agreements are more detailed and specific than the preceding example. The following arbitration provisions specify both the issues subject to arbitration and the authority of the arbitrator.[9]

Article IX—Arbitration

Section 1. The arbitration procedure hereinafter provided for shall extend only to those issues which are arbitrable under the terms of this Agreement. In order for a grievance to be arbitrable:

(a) It must have been properly and timely processed through the grievance procedure;
(b) It must genuinely involve the interpretation or application of a specified provision or provisions of this Agreement;
(c) It must not rest on any alleged understanding or upon any practice or other matter outside the scope of this Agreement; and
(d) It must not require the arbitrator, in order to rule in favor of the grievant, to exceed the scope of his/her jurisdiction under this Agreement.

[8] From the 1989–92 agreement between the Communication Workers of America and Southwestern Bell Telephone Company.

[9] From the February 15, 1994, through February 15, 1998, agreement between Stone Container Corporation (St. Louis, Missouri, Corrugated Plant) and Local Union No. 531, United Paperworkers International Union.

Section 2. The Union may elect to seek arbitration of any arbitrable issue, and in the event shall proceed as follows:

(a) Within forty-five (45) calendar days from the date of the answer in the final step of the grievance procedure, the Union shall so notify the Company in writing, stating the issue proposed to be submitted to arbitration, the provision or provisions of this Agreement on which the claim rests or out of which the dispute arises, and the relief or remedy sought.

(b) As soon as possible after receipt of such notice, the parties shall meet for the purpose of drafting the submission agreement and selecting an arbitrator. If the parties are unable thus to select an arbitrator, they shall jointly request the Federal Mediation and Conciliation Service to furnish a panel of five (5) names from which the parties shall attempt to agree upon an arbitrator, utilizing, if necessary, the method of alternating strike-offs (the party seeking arbitration striking the first name), unless one party objects to all of the names on the panel, in which event an additional panel of names shall be requested and the parties shall then proceed as above.

(c) If a question is raised concerning the arbitrability under the Agreement of the issue sought to be arbitrated, and if such question is not otherwise decided, the parties may submit this issue along to an arbitrator selected as provided above, and his/her decision on such issue shall be final and binding. If in favor of arbitrability, such decision shall be followed by a hearing on the merits of the issue as soon as another arbitrator can be selected and a hearing arranged. The fact that a claim or dispute has been handled under the grievance procedure shall not preclude either party from raising the question of arbitrability with respect to such claim or dispute.

Section 3. The arbitrator's jurisdiction to make an award shall be limited by the submission and confined to the interpretation or application of the provisions of this Agreement. The arbitrator shall not have jurisdiction to make an award which has the effect of amending, altering, enlarging, or ignoring the provisions of this Agreement; nor shall he/she have jurisdiction to determine that the parties by practice or implication have amended or supplemented this Agreement. The arbitrator's award so made shall be final and binding.

Section 4. The entire fee and expenses of the arbitrator shall be borne equally by the Company and the Union.

Both the American Arbitration Association and the Federal Mediation and Conciliation Service have developed policies and procedures to govern arbitration cases they administer.[10] Further, the arbitration section of a collective agreement usually will contain a statement of policy indicating what types of disputes may be arbitrated and will outline other rules governing the conduct of arbitration proceedings. Issues that must be met in the arbitration clause or by agreement by the parties include:

1. What is arbitrable? Most agreements provide that any dispute arising out of or relating to the interpretation or application of the agreement may be submitted to arbitration. On the other hand, the parties sometimes wish to exclude certain matters from arbitration, such as wage rates or determination of production or piece rate standards.

[10] See pamphlets: *Voluntary Labor Arbitration Rules of the American Arbitration Association* (New York: American Arbitration Association); and *Policies, Functions, and Procedures of the Office of Arbitration Services* (Washington, D.C.: Federal Mediation and Conciliation Service).

2. How is the arbitrator appointed, and what procedures shall be followed if the parties are unable to agree upon an arbitrator? Shall the parties appoint a permanent arbitrator or a rotating panel of arbitrators to hear all disputes, or should an ad hoc arbitrator be appointed for each case dispute? Most arbitrators are certified and obtained through either the Federal Mediation and Conciliation Service or the American Arbitration Association.
3. What are the rules and procedures governing the conduct of an arbitration? This issue includes methods for initiating an arbitration, time and place of hearings, swearing of witnesses, representation by legal counsel, recording of the proceedings, filings of briefs, rules of evidence, time within which an award will be made, and to whom it shall be delivered. Most of these issues will be determined by the parties themselves, but sometimes the arbitrator will be asked to rule on such procedural matters.
4. Who bears the cost of an arbitration? Typically, but not always, the parties will agree to share equally in these costs.

Disputes are brought to arbitration by one of two routes: either by a "submission" from the parties, or by a "demand for arbitration" filed by either party. A submission agreement is a statement signed by both parties indicating the specific nature of the issue under contention and the specific relief that the injured party is seeking. A demand for arbitration is a formal request made by either of the two parties to the other for arbitration of an issue in dispute.

Among the major types of evidence and testimony presented and considered by arbitrators are:

1. The language of provisions of the agreement.
2. The intent of the parties in negotiating agreement provisions.
3. Past practice or precedents in handling similar or parallel matters.
4. Practices at other firms in the same industry or in other industries.
5. Equity or fairness in certain matters; "just cause" in disciplinary cases.
6. Arbitration rulings and precedents established by other arbitrators.
7. Industrial relations practices accepted as desirable or undesirable.

The American Arbitration Association has identified 10 common errors committed by parties in arbitration.[11]

1. Using arbitration and arbitration costs as a harassment technique.
2. Overemphasis of the grievance by a union or exaggeration of an employee's fault by management.
3. Reliance on a minimum of facts and a maximum of arguments.
4. Concealing essential facts; distorting the truth.
5. Holding back books, records, or other supporting documents.

[11] American Arbitration Association, *Labor Arbitration, Procedures and Techniques* (New York, 1987), pp. 19–20.

6. Typing up proceedings with legal technicalities.
7. Introducing witnesses who have not been properly instructed on demeanor and on the place of their testimony in the entire case.
8. Withholding full cooperation from the arbitrator.
9. Disregarding the ordinary rules of courtesy and decorum.
10. Becoming involved in arguments with the other side. The time to try to convince the other party is before arbitration, during grievance processing. At the arbitration hearing, all efforts should be concentrated on convincing the arbitrator.

The parties to a dispute seek an award from the arbitrator. The purpose of the award is to provide a final and conclusive decision with respect to the controversy. The arbitrator must not exceed the authority given him or her under the terms of the collective agreement. Most agreements, for example, state in some way that the arbitrator may not add to, detract from, or otherwise modify any part of the collective agreement. Even if this is not specifically stated in a collective agreement, this restriction is generally implied in the submission of a dispute to the arbitrator. The award of the arbitrator is to be accepted by both parties, and it will be upheld in the courts unless the arbitrator exceeds the authority granted him or her by the parties, fraud or some other breach of ethics is proved, or the result is contrary to law (e.g., an arbitrator enforces an illegal union security provision).

Expedited Arbitration Expedited arbitration is a fairly recent, and in some situations still an experimental, approach designed to simplify and speed up the arbitration process. A typical arbitration will require several months or more to complete and cost each side thousands of dollars, when costs of personnel, lost time, and attorneys' and the arbitrators' fees and expenses are calculated. In fiscal year 2000 according to FMCS data, an arbitrator's fees and expenses alone averaged over $3,100 per case.

Because of concern about arbitration costs and other factors involved, a number of steel companies and the United Steelworkers Union in 1971 agreed to a three-year experiment that they named "expedited arbitration" or "miniarb." The experiment was successful, and they subsequently incorporated this procedure into their collective agreements. Numerous companies and unions are currently utilizing this procedure. Expedited arbitration is also being utilized in the public sector, as illustrated by the provisions from the following "master agreement."[12]

C. Regional Level Arbitration—Expedited

1. The parties agree to continue the utilization of an expedited arbitration system for disciplinary cases of 14 days' suspension or less which do not involve interpretation of the Agreement and for such other cases as the parties may mutually determine. This system may be utilized by agreement of the Union involved through its National President or designee and the Senior Assistant Postmaster General, Employee and Labor Relations Group, or designee. In any case, the FMCS or AAA shall immediately notify the designated arbitrator. The designated arbitrator is that member of the Expedited Panel who,

[12] From 1987–90 Collective Bargaining Agreement between American Postal Workers Union, AFL-CIO, and the United States Postal Service.

pursuant to a rotation system, is scheduled for the next arbitration hearing. Immediately upon such notification the designated arbitrator shall arrange a place and date for the hearing promptly but within a period of not more than ten (10) working days. If the designated arbitrator is not available to conduct a hearing within the ten (10) working days, the next panel member in rotation shall be notified until an available arbitrator is obtained.

2. If either party concludes that the issues involved are of such complexity or significance as to warrant reference to the Regular Regional Arbitration Panel, that party shall notify the other party of such reference at least twenty-four (24) hours prior to the scheduled time for the expedited arbitration.
3. The hearing shall be conducted in accordance with the following:
   a. The hearing shall be informal.
   b. No brief shall be filed or transcripts made.
   c. There shall be no formal rules of evidence.
   d. The hearing shall normally be completed within one day.
   e. If the arbitrator or the parties mutually conclude at the hearing that the issues involved are of such complexity or significance as to warrant reference to the Regular Regional Arbitration Panel, the case shall be referred to that panel.
   f. The arbitrator may issue a bench decision at the hearing but in any event shall render a decision within forty-eight (48) hours after conclusion of the hearing. Such decision shall be based on the record before the arbitrator and may include a brief written explanation of the basis for such conclusion. These decisions will not be cited as a precedent. The arbitrator's decision shall be final and binding. An arbitrator who issues a bench decision shall furnish a written copy of the award to the parties within forty-eight (48) hours of the close of the hearing.
4. No decision by a member of the Expedited Panel in such a case shall be regarded as a precedent or be cited in any future proceeding, but otherwise will be a final and binding decision.
5. The Expedited Arbitration Panel shall be developed by the National parties, on an area basis, with the aid of the American Arbitration Association and the Federal Mediation and Conciliation Service.

Expedited arbitration is not a substitute for regular arbitration. It is usually employed to settle certain types of disputes at some agreed-upon step of the grievance procedure after the parties have not settled at a previous step, and then only after a joint labor-management committee agrees to the abbreviated procedure.

This arbitration technique is marked by informality. The hearing is usually conducted in the office or shop, sometimes at the workplace, rather than in a hotel room or other neutral site. The arbitrator may interview witnesses on the spot. The rules of evidence often employed in arbitration proceedings are considerably relaxed. The arbitrator normally renders his or her decision within 24 to 48 hours of the hearing. Sometimes the arbitrator renders it the same day, on occasion within minutes after the conclusion of the hearing. This is called a bench decision.

The procedure is more applicable to some cases than others. It has been most useful in settling minor disciplinary cases, although it has also been employed to decide nondisciplinary issues, including compensation and employee rights questions. It is less useful in resolving issues involving interpretation of the meaning of an important contractual clause or questions of principle. Some disputes involve issues so fundamental to the parties that one or both may refuse to submit them to an expedited arbitration. For example, questions involving the meaning of management or union "rights" provisions in the contract, subcontracting, or production standards are more appropriately resolved by a more thorough arbitration procedure.[13]

Although expedited arbitration normally is associated with settlement of rather minor grievances, some companies and unions are utilizing the concept for discharge and other selected cases where the parties wish to bring the arbitration process to a swift conclusion. Here the parties may well have a very thorough and formal arbitration hearing of the case matter, but the selection of the arbitrator, the scheduling of the hearing, and the rendering of the arbitrator's decision are all accomplished within a specified and relatively short period of time. The following "Expedited Procedure" is representative of this type of approach.[14]

> **Section 4(a).** If a grievance involving the discharge of an employee shall have been submitted but not adjusted under Step 3, the following Expedited Procedure shall apply unless the Employer and the Union mutually agree to waive any of these provisions:
>
> 1. If the Union wishes to proceed to arbitration, it must give written notice to the Employer of its demand for arbitration within five (5) days after its receipt of the Employer's written reply following the Step 3 meeting.
> 2. The Employer will promptly notify the appropriate arbitrator selected as set forth below and schedule a hearing which is to take place within the five-day period following the Employer's receipt of the Union's demand for arbitration.
> 3. The arbitrator shall render a written decision within ten (10) days following the close of the hearing, and within sixty (60) days following the close of the hearing, the arbitrator will render a written opinion explaining the reasons for the decision.
>
> In conjunction with any Expedited Arbitration hereunder, either party may, at its option, submit a pre-hearing brief. And, either party may, at its option, request a court reporter for the hearing at its own cost, unless both parties request a transcript, in which case the cost of the court reporter will be shared equally.
>
> The decision of the arbitrator shall be final and conclusive on both the Employer and the Union. The arbitrator shall have no power to add to, detract from, or alter this agreement in any way. Pending final decision by the arbitrator, there shall be no action taken by either party to the controversy. Any expense incidental to and arising out of the arbitrations shall be borne equally by the Employer and the Union except as otherwise provided in this Article.
>
> (b) Expedited Arbitration Panel—Within thirty (30) days following the effective date of this Agreement, and annually thereafter, the Employer and the Union shall select a panel of five (5) arbitrators designated to decide Expedited Arbitration cases under this

[13] See Arthur A. Sloane and Fred Witney, *Labor Relations,* 9th ed. (Upper Saddle River, N.J.: Prentice Hall, 1997), pp. 271–72. Also see pamphlet, *Expedited Labor Arbitration Rules of the American Arbitration Association* (New York: American Arbitration Association).

[14] From 1985–87 agreement between Anheuser-Busch, Inc., of St. Louis, Missouri, and Bottlers Local Union No. 1187, affiliated with the International Brotherhood of Teamsters, Chauffeurs, Warehousemen, and Helpers of North America.

> Article. The panel of five (5) arbitrators shall be selected as follows: The Federal Mediation and Conciliation Service will be asked to provide five (5) lists of arbitrators with each list containing seven (7) names from the Midwest area comprised of the states of Michigan, Illinois, Indiana, Iowa, Arkansas, Kansas, Nebraska, and Missouri. One arbitrator will be chosen from each FMCS list by the procedure of alternating strikes—the party having the first strike on the first list will be determined by a coin flip and thereafter the party having the first strike on the remaining lists will alternate. The five (5) arbitrators thus chosen will constitute the Expedited Panel for proceedings under this Article.
>
> (c) Selection of an Arbitrator from the Expedited Panel—The arbitrator for an Expedited Arbitration shall be selected from the Expedited Panel as follows: The five (5) arbitrators on the Expedited Panel shall be listed in alphabetical order and cases will be referred to the arbitrators in that sequence until a new Expedited Panel is chosen (for example, the first expedited arbitration will be referred to arbitrator No. 1, the second will be referred to arbitrator No. 2, the fifth will be referred to arbitrator No. 5, the sixth will be referred to arbitrator No. 1, the seventh will be referred to arbitrator No. 2, the tenth will be referred to arbitrator No. 5, and so on). However, in the event the arbitrator designated by this procedure is unable to schedule a hearing within the five-day time period provided for above, the case will be referred to the next arbitrator in sequence and so on until an arbitrator is designated who can schedule the hearing within the appropriate time period, and any arbitrator thus bypassed will not be designated again until his name comes up in the regular sequence. Provided further that in the event none of the arbitrators on the Expedited Panel is able to schedule a hearing within the five-day time period described above, then that case will be referred to the arbitrator on the Expedited Panel who is able to schedule the earliest possible hearing, and again the sequence of selection of arbitrators for subsequent cases will start with the next arbitrator on the list and any bypassed arbitrator will not be designated again until his name comes up on the regular sequence.

It is likely that expedited arbitration in one form or another will continue to be utilized in future years. Expedited arbitration that serves the mutual interests of the parties thus represents another form of conflict resolution that can foster a more constructive atmosphere in union-management relationships.

Grievance Mediation[15] Another relatively recent approach for dispute resolution is that of grievance mediation. Grievance mediation is a process by which a union and an employer, assisted by a mediator, seek to resolve grievances without resort to arbitration. It is typically used only after all other prearbitration steps in a contractual grievance procedure have been completed.

Proceedings before a grievance mediator are informal. The facts are brought out in narrative form, the rules of evidence do not apply, and no record is made.

The mediator attempts to settle the grievance by using techniques commonly associated with the mediation process, including private meetings with each party. The mediator encourages the parties to focus not only on the contract, but also on the problems

[15] Part of this discussion has been excerpted and adapted from the brochure *Grievance Mediation: An Alternative in the Resolution of Labor/Management Disputes,* as prepared and distributed by the New Spirit of St. Louis Labor/Management Committee and the St. Louis Community College of St. Louis, Missouri.

underlying the grievance. If a settlement is not achieved, the mediator gives the parties an on-the-spot oral opinion as to how the grievance is likely to be decided if it goes to arbitration.

If the parties do not accept the mediator's advisory opinion, they are free to arbitrate. If they arbitrate, the mediator will not serve as arbitrator, and nothing said during grievance mediation, including the mediator's advisory opinion, can be used at arbitration.

It is normally recommended that grievance mediation first be tried for an experimental period of 6 to 12 months. During this period, the employer and union can determine from their own experience whether they wish to incorporate mediation into their grievance procedure on a long-term basis.[16]

SELECTED STATISTICS ON ARBITRATION AS REPORTED BY THE AMERICAN ARBITRATION ASSOCIATION AND THE FEDERAL MEDIATION AND CONCILIATION SERVICE

Over the past decade case filings with the American Arbitration Association have increased significantly. In the period of the early 1990s the Association processed approximately 8,000 cases per year. In 2004, case filings increased to 12,542. The American Arbitration Association is the largest processor of labor arbitration matters in the United States.[17]

According to the Federal Mediation and Conciliation Service (FMCS), in fiscal year 2004 its Office of Arbitration Services assigned some 18,033 arbitration panels from which arbitrators were appointed in about one-third of the case panels assigned. The FMCS actually closed only 2,581 cases in FY 04, a number that was slightly lower than those of several previous years. The predominant issues involved in the cases closed were: discipline/discharge (39 percent), seniority rights (3 percent), overtime disputes (2 percent), and work assignments (4 percent). FMCS sample data for FY 04 indicated that the average elapsed time between the date of the filing of a grievance and the date on which the parties requested an FMCS arbitration panel was 159 days. The average elapsed time between the date an FMCS arbitration panel was requested and the date of the arbitrator's award was 317 days. Transcripts were taken at about 36 percent of the hearings, and post-hearing briefs were filed by the parties in about 57 percent of the cases.[18]

[16] See John C. Sigler, "Mediation of Grievances: An Alternative to Arbitration?" *Employee Relations Law Journal* 13 (Autumn 1987), pp. 266–85. See also Robert D. Steinberg, "Grievance Mediation: Coming of Age," *Labor Relations Bulletin* (Bureau of Business Practice 679, October 1997), p. 8.

[17] This information was provided by the American Arbitration Association from their "2004 AAA Case Filing." The Authors wish to thank Larry Parke, AAA Director of Corporate Communication, for providing this information.

[18] From Federal Mediation and Conciliation Service, *Arbitration Statistics for Fiscal Year 2004* (Washington, D.C.: FMCS, December 2004).

DECIDING ARBITRATION CASES FROM AN ARBITRATOR'S POINT OF VIEW

The cases included in this section all resulted from actual disputes that were processed through grievance procedures in collective bargaining agreements, that remained unsettled, and that then were subsequently submitted to arbitration. In a condensed form, these cases provide the essential information available to the arbitrator. By studying the issues in such cases, one has the opportunity of experiencing actual arbitration situations and of arriving at one's own decisions with respect to the disputes. In so doing, however, it is desirable to follow certain principles that most arbitrators and practitioners of labor relations have come to understand as being appropriate to an arbitrator's decision-making responsibilities.[19]

In general, the three major aspects that an arbitrator must consider, in order of importance, are as follows:

1. What does the labor agreement say?
2. What is the role of past practices or precedents?
3. What standards of fairness or equity should be applied?

What Does the Labor Agreement Say?

It is usually recognized by the parties that a labor agreement is essentially a general outline for handling many problems and situations that arise during the course of an agreement, and that no contract could possibly cover all of them. Nevertheless, an arbitrator is first of all bound to the wording and general interpretation of the agreement itself. As a rule, most arbitrators take a somewhat restrictive view when applying and interpreting a labor agreement. That is to say, they normally do not expand upon the meaning of a clause in the agreement unless there is some reasonable evidence that this is what the parties had intended.

What Is the Role of Past Practices or Precedents?

If a clause in a labor agreement is not clear, or if it is subject to ambiguous interpretation, most arbitrators will look to past practices or precedents for guidance to determine the intent of the parties. Past practices or precedents can become an extension of a labor agreement almost as if the parties had negotiated additional contract language accordingly. This does not mean that a past practice or precedent always is a permanent fixture and cannot be changed for good reasons. But if the parties have handled a certain problem or parallel problems along consistent lines on a number of occasions, an arbitrator usually is reluctant to make a ruling contrary to such a practice, just as an arbitrator would not choose to change the wording of a labor agreement.

[19] Parts of this section were adapted from Raymond L. Hilgert, "An Arbitrator Looks at Grievance Arbitration," *Employee Responsibilities and Rights Journal* 8, no. 1 (April 1995), pp. 67–73.

What Standards of Fairness and Equity Should Be Applied?

The third and probably most subjective area of the arbitration process involves standards for fairness and equity to be applied in certain types of cases. This is especially true in discipline and discharge cases, since most labor agreements specify that a company may discipline or discharge an employee for "just cause" or "proper cause."

Over the last several decades, the majority of arbitrators have adopted in one form or another the "Seven Tests for Just Cause," which were first formulated by arbitrator Carroll R. Daugherty in the Enterprise Wire Company case (46 LA 359, 1966). These seven tests were posed in the form of questions that could be applied to the facts of any case involving discipline or discharge. A "no" answer to one or more of these questions presumably would signify that a standard of just (or proper) cause was not met, and the arbitrator, therefore, probably would set aside or modify the employer's disciplinary or discharge action. The seven tests for just cause are as follows:

1. Did the company give to the employee forewarning or foreknowledge of the possible or probable disciplinary consequences of the employee's conduct?
2. Was the company's rule or managerial order reasonably related to (*a*) the orderly, efficient, and safe operation of the company's business, and (*b*) the performance that the company might properly expect of the employee?
3. Did the company, before administering discipline to an employee, make an effort to discover whether the employee did in fact violate or disobey a rule or order of management?
4. Was the company's investigation conducted fairly and objectively?
5. At the investigation, was there substantial evidence or proof that the employee was guilty as charged?
6. Has the company applied its rules, orders, and penalties even-handedly and without discrimination to all employees?
7. Was the degree of discipline administered by the company in a particular case reasonably related to (*a*) the seriousness of the employee's proven offense, and (*b*) the record of the employee in his service with the company?[20]

One aspect that often is crucial in regard to the above tests is the matter of burden of proof in presentation of evidence. Most arbitrators believe that in discipline and discharge cases, the primary burden falls upon management to demonstrate from the preponderance of credible evidence available that what it did in a particular matter would be considered a reasonable course of action by a neutral or impartial person.

[20] For an expanded discussion of these tests, see Adolph M. Koven and Susan L. Smith (revised by Donald F. Farwell), *Just Cause: The Seven Tests,* 2nd ed. (Washington, D.C.: Bureau of National Affairs, 1992). See also Raymond L. Hilgert, "Reflections of an Arbitrator: The 'Hot Stove Rule' for Imposing Discipline," in *Discipline and Grievances* (Bureau of Business Practice 603, June 1991), p. 9; and Raymond L. Hilgert, "Making Credibility Determinations," *Labor Relations Bulletin* (Bureau of Business Practice 677, August 1997), p. 8.

Thus, in discharge and disciplinary matters, the cases most likely to go to arbitration, it becomes prudent for management to ask itself how a reasonable, neutral person would view what was done.[21,22]

Appendix C*

Preventive Mediation and Alternative Dispute Resolution Services of the Federal Mediation and Conciliation Service

Preventive Mediation

Although not as highly visible as dispute mediation, the Federal Mediation and Conciliation Services preventive mediation programs are increasingly being utilized by labor and management. The American workplace is the basic foundation of the U.S. economy, and the ability of American business to compete worldwide relates directly to workplace performance. The workplace labor-management relationship has major economic implications, because it affects the product quality, productivity, and profits of firms, and the jobs and employment security of workers. To assist management and labor in improving their relationship so they can learn to work together on issues of mutual interest as a team instead of as adversaries, FMCS offers a range of preventive mediation services which are broadly defined as collaborative union-management processes.

To assist a company and union in achieving these goals, FMCS mediators guide the parties through an assessment of the quality and development of their relationship and identify areas which need improvement. Problems often encountered include lowered employee morale, decreased productivity, excessive numbers of grievances or unfair labor practice complaints, or poor communication between union leadership and management. After analyzing the relationship and discussions with the parties, the mediator

[21] In 1991, a national legal commission, called The National Conference of Commissioners on Uniform State Laws, proposed a new employment statute for states that would let most fired employees take their cases to a neutral arbitrator. This commission was a quasi-official body appointed and funded by the states. Under this proposed system of arbitration, an estimated 60 million additional workers could be covered, most of them so-called employment-at-will employees. A number of states already have passed arbitration statutes, and other states are considering the proposal. See "Tell It to the Arbitrator," *BusinessWeek,* November 4, 1991, p. 109.

[22] In recent years, many firms have implemented their own alternative dispute resolution (ADR) procedures to resolve various types of employee complaints and also to avoid litigation. See "Employers Resolve Worker Complaints Through Alternatives to Litigation," *Employee Relations Weekly* (Bureau of National Affairs, Inc., November 25, 1991), pp. 1–2; Edward T. Lynch and Courtney E. Redfern, "Committing Employees to Out-of-Court Resolution," *HRMagazine* (Society for Human Resource Management, May 1993), pp. 97–103 or "Alternative Dispute Resolution Gaining in Popularity," *Human Resources Management: Ideas and Trends in Personnel* (Commerce Clearing House, March 29, 1995), pp. 49–53.

* Appendix C consists of adapted excerpts from publications of the FMCS, Washington, D.C.

recommends appropriate training in skills and processes that will assist in addressing the particular problem. Recommendations may include customized skills training in such subjects as:

- Alternative bargaining processes.
- Conflict management.
- Consensus decision making.
- Contract administration.
- Effective negotiation.
- Interpersonal communications.
- Labor-management partnership building.
- Team building.
- Union-management roles and responsibilities.

The mediator may recommend one or more comprehensive approaches composed of particular combinations of these skills components.

FMCS preventive mediation cases assigned to mediators averaged about 2,800 cases annually for fiscal years 1998 through 2000.[23]

Alternative Dispute Resolution

In late 1990, two pieces of legislation were signed into law by President George Bush that have had considerable impact on FMCS and its expanding role in alternative dispute resolution. The first Act, the *Administrative Disputes Resolution (ADR) Act of 1990,* required each federal agency to develop a policy for institutionalizing mediation and other forms of conflict resolution as an alternative to costly litigation proceedings. Along with developing a policy for the use of ADR, all federal agencies were ordered to appoint a dispute resolution expert and provide ADR training to appropriate staff. The second Act, the *Negotiated Rulemaking Act of 1990,* encouraged all federal agencies to utilize the regulatory negotiations, or "reg-neg," process in developing agency rules. Both Acts contained specific provisions for FMCS to proffer its personnel for training, consultation, systems design, and third-party neutral services to all federal agencies. In particular, the ADR Act also required all agencies to submit their policies to FMCS, along with the Administrative Conference of the United States, for review and comment. While no funds were appropriated for this work, FMCS was allowed to charge for its services via interagency agreements.

Alternative dispute resolution (ADR) is used to describe a variety of joint problem-solving approaches which can be used in lieu of more formal and often expensive courtroom litigation, or as an alternative to agency adjudication and traditional rule making. ADR processes usually involve the use of a neutral third party to help disputants find mutually acceptable solutions. Services are based on the specific needs of the parties, and these can include dispute resolution assistance, systems design, and training for agency personnel. ADR has proven to be far less expensive than litigation for settling

[23] For a more recent report on FMCS preventive mediation efforts, see Kathy Chen, "Government's Labor Mediators Branch Out," *The Wall Street Journal,* June 1, 2001, pp. B1 and B3.

certain disputes, such as employment discrimination complaints and environmental and public policy controversies, and generally ADR is completed in a shorter time frame. For fiscal years 1998 through 2000, FMCS alternative dispute resolution cases averaged about 700 cases annually.

Among the FMCS's ADR capabilities also finding wider interest and use is negotiated rule making. This process has the mediator bring together government regulators and those they regulate to draft necessary rules, regulations, and policies through negotiation and consensus. Results indicate that when those who will be affected by a regulation have the opportunity to participate in its development, the federal agency usually will develop a better regulation with less likelihood of legal challenges afterward.

Selected Bibliography

Ballot, Michael, with Laurie Lichter-Heath, Thomas Kail, and Ruth Wang. *Labor-Management Relations in a Changing Environment.* 2nd ed. New York: John Wiley & Sons, 1996.

Bognanno, Maris, and Charles Coleman, eds. *Labor Arbitration in America: The Profession and Practice.* New York: Praeger, 1992.

Bowers, Mollie H., and David A. DeCenzo. *Essentials of Labor Relations.* Englewood Cliffs, N.J.: Prentice Hall, 1992.

Brand, Norman, ed., *Discipline and Discharge in Arbitration.* Washington, D.C.: Bureau of National Affairs, 1998.

Carrell, Michael R., and Christina Heavrin. *Collective Bargaining and Labor Relations: Cases, Practices, and Law.* 6th ed. Upper Saddle River, N.J.: Prentice Hall, 2001.

Code of Professional Responsibility for Arbitrators of Labor-Management Disputes. National Academy of Arbitrators, American Arbitration Association, and Federal Mediation and Conciliation Service.

Colosi, Thomas R., and Arthur Eliot Berkeley. *Collective Bargaining: How It Works and Why.* 2nd ed. New York: American Arbitration Association, 1992.

Deitsen, Clourence R., and David A. Dilts, *The Arbitration of Rights Disputes in the Public Sector.* Westport, Conn.: Qubrum Books, 1990.

Fossum, John A. *Labor Relations: Development, Structure, Process.* 6th ed. Burr Ridge, Ill.: Richard D. Irwin, 1995.

Fossum, John A., ed. *Employee and Labor Relations—Volume 4 of the SHRM–BNA Series on Human Resource Management.* Washington, D.C.: Bureau of National Affairs, 1990.

Grievance Guide. 10th ed. Washington, D.C.: Bureau of National Affairs, 2000.

Guidelines: Innovative Collective Bargaining Contract Provisions, Issues 1 and 2. Washington, D.C.: Federal Mediation and Conciliation Service and U.S. Department of Labor, U.S. Government Printing Office, 1995.

Hill, Marvin, Jr., and Anthony V. Sinicropi. *Remedies in Arbitration.* 2nd ed. Washington, D.C.: Bureau of National Affairs, 1991.

Hill, Marvin, Jr., Anthony V. Sinicropi, and Amy L. Evenson, *Winning Arbitration Advocacy.* Washington, D.C.: Bureau of National Affairs, 1997.

Hogler, Raymond L. *Labor and Employment Relations.* St. Paul: West Publishing, 1995.

Koven, Adolph, and Susan Smith. *Just Cause: the Seven Tests.* 2nd rev. ed. Edited by Donald F. Farwell. Washington, D.C.: Bureau of National Affairs, 1992.

Labor Arbitration Awards. Chicago: Commerce Clearing House.

Labor Arbitration in America: The Profession and the Practice. New York: Praeger and the American Arbitration Association, 1992.

Labor Arbitration Reports. Washington, D.C.: Bureau of National Affairs.

Labor Relations Reporter. Washington, D.C.: Bureau of National Affairs.

Leap, Terry L. *Collective Bargaining and Labor Relations.* 2nd ed. Upper Saddle River, N.J.: Prentice Hall, 1995.

Loughran, Charles S. *How to Prepare and Present a Labor Arbitration Case.* Washington, D.C.: Bureau of National Affairs, 1996.

Mills, Daniel Quinn. *Labor-Management Relations.* 5th ed. New York: McGraw-Hill, 1994.

National Rules for the Resolution of Employment Disputes. New York: American Arbitration Association, 1996.

Rhodes, S. R., and R. M. Steers. *Managing Employee Absenteeism.* Reading, Mass.: Addison-Wesley, 1990.

Schoonhover, Ray J., ed. *Fairweather's Practice and Procedure in Labor Arbitration.* 4th ed. Washington, D.C.: Bureau of National Affairs, 1999.

Sheppard, Blair, Roy Lewicki; and John Minton. *Organizational Justice: The Search for Fairness in the Workplace.* New York: Lexington Books, 1992.

Sloane, Arthur A., and Fred Witney. *Labor Relations.* 9th ed. Upper Saddle River, N.J.: Prentice Hall, 1997.

St.Antoine, Theodore J., ed. *The Common Law of the Workplace: The Views of Arbitrators.* Washington, D.C.: Bureau of National Affairs, 1998.

Volz, Marlin M., and Edward P. Goggin, eds. *Elkouri and Elkouri: How Arbitration Works.* 5th ed. Washington, D.C.: Bureau of National Affairs, 1997.

Zack, Arnold M. *Grievance Arbitration: Issues on the Merits in Discipline, Discharge, and Contract Interpretation.* New York: American Arbitration Association, 1992.

Zack, Arnold M., and Richard I. Bloch. *Labor Agreement in Negotiation and Arbitration.* 2nd ed. Washington, D.C.: Bureau of National Affairs, 1996.

Zimny, Max; William F. Dolson; and Christopher A. Barreca, eds. *Labor Arbitration: A Practical Guide for Advocates.* Washington, D.C.: Bureau of National Affairs, 1990.

Index to Cases for Part Two

Case Number and Title	Management Rights	Union Rights and Activities	Seniority and Employee Rights	Discipline and Discharge	Work Assignments/ Job Bidding	Job Performance	Change/ Past Practices	Wages and Benefits	Employee Health, Safety, and Security	Discrimination/ Sexual Harassment
39. Who Should Maintain the Parks and Ballfields?	X	X			X					
40. Health Insurance Coverage Unilaterally Changed by Public Employer	X		X				X	X	X	
41. A Changed Remedy for Misassignments	X		X		X		X	X		
42. Probation for the Teacher	X		X	X		X				
43. Appeal to Arbitration: A Day Late?	X	X	X	X						
44. Denial of the Safety Incentive Prize	X	X						X	X	X
45. Demoted or Reclassified?	X	X	X	X	X	X		X		
46. Voluntary Resignation or Layoff?	X		X	X				X		
47. The Doubtful Worker	X		X	X	X	X			X	
48. The Recalled Management Trainee	X	X	X		X					

49. The Right to Bid Down	X		X		X		X			
50. Taking Care of Union Business	X	X		X	X	X				
51. Sick Leave for Adoption Care			X					X	X	X
52. An Issue of Reasonable Accommodation	X		X	X		X			X	X
53. Refusal to Post the Union's Memorandum	X	X					X	X	X	
54. Terminated for Possessing a Gun	X		X	X					X	
55. Are Teachers Obliged to Supervise Students in the Cafeteria?	X		X		X			X		
56. Anti-Arab Comments: Cause for Discipline?	X		X	X			X			X
57. Abuse of a Senior Citizen Resident	X		X	X		X				
58. Ability and Seniority for Promotion: Which Controls?	X		X		X	X				
59. Company Picnic: Employee Benefit or Gratuity?	X	X	X		X		X	X		
60. An Error in Equalizing the Overtime	X		X				X	X		
61. Forced to Work on a Holiday	X		X		X		X	X		

(*continued*)

Index to Cases for Part Two *(Continued)*

Case Number and Title	Management Rights	Union Rights and Activities	Seniority and Employee Rights	Discipline and Discharge	Work Assignments/ Job Bidding	Job Performance	Change/ Past Practices	Wages and Benefits	Employee Health, Safety, and Security	Discrimination/ Sexual Harassment
62. Full Consideration to Seniority and Qualifications	X		X		X	X				
63. No Accommodation without an Examination	X	X		X	X	X		X	X	X
64. Last Chance Violation: Strike Three or Overreaction?	X			X						X
65. Health Insurance Benefits for Same-Sex Domestic Partners			X				X	X	X	X
66. Arbitrability of the Scheduling Past Practice	X	X	X		X		X			
67. How Should the Lead Skycap Be Selected?	X	X	X		X	X	X			
68. Post-Reinstatement Drug Testing	X	X	X	X			X		X	
69. Conflict of Interest Rules and Discharge for News Photographer	X		X	X		X			X	

70. Sickness and Accident Benefits Denied	X		X					X	X	
71. Self-Defense or Excessive Use of Force?	X		X	X					X	
72. Egregious Horseplay	X		X	X		X			X	
73. No Reporting Pay	X				X		X			
74. Who Decides If an Employee Is Unable to Work?	X		X		X	X			X	
75. Internet Kiddie Pornography at Work: Just Cause for Discharge?	X		X	X					X	X
76. Unilateral Changes to the Absence Control Policy	X	X					X			
77. Wage Concession: Contract Violation or Authorized Wage Freeze?	X						X	X		
78. Layoff of the Higher-Seniority Employees	X	X	X			X	X			
79. Cash Same as Stock? The Case of the 401k Contributions	X	X	X				X	X		
80. Vacation, or Layoff, during a Shutdown	X	X	X					X		
81. Discharge for Job Abandonment?	X		X	X						

Case 39

Who Should Maintain the Parks and Ballfields?

Employer Town of Lee, Massachusetts

Union Local No. 404, General Teamsters, Warehousemen & Helpers, Building Materials, Heavy and Highway Construction Employees

BACKGROUND

In early 1990, the town's Department of Public Works had a bargaining unit of five employees. As permitted by the parties' collective bargaining agreement,[1] the town also had employed two temporary employees, Joe and Carl Judson,[2] who were not members of the bargaining unit.

In accordance with paragraph 91 of the agreement, the Truck Drivers/Laborers did the grass and lawn maintenance along the town's roads. For the past dozen years or so, various students had been hired as spring and summer help and assigned the grass and lawn maintenance of the town's seven parks and ballfields. The regular crew of union workers and the two temporaries did this work during the periods before and after the availability of the temporary student help. The Judson brothers were assigned this work in 1987 when the summer help became unreliable. By the summer of 1988, the Judson brothers had left the payroll and the work was again done by students. In 1989, two major maintenance vehicles and other equipment were inoperative. Without sufficient working equipment, neither the students nor the bargaining unit employees could do the work. Therefore, all park maintenance was contracted out for that year to a local tree and lawn service firm.

In early 1990, the town council decided to contract out the park and ballfields work again. The proposed contract called for work to be done periodically between May 1, 1990, and October 9, 1990. Also, the town council decided that it would contract out that portion of the road work that involved side slopes, ditches, and brush clearance. This latter work was not done regularly by anyone, but every four or five years a regular crew or the Judsons would do it.

The superintendent of public works, Abner Collins, informed the union steward, Bill Phillips, of his intent to contract. This notice took place verbally, after the contractual bid had been advertised in a local newspaper.

Phillips notified Wilson Billingham, president of Local 404 of the union, about the town's decision to contract out the various maintenance work. Subsequently, the union

[1] See the appendix for relevant contractual provisions.

[2] The names of all individuals are disguised.

filed a grievance, which was eventually submitted to arbitration.[3] The parties agreed on the following framing of the issue to be decided:

> Is the maintenance of lawns and ballfields in the town parks bargaining unit work? If so, is subcontracting of the maintenance of town lawns and ballfields a violation of the agreement? If so, what shall the remedy be?

POSITION OF THE UNION

The union contended that paragraph 91 of the parties' labor agreement guaranteed that park maintenance be done solely by bargaining unit members. The only permissible exception was that paragraph 43 allowed assignment of temporary employees, which had been done with the Judson brothers or with summer student help.

The union claimed that paragraph 43 of the agreement was intended to permit the town to have temporary workers who would not be in the bargaining unit, but this was the only exception to the union's work jurisdiction. This exception had been utilized each summer, and there had been no contracting out except in 1989 when maintenance vehicles and equipment had broken down. Therefore, the union claimed the labor agreement did not permit contracting out.

In addition, the union complained that notice of the intent to contract out the disputed work should have been given to the union office, not to the shop steward.

The union urged that the grievance be sustained by the arbitrator, that the arbitrator issue a "cease and desist" order on the town, and that the town be directed to negotiate the matter with the union. Absent any agreement with the union, the arbitrator should direct that the contested work be performed only by bargaining unit members.

POSITION OF THE EMPLOYER

Counsel for the town contended that the collective bargaining agreement was silent on the question of contracting out. Further, contracting out had taken place the previous summer (1989) when necessary vehicles and equipment were not working.

The town saw no difference between a temporary employee and a contractor. In either case, the disputed work had been done each year by non–bargaining unit members. Therefore, there was no practice or precedent to prevent the town from contracting out.

The town believed that it could contract out for the slopes, ditches, and brush clearance, because it did not have the appropriate equipment to accomplish those tasks.

As to the notice, the superintendent, Abner Collins, had always notified the union informally by talking with the shop steward. This complaint of the union was a "red herring" with no relevance to the merits of the case.

Counsel for the town urged the arbitrator to totally dismiss the union grievance.

[3] The dispute was submitted to the Massachusetts Board of Conciliation and Arbitration in accordance with Article VII of the collective bargaining agreement between the parties. An arbitrator was appointed by the MBCA to hear and decide the case.

Appendix

Relevant Contractual Provisions

Article I—Union Recognition

Paragraph 10. Pursuant to the certification of representation . . . the Employer hereby recognizes the Union as the sole and exclusive bargaining agency . . . for all truck drivers/laborers . . . employed by the Highway and Landfill Division . . .

Article IX—Wages and Classifications

Paragraph 91. Classification Descriptions . . . Truck Driver/Laborer. A truck driver/laborer . . . will perform a variety of maintenance and construction repair duties related to public works projects including, but not limited to, highway . . . recreation, forestry work . . .

Article IV—Seniority

Paragraph 43. The provisions of this agreement do not apply to temporary employees . . . However, in order that the Union may determine which new hires may acquire seniority, the Employer . . . will notify the Union, within ten (10) days after hiring any new employee, whether he was hired as a temporary or probationary. Any temporary employee will not work in excess of one hundred and twenty (120) days within a calendar year.

QUESTIONS

1. Carefully examine the relevant contractual provisions. Which (if any) provisions are supportive of the union's position? Of the employer's position?
2. Is there any real difference between a "temporary employee" and a "contractor" in this case? Discuss.
3. Should the employer have sent its notice of proposed contracting out to the union office, or is this not a real issue? Why would the union local complain about this notification procedure?
4. What should the arbitrator decide? (Evaluate the union's suggested remedy if the arbitrator should find for the union's position.)

Case 40

Health Insurance Coverage Unilaterally Changed by Public Employer

Employer County of Lawrence, Pennsylvania

Union Lawrence County Court Appointed Employee Organization (LCCAEO)

BACKGROUND

The employer unilaterally changed the health care insurance on January 1, 2003. The union received communications from the employer indicating a change in the health care program was about to occur. Because of financial difficulties the employer decided to drop its nonbargaining employees from the group health insurance, and, in turn, Blue Cross–Blue Shield dropped the employer from coverage.

The union filed a grievance concerning the alleged violation of Article 11 (contained in the appendix to this case) of their collective bargaining agreement, which was denied—as were subsequent appeals through the grievance procedure. The employer alleged the grievance was not timely filed because it was filed three months after the union was first notified of the likelihood that the insurance was going to be changed.

POSITION OF THE UNION

The union contended that the grievance was timely filed, claimed that this was a class-action grievance, and that the five-day time limit concerning the filing of grievances spoke to individual grievances. The union negotiated in good faith and cooperated with the employer concerning the financial difficulties and the health insurance program until it became clear that the employer was going to violate the contract. It was then that the union filed its grievance.

The union contended that the employer violated Article 11 when it substituted Health America for the Select Blue/Point of Service Plan identified in Article 11. Clearly the Health America plan differed from the Select Blue Plan in several respects, all of which resulted in fewer benefits or greater costs to the bargaining unit employees. This was simply not consistent with the clear and plain language of Article 11 of the contract. Therefore, the union urged the arbitrator to find the grievance both timely and meritorious. The remedy requested was that the employer be ordered to return to the Select Blue/Point of Service Plan specified in Article 11 of the contract.

POSITION OF THE EMPLOYER

The employer contended that the grievance was not timely; that the union had only five days from the time it first learned of the contract violation in which to file a grievance. It did not matter that the union was involved in negotiations with the employer or was exploring alternatives with the employer to filing a grievance to remedy its alleged problems with the changes in Article 11. The grievance was untimely and therefore could not be heard on its merits.

The employer had the right, which it exercised, to remove its nonbargaining personnel from the coverage of the Select Blue Plan. It did so as a matter of financial exigency. What the union then argued is that because Blue Cross–Blue Shield decided to cancel the employer's plan with respect to the remaining (bargaining unit) employees, the employer somehow violated the contract. This contention was absurd on its face. The employer did not have the right of control and therefore the "impossibility doctrine" must hold sway and the arbitrator must deny the grievance as being without merit.

Appendix

Relevant Contract Language

Article 11

HEALTH INSURANCE. Employees shall be enrolled, at the appropriate level in Select Blue/Point of Service Plan. Employees will have a common provider directory of both Ohio and Pennsylvania physicians and hospitals. Employees will have a $10.00 copayment for visits to a physician's office, and a $10.00 copayment for prescription drugs (brand name and generic).

QUESTIONS

1. Is the grievance timely? When does the clock begin to toll: when the negotiations cease or when the union becomes aware that something was amiss?
2. What is the impossibility doctrine? Does it really apply to these facts and circumstances? Why?
3. Did the employer violate Article 11? Why? If you were the arbitrator, how would you rule in this case? Why?

Case 41

A Changed Remedy for Misassignments

Company Pierce Company, Upland, Indiana

Union Retail, Wholesale & Department Store Union, Unit D

BACKGROUND

On April 24, 1990, the company's human resources manager, Esther Daly,[1] sent a letter to Viola Musgrove, president of the union, which stated in part:

> This will serve to confirm items discussed in our meeting Tuesday, April 17, 1990.
>
> Should the company erroneously assign overtime, the injured party will be made whole in the following manner: Within thirty days after the matter is brought to the Company's attention, the Company, at the employee's request, will make available the same amount of overtime work to the employee.

The union filed a grievance on April 26, 1990, charging that the company had violated provisions of the collective bargaining agreement, including, but not limited to, Article 7—Seniority, Section 2.[2] The union requested that the company "rescind the policy on overtime as stated in your letter of April 24, 1990."

In denying the grievance, the company responded that its "policy on overtime will be administered in a fair and equal way." The grievance was not resolved and eventually was carried to arbitration.

TESTIMONY AND POSITION OF THE UNION

Union President Viola Musgrove testified that at a grievance meeting on April 17, 1990, Giles Holiday, general manager, had announced that the company intended to change the practice on overtime payments that were to be made to rectify errors in overtime assignments. Holiday had stated that, if overtime was available and the senior employee was overlooked, that employee would not be paid automatically. Rather, he or she would be offered overtime on a makeup basis within the next 30 days, if the employee advised the company of the error in overtime assignment within three days of the error. According to Musgrove, this was the first time in 24 years that the company had announced such a policy. In the past, the company had always paid the senior employee for overtime assignment errors and did not remedy them by makeup overtime.

Musgrove testified that at the April 17 meeting the company's human resources manager, Esther Daly, had stated that the company did not have a big problem with errors in overtime assignments, but she wanted to have a better and fairer policy in place.

Dorsey Alexander, a full-time union staff representative who had serviced the company for 13 months, was also at the April 17, 1990, grievance meeting. He testified

[1] The names of all individuals are disguised.

[2] See the appendix for relevant contractual provisions.

substantially to the same effect as union President Musgrove. Alexander noted that when Ms. Daly had indicated that overtime misassignments were "not much of a problem," she had stated that in the previous 10 years there had been only two erroneous overtime assignments, and the eligible senior employees were paid for these errors.

In its post-hearing brief, the union argued that the company was bound by past practice to continue paying for erroneous overtime assignments, rather than giving makeup overtime assignments as a remedy. The union claimed that simply offering an employee an opportunity to make up improperly lost hours at a later date would not be an adequate remedy. The injured employee was entitled to work those hours at the time the hours were available. The injured employee should not be expected to work at a time more convenient to the employer, or at the discretion of a supervisor. The proper way to discourage supervisory errors or favoritism in making overtime assignments was to hold the company liable for breaches of contract by awarding pay to the employee who failed to get his or her proper assignment.

The union urged that its grievance be sustained, and that the company be directed to rescind the new overtime misassignment policy asserted in its letter of April 24, 1990.

TESTIMONY AND POSITION OF THE COMPANY

General manager Giles Holiday testified that at the April 17 meeting the company had notified the union that it intended to change the manner of paying for erroneously assigned overtime, but there was no intent whatsoever to change the collective bargaining agreement with respect to the manner of making overtime assignments.

Human resources manager Esther Daly testified that the company was not bound to any so-called past practice, since—to her knowledge—there had been only two erroneous overtime assignments during the past 10 years. The company felt that it had the reserved right under the contract to change the remedy for mistaken overtime assignments. It made no economic sense to pay an employee for not working just because there had been an unintentional supervisory error. The company's new policy, which was provided to the union in April 1990, would be a fair and equitable remedy, and this new policy did not in any way alter the contract. In its post-hearing brief, the company contended:

> The Company does not propose to change any overtime policy but only proposes a different remedy for aggrieved employees who erroneously were not assigned overtime.
>
> The Company on April 17, 1990, notified the union committee that in the future employees erroneously assigned overtime would be made whole as follows:
>
> "Should the Company erroneously assign overtime the injured party will be made whole in the following manner: Within thirty days after the matter is brought to the Company's attention, the Company, at the employee's request, will make available the same amount of overtime work to the employee."
>
> This was confirmed in a letter to the union dated April 24th. The union presented a grievance dated April 26th citing Article VII, Section 2. This article states the Company agrees to invoke the rule of seniority in a reasonable and equal way, giving preference to the senior employee where he possesses the necessary qualifications to do the work.

By making available the overtime within 30 days the Company is not violating Article 7, Section 2. Nor is the Company violating any section of the current contract as the contract is silent on the remedy to correct overtime errors.

The company urged that the union grievance be denied.

Appendix

Relevant Contractual Provisions

Article IV—Hours of Work and Overtime

Section 7. When overtime work is necessary the overtime work shall be offered to senior employees currently holding the classification and the work to be performed in the department. A shift overtime will be performed by employees working on the A shift, unless declined. B shift overtime will be performed by the employees working on the B shift, unless declined. C shift overtime will be performed by the employees working on the C shift, unless declined. If these employees refuse the overtime, the following will apply.

STEP 1: Saturday overtime for less than three shifts shall be offered to employees currently holding classification in department by seniority.

STEP 2: From the qualified coded availability list by plant seniority.

STEP 3: Qualified probationary employees.

STEP 4: The company can require the least senior qualified employees on the plant seniority list to work the overtime starting with qualified probationary employees.

Section 8. The above procedure will be followed except that employees will be permitted to continue working on work being performed at the end of their shift irrespective of seniority, not to exceed forty-five (45) minutes. When this work exceeds forty-five (45) minutes the above procedure will be followed except where it is impractical for the company to follow this procedure, either through the inability to contact employees, available employees are not qualified to do the work involved, or an emergency occurs.

Section 9. Scheduled overtime will be posted by 11:00 A.M. of the third day of the work week. Employees affected by the overtime will advise the company on the fourth day of the work week of their intent to work by their first break.

Article VII—Seniority

Section 2. The Company agrees to continue to invoke the rule of seniority for employees in a reasonable and equal way, giving preference to the senior employee where he possesses the necessary qualifications to do the work. The qualifications of any employee to do the work shall continue to be determined by the Company in accordance with the following factors: skill on work previously performed for the Company, job knowledge, attendance, and physical fitness. Any determination made by the Company as to an employee's qualifications may be challenged through the grievance procedure.

QUESTIONS

1. Why would the company and union pursue this case to arbitration when the problem involved occurred quite infrequently? Discuss.
2. Analyze the union's arguments and the company's arguments. Which are the most, and which the least, persuasive?
3. Arbitrators have often differed concerning the weight that should be afforded to past practices in interpretation and application of contract language.[3] Was the company bound to continue its previous practice (policy) concerning payments for erroneous overtime assignments? Why, or why not?

---

[3] See Frank Elkouri and Edna Asper Elkouri, *How Arbitration Works,* 4th ed. (Washington, D.C.: Bureau of National Affairs, 1985), pp. 437–56.

Case 42

Probation for the Teacher

Employer Jefferson County Board of Education (Kentucky)

Union Jefferson County Teachers' Association

BACKGROUND

During the 1989–90 school year, Roy Hastings,[1] a middle-school teacher with 19 years' experience in the system who had been recently transferred from teaching in an elementary school, was involved in a classroom incident during which he overturned a desk and threw a stapler. No one was injured and no property damage occurred. Following an investigation, the school principal, Helen Frieman, issued a report called an E-2 report, dated May 31, 1990. Hastings received a copy, which read:

> We discussed the outcome of Mr. Rupert Tuttle's investigation dated May 30, 1990. While you did admit throwing the stapler, you stated that you do not throw objects when you become upset as stated in the writeup. You also wanted to make it clear that you attempted to set up the desk with one hand and it lost its balance.
>
> I then told you that you need to refrain from throwing anything in the classroom or acting in any way other than professional which will only serve to downgrade your reputation. We then discussed the need for more alternatives to student conduct.

Hastings disputed some of the statements contained in the E-2 report. However, because of the intervening summer recess, he did not meet with his principal to discuss the matter until September 5, 1990, at a Level 1-B grievance meeting.[2] The meeting was attended by his union representative, Jane Seeger, and Principal Frieman. The meeting was apparently successful and the matter appeared to be resolved to everyone's satisfaction. Seeger followed up with a letter to the principal, dated October 11, 1990, summarizing her notes of the meeting:

> This letter is to verify the agreement we reached on September 5, 1990, concerning the grievance initiated by Hastings. This was a Level 1-B meeting to resolve the issue of an E-2 dated 5/31/90 which Hastings received at the end of the 1989–90 school year.
>
> We agreed that you would keep this E-2 in your school file for the 1990–91 school year. If there are no incidents during this time, the E-2 dated 5/31/90 will be destroyed; i.e., it will *never* be sent to his permanent employee personnel file.
>
> If this does not meet with your understanding of our agreement, please notify me immediately. Thank you for your cooperation in this matter.

However, while this first incident was being resolved, Hastings was involved in a second classroom incident. A student's parent telephoned the principal complaining that his son had been mistreated by Hastings. At Frieman's recommendation, the complaint was

[1] The names of all individuals are disguised.

[2] See the appendix for relevant contractual provisions.

reduced to writing in a letter from the child's father, dated October 19, 1990. The principal met with Hastings on October 24. Hastings was informed of the complaint, but he did not admit to the event in question. He volunteered to phone the parent and resolve the problem. On October 30, Frieman sent Hastings the following letter summarizing the matter:

> This letter serves as a summary of parent concern disposition. On October 22, 1990, the attached letter was received from Mr. John McDonald. On October 24, 1990, you and I met to address the complaint. You told me at that time you did not recall the incident. I reminded you to keep your hands off the students. You offered to call Mr. McDonald to discuss the letter. I asked you to call by the end of the day on 10/25/90. I called the John McDonald residence and spoke with the grandmother. I told her that you and I had a conference and asked her to tell Mr. McDonald to expect a call from you.
>
> On October 29, I met with you to bring closure to the complaint. You told me you had called Mr. McDonald and he seemed "satisfied" with the call.
>
> We concluded our conference with me reminding you to watch how you talk to students and to watch your contact with students.

Subsequently, Roy Hastings had occasion to review the contents of his permanent personnel file. He discovered that the E-2 document of May 31, 1990, had been inserted into this file. After discussing this with his union representative, he filed the following grievance:

> The Board, through its agents, violated the JCTA/JCBE Agreement by taking adverse action against the grievant, improperly disciplining the grievant, and placing improper material in the employee's personnel file. Such actions are in direct violation of Article IX, Employee Discipline; and Article XXIX, Grievance Procedure.

The parties were unable to resolve the grievance in the first three steps of the grievance procedure. The union, therefore, exercised its right to arbitrate under the terms of the agreement. The parties agreed on the following submission:

> Did the Jefferson County School Board, through its representative, Principal Helen Frieman, violate the Collective Bargaining Agreement by placing a Form E-2, which recorded a classroom incident, in the grievant's personnel file, and if so, what shall the remedy be?

POSITION OF THE UNION

The union argued that the testimony of both Jane Seeger and Roy Hastings proved that, following the September 5, 1990, meeting, they understood that the E-2 report would be held in the principal's office. Thus, the form should never have found its way into Hastings's personnel file. The union also held that the E-2 was apparently already in his file at the time of the September 5 meeting, and that Frieman had deliberately withheld that information from them. Placing the E-2 in Hastings's file constituted a violation of the Level 1-B resolution of his first grievance.

The union asserted that Hastings had not been informed that the McDonald incident of October 1990 constituted a violation of his probation. As a consequence, he had no way of defending himself with respect to the parent's accusation and Frieman's decision. Following his meeting with Principal Frieman on October 29, 1990, he was convinced that the matter had been handled appropriately and was closed. The union argued that

Hastings had complied with the conditions of the first grievance settlement, and thus the E-2 report should have been destroyed.

Finally, the union pointed out that the purpose of the E-2 form was to record the notes taken during a conference or investigation and should not have been used as an instrument for adding a disciplinary action to an employee's personnel file.

The union requested that the arbitrator order the removal of the E-2 report from Hastings's file, remove him from a probationary status, and expunge from his files all references to the McDonald incident.

POSITION OF THE BOARD

The board held that it had not violated either the collective bargaining agreement or the resolution of the Level 1-B meeting on September 5, 1990.

Principal Helen Frieman testified that in consideration of Hastings's 19 years as a teacher in the system and in order to provide him with an opportunity to adjust to the new classroom environment in the middle school, she had agreed to expunge the record of the incident from his file, provided he completed the 1990–91 year without further incident. She admitted that she accepted the letter of October 11, 1990, from union representative, Jane Seeger, without having read it. She stated that they had reached complete agreement regarding the probationary period.

Frieman testified that following the October 29 meeting with Hastings concerning the second 1990 (or McDonald) incident, she had interviewed two other children from the class, and she had determined that this incident did constitute a violation of Hastings's probationary period.

In addressing the use of the E-2 report, the principal stated that the form was routinely used as a record in an employee's personnel file, such as it was used in this case. She said that she did not remember when the E-2 report had been placed in Hastings's file.

The board argued that whether or not the E-2 form resided in the principal's office or the grievant's personnel file was irrelevant, since the desired outcome was that it would be destroyed if Hastings behaved appropriately during his probationary period.

Finally, the board pointed out that the principal was the individual charged with the responsibility of judging whether or not the second incident constituted a violation of the Level 1-B meeting held on September 5, 1990, and that she alone should determine whether Hastings had complied with the probation or not.

The board urged that the arbitrator deny the grievance in its entirety.

Appendix

Relevant Provisions of the Agreement

Article IX—Employee Discipline

Section A. Conditions for Just Cause. A.1. The employee has had opportunity to have foreknowledge of the possible or probable disciplinary consequences of the conduct or performance . . .

A.3. Before disciplining or terminating the employee, a fair and objective investigation was made . . . and the decision was based on substantial evidence or proof . . .

A.5. The degree of formal discipline . . . reasonably relates to (*a*) the seriousness of the employee's proven offense and (*b*) the record of the employee's service with the Employer.

* * * * *

Section C. The employee must be afforded an opportunity to answer the complaint and meet with the complainant within two weeks of receipt of the complaint.

Article XXIX—Grievance Procedure

A. Any employee covered by this Contract who feels that Management has violated the terms of the Contract or who believes that he/she has been treated unjustly, may file a grievance which shall be in writing and presented to that individual's immediate supervisor . . .

B. The first step of the grievance procedure (Level 1-B) . . .

C. The second step . . .

D. The third step . . .

E. If the parties are unable to resolve the grievance, either party may request that it be submitted to arbitration . . .

QUESTIONS

1. Did the principal, Helen Frieman, follow appropriate contractual due process in handling this case? Why, or why not?
2. The board held that it was Frieman's sole responsibility to determine whether or not Hastings had violated his probationary period. Are there any limitations to this right? If so, what are they?
3. Did Frieman improperly discipline Hastings in violation of the just cause provisions of the contract? Why, or why not?
4. How should the arbitrator rule in this case? Explain.

Case 43

Appeal to Arbitration: A Day Late?

Company Baltimore Mack Trucks

Union International Association of Machinists, District Lodge 12

BACKGROUND

The company in this matter discharged an employee for having threatened to damage another employee's vehicle on February 12, 2004. On February 13, 2004, the union filed a grievance on behalf of this discharged employee protesting the discharge. After several mutual extensions of the applicable time limits, the parties held a Step 3 grievance meeting on March 17, 2004. The parties were unable to reach a mutually satisfactory resolution to the grievance. At the conclusion of the meeting, the union informed the company that they would probably demand arbitration of this matter. On March 18, 2004, the company sent the union its written Step 3 decision denying the grievance. On April 13, 2004, the union submitted a request for arbitration to the Federal Mediation and Conciliation Service, and sent a copy of the request to the company.

Applicable Contract Language

> Step 3 (a). In the event that the grievance has not been adjusted at Step 3, it may, within ten (10) scheduled working days from the completion of Step 2 be referred to a meeting between a representative of the Union and a Company representative for resolution. If the grievance is not settled at the Step 3 meeting, it may be referred to arbitration within ten (10) working days by submitting the matter to the Federal Mediation and Conciliation Service, Area VII . . .
> (B) . . . The arbitrator shall have no power to add to or subtract from, or modify any terms of the Agreement . . .

POSITION OF THE COMPANY

The company's position in this matter was that the union appealed the grievance from Step 3 to arbitration in an untimely manner. The clear and unambiguous language of the parties' collective bargaining agreement required that "if the grievance is not settled at the Step 3 meeting, it may be referred to arbitration within ten working days . . ." The union did not comply with this time limit.

The record clearly shows that the union did not appeal this grievance to arbitration by submitting the matter to the Federal Mediation and Conciliation Service until April 13, 2004. The third-step meeting was concluded on March 17, 2004, and therefore the appeal to arbitration was 26 days after the conclusion of the third-step meeting. The union was therefore 16 days tardy in their appeal to arbitration. Further, the arbitration clause of the collective bargaining agreement limited the authority of the arbitrator. The arbitrator may not add to, subtract from, or modify the agreement between the parties. To find that this matter is arbitrable would require the arbitrator to modify the parties' time limits, and he has no authority to do so. Therefore, the company urged that this grievance was not procedurally arbitrable.

POSITION OF THE UNION

The union's position in this matter was that this grievance was arbitrable. The union made two separate contentions, either of which was sufficient to find this matter was appealed to arbitration within the time limits and to compel the arbitration of this grievance.

The union contended that the parties' Step 3 meeting was tardy, and as a result management implicitly waived the deadline with it when it did not hold the Step 3 meeting within the specified time limits. By not adhering to the contractually specified time limits to hold the Step 3 meeting, everything beyond that meeting deadline was delayed.

The union also contended that management did not raise the issue of arbitrability at any point in the process. Management first raised the issue of procedural arbitrability at the arbitration hearing. By delaying this contention until the hearing, management had waived its right to challenge the arbitrability of this grievance.

It was the union's position that this matter was procedurally arbitrable and that the arbitrator should hear this grievance on its merits.

QUESTIONS

1. The clear and unambiguous language of grievance procedure places time limits on holding a Step 3 meeting. Did management unilaterally violate this time limit? If not, what is the implication for the union's first argument?
2. Did the union file for arbitration within the prescribed time limits? What are the time limits, and when did the union file?
3. Is the limitation on the arbitrator's authority binding in this case? Explain.
4. Did management implicitly or explicitly waive its right to argue arbitrability by waiting until the arbitration hearing to make this contention? Explain.

Case 44

Denial of the Safety Incentive Prize

Company Chevron Chemical Company (Ortho Division), Maryland Heights, Missouri

Union Automotive, Petroleum, and Allied Industries Employees Union, Teamsters Local No. 618

BACKGROUND

The company plant produced consumer products under the Ortho product line; some 120 operations and maintenance employees in the plant were represented by the union.

The union grievance heard in arbitration in this case had been filed on February 13, 1991, by Jack Cason,[1] a production operator. The grievance included in relevant part the following complaint:

> Failure to comply with safety program. People that had OSHA recordable injuries still received their full safety award money while others did not.

Introduced in the arbitration hearing was a copy of a document entitled, "1990 Safety Incentive Programs."[2] The administration of these programs was the focal point of the dispute before the arbitrator. The parties stipulated that there was no provision in the labor-management agreement directly covering this matter. However, the parties also stipulated that the matter was properly before the arbitrator for determination as provided in the grievance-arbitration procedure in the collective bargaining agreement.

The issue for the arbitrator was submitted as follows:

> Did the company violate the terms of its "1990 Safety Incentive Programs" when it denied Jack Cason a 1990 monetary prize?
>
> If so, what should be the appropriate remedy?

TESTIMONY AND POSITION OF THE UNION

Giving primary testimony for the union was the grievant, Jack Cason, who said that he had been employed by the company for approximately 12 years. According to Cason, he had incurred an OSHA recordable incident in 1990, but still he should have received an incentive prize under the company's "Safety Incentive Programs," yet he did not. Cason's injury was to his right elbow area; it was identified as "ulnar tunnel syndrome" (somewhat similar to carpal tunnel syndrome) caused by repetitive motions.

The injury was work-related and caused by repetitive arm movements in his job. Cason said he had filed his grievance because another employee, John Alvino, had received a $160 safety prize for 1990, despite the fact that Alvino also had an OSHA recordable incident.

[1] The names of all individuals are disguised.

[2] See the appendix for relevant provisions of this program.

Cason said that the company had told him that Alvino was not personally responsible for his injury, and therefore Alvino was still eligible for the safety incentive prize.

Testifying next for the union was Dorothy Dobbs, union shop steward. She stated that in contrast to John Alvino's receiving a prize despite his OSHA recordable incident, other employees were denied a monthly incentive prize of $40 for which by the same logic they should have been eligible. She indicated that this had occurred in March or May of 1990. Dobbs said she believed that Alvino had received favorable treatment because Alvino was very active in a movement attempting to decertify the union in 1990. She stated that Alvino had "bragged" about his role in attempting to have the union decertified. A decertification election was held by the National Labor Relations Board in early 1991, but the union won the election. Dobbs stated that Alvino was one of the observers at the decertification election as part of the group that was trying to decertify the union.

Summarizing the union position, Jeffrey Cage, union assistant business representative, stated that neither he nor other union officers had ever received copies of the company's "Safety Incentive Programs" until Jack Cason's grievance was filed. This was a clear example of disparate and discriminatory treatment. The company had used its own safety program to show direct favoritism for John Alvino, who had been involved in an attempt to decertify the union. The union requested the arbitrator to grant Jack Cason $160 for equitable treatment under the "Safety Incentive Programs," and to direct the company to treat employees equally in the future.

TESTIMONY AND POSITION OF THE COMPANY

Giving testimony for the company was Bradley Genther, operations supervisor, who stated that he was responsible for production and warehouse facilities. Jack Cason reported to a first-line supervisor who in turn reported to Genther. Genther stated that the "1990 Safety Incentive Programs" were implemented in an effort to reduce frequency of accidents. The programs were developed with the participation of a safety committee. Seven of the 10 members of this committee were employees in the bargaining unit. Genther stated that an occupational injury absence caused by repetitive work motions was an OSHA recordable incident; this excluded Jack Cason from a 1990 safety award. Cason had been absent for a period as a consequence of his injury, and had received payment from the state workers' compensation system.

Genther testified that John Alvino did have an absence period in 1990. This had come about when he was sent to a training department facility to have blood drawn as part of a blood test monitoring program. Alvino developed an infection that caused him to be absent for several weeks. This had been defined as an OSHA recordable incident because of OSHA regulations. However, Genther stated, company management had met and decided to pay Alvino the $160 safety incentive award, because his OSHA recordable incident was not in any way a direct result of performing his job duties. No one was penalized because Alvino received this payment. Alvino's absence was technically an OSHA recordable incident, but the company was trying to treat Alvino fairly in regard to the overall intent of the "Safety Incentive Programs."

The position of the company was summarized by Dexter Sohn, labor relations counselor. Sohn contended that the company's "1990 Safety Incentive Programs" had been developed in conjunction with bargaining unit employees. The purpose was to assist in prevention of accidents and illnesses, and the programs were not a contractual matter under the parties' negotiated agreement. Sohn claimed that the company felt that John Alvino was entitled to the safety incentive award of $160, since his OSHA recordable incident was not directly related to performance on the job. Sohn asserted that the reason why some employees had not received the $40 monthly prize in question was that during the same period other employees had incurred OSHA recordable incidents besides Alvino. Sohn contended that he had been unable in his review of the case to find any evidence that indicated Alvino had been treated favorably because of his involvement in the union decertification campaign. The company urged the arbitrator to deny the union grievance.

Appendix

Relevant Provisions of the "Safety Incentive Programs" Document

Maryland Heights 1990 Safety Program

X. Safety Incentive Programs—1990. Safety incentive programs are developed and used for the purpose of heightening safety awareness and rewarding exemplary safety performance. The programs that will be used in 1990 were developed by a safety incentive committee made up mostly of O&M employees. The programs are based on individual and plant safety performance.

A. For every *individual* that completes the calendar year of 1990 without having an OSHA recordable injury or illness, $160.00 will be awarded.

B. For each calendar month in which the *entire plant* experiences no OSHA recordable injuries or illnesses, each person will be awarded $40.00.

C. When the entire plant completes the first six months of 1990 with 6 OSHA incidents or less, a $5,000.00 pot will be divided by all employees. The same program will be in effect for the second half of 1990.

Definitions

OCCUPATIONAL INJURY:

Any injury such as a cut, fracture, sprain, amputation, etc., which results from a work accident or from an exposure involving a single incident in the work environment.

OCCUPATIONAL ILLNESS:

Any abnormal condition or disorder, other than one resulting from an occupational injury, caused by exposure to environmental factors associated with employment. It includes acute and chronic illnesses or diseases which may be caused by inhalation, absorption, ingestion, repetitive motion, or direct contact.

OSHA RECORDABLE INCIDENT:

An occupational illness or injury as stated above that requires treatment by a physician or results in lost workdays, work restrictions, prescription of medicines, or therapeutic measures. This list is not complete but implies the recordability criteria.

QUESTIONS

1. Why would the company agree to arbitrate this case when the issue arose under a document that was not part of the parties' collective bargaining agreement?
2. Should the company have denied a safety prize to John Alvino, even though his OSHA recordable incident was not due to his work performance? Explain.
3. To what degree should the fact that John Alvino was openly supportive of the union decertification effort be weighed by the arbitrator? Discuss.
4. How should the arbitrator decide this case? Why?

Case 45

Demoted or Reclassified?

Company Lord Aerospace Products (Division of Lord Corporation), Erie, Pennsylvania

Union International Association of Machinists and Aerospace Workers, District Lodge 83, Local Lodge No. 1968

BACKGROUND

For several years prior to the grievance in this case, the company had sought to have its toolroom operate in what it characterized as a "self-directed mode." Management had hoped to develop a shop environment in which toolmakers would help manage their own day-to-day activities and develop a greater sense of responsibility for the quality and quantity of their work. Management expected that obtaining greater employee involvement through "participative management" would improve quality and efficiency and achieve greater customer satisfaction.

The company had created four Lead Toolmaker positions at the start of the self-direction project, and four men assumed these positions after bidding for the jobs.[1]

After giving the new organization structure a trial of several years, management came to believe that the Lead Toolmaker position, as it had been conceived, was part of the problem with the project. Self-direction had not worked out as planned. Management concluded that the Lead Toolmakers, in practice, had relieved the majority of the toolmakers of their responsibilities for quality and quantity. Their continuous role as advisors and helpers had prevented the rest of the toolmakers from feeling ownership of their work.

In April 1991, management informed the four Lead Toolmakers of its decision to vacate the position of Lead Toolmaker and to assign them to their former positions as journeyman toolmakers at a rate of $1.02 less than they had received as Lead Toolmakers.

The union on May 16, 1991, filed the following grievance:

> On April 25, 1991, Dan Goetz, Harold Hannigan, Byron Smith, and Ben Borgatta,[2] were informed by their Facilitator Henry Beecher and their Manager George Hall that effective April 29, 1991, their duties as Lead Toolmakers were no longer needed, and that their rates of pay would be decreased to those of a top "A" Toolmaker. The aforementioned aggrieved members and the Union feel that this action is contrary to the present agreement, and that the Company should do whatever is necessary to make the aggrieved members whole.

The grievance was eventually carried to arbitration.

[1] See the appendix for the job summary of the Lead Toolmaker position and for relevant contractual provisions.

[2] The names of all individuals are disguised.

POSITION OF THE UNION

The union pointed out that all four grievants possessed the requisite skills, training, and knowledge to perform their jobs. All had graduated from apprentice to journeyman under the job-training program at Lord Aerospace. In fact, two of them, Goetz and Borgatta, had completed their apprenticeship programs in three years, rather than the normal four.

The company's action violated Article I (2) and Article IV (3) (a), which required that it negotiate with the union on matters of wages, hours, and other conditions of employment. In the past, the company had always discussed and negotiated changes that affected employees in the bargaining unit, and the union insisted that it do so in this instance. By reclassifying the Lead Toolmakers as toolmakers, management had demoted them and reduced their wage rate. The company could not do so without the consent of the union.

The union argued that the job classification of Lead Toolmaker had first appeared in the contract in 1975, and that it had remained there to this day. The company could not now eliminate that classification and remove the Lead Toolmakers from the contract without agreement from the union.

Finally, the union argued that if management felt that the Lead Toolmakers were not effective in their role as it had been defined in their job descriptions, management should have given them clear-cut supervisory responsibilities and paid them accordingly.

The union petitioned that the arbitrator uphold the grievance in its entirety. The four demoted grievants should be returned to the classification of Lead Toolmaker and made whole for all losses they had sustained because of the improper demotions.

POSITION OF THE COMPANY

The company contended that it had not violated the contract, and that Article V (1) bestowed on management the right to restructure the toolroom and to assign and reassign employees to meet the needs of the organization. The company had always negotiated on matters designated in the contract; this was simply a case where the contract did not apply.

The company stated that the four Lead Toolmakers were not disciplined, demoted, or punished. They were reassigned to their former positions of journeyman toolmakers, because the company had decided that the position of Lead Toolmaker currently was no longer needed. The job classification of Lead Toolmaker had not been eliminated; it was only being vacated at this time. In previous years, the Lead Toolmaker position had not always been filled, depending on the company's needs. What the company had done was to determine again that there was no present need for the Lead Toolmaker position in the toolroom. If in the future the company decided to again fill the position of Lead Toolmaker, the grievants would be afforded the opportunity to apply for and/or bid for the position.

Management reiterated its position that the performance of the grievants was entirely satisfactory. They had not been demoted. While their wage rate had been reduced by $1.02 per hour, they were receiving the top rate for the toolmaker classification.

The company requested that the arbitrator deny the grievance.

Appendix

Relevant Provisions of the Agreement

Article I—Recognition

2. The Company will bargain collectively with the Union with respect to rates of pay, wages, hours, and other conditions of employment involving the employees in the above-stated classifications, provided however, that this Agreement shall finally dispose of all demands of the Company and the Union which have heretofore been made or which might be the subject of collective bargaining throughout the period of this Agreement, not intending, however, to preclude the presentation of or processing of grievances hereunder.

Article IV—Settlement of Grievances

3. a. Only matters concerning the interpretation and application of the terms of this Agreement are subject to arbitration. However, differences with respect to changes in the existing wage structure, or differences with respect to terms of a new Agreement, will not be subject to arbitration. The impartial arbitrator shall have no jurisdiction or power to amend, modify, supplement, vary, disregard, or contravene any provision of this Agreement, or any supplement thereto, in any respect whatsoever.

* * * * *

Article V—Management Responsibilities

1. The management of the plant and the direction of the working forces, including: the right to direct, plan and control plant operations; the right to select, assign, transfer, suspend, promote, demote, or terminate employees on the basis of knowledge, training, skill, and performance; to terminate or discharge employees for justifiable causes and to relieve employees of duty because of lack of work or for other legitimate reasons; and the right to introduce new and improved methods and facilities and the management of the properties is vested exclusively in the Company. It is also understood that it is the sole responsibility of the Company to use whatever instructional and corrective procedures it deems appropriate in any and all cases involving employee performance that is unsatisfactory in the opinion of Management, provided however, that if an employee is demoted, suspended, or discharged following the application of such procedures, he may file a grievance and the case may be processed through arbitration for a review as to whether the demotion, suspension, or discharge was for just cause. Any action taken under this Article shall not circumvent, supersede, or in any manner conflict with the expressed terms of this Agreement.

Job Summary for Lead Toolmaker

Assume complete responsibility for the manufacture of any complex tooling. Set up and operate all machines involved. Perform necessary assembly and bench work. Direct other Tool Room personnel when assigned to him by the Supervisor. Heat treat as needed. Also responsible for final assembly and acceptance at inspection by the Gage Room.

Specific Duties. The duties of the job include, but are not limited to:

1. Make and repair any type of mold, die, gage, jig and fixture, including the most complex.
2. Machine and fabricate complex parts to close tolerances to ensure acceptable final assembly.
3. Direct other Tool Room personnel as required to complete assignments.
4. Usually work from complex prints; may also work from simple prints, models, sketches, and verbal instructions. Use shop and machinist's handbooks.
5. Perform work of toolmakers A, B, and C as required.
6. Perform other similar and related duties.

QUESTIONS

1. What limits do Articles I, IV, and V place on the union's right to participate in or contest any decision regarding the reorganization of the toolroom and the transfer of the four grievants out of their jobs as Lead Toolmakers? What limits do these Articles place on management?
2. Were the four grievants demoted or reassigned? Explain.
3. Should company management have discussed the decision with the union prior to implementing it, even if management felt it was not obligated contractually to do so? Discuss.
4. How should the arbitrator rule in the case? Explain.

Case 46

Voluntary Resignation or Layoff?

Company Quantum Chemical Corporation/UST Division, Port Arthur, Texas

Union Oil, Chemical, and Atomic Workers International Union (OCAW), Local No. 4-288

BACKGROUND

On June 27, 1991, the company announced plans to shut down parts of three of its less efficient production units, one of which was located at the Port Arthur, Texas, plant. The human resources manager, Otis Gullion,[1] entered into discussions with the union with regard to the payment of severance pay. He advised the union that each case would be handled on an individual basis.

On August 2, 1991, the company issued a 45-day-notice letter to the employees who were scheduled for layoff. The grievant in this case, Ramona Hawthorne, and other OCAW employees received this letter. Hawthorne's letter indicated a layoff date of September 16, 1991.

On receiving the notice of layoff, Hawthorne commenced looking for a job. She had worked as a laboratory technician for the company, but her efforts to find work in that capacity elsewhere revealed that no such positions were open. Hawthorne had been a teacher prior to coming to work for the company, so she began to look for work in the teaching profession. Most permanent teaching jobs in the area had been filled, since most schools in the area opened August 21, 1991. Hawthorne was eventually offered a substitute teaching job in mathematics at a junior high school, and she worked in that capacity on Wednesday, August 21, Thursday, August 22, and Friday, August 23. Since she was scheduled to work at the company on those days, she called in "sick" to cover her absences when in fact she was performing substitute teaching work. On Monday, August 26, she was offered a permanent job as a teacher at the school; by letter, Hawthorne resigned her employment with the company as of that date.

Ricardo Niechez, company labor relations supervisor, returned from his vacation on August 19, 1991. While reviewing attendance reports, he noticed that Ramona Hawthorne had reported sick on two separate occasions over a short period of time. He subsequently learned that there was some reason to believe that Hawthorne had found other employment. He talked to Hawthorne by telephone on August 23. She admitted that she was working as a substitute school teacher. She also stated that she had reported off sick on several days, even though she was not sick. Niechez advised Hawthorne that he was going to investigate the situation, and that she could be in "serious trouble" for reporting off sick when in fact she was working elsewhere. On receipt of Hawthorne's resignation letter on August 28, he canceled his investigation into the matter.

[1] The names of all individuals are disguised.

Subsequently, Otis Gullion advised Hawthorne that she was not eligible either for severance pay or recall rights, as a consequence of her voluntary resignation. Hawthorne and the union filed a grievance in protest of this management action.

The grievance was not resolved by the parties, and it was eventually submitted to arbitration. The parties stipulated that the issue for the arbitrator's determination was as follows:

> Did the Company violate the Agreement[2] by denying Ramona Hawthorne severance pay? If so, what is the appropriate remedy?

POSITION OF THE UNION

The union maintained that Ramona Hawthorne was entitled to severance pay under Article XVII, Section C, of the parties' collective agreement. She had met all the requirements for that benefit. She had a minimum of one year continuous employment, and she was laid off through no fault of her own, because of a reduction in work forces. As a result, under the contract's schedule of benefits, having two years of employment, Hawthorne was entitled to two weeks' severance pay. The denial of severance pay to her was arbitrary and unjust.

The union advanced arguments as rebuttal to the contentions of the company why it had denied Hawthorne her severance pay. The company had argued that Hawthorne had left prior to the effective day of the layoff, September 16, 1991, and therefore she was not entitled to severance pay. The union pointed out that there was no such requirement in the labor agreement, nor was there any practice to that effect. In fact, in a later layoff in spring 1992, a number of employees had left the company well before the effective date of their layoffs and had been given severance pay.

The company also had argued that Hawthorne had engaged in a false and deceitful act by reporting off sick, when in fact she was working as a substitute school teacher. The union countered that she had not been paid for the days she called in sick, nor did she request pay. No discipline was ever imposed on her. Hawthorne was not terminated for cause. She left the company because of a reduction in force, and she needed to find new employment. She voluntarily resigned on August 26, 1991. There was no provision in the contract barring her right to severance pay because of an early resignation or for improperly calling in sick under such circumstances as these.

POSITION OF THE COMPANY

The company contended that under the language of Article XVII, Section C, severance pay was not automatic. Certain eligibility requirements were set forth, and Ramona Hawthorne did not meet these requirements. She had received a contractually mandated 45-day layoff notice from the company, but she had not fulfilled this requirement because she had not worked until the layoff date. Hawthorne terminated her employment by a voluntary resignation prior to the layoff date of September 16, 1991.

The union had cited the layoff in February 1992, in support of its position. In this particular layoff, the company had determined that the layoff date would be April 16, 1992.

[2] See the appendix for relevant contractual provisions.

However, the company decided to release those employees scheduled for layoff in March 1992, but continued to make them whole in terms of wages and benefits until the layoff date of April 16, 1992. Severance pay and recall rights were given those employees until April 16, 1992. Thus, the affected individuals remained in the company's employment.

The company claimed that the weakness of the union's claim of severance pay for Ramona Hawthorne was a proposal made by the union in contractual negotiations in November 1991. At that time, the union had proposed that employees who were given a 45-day notice of layoff would not lose their rights to severance pay or recall rights, if they found employment elsewhere. This was precisely the Hawthorne case. The company had rejected the union proposal. The company maintained its position that employees who resigned or who left before the layoff date would not be eligible for severance pay.

The imposition of eligibility requirements for severance pay was essential to the company's efficient operation. When a layoff notice was given, the company had every right to expect those employees to remain until the effective date of their layoff. The well-planned and controlled downsizing by the company required that employees remain until their layoff date, so as not to jeopardize production, maintenance, and safety. An employee who resigned his or her employment prior to the effective date of the layoff forfeited severance and recall rights.

The company urged the arbitrator to deny the union grievance.

Appendix

Relevant Provisions of the Agreement

Article XVII—Additional Benefits

Section C. Severance Pay Plan. 1. The Severance Pay Plan has been incorporated herein and made part of this Agreement.

An employee shall be eligible for benefits hereunder, provided:

(1) They have had a minimum of one (1) year continuous employment by the Company immediately prior to the layoff date; and

(2) They are laid off through no fault of their own, because of a reduction in forces.

Amount of Benefits.

An eligible employee shall be entitled to receive severance pay based on their current rate at the time of separation in accordance with the following schedule:

1 yr. but less than 2 yrs. 1 wk's pay.

2 yrs. but less than 4 yrs. 2 wk's pay.

4 yrs. but less than 7 yrs. 3 wk's pay.

7 yrs. but less than 10 yrs. 4 wk's pay.

10 yrs. but less than 15 yrs. 5 wk's pay.

15 yrs. but less than 20 yrs. 7 wk's pay.

20 yrs. and over 9 wk's pay.

Payment of Benefits.

Payments under this Plan may be paid in a lump sum or in installments. Lump sums will not be paid when the layoff is presumed temporary.

Reemployment.

Upon recall an employee who has received all severance pay due shall be considered a new employee for severance pay purposes.

Under no conditions will severance pay for any employee exceed the maximum of nine (9) weeks.

QUESTIONS

1. Evaluate the arguments presented by the union on behalf of the grievant. Which do you consider the most/least persuasive?
2. Evaluate the arguments presented by the company. Which do you consider the most/least persuasive?
3. Should Ramona Hawthorne's "dishonesty," that is, calling in sick when she was working elsewhere, disqualify her from receiving severance pay?
4. What should the arbitrator decide? Why?

Case 47

The Doubtful Worker

Company Fraenkel Company, Olive Branch, Tennessee

Union Furniture Workers Division of the International Union of Electronic, Electrical, Machine, and Furniture Workers, Local No. 282

BACKGROUND

The company manufactured mattresses, boxsprings, and other bedding materials in Olive Branch, Tennessee, outside Memphis.

Anne Manion,[1] the grievant in this incident, was hired on February 15, 1991, and assigned to a job in sewing supply of the bedding department. She continued to work there until she was laid off on October 28, 1991, along with several others in the plant. She was recalled from layoff on November 22, 1991, but to a different job. Although in the same section and department, the new job was a production rather than a supply job, and it required that she work under output standards.

Manion was first notified of the recall by the assistant manager, Ron Steffin, in a telephone call. Manion immediately focused on the differences between the two jobs. Her supply job had no production standards, and Manion expressed deep fear that she would be unable to meet the production standards.

Manion's reluctance to return to work on the new job was discussed at length during two telephone conversations with Steffin on Friday, November 22. Most of their discussion focused on whether or not she was qualified to perform the work. Manion persisted in arguing that she would be unable to perform the work; Steffin was adamant that she could. He discussed the problem with Alice Moon, her supervisor, who also felt that Manion was qualified, since the duties of the job she had been performing and those of the new job were similar.

Steffin then wrote a letter that was delivered by certified mail on Monday, November 25. Manion neither reported for work on Monday nor otherwise communicated with the company that week. She was terminated on Friday, November 29, 1991.

The union then filed a grievance stating that the company had violated Article XI, Sections 5 and 7, of the labor agreement, and that Anne Manion was unqualified to perform the new job.[2] The union claimed that her termination was improper, and she should be reinstated and remain on layoff until such time as a job for which she was qualified opened up.

The parties were unable to resolve the dispute and selected an arbitrator to render a final and binding decision. The union and company agreed that the issue to be resolved was:

> Whether the grievant, Anne Manion, was discharged for just cause; if not, what is the proper remedy?

[1] The names of all individuals are disguised.

[2] See the appendix for relevant contractual clauses.

POSITION OF THE UNION

The union contended that Anne Manion did not possess the ability and qualifications to perform the job of sewing mattress panels, the job she had been recalled to perform. She had never before performed the work, and she could not have been said to be qualified without having had considerable training and experience on this new job.

In discussing the new job with Ron Steffin on Friday, November 22, Manion had asked him what would happen if she couldn't perform the work. According to her, he had told her she would be terminated. She stated that she told him she wanted to pass up this job and stay on layoff until something in supply came up. She told him she could not perform the job of sewing mattress panels, and she was afraid to try since she was sure she would fail at it.

The union argued that rather than being required to take a job she could not perform, Manion should have been offered a job in sewing boxsprings made vacant by the retirement of Debra Gribbons. Gribbons's job had instead been given to Pam Benson, who had less seniority than Manion, and Manion was now being offered Benson's job. The union asserted that the provisions of Article XII of the agreement had been violated.

The union pointed out that Manion had been laid off in October 1991, despite the fact that employees with less seniority who were sewing mattress panels had not been laid off. The company could not have it both ways. It was not proper for the company now to declare that Manion was qualified for this new job when she had not been thought to be sufficiently qualified to avoid layoff.

The union requested that the arbitrator uphold its position, and that Anne Manion be reinstated and made whole in every way.

POSITION OF THE COMPANY

Management maintained that Anne Manion was qualified to perform the job to which she had been recalled, sewing mattress panels. Several management witnesses asserted that her old job and the new one were very similar. Jerry Winters, assistant plant manager, testified in response to the question, "What was her former job?" as follows:

> Sewing borders and closing them up . . . It was about a 15-inch-wide strip of quilted material, about a quarter-inch thick, sewn together on the ends where it would have made a complete loop. And put it into a sewing machine and ran it through and it sewed the ends closed and cut off the edge where it would make a nice straight line and take all the threads and everything off and closed it, closed with threads kind of wrapped around it to make it nice and neat and straight . . . and then there was another sewing machine that she had so she could sew the corners up on. It was two processes she did.

When questioned about the new job to which Manion had been recalled, that is, sewing mattress panels, Winters said that supervisor Alice Moon had told him that Manion could do this job. Winters testified:

> Well, it's the same machine for doing the borders. It just has one needle added to it for doing the mattress panels. And there's a five-and-a-half-inch strip of cloth that's attached underneath the panel as it's run through the machine. But it's the same process. It's a rectangular panel, and you have to turn corners on it, whereas the other one was just running it straight through. It's the same identical machine used for the other process.

The assistant manager, Ron Steffin, stated that he had never told Manion that she would be terminated if she were unable to meet production standards on the new job. He had not heard Manion state that she wished to remain on layoff until a job opened up in supply. In any event, she did not have that choice.

Finally, the company pointed out that Article XI, Section 8(3), of the collective agreement required that she report for work on Monday, November 25. The contract provided that she must return to work within three days of having received the letter of recall. When she failed to report, the company had justifiably terminated her.

The company reiterated that it had met all the provisions of the collective bargaining agreement, and that the arbitrator should uphold its position and deny the union grievance.

Appendix

Relevant Provisions of the Agreement

Article XI—Seniority

Section 4. Current departments as established by the Company are:

(a) Bedding plant;

(b) Wholesale plant/Over-The-Road drivers.

Section 5. When the company determines that it is necessary to lay off employees, employees will be laid off by departments. Layoff of employees in a department will be done as follows:

1. The least senior person in the department will be laid off provided there is another employee in the department who has the qualifications and ability to perform the job of the individual to be laid off.
2. If another employee in the department does not have the ability or qualifications to perform the job, the Company will then choose the next least senior person in the department provided there is an employee in the department who has the ability and qualifications to perform the job. Therefore, the least senior person in the department will be laid off provided another employee in the department has the qualifications and ability to perform the job.

Section 6. Once layoff occurs, the Company has the right to transfer employees in the department to cover any job(s) as the result of the layoff. For the first forty-five (45) days, the employee transferred will be paid his personal rate or the base rate in the classification, whichever is higher. After forty-five (45) days, the transferred employee will be paid at the classification rate of the job he is performing whether higher or lower.

Section 7. In the event that a job opening becomes available in the department and there are laid-off employees, the Company will recall employees as follows:

1. The employee laid off with the most departmental seniority will be recalled to the job provided the employee has the ability and qualifications to do the job.
2. In the event that a job opening becomes available and individuals on the layoff list do not have the ability and qualifications to perform the job, the Company has the

right to transfer personnel in the department to perform the job, and recall the most senior laid-off employee in the department to perform the open job, providing the employee has the ability and qualifications to perform the job.

3. Recalled employees will be paid the classification rate of the job to which they are recalled.

Once an employee is recalled to a classification, there will be no other rights to transfer to another job unless transferred by the Company.

Section 8. An employee shall be terminated and lose all accumulated seniority upon the occurrence of any of the following events:

1. Voluntary quit.
2. Discharge for just cause.
3. Failure to return to work within 3 days after receipt by certified mail of written notice of recall mailed by the Company to the employee's last known address on the records.
4. The employee is absent for two consecutive working days without written or oral notification to the Company management, the burden of proving notification to be on the employee.
5. The employee is separated from payroll from the Company for any reason for a period of twelve (12) consecutive months.

Article XII—Job Posting and Bidding

In the event of a permanent vacancy, the Company shall post a notice on the bulletin board in the department that has the vacancy (Bedding or Wholesale/OTR) for three working days advising the employees of the vacancy. A vacancy exists when the Company determines that a new job has been created or that an existing job has become permanently vacant. Procedure for filling the job is as follows:

1. All employees in the department have the right to bid on the job.
2. The Company will select the most senior person bidding on the job provided the employee has the qualifications and ability to perform the job. When two or more employees' qualifications and ability are relatively equal, the employee with the most departmental seniority will be awarded the job.
3. Once an employee is awarded the job, the Company shall consider that employee's job vacant and the job will be posted for job bidding.
4. After the second job is bid, the Company no longer has the obligation to post for bid any other job opening created by job bids. The Company may fill any job in its discretion with any employee or hire from an outside source. However, prior to filling the job with another employee or from an outside source, the Company will offer the job to any laid-off employee who has the ability and qualifications to perform the job. In the event a laid-off employee is requested and accepts the job, they lose any recall rights to the job from which they were laid off.

An employee who accepts a job under this Article will be paid the hire-in rate for a period of forty-five (45) days and then will move to the classification rate of the job.

QUESTIONS

1. Was Anne Manion qualified to perform the job of sewing mattress panels? How can the arbitrator determine this?
2. Did Article XI, Sections 5 and 7, of the collective agreement protect Manion from disciplinary action if she did not possess the qualifications and ability to perform the job? Explain.
3. Did the company violate the bidding procedure of the contract? Discuss.
4. How should the arbitrator rule? Why?

Case 48

The Recalled Management Trainee

Company Stacor Corporation, Dunmore, Pennsylvania

Union United Brotherhood of Carpenters & Joiners of America, Local No. 2075

BACKGROUND

The Dunmore facility was one of several installations operated nationwide by Stacor Corporation. In April 1992, the corporation decided to temporarily suspend all production operations and lay off all bargaining unit employees.

Prior to that time, one hourly rated bargaining unit employee, Willis Hussmann,[1] had worked in a part-time capacity as a management trainee. This arrangement had existed for approximately one year prior to the layoff without any objection by the union. During this time, Hussmann performed bargaining unit work, and on a part-time basis he also was being groomed by management to assume a supervisory position at some time in the future.

The layoff was of short duration. Management determined that the situation required additional supervisory personnel preparatory to resuming production. It called Hussmann back to work in a supervisory capacity to assist in making the plant ready for the recall of the other workers and production to begin again. Hussmann had remained on the bargaining unit seniority roster during the year prior to the layoff, he was on it during the layoff, and he was still on the union seniority list at the time the union filed a grievance, April 27, 1992.

The union grievance charged that the company had violated Article XVII, Layoffs, of the agreement,[2] when it recalled Hussmann and failed to recall Henry Porter, a 30-year employee who had considerably more seniority than Hussmann. In all, Hussmann worked some 17 days before Henry Porter, too, was recalled from layoff.

When the parties could not agree on a settlement, the grievance was referred to an arbitrator for a final and binding decision. The parties agreed that the issue was:

> Did the company improperly recall Willis Hussmann to work and deny Henry Porter employment and pay for 17 days? If so, what shall the remedy be?

POSITION OF THE UNION

The union charged that the company had violated the rights of Henry Porter by recalling Hussmann, a less senior employee who had only nine years' seniority, before Porter. The

[1] The names of all individuals are disguised.

[2] See the appendix for this provision.

layoff and recall language contained in the contract was clear and unequivocal. Hussmann had not been removed from the union's seniority list. He was far down the list from Porter. Further, the union had not agreed to any departure from the language in Article XVII.

In remedy, the union requested that the company award Porter 17 days' back pay, as the agreement required. It also requested that such payment not be reduced by the amount of his unemployment earnings during that time.

POSITION OF THE COMPANY

The company held that it had not violated the terms of the collective bargaining agreement by placing Willis Hussmann in a supervisory position during the period when all other employees were still on layoff. The company had been grooming him for a supervisory position for more than a year with no objection from the union. The union could not now change a long-standing practice. The company contended that it had needed an additional supervisor in April 1992, and that Hussmann was qualified to serve in that capacity. In this regard, there was nothing in the agreement to prevent management from promoting an hourly rated employee to a supervisory position at its discretion. All management rights not specifically contracted away in the agreement resided with Stacor Corporation.

The company pointed out that by recalling Hussmann to a supervisory position and placing him on the management team, this in effect had shortened the layoff period for all employees by increasing management's ability to get ready for call-back and full production. Even though Hussmann was still on the union seniority roster list when he was recalled and promoted to a supervisory position, this was a technical oversight of no consequence to management's decision in this situation.

Finally, the company argued that the remedy sought by the union, including back pay for 17 days without the deduction of any unemployment income, would constitute punitive damages. To pay Porter the sum sought by the union would unjustly enrich him at the company's expense.

The company requested that the arbitrator deny the grievance.

Appendix

Relevant Provision of the Agreement

Article XVII (Layoffs)

Layoffs will start with the last employee hired plant-wide and proceed, with the exception of Chief Steward previously mentioned, by date of hire; the inverse will be applied on rehire. Any exceptions to this seniority procedure will be mutually agreed to by the Company and Union. New employees shall not be hired until all layoffs are recalled.

QUESTIONS

1. Evaluate the union's claim that Article XVII denied the company the right to promote Willis Hussmann.
2. The company employed Hussmann as a part-time management trainee before the layoff. Why didn't the union grieve the company's action?
3. Since the contract was silent on the matter of promotion out of the bargaining unit, why would the union grieve at this time?
4. Evaluate the union's request that Henry Porter be awarded payment for lost time without reduction for unemployment benefits he received.
5. Evaluate the company's claim that by recalling Hussmann into a supervisory position, it was able to recall bargaining unit workers faster.
6. Why had Hussmann remained on the union's membership roster during all this time?
7. How should the arbitrator rule in this case? Explain.

Case 49

The Right to Bid Down

Company Alltel Florida, Inc., Alachua, Florida

Union Communications Workers of America, District No. 3

BACKGROUND

The company was a telephone company that provided telephone service to customers in a wide area of north Florida. Gerardo Thornwall,[1] the grievant in this case, had worked for the company for 16 years. He was classified as a P.B.X. Installer-Repairperson, a labor "Grade 6" job, which was the highest plant grade. His job was repair and service of "private exchange" facilities for large commercial and industrial customers in the company's Alachua, Florida, exchange area.

In summer 1992, the company posted a job vacancy for the position of Installer-Repairperson in its Alachua exchange. This job was a labor "Grade 5" position. Thornwall bid on the job, notwithstanding the fact that it was a lower-paid job, and would involve a demotion (or downgrade) and reduction in pay. Thornwall's stated reasons were personal; he claimed that he did not think the additional pay he received in his current job was sufficient for the added responsibility and stress that it required.

Two other employees also bid on the job. Although Thornwall was the senior bidder and company management recognized that he was well qualified to hold the position of Installer-Repairperson, the job was awarded to another employee with less seniority. Thornwall was told by his supervisor, Alex Claremont, and the director of human resources, Meredith Juniper, that his bid in effect was asking for a downgrade, and that voluntary demotions or downgrades were granted only at the discretion of the company and not by seniority. They also told Thornwall that the company had good reasons to reject his bid in this case.

A union grievance was filed and processed through the steps resulting in arbitration. The parties agreed that the issue before the arbitrator was:

> Did the company violate the contract[2] on or about July 9, 1992, in its award of the Installer-Repairperson job on which Gerardo Thornwall had bid? If so, what should be the remedy?

POSITION OF THE UNION

The union contended that the parties' labor-management agreement did not specify that employees could not bid down. There were several past cases in which qualified employees had bid down and the seniority and qualifications of the bidders were determinative

[1] The names of all individuals are disguised.

[2] See the appendix for relevant provisions of the agreement.

in the award of such bids. Thornwall was the most senior qualified bidder; the seniority principle should have been followed in awarding him the position for which he had bid.

The union argued that since the contract was ambiguous in this area, such past practices of awarding by seniority in downward bids should have been followed in this case.

The union asked that the company be directed to rescind its prior decision, and the job in question be awarded to the grievant, Gerardo Thornwall.

POSITION OF THE COMPANY

The company contended that there was nothing in the contract that required it to follow seniority in a downward bid. In any downward bids, the selection was solely discretionary with the company.

The company claimed that even if management had on occasion deferred to seniority in downward bids, Articles 29 and 39 of the parties' labor-management agreement made any such practice discretionary on the part of the company.

The company contended that it had valid reasons for not awarding the job in question to Thornwall. He was a valuable and experienced employee whose skills were needed in his higher-rated "P.B.X." position. It would have been an economic waste to have Thornwall working at a lower-skilled position. Further, Thornwall currently was the only employee trained on certain equipment; it would have placed the company in a difficult position with certain customers if his bid down had been permitted.

The company urged the arbitrator to deny the union grievance.

Appendix

Relevant Provisions of the Agreement

Article I—Definitions

P. *Promotions.* Reassignment to a job having a higher maximum rate or top basic rate within the bargaining unit.

Article XV—Promotions

A. Where qualifications are substantially equal, seniority shall be the controlling factor in all matters of promotion.

B. A classification shall be considered to be higher if the scheduled rate of pay is higher.

C. Seniority shall be determined from the seniority roster posted on the bulletin board.

D. It is recognized that the Company retains the right to conduct oral and/or written tests providing the evaluations are pertinent to the job tested for. The Company will give the employees tested a copy of their grades and evaluation.

E. The Company agrees that it will not promote or transfer any duly certified Union representatives without two (2) weeks' written notice to the local.

Article XVII—Job Vacancies

A. A job vacant within the bargaining unit shall be posted by the Company, in each location where employees report for work, at least ten (10) working days prior to the time the job vacancy is to be filled. All such postings shall show the report location of the job. However, such posting of report location shall not restrict the Company's subsequent right to assign reporting locations within work areas and/or to transfer as provided in Articles 11 and 12 of this Agreement.

B. Employees desiring to be considered for the posted job shall submit a written bid within ten (10) working days from the date of the job posting, stating his qualifications, and the reasons he desires the job. Written bids should be sent to the employee's immediate supervisor.

C. The Company will fill the posted job within thirty (30) days after the closing date on the bid and notify, in writing, all who bid, as to the person given the job. Both successful and unsuccessful bidders will be notified on the same date. The successful bidder will be transferred to his new job as soon as practical but within thirty (30) days. The Company may withdraw the job vacancy if it is determined that the vacancy does not exist. The Employee may decline the job if within ten (10) days he notifies the Company in writing of such from the date he is notified of selection.

D. If the Company has not filled a posted job bid within three (3) months by either selection of a bidder, or the hiring of a new employee, the job will again be posted for bidding before the Company can hire into the job.

E. The following jobs shall be considered as entrance jobs and not subject to job posting and bidding: Commercial-Accounting, Grade 2 positions; Janitors; Right-of-Way Person; Lineperson; Cable Helper; Coin Collector.

However, in the event of a vacancy in any such entry level job, consideration shall be given, in order of seniority, to any employees then in other entry level jobs. Notice of such vacancies shall be posted.

F. The Company shall not be required to accord transfer or promotional consideration to any employee who has held his/her job classification for less than one (1) year.

Article XXIX—Rights of Company

The management of the business and the direction of the working force shall remain with the Company, including the right to hire, promote, and discharge for just cause, to use improved methods or equipment, to determine work assignments and tours, to decide the number of employees needed at any particular time or place and to be the sole judge of the communications service rendered the public; provided, however, that this section will not be used for the purpose of discriminating against members of the Union nor shall it alter the meaning of any provisions of this Agreement.

Nothing contained in this Agreement shall be deemed to limit the Company in any way in the exercise of the regular and generally recognized customary functions and responsibilities of management. Moreover, such functions of management as may be included herein shall not be deemed to exclude other functions of management not specifically included herein.

Article XXXIX—Past Practices

It is recognized by the parties that this agreement contains the entirety of their respective commitments. Any and all past practices not specifically mentioned in this

Agreement may be continued, discontinued, or modified by the Company, except as noted below:

The Company will continue its practice of paying employees to climb microwave towers at the rate of $25.00 per climb.

QUESTIONS

1. Examine carefully the relevant contractual provisions. Which provisions appear to be most supportive of the union position? Of the company position?
2. Should the seniority principle prevail in a downward bid, if the most senior employee is the most qualified job bidder? Why, or why not?
3. Was the "past practice" of allowing some previous downward bids by seniority binding on the company, or was this type of decision solely discretionary with the company? Discuss.
4. What should the arbitrator decide? Why?

Case 50

Taking Care of Union Business

Employer Bloomfield Board of Education, Bloomfield, Connecticut

Union National Association of Government Employees (NAGE), Local No. RI-214

BACKGROUND

Local No. RI-214 represented certain employees in the Bloomfield, Connecticut, educational district who were classified as custodians, bus drivers, maintenance personnel, and other positions. Rocco Mahoney,[1] the grievant in this case, was a licensed electrician who also served as president of the local union.

The grievance heard in arbitration was filed by the union and Rocco Mahoney protesting the employer's 30-day suspension of Mahoney for alleged insubordination in his conducting union business on company time. This suspension was effective September 1, 1992.

As mutually stipulated by the parties, the issue before the arbitrator was:

> Did the Bloomfield Board of Education have just cause pursuant to Article XX of the collective bargaining agreement[2] to suspend Rocco Mahoney for 30 days? If not, what shall the remedy be?

TESTIMONY AND EVIDENCE PRESENTED IN THE ARBITRATION HEARING

Ray Steele, director of facilities, testified that he had given Rocco Mahoney numerous verbal warnings about conducting union business on company time without proper permission. Steele said it was especially important that Mahoney devote his time to his electrical work, since Mahoney was the only licensed electrician working for the Bloomfield district.

Steele said that in September 1990, he had documented his warnings to Mahoney in a written memorandum specifically stating that Mahoney must have management permission to conduct union business during working hours. In relevant part, the memorandum included the following:

> September 18, 1990
>
> To: Rocco Mahoney, President
> NAGE Bloomfield local
>
> From: Ray Steele, Director of Facilities
>
> Subject: Role of Union Representative

[1] The names of all individuals are disguised.

[2] See the appendix for relevant contractual provisions.

> I am very appreciative that the recent grievance taken by your local was resolved in my office. I must call to your attention, however, what I see as the role of the Union President during working hours. If I or one of my assistants listens to a grievance by an employee during the work day, you or someone in your place has the right to represent the employee at the meeting. This is done by contacting your immediate superior and informing him of your need to be present.
>
> You may not, however, use company time to meet with Union representatives during the work day to discuss Union business unless I personally approve of such a request.
>
> If you have any questions regarding the above, please contact me immediately.

Ray Steele testified that he had received reports from several supervisors that Rocco Mahoney's habit of conducting union business during working hours disrupted the work schedule of other employees. Therefore, he again told Mahoney in late 1991 that he (Steele) was the only person who could give Mahoney permission to discuss union business during working hours. If Steele was not available, Durwood Gable, another management person, was designated to give permission to Mahoney for this purpose.

Durwood Gable, superintendent of highways, testified that on numerous occasions he had heard Rocco Mahoney disrupting workers' job duties during their work time. On two occasions in 1991, he had ordered Mahoney out of the highway department building. Gable testified that he reported these incidents both to Steele and to Ollie Carbol, Mahoney's immediate supervisor, who reported directly to Steele.

Milicent Rohrbach, secretary to Ray Steele, testified that at approximately 9:00 A.M. on September 1, 1992, Mahoney had requested her to contact Ray Steele to get his permission for Mahoney to attend a meeting at the local office of the State Labor Department. She was unable to reach Steele, but she did talk with Durwood Gable, who said he would reach Steele and have him call back. This message was given to Mahoney. However, when Steele eventually called, Mahoney had already left the building without getting the approval of Steele to attend the meeting at the Labor Department.

In his testimony, Rocco Mahoney asserted that he had not known about a hearing at the Labor Department until he was informed by a fellow worker earlier that morning. He immediately spoke with Milicent Rohrbach, Ray Steele's secretary, who advised him that Steele was not available. However, Rohrbach did reach Durwood Gable, and she advised Gable that Mahoney had to attend a hearing. The message relayed to him (Mahoney) by Ms. Rohrbach was that Gable would contact Steele to advise him of (Mahoney's) need to attend a hearing at the Labor Department.

Mahoney testified that he had then contacted Barbara Marchesi, secretary-treasurer of the union. Marchesi said that she was not aware of a hearing at the Labor Department; but she did suggest to him that as union president, he should attend all hearings and meetings where employees' interests were at stake. Mahoney went to the Labor Department building, but found there was no hearing scheduled. With some prior information in mind that he had received from Barbara Marchesi, he then proceeded to a meeting being held at an employer facility in Bloomfield. There he was advised by the NAGE staff attorney that this meeting had been arranged for the purpose of stipulating facts relative to an upcoming arbitration hearing concerning bus drivers. Mahoney said that this meeting lasted several hours. Following the meeting, he returned to his job site where he was informed that he had been suspended for insubordination.

Geofrey Milchrist, a consultant to the Bloomfield Board of Education, testified that he was present at the meeting attended by Mahoney. He said that he had been disturbed that Mahoney was there, since Mahoney's presence was unnecessary. However, Beth Margo, staff attorney of the union present at this meeting, testified that she had explained to Milchrist that Mahoney sincerely believed he was required to be present even though this might not have actually been the case.

POSITION OF THE EMPLOYER

Counsel for the Bloomfield Board of Education contended that there was ample just cause for the employer to suspend the grievant, Rocco Mahoney, for 30 days for his willful insubordination in the incident of September 1, 1992. As required under Article XX of the agreement, Mahoney had been warned both verbally and in a written memorandum concerning the proper procedures to follow if he wanted to conduct union business on company time. His behavior had caused disruption of work among other employees in the workplace, and he was on ample notice to follow the required procedure.

On September 1, 1992, Rocco Mahoney failed to get permission to attend a hearing or meeting on that date. Even though he may have believed that his presence was necessary at a hearing or meeting, this did not give him the right to leave his job without management permission. As an employee who was also union president, Mahoney had to follow legitimate rules and procedures just like anyone else. His behavior in this situation was inexcusable, and it showed willful insubordination and a reckless lack of concern for his job responsibilities.

Counsel for the Bloomfield Board of Education reiterated that the employer had ample just cause under the agreement to suspend Rocco Mahoney for 30 days. He urged that the union grievance on behalf of Mahoney be denied.

POSITION OF THE UNION

Counsel for the union urged that Rocco Mahoney had been unjustly suspended for 30 days because of circumstances that were beyond his control. Mahoney had tried diligently to contact Ray Steele for permission to attend a hearing he thought had been scheduled at the State Department of Labor. He was under the impression from the message he received from Milicent Rohrbach, Mr. Steele's secretary, that the permission to attend the meeting would be forthcoming. Mahoney had felt that his duty to represent union members at an important hearing would be understood by Mr. Steele; therefore he had left to go to the hearing, and then to a meeting, even though he had not specifically talked with Mr. Steele.

Counsel for the union claimed that at most Rocco Mahoney was a "victim of communication difficulties" that had placed him in an untenable position where he had to make a choice of action. He had not recklessly abandoned his job responsibilities, since he had tried to communicate with the proper management persons as he had recognized he was required to do. In the union's view, the employer's 30-day suspension of Rocco Mahoney was totally unjustified given the mitigating circumstances. Counsel for the union asserted that the employer had not had just cause to administer a major suspension on Mr. Mahoney, and urged that the union grievance be sustained, the disciplinary suspension rescinded, and Mr. Mahoney made whole for all lost pay and benefits during the period of unjust suspension.

Appendix

Relevant Provisions of the Agreement

Article XX—Discipline

Section 3.

(1) All disciplinary actions shall be applied in a fair manner and shall not be inconsistent with the infraction for which the disciplinary action is being applied.

(2) All suspensions and discharges must be for just cause and must be stated in writing with the reason given and a copy provided to the employee at the time of the suspension or discharge. A copy shall also be forwarded to the Union at the time it is provided to the employee.

(3) Serious misconduct shall be grounds for immediate suspension or discharge and need not follow the procedure listed in (4) below. Examples of serious misconduct include: theft, moral turpitude, insubordination.

(4) Disciplinary actions shall include:

(*a*) verbal discussion of problem,
(*b*) written warning,
(*c*) suspension without pay,
(*d*) termination,

and shall follow in this order except as noted in (3) above as serious misconduct.

QUESTIONS

1. Was the requirement that Rocco Mahoney receive specific permission to attend to union business a reasonable directive, especially as applied to the circumstances of September 1, 1992? Discuss.
2. Why would the employer want to control the time spent by a union president on union business? Why would the union want to have its union president available to conduct union business as the need might arise, often at unexpected times?
3. Was Rocco Mahoney guilty of willful insubordination, or was he caught between "a rock and a hard place" and forced to make a judgment that caused the employer to react?
4. If you were the arbitrator in this case, how would you decide? Why?

Case 51

Sick Leave for Adoption Care

Employer City of Columbus, Ohio

Union Fraternal Order of Police, Capital City Lodge No. 9

BACKGROUND

This case involved the grievance of Ms. Jean Larson,[1] who at the time of the case was a police officer serving as an aide to the chief of police, Jerry Jostes. In late 1991, Larson told Jostes that she and her husband were considering adopting a baby. Jostes wholeheartedly supported their becoming adoptive parents, which he further indicated in his letter of January 28, 1992, to the Franklin County Probate Court in support of Ms. Larson's adoption application. During her discussion with Jostes as to his willingness to write such a letter of support, Larson inquired as to whether she would be permitted to use accumulated sick leave to remain at home to take care of her newborn adopted baby. Jostes responded that he thought she "might be permitted" to do so for that purpose.

On July 15, 1992, Larson and her husband adopted a baby infant girl, born July 12, 1992. In an interdepartmental memo dated July 16, 1992, Jean Larson requested to use six to seven weeks of her accumulated sick leave to care for her newborn infant. Attached to her request was the certificate of adoption from the court and a letter from her physician, Dr. Marie Chandler, indicating the need for a minimum of six weeks for the parents to "acclimate" to the new baby.

Larson's request was approved through the chain of command until it reached Chief Jostes, who disapproved the request. The petition was subsequently also disapproved by Marjorie Gillette, the city's public safety director. Larson's request was denied on the basis that the sick leave provision of the collective bargaining agreement between the City and the police officers' union[2] did not authorize sick leave under the circumstances presented by Jean Larson. As a result, Larson had to take leave without pay for about thirty working days.

The union filed a grievance on behalf of Jean Larson which in relevant part included the following:

> GRIEVANCE NO. 92-38
>
> Officer Jean Larson applied for and was subsequently denied the ability to use sick time to care for a new born adopted infant. Officer Larson submitted plenty of documentation to convince a reasonable individual. The legitimacy of the need cannot be disputed.
>
> Further this incident became a subject of conversation during the most recent negotiations and it was agreed at the table that in these situations the leave would not be unreasonably withheld. In Officer Larson's case, it has been.
>
> This action by the Department and subsequently, the safety director, is a violation of the current contract between the City of Columbus and the Fraternal Order of Police, Capital City Lodge #9. Article 10.1 states, "No bargaining unit(s) member shall be

[1] The names of all individuals are disguised.

[2] See appendix for relevant contractual provisions.

removed, reduced in pay or position, suspended, required to forfeit accrued leave (excluding sick leave), reprimanded, or suffer any career disadvantage except for just cause."

Forcing Officer Larson into a leave-without-pay status for the duration of this leave is an unfair hardship that forces her to lose seniority.

As resolution to this grievance, Officer Larson should immediately be placed into paid status, by permitting the use of sick time, reimbursed for any time she had used and reinstated to her proper seniority number.

The grievance eventually was carried to arbitration.

POSITION OF THE UNION

The union first of all contended that if Jean Larson had given birth to her baby daughter instead of adopting her, Larson would have been granted the right to use her accumulated paid sick leave without question. The issue in this case was whether the agreement authorized a female police officer to use her accumulated paid sick leave for adoption care.

The union noted that it had been the practice within the Division of Police for a female police officer to "mark off" at the time she gave birth to her child, and she would remain off for as long as her doctor said she needed to be off. The period of time granted for such type of leave usually was between six to eight weeks, regardless of the health of the infant or mother. Implicitly this policy embodied the principles articulated by Dr. Chandler in her July 1992 letter. This policy also was consistent with the recommendation of Deputy Chief Arlen Trumbull when he reviewed Larson's request of July 16, 1992. Trumbull's recommendation noted that "if approved, she is not being 'given' any time. The hours are available in her bank. She should not be treated differently from other female officers."

In the union's view, even though Article 26, Section 26.2, was written in terms of "sick leave," when it had been applied to female officers who were mothers of newborn infants, it had in effect meant "maternity leave." Thus, since "maternity leave" for mothers of newborn infants had been routinely granted for periods of up to and in excess of six weeks regardless of their health, the City's argument that neither Jean Larson nor her newborn were "sick" was not persuasive. There was no sound reason for the City to deny Larson her right to use accumulated sick leave for the period of time in question. It had been a longstanding practice to allow female officers with newborn children to use their accumulated sick leave to care for infants, and Chief Jerry Jostes even told Larson that she likely would be permitted to do so as well.

The union further argued that Jean Larson had never been the subject of any disciplinary action, and the effect of requiring her to go into an unpaid leave status constituted the imposition of "career disadvantage" upon her without just cause. Therefore, this was a violation of Article 10, Section 10.1, of the collective bargaining agreement.

The union requested that the grievance should be sustained. As a remedy, Jean Larson should be restored to the status she would have been in had she been permitted to use her accumulated sick leave following the adoption in July 1992. This should include compensation for the time she was in an unpaid leave status, restoration of all lost seniority, class ranking, and all lost retirement credit and retirement contributions, plus any and all other appropriate relief necessary to remedy her grievance.

POSITION OF THE EMPLOYER (THE CITY)

The City conceded that Dr. Marie Chandler had strongly recommended that Jean Larson should be home for six to eight weeks with her newborn daughter. Further, the City also conceded that the custom and practice regarding a pregnant officer was that she "marked off," that is, she took time off work on a sick leave basis as long as her doctor indicated she needed to be off work. This usually was six to eight weeks, and the City typically required nothing more from the doctor than written confirmation that the officer was fit to return to duty. However, in the City's view, Article 26.2 could not be more clear in stating that sick leave would be granted only for the reasons articulated therein. There was no evidence that Larson met any of these criteria for the proper use of sick leave. Notwithstanding the emotional appeal of permitting an adoptive mother to spend time with her newborn daughter, there was no provision in the agreement for the grievant's being granted sick leave under the circumstances presented.

The difference between Jean Larson's circumstances and those presented by pregnant officers was that there was a "sickness" present for the pregnant officer upon delivery of the child for which she was entitled to sick leave during her recuperation. The fact that the City as a matter of course did not typically question the length of time a pregnant officer recuperated from delivery did not negate the fact that the essential condition of "sickness" was present when the officer delivered the child. If Larson had been pregnant, delivered a child, and was subsequently denied sick leave, then her grievance would have merit. But in this instance, she simply did not present the same circumstances as those female officers to whom she compared herself.

The City posed the question: If the City had granted sick leave for Larson, where would the line be drawn for others who desired to use sick leave to bond with newborn children? Would the City be required to approve sick leave for fathers of natural children when the father, mother, or child were not sick, or for adoptive fathers when neither the father nor the child was sick? Clearly, the agreement did not provide for sick leave in those circumstances.

According to the City, Chief Jerry Jostes might have inadvertently left the impression with Jean Larson that her sick leave request for adoption care might be approved. However, Jostes also strongly asserted that he had told Larson that sick leave would not be granted on any other basis than what was permitted under the contract. After carefully reading the collective bargaining agreement, Jostes and top City administrators had concluded that for sick leave to be approved would require that either Larson or her child must be sick. Larson had claimed that Chief Jostes stated that sick leave would be approved for her, "just like anyone else." Even if Larson was correct in her assertion, there was no provision in the agreement for the police chief to unilaterally change the provisions of the agreement.

The City was not without empathy for Larson's request and never maintained that it was inappropriate for Larson to have time with her new daughter. In fact, the City granted her request for leave without pay for about seven weeks.[3] However, the negotiated agreement did not provide for sick leave under the circumstances presented by the grievant. For all of these reasons, the grievance should be denied.

[3] Under Article 29, Section 29.1 of the parties' collective bargaining agreement, "special leaves" could be authorized by the public safety director without pay.

Appendix

Relevant Provisions of the Agreement

Article 10—Corrective Action and Records

10.1 Corrective Action for Cause: No bargaining unit(s) member shall be removed, reduced in pay or position, suspended, required to forfeit accrued leave (excluding sick leave), reprimanded, or suffer any career disadvantage except for just cause.

Article 26—Sick Leave

26.2 Use of Sick Leave. (A) Sick Leave with pay shall be granted upon the recommendation of the Public Safety Director only for the following reasons:

(1) Sickness of the member.

(2) Injury to the member which is not subject to the provisions of Article 28, Injury Leave.

(3) Medical, dental, or optical consultation or treatment of the member.

(4) Sickness of a member of the immediate family. Members shall be granted not more than five (5) workdays in any calendar year for sickness in the immediate family. A certificate of the attending physician shall be required before paying any member under this paragraph for absences of a duration of three (3) days or more. In special cases where the Public Safety Director deems that more than five (5) workdays are necessary, the Director shall grant such leave.

(5) Quarantine of a member because of exposure to a contagious disease. The Public Safety Director shall require a certificate of the attending physician before paying any member under this paragraph.

(6) Any member scheduled to work on a holiday as designated in Article 24 who reports sick shall be charged sick leave with pay for the number of hours that comprise the holiday.

(7) In the event a member uses all injury leave time and is still unable to return to active duty, the member may, with the approval of the Public Safety Director, use any paid leave to which the member is entitled.

(8) In the event of death in the immediate family, each member shall be entitled to up to five (5) workdays for a funeral service and/or interment.

(9) The immediate family shall include: spouse, son, daughter, brother, sister, parent, grandparent, grandchild, stepfather, stepmother, stepbrother, stepsister, stepson, stepdaughter, father-in-law, mother-in-law, son-in-law, daughter-in-law, brother-in-law, sister-in-law, grandparent-in-law, half brother and half sister and persons who stand in loco parentis.

QUESTIONS

1. Evaluate the union's position that in practice the City had really equated "sick leave" for female officers of newborn infants to be the same as "maternity leave."
2. The grievant (Jean Larson) apparently believed that the police chief (Jerry Jostes) had given her an implied promise that she would be able to utilize her accrued sick leave

for care of her adopted infant child. Should this aspect of this case be significant or crucial in the arbitrator's decision? Why, or why not?

3. Was the City justifiably concerned about the precedent implications surrounding Larson's request for sick leave for adoption care? Discuss.
4. If you were the arbitrator, how would you decide, and why?
5. Review the major provisions of the Family and Medical Leave Act of 1993. If provisions of this law could be applied retroactively to the circumstances of this case, would it make any difference in your arbitration decision? Why, or why not?

Case 52

An Issue of Reasonable Accommodation

Company Multi-Clean, Inc., Division of Hako Minuteman, Inc., Shoreview, Minnesota

Union International Association of Machinists and Aerospace Workers, District Lodge No. 77 and Local Lodge No. 459

BACKGROUND

The company manufactured and distributed chemical cleaning and coating products for use with cleaning commercial floors, carpets, and other surfaces. One of its nationwide plants was located in Shoreview, Minnesota. In 1984, Hako Minuteman, Inc., had purchased substantially all of the assets and business of the Multi-Clean Products Division of H. B. Fuller Company. The grievant in this case, Roger Robek,[1] was originally employed by H. B. Fuller on March 18, 1964. Multi-Clean retained Robek after its 1984 acquisition. At the time of his grievance (1992), Roger Robek held the position of leadman in the Chemical Processing Department, a bargaining unit position.

Over the years, Robek had incurred certain back injuries at work. The most serious of these injuries was a back injury from a fall from the roof of the plant in 1987 for which Robek was determined subsequently to have suffered a 10.5 percent permanent partial disability. Robek continued to work in the plant in the position of leadman, chemical processing, on a full-time basis despite suffering this permanent partial disability and other work-related injuries.

On February 26, 1992, Roger Robek suffered an aggravation of his back injuries when he went outside to clean up a chemical spill. After cleaning up the spilled substance, he was coming back into the plant when he stepped on the three steps to come into the building. His back gave out, and he fell to his knees on the steps where he remained for a few minutes. He then got up, came into the building, and made a report of his fall to Louis Zweig, company operations manager, at approximately 9:30 A.M. Robek worked until 2:30 P.M., and then he went home before his shift ended. When Robek reported for work the next day, he complained of severe back pain, and he was directed by Zweig and the plant's human resources manager, Mildred Roos, to seek medical attention.

On February 27, 1992, Robek began medical treatment at a local medical clinic called Health Works. Robek had physical therapy scheduled two times a week, and on April 6, 1992, he was referred by his treating physician at Health Works to Dr. Florence Buhro of Fairview Southdale Hospital Spine Care Center. During all of this time, Robek was absent from work as a result of his work-related injury, and he was also receiving workers' compensation benefits.

Roger Robek was examined by Dr. Buhro on April 10, 1992. Dr. Buhro diagnosed Robek as having degenerative disc disease, and appropriate medical treatment was prescribed for several weeks. At the same time, Dr. Buhro released Robek to return to work, but with weight and lifting restrictions and the restriction to work only eight hours a day.

[1] The names of all individuals are disguised.

When Robek informed company managers on April 10, 1992, that he was released to go back to work with weight and lifting restrictions, they indicated to him that they felt he was not ready to resume work. Robek then informed the company that he had received notice from the workers' compensation insurance carrier (Wausau Insurance Companies) that his payments were being terminated. The company intervened on behalf of Robek, and the workers' compensation payments were extended through June 5, 1992. At that time, Robek requested again that he be returned to work. Company management refused, and they claimed that there was not any work for him to do because of his weight-lifting and bending restrictions.

On August 6, 1992, Dr. Buhro determined that Robek had reached his maximum medical improvement status, and she directed that he could return to work with strict weight-lifting and bending restrictions being imposed upon him. The weight restrictions were that he should not exceed a 50-pound lift at waist level with no repetition, and lifting of up to 40 pounds only on occasion. The other restriction was no repetitive bending. Company management again refused to return Robek to work because of these restrictions.

On September 29, 1992, the company, through its vice president of finance, Terrence Nestor, sent Roger Robek a letter which terminated his employment as of September 30, 1992. The reason given in the letter for his termination was: "Unfortunately as you remain physically unable to properly perform the duties associated with your position due to degenerative disc disease, we must terminate your employment in accordance with terms of the collective bargaining agreement."

Roger Robek filed a written grievance on October 7, 1992, protesting his termination. The grievance was eventually carried to arbitration. The parties stipulated that the issue to be decided was:

> Did the Employer violate the contract when it failed to return the grievant, Roger Robek, to work after he was released for duty by his treating physician from a work-related accident? If so, what shall the remedy be?

Robek continued to receive medical treatment after his date of termination. He was examined by Dr. Buhro in October and December 1992, and again in March 1993. On March 29, 1993, just prior to the arbitration hearing, Dr. Buhro conducted a Functional Capacities Evaluation (R-33) concerning Robek's medical status at that time. The test revealed that as of March 29, 1993, he was still physically incapable of lifting any weights beyond 35 pounds on an occasional basis, or pulling or pushing 100 pounds on more than an occasional basis. In addition, Robek was restricted from sitting, standing, or walking for more than six hours in an eight hour day.

POSITION OF THE COMPANY

The company maintained that Roger Robek was terminated for ample just cause because he was no longer physically capable of performing his job.[2] Robek's degenerative disc disease and medically imposed work restrictions rendered him physically incapable of performing the job of leadman in the Chemical Processing Department.

A review of the evidence showed that lifting of weights over 40 pounds was continually an integral daily part of each job in the Chemical Processing Department. This was

[2] See the appendix for relevant contractual and legal provisions relevant to this case.

verified by a tour of the plant in the arbitrator's presence to review the different procedures and requirements of that department.[3]

The company claimed that the majority of time spent by any leadman was on the production lines assisting other employees whenever and wherever needed. There simply was no job in the Chemical Processing Department which did not include much lifting. Due to the Roger Robek's weight-lifting and bending restrictions, plus restrictions from sitting, standing, or walking for more than six hours in an eight hour work day as imposed upon him by his physician, there was no job in the Chemical Processing Department for which Robek was medically qualified to serve.

Further, the Functional Capacities Evaluation of Robek reflected that he was physically limited from repetitive sitting, standing, walking, bending, crawling, crouching, and lifting weights over 35 pounds. Under Section 7.7 of the collective bargaining agreement, the company was not required to retain Robek in another position for which he might be physically capable. Regardless, at the time of the grievant's termination, no vacant position was available anywhere within the plant that Robek was physically capable of performing.

The company's obligation to protect its employees from danger and ensure a hazard-free workplace required it to employ individuals who were physically capable of performing their jobs without safety threats to themselves and other employees, or damage to company property. Neither the contract nor the Americans with Disabilities Act required the company to retain an employee who could not perform the job duties that existed in the plant operation.

The company urged that the arbitrator should determine that Roger Robek was justly terminated, and to render an award in favor of the company position.

POSITION OF THE UNION

The union argued that the company had not complied with the "reasonable accommodation" requirement of the collective bargaining agreement as described in Section 7.7. The company never gave Roger Robek an opportunity to work with any reasonable accommodations, which the company had done in the past when he was previously injured on the job. The company never discussed work station modifications or other modifications to the job of leadman in the Chemical Processing Department, which could make the job

[3] During the arbitration hearing, through witnesses and a plant tour, the company showed that at the time of his discharge, Roger Robek was a Grade 6 leadman in the Chemical Processing Department. This department consisted of several production lines such as the Bag-in-the-Box, Chemical Mix and Processing, Fill Machine Operations, Silkscreen Operations, and general manual labor filling of product. Lifting of weights in excess of 40 pounds was an integral part of the assigned duties of workers and any leadman. For example, empty steel drums weighing at least 40 pounds were routinely lifted and removed by hand from the work area. The chemical containers weighed approximately 40 to 50 pounds when filled and had to be manually lifted onto pallets. In addition, 500-pound drums were manually tilted to accommodate the mixing vats. The filling machines and Bag-in-the-Box operations required packaging products into boxes and lifting these 40- to 50-pound boxes onto skids and pallets two-boxes high and often lifting above waist level. The silkscreen operation, which had been added but which did not exist at the time of the grievant's discharge, included lifting of weights of 45 pounds.

fit Robek's medical restrictions. There were any number of such modifications that could have been made without causing undue hardship on the company.[4]

In the union's view, Roger Robek should have been given a chance with reasonable accommodations to perform those job duties which existed prior to his latest injury to determine whether he could in fact—as stipulated in Section 7.7 of the contract—"perform the work in his department in a manner comparable with that performed by other workers at the average speed and ability" within the Chemical Processing Department. Further, the company did not make any efforts to determine if there were any other job positions in the plant that Roger Robek could have performed with or without reasonable accommodations.

The union asserted that there was not one shred of evidence that the level of performance of Roger Robek prior to his February 26, 1992, injury was unacceptable, or that he had been warned of any dissatisfaction with his work.

The union also claimed that the company had changed some of the work duties of the leadman position in Chemical Processing while Robek was injured. It appeared to the union that this was an attempt by the company to make the duties even more difficult for Robek to perform as compared to the job he had been performing before his most recent injuries.

The union further urged that the company had violated Section 24.1 of the contract and also the Americans with Disabilities Act of 1990 by discriminating against the grievant who was a qualified person with a disability. Further, Robek was a senior employee of almost 30 years of service with the company and its predecessor. It could also be imputed that the company had Robek's age in mind when it decided to terminate him. This, too, would be discrimination prohibited by the contract and federal law (the Age Discrimination in Employment Act).

[4] In the union's post-hearing brief, the union submitted a list of possible "reasonable accommodations" that the union felt could have been made by the company. These were stated as follows:

A. An adjustable work station upon which the bin into which the unprinted plastic bottles are loaded would allow loading of those bottles at waist height then raising to conveyor level;

B. A return roller conveyor for the empty printed bottles in cases would eliminate the need for any employee to carry the cases back to be reloaded to print a second color;

C. Pallet lifts at the end of the roller conveyor from the filling machine could be countersunk into the floor to provide the height of the pallet, empty or loaded to four tiers of Bag-in-the-Box or plastic bottle cases, and would be at conveyor height so the last level could be slid from the conveyor onto the tops of the pallet, eliminating the need for excessive lifting;

D. An attachment for the forklift could be purchased or fabricated which would grasp fifty-five gallon drums and move them to other lifting devices instead of pushing and pulling them from the skid and tipping onto a barrel dolly, much safer for all employees;

E. The adding of dry ingredients to the mixing vats could be accomplished much more safely for all employees if the filling hole were closer to the platform on which employees must stand and bend over the guard rails to pull bags to the opening and open to dispense the contents into the vat.

The union acknowledged that these job accommodations had not been presented to company management prior to Roger Robek's termination. The union also pointed to provisions of the Americans with Disabilities Act (ADA) of 1990, which outline examples of "reasonable accommodations." See appendix to the case.

The union submitted that the grievance should be fully sustained. As a remedy, Roger Robek should be reinstated to his former position with full seniority and benefits. In addition, he should be awarded back pay at the applicable rate from April 10, 1992, when the treating physician released Robek to return to work (or, alternatively, from no later than June 5, 1992, the date the company's workers' compensation carrier terminated his weekly disability payments) until Robek returned to full-time employment with the company. The back pay award should include any applicable overtime which he would have worked if he had not been unjustly discharged. Additionally, the discharge should be expunged from Roger Robek's work record.

Appendix

Relevant Provisions of the Agreement and of the Americans with Disabilities Act (ADA)

Management Rights

Section 3.1. The management of the business and the direction of the working forces, including, but not limited to, the right to plan, direct and control operations, the operations or services to be performed in or at the plant or by employees of the Company, to schedule the working hours, to hire, promote, demote and transfer, to suspend, discipline, discharge for just cause, or to relieve employees because of lack of work or for other legitimate reasons, to make and enforce reasonable shop rules and regulations not inconsistent with the provisions of this Agreement, to introduce new and improved methods, materials or facilities, or to change existing methods, materials or facilities are vested exclusively in the Company; provided, however, that such rights shall not be applied in any manner violative of any of the provisions of this Agreement.

Seniority

Section 7.7. Any employee who, because of age or who has been incapacitated at his regular work by injury or compensable disease while employed by the Company, or as a result of surgical operations or severe illness is unable to perform the work in his department in a manner comparable with that performed by other workers at the average speed and ability within said department after the Company has made reasonable accommodation, may be employed by the Company at its sole discretion, but the Company is not obligated to retain such employee in the employ of the Company, in other work in the plant which he is physically able to do without regard to seniority and the Company may fix a rate for such employee in such new work commensurable with the ability of such employee to perform such work.

Nondiscrimination

Section 24.1. The Company shall not discriminate against any employee because of membership in, or lawful activities on behalf of, the Union and neither the Company nor the Union shall discriminate against any employee because of race, religion, color, sex, national origin or age.

In addition, the Employer and the Union shall comply with all applicable Federal Laws and Regulations with regard to the employment of and nondiscrimination against disabled persons and Veterans seeking employment.

Americans with Disabilities Act (ADA) of 1990

The ADA defines the term "reasonable accommodation" as follows:

(A) Making existing facilities used by employees readily accessible to and usable by individuals with disabilities; and

(B) Job restructuring, part-time or modified work schedules, reassignment to a vacant position, acquisition or modification of equipment or devices, appropriate adjustment or modifications of examinations, training materials or policies, the provision of qualified readers or interpreters, and other similar accommodations for individuals with disabilities. (42 U.S.C. Section 12101 et seq., 42 U.S.C. Section 12111 et seq.).

QUESTIONS

1. Closely examine Section 7.7 of the parties' labor agreement. Which parts of this provision best support the company's position? The union's position?
2. To what degree should requirements of the Americans with Disabilities Act influence/determine the arbitrator's decision in this case? Discuss.
3. Did company management violate the labor agreement when it terminated Roger Robek's employment? Why, or why not?
4. As the arbitrator, if you find that the union grievance should be sustained, would you agree with the union's proposed remedy? If not, what type of remedy would you direct?

Case 53

Refusal to Post the Union's Memorandum

Company Arcata Graphics, Kingsport, Tennessee

Union Aluminum, Brick and Glass Workers International Union, Local No. 299

BACKGROUND

The main company plant had been in continuous operation at its present site since 1923. For many years, it operated as Kingsport Press, and in the late 1960s it was acquired by Arcata. The union had represented the employees since 1988, and the current contract was the second between the parties. There were about 1,175 bargaining unit employees at the Kingsport location, which produced approximately 90 million books per year at this facility. The bargaining unit also consisted of the Hawkins County Plant (800 employees), the Sherwood Plant (150 employees), and the Distribution Center (100 employees). Employees at the four locations were covered by the same labor contract.

This grievance arbitration concerned the application and interpretation of Article XXIII of the current labor-management agreement between the parties. This provision stated as follows:

> **Article XXIII—Bulletin Boards**
> The Company agrees to furnish the Union exclusive access to one (1) bulletin board in each department for use by the Union for the posting of official announcements and notices concerning meetings of the Union, scheduling and results of elections, appointments to office, and social, educational and recreational affairs. Prior to the posting of any information on the bulletin board provided in this Article, such information shall be submitted to the Human Resources Manager for his review and approval, which shall not be arbitrarily withheld.

Under Article XXIII, the company had agreed to furnish the union access to one bulletin board in each department for use by the union. The only change in Article XXIII from the previous contractual language was that the current contract provided for a bulletin board in each department in the plant.

In the fall of 1992, the union was conducting a membership drive and mailed a report to all employees represented by the union in the collective bargaining unit.[1] The report contained information on the union-administered and -sponsored long-term disability plan. Due to the number of phone calls it received after the mailing, the union decided to post a memorandum dated November 24, 1992, and entitled "Long-Term Disability Facts," on the bulletin boards in the company plant.

Pursuant to Article XXIII, the union requested permission from the company's human resources manager, Jackson Russell,[2] to post the informational memorandum on the company bulletin boards. However, Russell denied this request. Thereupon, the union filed unfair labor practice charges with the Regional Office of the National Labor

[1] Tennessee is a "right-to-work," or "open shop," state. Therefore, certain employees were not union members, although they were part of the bargaining unit and were represented by the union.

[2] Names of individuals are disguised.

Relations Board, claiming that this denial constituted unlawful interference and a refusal by the company to honor the terms of the parties' negotiated contract. However, after review of these charges, the NLRB administratively remanded and deferred the case back to the parties to be processed under their grievance-arbitration procedure.

The union in the person of its local union vice president, Darwin Caswell, filed a grievance which was then appealed directly to arbitration. The union grievance was stated as follows:

> The Company failed to live up to the contract, when it failed to post educational information on the Union's Long Term Disability Plan for its membership. Remedy: Company abide by the contract in the future.

POSITION OF THE UNION

The union strongly argued that the company had violated the collective bargaining agreement when it denied permission for the union to post a memorandum (or notice) about its long-term disability plan. The union pointed out that the agreement gave the union the right to post notices for meetings, scheduling and results of elections, appointments to office, and social, educational, and recreational affairs. The union noted that its request to post the memorandum (or notice) was the result of the many questions it had received about its long-term disability plan, which had been included in a letter sent to employees as part of a union membership drive. The union claimed that the language in the labor contract gave it the right to post notices of an educational type; explanation of the long-term disability plan was certainly an educational matter.[3]

When permission was denied, the union was forced to distribute the informational sheet at the plant gates. Subsequently, the union filed unfair labor practice charges with the National Labor Relations Board, which deferred the case to arbitration.

In the union's view, the company's refusal to permit the posting of its memorandum was a result of its misguided and narrow interpretation of Article XXIII, which violated the wording, intent, and spirit of that provision. There was nothing in the posting of the "Long-Term Disability Facts" sheet that was adverse to the company. It was strictly an informational and educational notice for all employees in the bargaining unit.

The union requested that the arbitrator should sustain the grievance and direct the company to adhere to the contract in the future.

POSITION OF THE COMPANY

The company maintained that Article XXIII was ambiguous. This provision only provided that the union could post notices of "official announcements and notices concerning meetings of the union, scheduling and results of elections, appointments to office, and social, educational and recreational affairs." This provision did not say that the union could post informational material, solicitations, general editorials, propaganda of any kind, educational materials, or similar informative matters.

In the company's view, the union's "Long-Term Disability Facts" sheet was simply a union informational memorandum that was not included within the contractual coverage

[3] The union memorandum contained a number of questions and answers about the union's long-term disability plan, primarily regarding costs, benefits, eligibility, and filing claims.

of Article XXIII. The company had the discretionary right under Article XXIII to deny the union's request to use the plant bulletin boards to disseminate this type of information-based memorandum, since other alternative means of communication were available to the union.

In regards to the above, the company pointed out that it had informed the union that it would have agreed to post a notice about a "Union Meeting on Long-Term Disability." However, the company refused to post the memorandum as it was submitted, because it only contained information and data about the long-term disability plan, and it was neither a "notice" nor an "educational affair."

The company requested the arbitrator to dismiss the union grievance.

QUESTIONS

1. Why would the company deny the union its request to post the "Long-Term Disability Facts" sheet on plant bulletin boards and eventually go to arbitration over the issue?
2. Why would the union press this issue, first to the NLRB and then to arbitration? (Speculate why the NLRB deferred the union's complaint to the parties' grievance-arbitration mechanism).
3. Could this case have been settled in a manner acceptable to both parties without going to arbitration? Discuss.
4. How should the arbitrator decide this case? Explain your reasoning.

Case 54

Terminated for Possessing a Gun

Employer City of New Haven, Connecticut

Union American Federation of State, County, and Municipal Employees, Council 4, Local No. 3144

BACKGROUND

Matthew Kress[1] had been employed for 14 years by the Water Pollution Control Authority (WPCA) in the city of New Haven. At the time of his discharge, he held the title of Wastewater Supervisor I, and he was assigned to the third shift (midnight to 8 A.M.).

On May 8, 1986, WPCA had distributed to all employees a policy concerning weapons on the premises. It included the following:

> Effective immediately—No weapons of any sort shall be allowed on WPCA premises, including lockers and private vehicles parked on WPCA property. No exceptions shall be made to this policy. Anyone caught with a weapon on WPCA property in violation of this policy shall be subject to immediate discharge.

Matthew Kress had received a copy of this policy and signed an acknowledgment form to that effect.

On November 17, 1992, Kress brought a gun onto WPCA premises. Kress had a state permit to carry a weapon. He had previously stated that the neighborhood in which he lived had caused him to purchase and carry a gun for his personal safety. On November 17, he removed his gun from his briefcase and showed it to a co-worker. Two other employees later testified that they also saw the gun that night.

On November 18, 1992, Roger Schienvar, general manager, initiated an investigation of the gun incident. The employees who had seen Kress display the gun stated their observations to WPCA investigators.

In addition to the gun incident investigation, Schienvar reviewed Kress's work history at WPCA. Schienvar found and reported in a memorandum dated November 20, 1992, including as follows:

> There have been a series of continuing and ongoing incidents of failure to perform duties in an appropriate manner, failure to follow orders, failure to follow and apply policies and procedures, failure to display appropriate level of care and judgment to the position of Waste Supervisor I.

Several of these previous incidents had involved difficulties and confrontations with other employees. Concerning Matthew Kress's disciplinary history, Schienvar found and wrote in his memorandum:

[1] The names of all individuals are disguised.

> He has been given verbal warnings to written warnings to suspensions in increasing terms, and the last discipline prior to this particular incident was a 30-day suspension that was invoked in early July of 1992.

On January 6, 1993, WPCA management provided Kress with a pretermination conference during which he had union representation. After this January 6 conference, management reached a decision to terminate Matthew Kress. In a termination letter to Kress, Roger Schienvar included the following statement:

> There was a request—appeal, if you will—from the union for leniency. But for a number of factors, primarily the seriousness of the offense and the definitive and clear nature of the policy, it was our decision to follow through on the termination.

The union filed a grievance on behalf of Matthew Kress, which was carried to arbitration. The issue was framed as:

> Was the discharge of Matthew Kress for just cause?[2] If not, what shall the remedy be?

POSITION OF THE EMPLOYER

It was WPCA's position that Matthew Kress had been discharged for just cause. Kress had admitted he knew the policy prohibiting bringing weapons to work. He admitted bringing a fully loaded weapon to work, and he admitted showing the gun to at least one employee. Such acts were clear violations of rules and of the contract, and they were extremely dangerous. WPCA could not allow such actions on the part of any employee. Therefore, the discharge of Kress was for ample just cause, and WPCA asked that the grievance be denied.

POSITION OF THE UNION

It was the union's position that WPCA's policy was not posted anywhere in the authority's facilities. Matthew Kress had a permit to carry a weapon issued by the state of Connecticut. He obeyed the law concerning his gun. Except for this one incident of showing the gun to another employee, Kress had kept the gun out of sight in his briefcase. He promised never to bring the gun to work or onto the work premises again. Kress had never threatened anyone with the gun. Kress had kept the gun with him because of the high-crime area in which he lived. He couldn't keep it in his car at work because of the numerous break-ins of cars in the parking lot. In this case, the WPCA and the City had overreacted. Their decision to terminate a long-service employee was arbitrary and unreasonable, and it did not meet a just cause standard. The union asked that the grievance be sustained, and that Matthew Kress be reinstated to his position and made appropriately whole.

[2] See the appendix for relevant contractual provisions.

Appendix

Relevant Provisions of the Agreement

Article 16—Discharge and Discipline

Section 2. (a) Disciplinary action shall be consistent with the type of infraction or malfeasance which is the subject of the discipline.

(b) Discipline should be progressive in nature, but where circumstances warrant termination, it need not necessarily have been preceded by lesser disciplinary actions.

QUESTIONS

1. Evaluate the employer's and the union's respective arguments. Which do you find the most and which the least persuasive?
2. Should Matthew Kress's prior disciplinary record be a major or minor consideration in the arbitration decision? Explain.
3. Is there a conflict between the statutory right of an employee to obtain a permit to carry a gun, and the employer's policy of no weapons on the premises? Discuss.
4. How should the arbitrator decide? Why?

Case 55

Are Teachers Obliged to Supervise Students in the Cafeteria?

Employer Newbury Ohio Local School District Board of Education

Union Newbury Education Association

BACKGROUND

During the 2001–2002 school year proctors were employed to supervise elementary school lunch periods at the district's elementary schools. Four proctors were employed, two for each of two lunch periods to supervise the cafeteria, and two for the playground to supervise students on the playground during the lunch-period recess. The principals at the elementary schools noticed that there was an increase in student control and behavior problems from students coming in from the playground from the lunch-period recess.

The district's supervisory personnel decided that volunteers could not be used to assist in playground supervision. Therefore, all four proctors were assigned to playground duty during the lunch period, and teachers were given one 20-minute lunch period every three days to supervise the cafeteria. This resulted in two teachers being present in the cafeteria for each lunch period.

The teachers filed a grievance concerning these cafeteria assignments. The parties' collective bargaining agreement specifically stated that cafeteria supervision was part of the secondary teacher's responsibilities, but the contract was silent on such issues for elementary school teachers. There was a standard management rights clause in the parties' collective bargaining agreement, reserving to management any rights not specifically abridged by provisions of the collective bargaining agreement.

The parties stipulated that the present grievance is properly before the arbitrator.

POSITION OF THE UNION

The union claimed that the elementary school teachers never had cafeteria supervisory responsibilities. Therefore, there was a clear past practice established that teachers were not to supervise the cafeteria. Clearly, the parties contemplated secondary teachers supervising their cafeterias because those duties were included in the secondary teacher job description. However, no such duty was included in the elementary school teacher job description.

The union also pointed to the fact that elementary teachers had always used the lunch period for numerous educational activities. Remediation, calling parents, make-up tests, and other such activities had always been conducted during these periods, and if they were given up for cafeteria supervision the quality of education would be impaired.

Finally, the principals prepared a handbook for elementary teachers. This handbook was a management-prepared document, without input from the union. The handbook provided an exhaustive list of elementary teacher duties and guidance for fulfilling those duties. No place in this document was there anything about cafeteria supervision.

It was the union's position that the district violated the parties' collective bargaining agreement by assigning cafeteria supervision duties to elementary school teachers. The remedy requested was for the district to cease and desist assigning such duties, and pay the teachers their per diem rate for the hours they performed cafeteria supervisory duties.

POSITION OF THE EMPLOYER

The district's position was that the management rights clause provided that the district "retains the management rights to direct, supervise, and manage the work force." The only exception to this management right was where the collective bargaining agreement or statute limited that right. There was no dispute that neither statute nor the collective bargaining agreement limits the administration's right to assign elementary school teachers to cafeteria supervisory duties.

Contrary to the union's assertions, there was no evidence that teacher performance or educational opportunities were adversely affected by assigning cafeteria supervisory duties to elementary teachers. The sole reason that these duties were assigned to teachers was to provide for better student supervision and to mitigate the behavioral problems that were observed when the proctor's time was split between the playground and the cafeteria.

The union bears the burden to show the district violated the contract. There was no such proof offered in this case. Therefore, the district had the contractual authority to assign cafeteria supervisory duties to the elementary teachers. This grievance should be denied as being without merit.

QUESTIONS

1. Is there a contractual basis, expressed in language, for the union's claim in this matter? If so, what is it?
2. Is there a binding past practice in evidence in this case barring the district from using the elementary school teachers for cafeteria supervision? Explain.
3. If you were the arbitrator, how would you rule in this case? Explain.

Case 56

Anti-Arab Comments: Cause for Discipline?

Company Pepsi Bottling Group, Fresno, California

Union United Steelworkers of America

BACKGROUND

It is undisputed that the company had promulgated rules concerning employee conduct shortly after the events of September 11, 2001, entitled "General Rules of Conduct." Included in those rules of conduct were provisions proscribing racially insensitive remarks to Arab-American customers of the company. These rules were consistent with prior company rules concerning employee behavior.

On September 28, 2001, Mr. S, the grievant in this matter, made remarks to an Arab-American (Mr. H) customer on his route who owned the store the grievant was servicing. Those remarks included statements to the customer concerning the possibility of Arabs being interned in concentration camps like Japanese-Americans were after Pearl Harbor in the event of a second terrorist attack. These remarks upset the Arab-American customer, Mr. H. Mr. H complained to the management of Pepsi. After discussions with management, Mr. H offered to forgive the grievant if a proper apology was forthcoming. On October 1, 2001, the grievant apologized to Mr. H at his store, and Mr. H indicated his acceptance of the apology.

Mr. S then proceeded to another store on his route owned by an Arab-American, Mr. A. Mr. A was sitting in his store reading an article concerning a Yemeni who had been murdered in the Fresno area, with the appearances that the crime had been a hate crime. According to Mr. A, the grievant said something to the effect that the person of Yemen probably deserved to die because he was probably talking trash. Mr. A ordered the grievant from his store and complained to Pepsi management about what he perceived to be racist and offensive conduct. The grievant subsequently returned to Mr. A's store and apologized for his remarks.

Upon hearing of the second incident, Mr. H (victim of the first incident) took the position that the grievant's conduct was insensitive and the apology was no longer acceptable. On October 26, 2001, the grievant was suspended pending an investigation of the conduct in those two stores. Subsequently, on October 31, 2001, the grievant's employment was terminated for being kicked out of two stores for offensive remarks that violated the company's rules concerning conduct.

The union filed a timely grievance, which was denied as were subsequent appeals in the grievance procedure. The parties stipulated that the case was properly before the arbitrator pursuant to the parties' negotiated grievance procedure.

POSITION OF THE COMPANY

It was the company's position that it had just cause to discharge this grievant. There was no dispute that the company promulgated rules proscribing this grievant's grievous conduct.

There was no doubt the grievant knew what he did was contrary to the company's rules, and the record shows he did apologize, acknowledging his culpability in these matters. The grievant was specifically ordered not to engage in the conduct he did with Mr. H after the first incident. Rather than adhere to those instructions, the grievant committed a second offense involving Mr. A.

There were no factual disputes concerning the incidents involving Mr. H or Mr. A. The grievant acknowledged comments of the nature he was charged with were made. His only defense was that in the second incident he said what he said to himself, not to Mr. A. Clearly, management had discharged its burden of proof in this matter. There was just cause for the discharge of this grievance. Therefore, the arbitrator should sustain the discharge, and deny this grievance as being without merit.

POSITION OF THE UNION

The union contended that the first incident was resolved when Mr. H accepted the grievant's apology. The first incident was therefore of no consequence in the proceedings. The second incident did not constitute insubordination as alleged by the company. The grievant's remarks were not addressed to Mr. A, but rather spoken to himself and not meant to be heard by others. It was therefore the union's position that there was no misconduct for which discipline was appropriate.

Should the arbitrator disagree, there were mitigating factors present in this case. The grievant was a 19-year employee with a spotless record. This is a substantial bank of goodwill and should serve to mitigate any penalty assigned this grievant. Further, many other Pepsi employees have had their routes changed to keep them away from stores where they had personality conflicts with the owners. Nothing was ever done to adjust this grievant's route, and he always provided courteous service to his customers. For all of these reasons, the union argued the grievance should be sustained.

QUESTIONS

1. Are the facts in this matter disputed? Explain. Has the company proven misconduct on behalf of the grievant? Explain.
2. Are there mitigating factors present in this case? If so, what are they and should they serve to lessen the penalty assessed in this case? Explain.
3. If you were the arbitrator in this case, how would you have ruled? Explain.

Case 57

Abuse of a Senior Citizen Resident

Employer Lutheran Senior City, Inc., Columbus, Ohio

Union United Industrial Service, Transportation, Professional and Government Workers of North America

BACKGROUND

Lutheran Senior City, of Columbus, was a multilevel retirement community providing services to senior citizens. The services included care levels from independent living to full nursing and custodial care.

Andrea Gwynn,[1] the grievant in this case, had been an employee for 22 years. At the time of her discharge, she was classified as a nursing assistant, and her responsibilities were essentially the primary care of residents. The events leading up to Gwynn's termination began at approximately 10:15 P.M. on July 12, 1993. At that time, Gwynn and two other staff employees were in the process of preparing a resident for bed. This particular resident was at times known to be physically and verbally aggressive toward the staff. As the three employees were lowering the resident into her bed (approximately 6–12 inches above the floor), the resident pulled her hands loose from one of the staff members, reached up, and scratched Andrea Gwynn's nose. As a result, Gwynn let go of the resident, which caused the other staff members to let go, and the resident dropped to the bed. Immediately after the incident, Gwynn reported her scratched nose to the LPN on duty. Thereafter, Gwynn left the work premises; her shift ended at 10:30 P.M.

Subsequently, during the following shift, two nurse assistants discovered marks on the resident's face, but they took no action. It was not until somewhere between 5:00 and 6:00 A.M. on July 13, 1993, that a supervisor became aware of the marks on the resident's face.

On July 13, 1993, Andrea Gwynn was questioned by Katherine Fresta, director of nursing, about the July 12 incident, but no conclusions were made after that meeting. Gwynn again met on July 15 with Fresta. At this meeting, Fresta asked Gwynn if she had hit the resident. Gwynn did not deny hitting the resident, but said if she had, she was sorry.

On July 14, 1993, Andrea Gwynn met with Rachel Crisp, administrator of Lutheran Senior City. At this meeting, when Crisp asked Gwynn if she had hit the resident, Gwynn replied that she couldn't remember, and she had "blacked out." However, Gwynn did not specifically deny that she had struck the resident.

After reviewing the incident with staff members involved, Administrator Crisp determined on July 16, 1993, that Andrea Gwynn should be terminated for a violation of the work rules (item III-n). In a letter of termination to Gwynn, Crisp indicated that Gwynn's violation of this work rule was sufficient to establish just cause under the parties' labor agreement.[2] The letter further indicated that the decision to terminate Gwynn was based

[1] The names of all individuals have been disguised.

[2] See appendix for relevant provisions of the agreement and the applicable work rule.

upon the physical evidence (marks on resident's face), the fact that Gwynn never denied she had hit the resident, and her statements that she had "blacked out" and "hoped she hadn't hurt anyone."

The union and Andrea Gwynn filed a grievance which eventually went to arbitration. Her grievance read in part:

> I was terminated July 16, 1993, 2 P.M. I was accused of slapping a resident's face. I didn't do it.

POSITION OF THE EMPLOYER

The employer pointed out that during the period of management's investigation (July 13, 14, and 15, 1993), at no time did Andrea Gwynn deny that she had struck the resident. Thus, Gwynn's inconsistent responses and testimony should be recognized in assessing her credibility. Similarly, Gwynn's statements about not remembering and blacking out were not consistent with her denial of the conduct at the arbitration hearing. This, too, adversely damaged the grievant's credibility.

The employer noted that at the arbitration hearing, Andrea Gwynn did admit that she shouted at and probably had uttered some profanities to the resident at the time of the incident. This admission of verbal abuse, by itself and pursuant to the applicable work rule (III-n), justified the determination that her discharge was for just cause.

The employer submitted several photographs of the resident that were taken on July 13, 1993. These photographs clearly showed a number of marks on the resident's face. This attested to the conclusion that the resident had been struck in the face, presumably by Andrea Gwynn.

The employer asserted again that Gwynn was terminated for a violation of rule III-(n), which was one of 19 rules with penalties ranging from a final warning and a suspension of five days without pay to discharge on the first offense. Gwynn's physical and verbal abuse of the resident justified her termination, even though Gwynn was a long-service employee. The employer pointed out that the bargaining agreement (Article VI, Section 6.9) indicated that great deference should be given to management's business decisions where there was no evidence of bias or impartiality and thc matter pertained to issues of residents' safety. This area was within the medical and business expertise of the employer, not the arbitrator.

The employer urged that it had no choice but to discharge Andrea Gwynn to ensure the safety of residents entrusted to its care, to protect its reputation as a provider of quality care to the elderly, and to protect itself from liability for the actions of an employee whose own statements and failure to deny the charges were tantamount to an admission of resident abuse.

The employer reiterated that the discharge was for just cause, and the grievance should be denied.

POSITION OF THE UNION

The union argued that in a discharge matter, the burden of proof lies with the employer to demonstrate by clear and convincing evidence that it had just cause for the discharge. The union asserted that this burden had not been met by the employer in this case.

First of all, the injury to the resident was not reported until hours after Andrea Gwynn had left the resident's room. Anything could have happened during the time period involved. The union claimed that the employer had been unduly influenced by and had relied upon the written statement of a fellow-employee to the effect that she had seen Gwynn previously hit other residents a "couple of times." This allegation should not be considered by the arbitrator due to its hearsay nature and the fact that the union had no opportunity to cross-examine the individual who made this statement but who refused to testify in the arbitration hearing.[3]

The union argued that Gwynn's testimony at the arbitration hearing that she did not hit the resident should carry more weight than the employer's inference regarding Gwynn's failure to deny that she had hit the resident in her earlier interviews with management.

Although Gwynn admitted that she may have cursed and shouted at the resident at the time of the incident, this was precipitated by the resident's behavior and scratching Gwynn's nose. This was not verbal abuse of a resident in the union's view.

The union urged that the employer had failed to demonstrate that it had just cause to discharge the grievant. There were no eyewitnesses to the alleged hitting of the resident. The reasons given by the employer for the discharge were not based on facts but on conclusions from circumstantial evidence and inferences. The discharge of an employee with 22 years of prior faithful service based upon unsubstantiated allegations should not be allowed to stand. The union requested that Andrea Gwynn should be reinstated with full back pay and benefits.

Appendix

Relevant Provisions of the Agreement and Work Rules

Article V

Management Rights.

5.1 Except as expressly and specifically limited by the provisions of this Agreement, the Employer has and shall retain the full right to manage its workforce. Such right of management includes but is not limited to: the right to maintain discipline and efficiency of employees; the right to hire, lay off, assign, transfer, promote, and determine the qualifications of employees; the right to increase, decrease, discontinue or relocate its operations; the right to assign work and duties in accordance with its determination of the needs of the business; the right to subcontract provided that present employees are not thereby displaced; the right to establish, change, modify, and enforce work rules; and the right to impose discipline up to and including discharge upon employees for what the

[3] In rebuttal, the employer asserted that this statement did not cause Gwynn's discharge. Rather, it was because of Gwynn's own statements, her failure to deny that she hit the resident, and the evidence of definite physical abuse.

Employer determines to be just cause. The Employer shall be the exclusive judge of all matters pertaining to the work to be done and the services to be performed, schedules of working time, and the methods, processes, means, and supplies to be used.

Article VI

Dispute Procedure.

6.7 In all cases the expenses of the arbitrator, as well as other joint expenses of the arbitration hearing, shall be shared equally by the Employer and the Union.

6.8 The award of the arbitrator shall be in writing, and any written award on the merits of any grievance within his/her jurisdiction and authority shall be final and binding upon the aggrieved employee or employees, the Union, and the Employer, subject to normal judicial review where provided by law.

6.9 The jurisdiction and authority of the arbitrator and his/her opinion and award shall be exclusively limited to the interpretation of the written provisions of this Agreement. The arbitrator shall have no power to add to, subtract from, or in any way modify the terms of this Agreement. The arbitrator shall not have jurisdiction or authority to substitute his/her judgment or discretion for that of management in an area that has not been clearly delegated to him/her under the terms of this Agreement. The arbitrator shall have authority only to interpret and apply the specific provisions of this Agreement which shall constitute the basis upon which his/her decision shall be rendered.

Work Rules

Corrective Action Plan—Group III

The following are considered extremely serious infractions. *A final warning and a suspension of five days without pay or discharge may result on the first offense.*

* * *

III-n
Any abusive action towards a resident or an employee, either verbally or physically.

* * *

QUESTIONS

1. Why is a case of this nature extremely difficult for the arbitrator to decide?
2. To what extent should the grievant's 22 years of past service be weighed in the arbitrator's decision? Discuss.
3. Should the admission by the grievant, Andrea Gwynn, at the arbitration hearing that she might have "verbally abused" the resident be sufficient in itself to justify her discharge? Why, or why not?
4. Why would the employer "caution" the arbitrator that management's decision to terminate Andrea Gwynn was within its own medical and business expertise? Discuss.
5. If you were the arbitrator, how would you decide this case? Explain your decision.

Case 58

Ability and Seniority for Promotion: Which Controls?

Company Tecumseh Corrugated Box Company, Van Wert, Ohio

Union PACE International Union, Local 5-1228

BACKGROUND

The company operated a corrugated box factory in Van Wert, Ohio (among other places). The union represented its production and maintenance employees. The parties' collective bargaining agreement contained Section 18.14(b), which governed who would receive jobs posted for bidding (contained in the appendix to this case). Between 1985 and the time of this case in 2001 there was no incident of a test being used to determine abilities, and the posted job was simply awarded to the senior bidder.

In May 2001 a maintenance trainee position was posted in the plant. There were nine employees who bid for the job. The posting for the job specifically stated: "Ability and seniority will determine which applicant is placed on this job." To determine ability, the company administered a test. Before the test was given, two of the bidders withdrew their bids for the job. Mr. Lake[1] was the senior bidder but scored 11 out of 36 on the test. Two junior employees, Mr. Smart and Mr. Bright, scored the highest on the test with 23 out of 36 questions correctly answered. The company deemed 23 was necessary to demonstrate ability to perform the job and awarded the job to the senior of the two employees scoring 23 on the test, Mr. Smart.

Mr. Lake filed a grievance protesting the awarding of the job to a junior employee. The grievance was denied as were subsequent appeals in the grievance procedure, and the parties stipulated that the matter should be placed before an arbitrator.

POSITION OF THE UNION

The union contended that the company violated the collective bargaining agreement by awarding the posted job to Mr. Smart. The company had never before required a test to demonstrate an employee's ability to perform a posted job. In fact, management's own witness testified that they had never before used a test in determining the successful bidder for a posted job. The parties' contract language had not changed in decades, and they had always interpreted and applied the language such that the senior bidder received the job. For management to change the practice was to amend the parties' contract.

The union asked that the arbitrator sustain the grievance and award the job to the senior bidder, and make him whole for all lost wages and benefits.

POSITION OF THE COMPANY

The company had simply applied the plain meaning of the contract language it negotiated. The plain meaning of the contract language permitted the company to consider both

[1] The names of individuals have been disguised.

ability and seniority and that is precisely what the company did in selecting Mr. Smart for the posted position.

The union did not challenge the validity of the test, nor protest the legitimate business reasons for considering ability, as authorized by the contract. The union simply argued that only seniority should be considered in this matter, which ignores the plain meaning of the contract language. To argue past practice ignores the fact that the language is clear and that the company has not forfeited its right to use ability when ability is important, as it is in this maintenance position.

The company therefore contended that the grievance should be denied because there was no violation of the parties' contract.

Appendix

Article 18.14 (b)

> (b) After the two (2) working days, the Company shall remove the job bid posting, with a copy given to the Local Union President (or Vice President). The Company shall immediately notify the Local Union President (or Vice President) and the employee with the most plant wide seniority and ability to perform the work required of his being awarded to fill the vacancy or created job. . .

QUESTIONS

1. Does the plain and unambiguous language of a contract prevail over a past practice in a case such as this? Why?
2. What does it take to establish that a past practice is binding upon the parties? Explain.
3. Could the union have challenged what ability is in this matter? What sorts of problems exist for such a challenge in this matter? Explain.
4. If you were the arbitrator in this case, how would you rule? Explain.

Case 59

Company Picnic: Employee Benefit or Gratuity?

Company Meade Westvaco Corporation, Escanaba, Michigan

Union PACE International Union, Local 7-0021

BACKGROUND

The company has sponsored an annual picnic for its employees, retirees, and their families each year since 1920. The picnic is held each year in the summer time, and the company pays for the event. Initially, the employees were involved in the planning and logistics; however, over the years employee involvement waned. As employee involvement lessened, responsibilities for the picnic fell heavily on managerial personnel, particularly those in the human resources department. Also, in recent years employee attendance at the picnic has declined to a point where approximately 35 to 40 percent of the workforce now attend.

In only two years was the picnic not held. In 1975 there was no company picnic due to a strike, and then again in 1989 when labor-management relations were seriously strained. At no time has there ever been mention made of the picnic in any memorandum of agreement or contract between the company and union.

To relieve the increasing burden on the human resources department staff the company began contracting with a vendor to plan, supply, and conduct the picnic, including games and entertainment. At the same time as the picnic activities, the company also ran a Safety and Health Fair for the benefit of its employees. In employing the outside vendor, the costs to the company over the past two years has been in excess of $50,000; during the last year it was nearly $60,000.

In 2003, a new mill manager was hired and he determined because of a downturn in the company's business an aggressive cost-cutting program was necessary. Upon review of the costs of the company picnic and the fact that the picnic was not mentioned in any agreement with the union, the manager unilaterally decided to discontinue the company picnic in order to save the costs of the event. The union immediately grieved the company's announcement that the company picnic was being discontinued.

POSITION OF THE UNION

The union contended that the company picnic was a well-established past practice and benefit relied upon by the employees, and under these circumstances cannot now be discontinued. It was the union's position that for more than 80 years the company provided this benefit to the employees and it was mutually understood between the company and union that this benefit would continue. As with a multitude of other practices between the parties, this benefit was an implied contract even though it was not reduced to writing and incorporated in a written agreement.

The company picnic had been continued over decades, and the employees relied upon this benefit. The company simply had no right to unilaterally discontinue this benefit. If this was the company's intent, it could have raised the issue in the last contract negotiations, but it failed to do so. The union requested that its grievance be sustained and the company be directed to reinstate the picnic and bargain over desired changes the company wished to make.

POSITION OF THE COMPANY

The company's position was that the picnic was not a binding past practice, but rather it was a gratuity. The picnic was created unilaterally by management and therefore it could be unilaterally discontinued by management. At no time, over the decades this picnic existed, did the union seek any input whatsoever concerning any aspect of the picnic. The decision to discontinue the picnic was well within management's retained rights because there was no mention of the picnic in any agreement between the parties.

The decision to discontinue the picnic was made because of real economic reasons and was a legitimate exercise of management's retained rights. Therefore, it was the company's position that the arbitrator had no authority to "modify, change or alter" the parties' contract and hence find that this picnic was somehow incorporated into the contract. There was no dispute that the contract did not mention the picnic. Therefore, the arbitrator had no authority to grant this grievance, and the grievance should be denied.

QUESTIONS

1. What is a past practice? What must be shown for the parties' practice to attain the status of an implied contract?
2. How does a gratuity differ from a benefit in the context of an employer-employee relationship?
3. Does having the legitimate economic need to cut costs have any bearing on the merits of this case? If so, how?
4. Does the picnic rise to the level of an implied contract in this matter? Why, or why not?

Case 60

An Error in Equalizing the Overtime

Company St. John's River Power Park, Jacksonville, Florida

Union International Brotherhood of Electrical Workers (IBEW), Local No. 1618

BACKGROUND

On July 14, 1993, Jerald Oxnard,[1] an electrical technician, filed a grievance citing Article 16, Section 6, of the parties' collective bargaining agreement[2] and contesting the company's failure to call him for overtime on July 11, 1993. At this time, Oxnard was the first-listed qualified employee on his department's overtime list for that week. His supervisor, Walter Higgins, did not call Oxnard to work some needed overtime hours on July 11, 1993, because Higgins believed that Oxnard was still on his vacation (or annual leave).

In his grievance, Jerald Oxnard requested as a remedy that he should be paid five and one-half hours of overtime pay as compensation for not being permitted to work the hours to which he was entitled. The grievance was processed without resolution through steps of the grievance procedure and was eventually carried to arbitration. The parties stipulated that the issue to be decided was:

> Did the Company violate Article 16, Section 6, of the Collective Bargaining Agreement when it failed to call the Grievant for overtime on July 11, 1993, and, if so, what is the remedy?

POSITION OF THE UNION

The union stated that there really was no dispute about the fact that Oxnard should have been called to work the overtime in question. He was qualified, and he had first eligibility on the overtime list to work the overtime. Supervisor Higgins, who was responsible for making the calls, had fully admitted that he made a mistake when he did not call Oxnard for the overtime. Oxnard had been on annual (vacation) leave earlier in the week, and Higgins mistakenly believed that Oxnard was still on annual leave on July 11, 1993.

Even though it might have been an inadvertent and honest mistake by the supervisor, the contract was clear concerning Oxnard's right to have been called for the overtime work. The union contended that the problems with call-outs for overtime had been a recurring one. These problems contributed to a lowered morale of bargaining unit members. The union cited a recently settled EEOC complaint involving overtime in which the company agreed to pay the complainant for overtime she did not work but should have been permitted to work. Therefore, the union was asking that the grievant, Jerald Oxnard, should be paid for the overtime he would have worked in this situation if the company had properly followed the contractually mandated overtime call-out procedure.

[1] The names of individuals have been disguised.

[2] See the appendix for the relevant contractual provisions.

POSITION OF THE COMPANY

The company contended that the supervisor, Walter Higgins, consistently had made reasonable efforts to see that the opportunity to work overtime was equitably distributed among the bargaining unit employees pursuant to Article 16, Section 6. In this situation, Higgins admittedly made a mistake by not calling Oxnard, but there is no dispute that the mistake was unintentional. Oxnard was not charged for any overtime hours, and he did not lose his place on the overtime list. In fact, Oxnard was given the next opportunity to work overtime about a week or so later.

The company further contended that if the arbitrator should find that there was a contractual violation and/or that not sufficient reasonable effort was made in this case by the supervisor, the appropriate remedy was not pay as requested by the grievant. Whenever overtime was needed, the call-out procedure required the supervisor to place many calls. Errors were sometimes made.

However, there was no allegation by the union that the error in this case was intentional, or that the supervisor had deliberately not called Oxnard or other employees when they were needed for overtime. An inadvertent error did not justify paying money to someone for work not performed. The collective bargaining agreement contained no language that required the company to pay an employee for hours not worked as compensation for being inadvertently skipped over. Further, sound business practice precluded paying an employee for time not worked. The EEOC settlement referred to by the union involved entirely different circumstances and not a grievance under the collective bargaining agreement.

The company urged that the grievance should be denied.

Appendix

Relevant Provisions of the Agreement

Article XVI—Hours of Work and Overtime

Section 6.

(a) The Employer shall make a reasonable effort to see that the opportunity to work overtime is equitably distributed to bargaining unit employees.

(b) In order to accomplish this goal, the Employer will prepare an overtime list on a weekly basis. Copies of the list shall be posted in every work area and shall be made available to the area steward upon request.

(c) When a supervisor needs to call out an employee for overtime, or is arranging planned/scheduled overtime, the supervisor will refer to the current overtime list. The supervisor shall contact the first qualified employee on the overtime list in that work area to determine whether the employee is available to work the overtime assignment. If the supervisor is able to contact the employee and the employee either accepts or rejects the overtime, the supervisor will make a note of the date and time of the contact.

(d) If the employee works, rejects, or does not respond to a request to work overtime, the employee shall be charged for that overtime. A failure to respond is defined as either not answering the telephone within eight (8) rings, or failing to respond within one (1) hour to a message left on the employee's answering machine or to a message otherwise left for the employee.

(e) An employee returning a message within one (1) hour shall be assigned the overtime if the Employer has not scheduled another employee to work by the time of the return call. If another employee has already been assigned to work the overtime, the employee returning the message shall not be charged for the overtime.

QUESTIONS

1. Evaluate why the union would pursue a case of this nature to arbitration.
2. Examine closely Article 16, Section 6, of the parties' collective bargaining agreement. What does this provision mandate? What is not mandated by this provision?
3. How should the arbitrator interpret the requirement in Article 16, Section 6, that the company must make a "reasonable effort" to equalize overtime as related to the circumstances of this case?
4. Did the company violate the agreement by the fact of the supervisor's honest mistake? If so, what should be the appropriate remedy?

Case 61

Forced to Work on a Holiday

Company Ravarino and Freschi (Division of Borden, Inc.), St. Louis, Missouri

Union Teamsters Local Union No. 688

BACKGROUND

At the time of this case, there were about 250 employees in the plant bargaining unit represented by Teamsters Local Union No. 688. The company plant manufactured a full line of pasta products.

On January 1, 1994, three virtually identical union grievances were filed by bargaining unit employees. Each protested the company's having required bargaining unit employees to work on January 1, 1994. These grievances were eventually taken to arbitration.

In relevant part, each union grievance stated:

> Forced work on any of the holidays stated in Article 33[1] is a violation of the contract. The contract specifically states that "no work is performed on such holiday." The union membership is owed a day of no work on the nine stated holidays in Article 33. If the company decides to exercise its right to reschedule the holiday, then the membership is still "owed" a day of no work with holiday pay on a different day. We request compliance with Article 33 on every holiday stated therein or a rescheduled day of no work, with holiday pay, on another day. We request that if this grievance is won that it becomes binding on every holiday until the end of the contract.

The issue for the arbitrator was framed somewhat differently by the parties. Counsel for the union submitted that the issue should be stated:

> Does the company have the right to force employees to work on holidays?

Counsel for the company submitted that the issue should be framed:

> Did the company violate the agreement when it scheduled a work day on one of the contractually stipulated holidays?

TESTIMONY IN THE ARBITRATION HEARING

Giving brief testimony for the union was Carla Hempelmann,[2] a production employee. She had been with the company since 1986, and she was union chief shop steward after having served previously as a union shop steward. She indicated that Article 15 of the collective bargaining agreement had provided the company with considerable flexibility to transfer and assign employees in order to accommodate the start-up of a new company plant, which had opened in late 1991. In December 1993, company management had moved the Christmas holiday schedule around in a manner that was consistent with the previous

[1] See the appendix for relevant contractual provisions.

[2] The names of all individuals are disguised.

agreement, but everyone did get two days off for Christmas as stipulated in the agreement. Hempelmann stated that except for the year when the new plant was involved in the start-up, no one had ever been forced to work a contractual holiday until January 1, 1994.

Giving major testimony for the union was Rafael Decker, union business representative, who said that he serviced the Ravarino and Freschi plant. According to Decker, provisions in the agreement required that the company first seek volunteers before requiring overtime. He stated that for the most part, the company had been able to secure adequate volunteers when the company had had overtime needs. Introduced as union exhibits were several grievances filed by another employee, Martin Dumas, and the settlement of these grievances in the latter part of 1993. Decker said that Dumas's grievances had been granted by higher company management because management had recognized that contractual procedures for seeking volunteers before requiring overtime had not been followed. Thus, Decker stated, when bargaining unit employees were told that they had to work the January 1, 1994, holiday, employees first should have been asked to work on a voluntary basis. Forcing employees to work overtime on a contractually designated holiday was not permitted under the agreement, and it had never been attempted by the company until January 1, 1994.

Decker acknowledged that for overtime needs of the company except on contractual holidays, the company could force employees to work overtime after the company had first sought volunteers, if not enough volunteers were willing to work. If the company wanted to work everyone, the company could do this except for holidays. To Decker's knowledge, there had never been a prior grievance on the subject of forcing employees to work on a contractual holiday. Decker and the union suggested as one remedy for this grievance that employees who had been forced to work on January 1 might be given another day off on a date mutually agreeable to the company and employees. Further, a number of employees who had not worked on January 1, 1994, had been given written warnings, and the union wanted all these warnings rescinded and removed from employee records.

Testifying for the company was Albert Gronski, who stated that since early 1993, he had been operations coordinator for the company in Columbus, Ohio. From 1981 until 1986, he had been vice president of manufacturing at the Ravarino and Freschi plant in St. Louis. The company had been purchased by Borden in November 1986, and he had served as operations manager in the St. Louis plant until his move to Columbus, Ohio. Gronski stated that he had been involved in contractual negotiations for the two prior labor-management agreements. The current agreement had been negotiated in May 1990, because the company had been building a new plant in St. Louis and shutting down production operations at its older St. Louis plant and several other facilities. The company had wanted a new labor agreement to provide flexibility for a transition to the new plant, which opened in November 1991.

Gronski said he believed the entire plant had worked on Thanksgiving Day 1991, although the plant was shut down for Christmas 1991. As a result of an edict from the former president of the division, all plant bargaining unit employees had worked on January 1, 1992. Gronski said he also thought this had been the case on July 4, 1992. According to Gronski, the decision to require employees to work on January 1, 1994, had been to rectify a situation of very low inventory and high production order requirements. The company had needed to keep the plant running in order to meet the demands of customers. The business was very competitive, and the decision was made to schedule the entire plant on January 1, 1994, because of the inventory and customer concerns. Under cross-examination, Gronski admitted that he was "unsure" whether any employees were forced to work on the Thanksgiving 1991 and July 4, 1992, holidays that he had mentioned earlier in his testimony.

POSITION OF THE UNION

The position of the union was summarized in a post-hearing brief submitted by counsel for the union. Excerpts from this brief were as follows:

> The holiday clause of the collective bargaining agreement contains the following sentence: "No work is performed on such holiday." That sentence has been in the contract for many years, and during that time employees have never been forced to work on a holiday. The plain meaning of that sentence must be accepted for what it readily implies, i.e., employees cannot be forced to work on a holiday contrary to their wishes. If that interpretation is not given to the language, the sentence has no meaning at all which cannot be the intent of the parties. It is a well-recognized principle of contract construction that a contract must be construed in a way which gives full meaning to all of provisions; and another recognized principle is that the words of the contract must be given their plain and ordinary meaning. Those principles require that the contract be interpreted as not permitting the Employer to require employees to work on a scheduled holiday. Of course, the Employer has the unusual flexibility to schedule when the holidays will be observed in order to meet its business needs.
>
> Furthermore, Article 27, Section 7, of the collective bargaining agreement requires that in order for an employee on vacation or a holiday to be eligible to work on weekend overtime, the employee must make his/her availability known prior to leaving for vacation or holiday. It appears that this language may have been carried over inadvertently after the institution of mandatory overtime and the elimination of personal and birthday holidays; but the language supports the conclusion that the parties intended that work performed on holidays must be voluntary.
>
> The Employer argues that the language of Article 27, Section 2, specifying how employees who work on a holiday are to be paid supports the conclusion that the Employer may force employees to work on a holiday; but that language merely provides for the manner in which employees who agree to work on a holiday will be paid. The Employer also argues that its severe production requirements demand that it be permitted to require employees to work on holidays; but production demands, however severe, may not override the restrictions of the contract. The Employer has been able to satisfy its production demands for many years without forcing employees to work on scheduled holidays; and the Employer has the flexibility of scheduling the holidays on days which accommodate its legitimate business needs. Therefore, the requirements of the contract must be followed, unless and until the Employer is able to negotiate a change, as it did with mandatory overtime.
>
> Therefore, the grievance should be sustained.

POSITION OF THE COMPANY

The position of the company was summarized in a post-hearing brief submitted by counsel for the company. Excerpts from this brief were as follows:

> The Company maintains they can schedule a holiday as a work day as long as they pay the proper premiums. That is, 8 hours' pay for the holiday plus the additional time and one-half for the hours worked.
>
> There is absolutely nothing in Article 33 that prevents the Company from scheduling one of the contractual holidays as a work day for the entire plant. In addition, there is absolutely nothing in Article 33 that requires the Company to schedule another day as a holiday if they do schedule all the employees to work on one of the days listed in the contract.
>
> The language of Article 27, Section 2, which reads "all work performed on a holiday or the day celebrated in lieu thereof shall be paid for at time and one-half (1½) plus holiday pay," clearly shows the intent was not to keep the Company from scheduling work on a holiday but to require them to pay a premium to the employees if they did so.
>
> Article 27, *Hours of Work,* Section 2(D), specifically buttresses the Company position that mandatory overtime can be required when the Company deems it necessary to schedule the employees to work overtime.
>
> * * * * *
>
> The management rights clause, Article 23, specifically provides that the management of the business and the direction of the workforce is vested exclusively in the employer except as specifically provided in the labor agreement.
>
> * * * * *
>
> In line with the language contained in the Management Rights Clause, and contra to the Union's position, there is absolutely no language in the agreement that prevents the Company from scheduling full production on a holiday and certainly no language that requires the Company to schedule another day off for the employees when a holiday is worked.
>
> * * * * *
>
> A reading of Article 33 in the totality shows that the phrase "no work is performed on such holiday" simply sets forth the situation which will entitle the employee to eight (8) hours' pay at straight time. Thus the employee will receive holiday pay if he/she performs no work on a holiday and works the scheduled day before and the scheduled day after the holiday.
>
> Setting forth the requirements that need to be met to receive regular holiday pay does not contractually restrict the Company from scheduling work on a holiday.
>
> * * * * *
>
> Article 27 of the labor agreement clearly anticipates the Company may need to schedule work on a holiday by spelling out the requirement that "all work performed on a holiday or the day celebrated in lieu thereof, shall be paid for at time and one-half (1½) plus holiday pay."
>
> Therefore, according to the contract, an employee will receive 8 hours' straight time pay if he doesn't work on a holiday and eight (8) hours pay at straight time plus time and one-half if a holiday is worked.
>
> Conversely, nowhere in the contract does it say the Company can't schedule work on a holiday and nowhere does it set forth the requirement that anyone who works on a holiday must be given another day off in lieu of the holiday.
>
> * * * * *

Frankly, the testimony on past practice was so confusing and conflicting that it was impossible to follow. Parties must knowingly enter into a past practice for it to be binding on the parties. Obviously, such is not the case before the arbitrator.

Then too, the failure to exercise a particular management right for a period of time does not waive the right. From the testimony, it would appear that on most of the holidays in the past, the Company production requirements did not require that all the employees be scheduled to work on a holiday. If you don't need to schedule the employees, that does not mean you have waived the right to schedule when needed.

* * * * *

We submit that the applicable contractual language and Industrial Common Law permits the scheduling of mandatory overtime on a holiday without requiring the Company to designate another day of non-work in lieu of the holiday worked. This being the case, we respectfully submit the grievance before the arbitrator should be dismissed in the entirety.

Appendix

Relevant Provisions from the Agreement

Article 15—Transfers

The Employer may make temporary transfers from one classification to another as business needs dictate. The senior employee with the ability in a classification (when transfer exceeds one (1) hour) shall be offered the transfer when the transfer involves a higher paying job. The employee transferred shall receive the higher rate for the entire day which he works at the higher rated job. The junior employee in the classification (when transfer exceeds one (1) hour) shall be the one transferred to an equal or lower paying job. The employee transferred shall retain his regular rate. It may be necessary to make double transfers as business needs dictate, however, such double transfers shall be reviewed with the Chief Shop Steward, where the transfer exceeds one hour EXCEPTION:

During the first year of the start-up phase of the new facility located at Davis Street, the Company will be transferring employees over to the new facility based on production and efficiency requirements without regard to seniority and overtime. Transferring of employees within either operation during the start-up phase will be done with total flexibility without regard to seniority.

Article 23—Management Rights

Except as provided specifically in this Agreement, the management of the Employer's business and the direction of the working force, including the right to hire, suspend, or discharge for cause, or to transfer, to promote or demote, and the right to relieve employees from duty because of lack of work or for other legitimate reasons, is vested exclusively in the Employer, provided, however, that none of the powers herein reserved to the Employer shall be used for the purpose of discrimination because of an employee's membership in the Union.

Article 27—Hours of Work

Section 1. The regular work week shall consist of any eight (8) hours per day, forty (40) hours per week, or four (4) days at ten (10) hours per day or a 4–10 day schedule.

Section 2. Time and one-half shall be paid for work performed in excess of eight (8) per day or ten (10) hours on a 4 day 10 hour schedule or forty (40) hours per week, but no employee will be paid overtime twice for the same hours. Vacation and holidays will be figured as time worked when computing overtime. Time and one-half (1½) will be paid for the sixth consecutive day worked and seventh consecutive day worked.

All hours paid for shall be considered hours worked for the purpose of computing fifth, sixth, and seventh consecutive day overtime.

All work performed on a holiday or the day celebrated in lieu thereof, shall be paid for at time and one-half (1½) plus holiday pay.

Employees who work their vacation shall receive vacation pay plus their regular straight time rate.

This section defines the normal hours of work and shall not be construed as a guarantee of hours per day per week.

* * * * *

Section 6(A). Overtime shall be voluntary by seniority within the classifications to the extent the operation permits (i.e., voluntary first).

(B) If sufficient amount of employees cannot be obtained as stated above, then such overtime shall be offered according to seniority (with the ability) within the department.

(C) If sufficient amount of employees cannot be obtained as stated in "B," then such overtime shall be offered by unit-wide seniority (of the employees in the plant) with the ability to perform the available work.

(D) If the Company can't get employees to work the required overtime, such overtime shall be mandatory within the classification in reverse order of seniority. Overtime shall be posted on the bulletin board at least twenty-four (24) hours in advance of said overtime, whenever reasonably possible.

* * * * *

Section 7. An employee taking vacation, holiday (personal or birthday), or sick leave will be eligible for weekend overtime only if that employee informs his supervisor in writing on a form supplied by the Employer that he or she will be available for work prior to leaving. The employee so informing his supervisor shall be obligated to work the overtime and shall call his supervisor between 2:00 P.M. and 3:00 P.M. on the Friday preceding the weekend to learn whether he has been assigned to that overtime work.

* * * * *

Article 33—Holidays

Employees shall be paid at straight time on the basis of an eight (8) hour day whenever any of the following holidays occur during a work week or not. No work is performed on such holiday. Provided such employee works the scheduled day before and the scheduled day after such holiday unless otherwise agreed to by the Company and the Union. The following holidays shall be observed:

NEW YEAR'S DAY	THANKSGIVING DAY
MEMORIAL DAY	FRIDAY AFTER THANKSGIVING

FOURTH OF JULY
GOOD FRIDAY
LABOR DAY
CHRISTMAS DAY
DAY AFTER CHRISTMAS

The Company reserves the right to schedule the holiday.

Article 34—Entire Agreement

The parties agree that this Agreement incorporates their full and complete understanding and that prior agreements or practices are superseded by the terms of this Agreement. The parties further agree that no oral understanding will be recognized in the future unless committed to in writing and signed by the parties as a supplement to this hereto.

QUESTIONS

1. Examine the various contractual provisions. Which of these most support the union position? Which of these most support the company position?
2. Do the prior grievances of employee Martin Dumas cited by the union have significant relevance to this case? Why, or why not?
3. Why is the outcome of this case of major significance to the company? To the union? Discuss.
4. How should the arbitrator decide? Why?

Case 62

Full Consideration to Seniority and Qualifications

Company Nordson Corporation, Amherst, Ohio

Union Local Lodge No. 1802, International Association of Machinists and Aerospace Workers

BACKGROUND

The grievant in this case, Roger Kass,[1] had served as a machinist leader on and off since 1986, and he had held this position steadily on the third shift for about five years. During the last three of these years, he was designated as permanent leader. Kass voluntarily resigned from the position of third-shift leader effective July 26, 1993, in order to "bump" into a first-shift job so that he could spend more time with his family. At that time, no leader was utilized on the first shift.

Second-shift supervisor Milton Shaw on several occasions had counseled Kass about his performance as leader. On one occasion in June 1993, Shaw recorded his views in writing, and gave a copy to Kass. The primary source of Shaw's dissatisfaction was that Kass did not arrive early enough to communicate with the second shift, so that announcements made on other shifts, instructions, problems encountered, or other feedback could be relayed. Kass participated in a car pool, and although he never arrived late, Shaw wanted him to arrive early for the purpose of communicating with the prior shift. Neither Shaw's conversations with Kass nor his written memo constituted disciplinary action. Kass was never disciplined, either as leader or in any other capacity, and he had achieved near-perfect attendance. Management personnel generally acknowledged that Kass was a capable machinist and an above-average employee. During the time that Kass served as third-shift leader, Shaw normally left around midnight, leaving Kass in charge of the building and in possession of the keys and the alarm codes. As leader, Kass never encountered a problem which he could not handle, even though there usually was no supervisor present on the third shift.

In April 1994, employees on the first shift presented a petition seeking that a machinist leader be appointed on their shift. They listed 10 attributes or functions, which they envisioned as part of the leader's job. The factory manager, Sandra Mumm, after consultation with other management representatives, concluded that the idea had merit, and that a leader should be designated on the first shift. She drew up her own list of qualifications for the position, which largely corresponded to those listed by the first-shift employees. Mumm perceived the position as being one for a knowledgeable employee to whom others could turn for help, and who would "trouble shoot" and offer suggestions, or do whatever else was necessary to make the operation run more smoothly and efficiently. She perceived the job as calling for a self-starter, who did not need to be told what to do.

Sandra Mumm announced the opening and posted a job-bidding notice on May 1, 1994. There were two applicants (or bidders), Roger Kass and Mario Diaz. Mumm interviewed

[1] The names of all individuals are disguised.

both applicants, and she asked questions designed to help her evaluate them as to their initiative, communications skills, and ability to make decisions. Mumm also asked about their flexibility in scheduling. Later, Mumm discussed the two applicants with Milton Shaw. Shaw rated Diaz stronger in interpersonal skills, and he said that employees would feel more comfortable going to Diaz with questions. Shaw further offered his view that Diaz had more initiative; in his estimation, Diaz was more likely to take it upon himself to act, while Kass waited to be asked. Shaw also considered Kass less flexible, and he mentioned Kass's problem of communication with the second shift when Kass was the third-shift leader. Shaw stated that when Kass resigned as leader and moved to the first shift, Kass told him that he just wanted to be left alone, to run his machine, and not be bothered. Shaw commented that some third-shift employees had complained to him that Kass had not given them all the assistance they expected when they had asked Kass for help.

Also, two first-shift employees had confided privately with Sandra Mumm that they had more positive views about Mario Diaz as compared to Roger Kass. Mumm decided to select Mario Diaz to be the first-shift machinist leader. She notified both Kass and Diaz of her decision on July 1, 1994. Shortly thereafter, the union filed a grievance on behalf of Roger Kass, protesting the selection of the junior seniority machinist, Mario Diaz, over Roger Kass for the first-shift machinist leader position.

THE GRIEVANCE MEETING

A first-step grievance meeting was held in mid-July 1994, during which Roger Kass was accompanied by several union representatives. Sandra Mumm stated that her decision favoring Diaz over Kass was based on her assessment of Diaz as having the edge in interpersonal and other communication skills, initiative, and attitude. She said that Diaz seemed to enjoy doing the kinds of things that would be required of a leader. In her view, Diaz would work better with the supervisors, and employees would feel more comfortable going to Diaz with their questions. Mumm also stated that she had "considered" seniority in making the decision, but that Diaz's superior qualifications swung the decision in his favor.

The union pointed out that Roger Kass had a seniority date of March 10, 1977, which was four years senior to Diaz, who had a seniority date of July 6, 1981. When the opening for first-shift leader was announced, Kass was classified as a machinist first class, and Diaz was classified as a machinist second class. The pay differential between these two positions was $.93 per hour. Diaz had been rated as qualified to be a machinist first class since March 1991, but he had not received a promotion because there were a limited number of slots, and no openings occurred. Diaz had held the position of leader previously only on the basis of temporary transfers. Kass had originally trained Diaz as well as the individual currently serving as leader on the third shift. The union acknowledged that Kass was classified as a machinist, rather than leader, when he was training Diaz.

The union claimed that Sandra Mumm, after making the decision in favor of Diaz, had met with Kass to communicate the decision to him. According to Kass, Mumm had said—among other things—that he might be "a little too pro-union," and that with contract negotiations coming up, she wanted someone who was a "little more wishy-washy." Kass acknowledged that perhaps he did not grasp all of what Mumm had said during this interview, because he was so distraught over her decision. Sandra Mumm claimed that what she had said to Kass was that she wanted someone who would "keep communications open even when there was noise in the environment." She had used upcoming negotiations as an example of such "noise."

In the ensuing discussion, union representatives suggested that Mumm's ratings of the two candidates as to initiative may have been flawed in that Mario Diaz's machine had a longer cycle time, which afforded him more time to assist other employees. Mumm responded that it was not the amount of cycle time, but what the employee did with it that influenced her decision. In her and other supervisors' observations, Diaz was more likely to look to help someone else; Kass was more likely to wait around, and he would help another employee only if someone requested him to do so. Supervisor Milton Shaw, who was present at the grievance meeting, stated that when Roger Kass was leader on the third shift, he had encouraged Kass to operate a machine with a longer cycle time so that he could spend more time with the other employees. Kass, however, had responded that it would not be fair to the other employees if he did not rotate. (At that time, machinists rotated among the machines. By the time the position of first-shift leader was created, the rotation procedure had been discontinued.)

The local union president, Ronald Guy, pointed out that in the past, the most senior applicant was selected as leader the "majority of the time," although he did know of one instance when the senior candidate was not selected as leader, and no grievance was filed. Guy said that the current promotion was the first time that the position of leader was awarded to a machinist second class. Further, Guy mentioned that in his experience as a machinist repairman, Roger Kass had always been very helpful in assisting him to fix machines.

THE ARBITRATION ISSUE

In an effort to resolve the grievance, the company in the person of Sandra Mumm offered Roger Kass the opportunity to serve as first-shift machinist leader on those occasions when Diaz was absent. Kass declined this offer.

The grievance eventually was carried to arbitration. The parties agreed that the issue was whether the selection of the junior seniority employee (Diaz) for promotion to the position of machinist leader violated the Agreement.[2] If so, what should be the appropriate remedy?[3]

POSITION OF THE UNION

The union argued that the evidence demonstrated that Roger Kass was well qualified to hold the position as leader, as indicated by the fact that he had served as leader for a number of years, first on a temporary basis, and later as a permanent assignment. The union pointed to the absence of any disciplinary record in his file to suggest that he had not performed satisfactorily as leader. Further, the union saw the company's offer to let Kass

[2] See appendix for relevant contractual provisions.

[3] At this time, an employee classified as machinist leader received $.46 per hour above the rate for a first class machinist. The leader position was similar to that of a "working foreman," and it was included in the collective bargaining unit.

serve as leader on a temporary basis after Diaz was selected for the position on a permanent basis as a demonstration that in the company managers' views, Kass continued to be qualified for the leader position. By contrast, Diaz, the candidate who was awarded the position, was not only junior to Kass, but also at the time was classified as only a machinist second class. The union contended that the company had not given "full consideration" to the grievant's seniority and qualifications. Kass had worked his way up to the leader position, and while he held it, he performed in a satisfactory manner.

The union claimed that company managers had relied upon a number of irrelevant considerations and obsolete opinions about Kass. In this regard, the union particularly cited Sandra Mumm's conversation with Kass about upcoming contract negotiations, which was extremely "out-of-line" and quite irrelevant. Mumm further was relying on "ancient history" to the extent that Milton Shaw's observations played a part in the decision-making process.

Finally, the union criticized the company's selection method as relying on subjective factors and unexplained criteria, which in the union's view seemed to change from case to case to fit the company's predispositions in favor of, or against, certain candidates.

The union requested that the grievance should be sustained, that Roger Kass should be awarded the position of leader, and that he should be made whole by payment of back pay and any other benefits to which he was entitled.

POSITION OF THE COMPANY

The company asserted that the burden of proof in this case was upon the union, and the union had failed to meet the required burden. The arbitrator was not free to substitute his own judgment for that of management, so long as management's decision was not arbitrary or capricious.

The company argued that the labor contract provided for seniority to play a lesser role in the selection of an employee to fill a machinist leader position than for other promotions within the bargaining unit. Management fully considered and did take into account the grievant's greater seniority, which was its only obligation under the collective bargaining agreement. Having done so, management evaluated Mario Diaz higher on other criteria pertinent to the job. Management then was free to select him for the promotion. Although the grievant, Roger Kass, had held the position before, the company asserted that the agreement did not provide that a preference must be given to one who held a position previously. In this regard, the company claimed that there was at least some degree of dissatisfaction with Kass's performance when he had held the leader position on the third shift.

The company maintained that historically seniority had not been the determining factor in selection of employees to fill leader openings, and it identified two instances in which junior seniority employees were selected without union grievances being filed. The company claimed that this showed that the union, too, had recognized that the position of leader required certain qualifications that went beyond seniority and technical know-how. The leader was a type of supervisory position within the bargaining unit, and the company should have broad discretion to choose the employee who was most qualified for that role.

The company urged the arbitrator to deny the union grievance.

Appendix

Relevant Provisions of the Agreement

Section 20.1. Awarding a Job Bid. When job openings occur or there are vacancies in classifications covered by this Agreement, excluding Leader classifications, the Corporation shall post on its bulletin boards a notice of such opening or vacancy, indicating the rate of pay for a period of three (3) days, in order to afford employees an opportunity to qualify for such opening or vacancy on the basis of seniority and ability to perform the available work. The Corporation shall not be required to consider the bid of a probationary employee. At the end of the third (3rd) day, the job opening or vacancy shall be filled by the employee who qualifies as soon as possible, but not to exceed ten (10) working days.

* * *

Section 20.4. The provisions of this Section, however, shall not be construed to prevent the Corporation from immediately filling vacancies in order to maintain scheduled production requirements, subject to the posting provisions of this Section. In filling vacancies in Leader positions covered by this Agreement, the Corporation agrees to give full consideration to seniority and the qualifications of employees in filling such vacancies.

* * *

QUESTIONS

1. Evaluate carefully the relevant contractual provisions in this case. What is meant by the provision that requires company management "to give full consideration to seniority and the qualifications of employees" when filling vacancies for the leader position? Discuss.
2. Discuss which of the union's contentions in this case you find to be the most and least persuasive. Discuss which of the company's contentions in this case you find to be the most and least persuasive.
3. Should it make any difference in the arbitrator's decision that there had been at least one or two prior occasions when the company chose a junior seniority person for the leader position without a union grievance being filed? Why, or why not?
4. If you were the arbitrator, how would you decide, and why?

Case 63

No Accommodation Without an Examination

Company Cessna Aircraft Company, Wichita, Kansas

Union District No. 70, International Association of Machinists and Aerospace Workers

BACKGROUND

This grievance-arbitration matter arose at the company's plant in Wichita, Kansas, where it manufactured commercial aircraft.

Claudia Gast[1] was hired in March 1990, and she was classified as a radio and electrical assembly installer. Her chief duties were to install wiring in and about the aircraft. In October 1991, Gast hurt her back, neck, and left shoulder when she fell while on the job. She consulted with and was treated by a number of doctors. She filed a workers' compensation claim and retained a lawyer to represent her in her claim. Gast also participated in a company paid-for "work-hardening" program, although she reported to the company that it aggravated her condition. Gast was placed on extended medical leave of absence on or about December 20, 1991. This leave was in accordance with Article X of the parties' collective bargaining agreement.[2]

For the next 22 months, except for a few days in December 1991, Gast remained off work and was treated by several doctors. On October 5, 1993, Dr. Emil Scheidt, the doctor designated by the Kansas Workers' Compensation Court to treat Gast, released her to return to work with some restrictions. These restrictions included limited use of her left shoulder with occasional overhead activities; reaching of no more than once or twice an hour; and no overhead lifting or more than 5 pounds with a maximum level lift of no more than 5 to 10 pounds using the left upper extremity. Further, Gast was required to avoid repetitive gripping or squeezing activities and to avoid the use of vibratory power equipment with the left upper extremity. She was to avoid prolonged work with outstretched arms. For workers' compensation purposes, Dr. Scheidt fixed her permanent partial impairment at 14 percent for the left upper extremity and shoulders, which converted to an impairment of 8 percent to the body as a whole.

There was some dispute concerning the factual circumstances surrounding Claudia Gast's proposed return to work. Gast's version was that when she was released to return to work, she called the company to find out how to proceed. Abner Kollander, the firm's employee benefits manager, told Gast that the company did not have the paperwork that was needed before she could go back to work. After delays and a number of conversations, Kollander told Gast that she could come back to work on a different job at a lower rate of pay. According to Gast, on December 6, 1993, she reported to the company for a physical examination before starting back to work. Dr. Alia Foriad, the company's doctor, after checking with Gast's doctor about restrictions, authorized her return to work with the aforesaid restrictions on lifting and on overhead work involving reaching.

[1] Names of individuals have been disguised.

[2] See appendix for relevant contractual provisions.

However, the company's version of these circumstances was somewhat different. Abner Kollander, the employee benefits manager, claimed that when Claudia Gast first contacted the company about coming back to work, she did not mention having any work restrictions. When Gast reported for a physical exam on December 3, Dr. Foriad, the company doctor, found out for the first time that the workers' compensation doctor had placed work restrictions on Gast, which Dr. Foriad concurred with. Since Gast was restricted in the kind of work she could perform, the company requested her to submit to a functional capacity examination (FCE) to see what work she actually was capable of doing. The company arranged with a local rehabilitation center to conduct the FCE tests.

Claudia Gast refused to submit to the company-requested FCE examination. Gast informed the company that she had previously taken an FCE, and her lawyer had advised her not to take another FCE examination.

Because Gast refused to take the FCE, on January 4, 1994, the company informed Gast that her two-year leave of absence had expired, and she was, pursuant to the contract, thereby terminated.

A union grievance was filed, processed through the steps, and carried to arbitration.

POSITION OF THE COMPANY

The company contended that, as stipulated in the agreement, it had placed Claudia Gast on leave of absence on December 20, 1991, for 24 months because her injury was work-related. After the expiration of Gast's leave, the company terminated her in accordance with the contract when she refused to take a functional capacity examination (FCE) to determine where she could be placed and to confirm her specific physical limitations.

The company contended that the doctor's work restrictions would have seriously handicapped Gast in performing her previous job as a radio and electrical assembly installer. Because of this, the company wanted Gast to take an FCE so the company could determine if she could do the work of her job classification with some accommodation, or any other job to which she might be assigned.

The company argued that it had the right and responsibility to determine what functions Gast could or could not perform with her restrictions before placing her back on the job. When Gast chose not to take the FCE, the company claimed it "had no alternative but to terminate her," because her leave of absence had expired under the contract.

The company claimed it made a reasonable attempt to accommodate Gast, but she failed to cooperate by refusing to submit to an FCE. This examination was routinely required of all such employees under these types of circumstances. By her adamant refusal to take the FCE, Gast's leave of absence period expired, and in effect she terminated herself. The company requested that the union grievance should be denied.

POSITION OF THE UNION

The union contended that the company violated the contract by failing to reasonably accommodate Claudia Gast by providing her a job that she could perform within her work restrictions. The union argued that the evidence showed that Gast could have been placed back on her old job, which she could have done within the doctor's restrictions.

The company doctor had agreed that Gast could return to work with the lifting, reaching, and overhead work restrictions that had been set out by Gast's own doctor. A number of union witnesses testified that in their opinion Gast could do her old job of installing wiring in airplanes while working within these medical restrictions.

The union contended that the company had acted in bad faith by terminating Claudia Gast immediately after the 24-month period of her leave of absence had expired. There was an ongoing dispute concerning the FCE examination, to which Gast's attorney had advised her not to submit. The company seized upon the delay in resolving this dispute to terminate Gast. This was an act of egregious bad faith by the company; the company did not want to accommodate Gast, but only wanted to get rid of her.

The union asked that the grievance should be granted, and that Gast should be reinstated and made whole in every respect.

Appendix

Relevant Provisions of the Agreement

Article X—Leave of Absence

Leaves of absence shall not extend beyond a period of eighteen (18) months except for those employees on leave of absence due to an occupational injury or illness which employees may be on leave up to twenty-four (24) months.

Article XIV—Discrimination

The Company and the Union agree to promote equal employment opportunity principles and that there shall be no discrimination by reason of race, color, sex, age, religion, national origin, ancestry, physical handicap, or veteran status in regard to hiring, tenure or other terms or conditions of employment.

Letters of Intent—Disability Accommodation

L.5. The Company and the Union acknowledge that the Americans with Disability Act, the Kansas Act Against Discrimination, and the Family Leave Act (effective 08/05/93) require employers to reasonably accommodate the physical and mental disability of employees and applicants so long as accommodation will not be an undue hardship. Consistent with the provisions of this Agreement the Company will take those actions required to meet its obligation under those statutes.

QUESTIONS

1. Should the disputed factual circumstances surrounding Claudia Gast's proposed return to work influence the arbitrator's decision in this case? Why, or why not?
2. For what reasons might the grievant, Claudia Gast, have been unwilling to take the company-arranged FCE examination prior to returning to work? Discuss.

3. Evaluate the contractual provisions relevant to this case situation. Which of these provisions—if any—do you believe should be controlling, or most compelling, in the arbitrator's decision?
4. If you were the arbitrator, how would you rule, and why?
5. Why is a case of this nature, which has both contractual and legal ramifications, difficult for all parties concerned? Discuss.

Case 64

Last Chance Violation: Strike Three or Overreaction?

Company Interstate Brands Corporation

Union Bakery, Confectionery, Tobacco Workers, and Grain Millers International Union, Local 37

BACKGROUND

The company had a long-standing, written policy proscribing sexual harassment, which defined sexual harassment, in relevant part, as unwelcome verbal, physical, or visual contact of a sexual nature that creates "an intimidating, hostile or offensive working environment." Three years before the incident in this case, the grievant was suspended for five working days for having sexually harassed a co-worker. At that time the grievant signed a last-chance agreement which provided that any further violations of the company's sexual harassment policy would result in his immediate discharge.

The present incident involved the grievant (a male) putting his hand on a woman's shoulder and asking her, "Why are you going out with [co-worker] when you are not going out with me?" The result was the woman went into emotional trauma, frightening her, and causing her to weep uncontrollably. The company, upon investigation, determined that the grievant's conduct violated his last-chance agreement and discharged him.

POSITION OF THE COMPANY

It was the company's position in this case that it had a responsibility to its employees to provide a healthy and safe work environment. This responsibility included providing a working environment free from sexual harassment. To this end the company promulgated a policy proscribing sexual harassment.

This grievant was certainly aware of the company's policy because three years earlier he had received a five-working-day suspension for the violation of this policy. In addition to the suspension the grievant also signed a last-chance agreement with the company agreeing that he would refrain from future violations of this policy. Further, the agreement specifically stated that any future violations of the company's policy on sexual harassment would result in his immediate discharge.

The company noted that neither the grievant nor the union denied the fact that the grievant touched a female employee and made the comments with which he is charged. Therefore, the company contended that it had proper cause to discharge this grievant. The company urged that its discharge should be sustained, and the grievance denied as being without merit.

POSITION OF THE UNION

The union admitted that the grievant was a "touchy, feely" type of person. However, the union denied that there was anything but a platonic relationship between this woman and the grievant. There was no intent on his part to harass her.

The woman alleged that the grievant's advances toward her were habitual, but she hoped that they would stop on their own without her having to take action. Had the woman thought these were sexual acts, a reasonable person would assume she would have complained. However, it is clear that the grievant's touching of her shoulder had no sexual content or implication; this was simply a friendly act.

The union believed that management overreacted and that the grievance should be sustained. This was a long-service employee with a virtually clean disciplinary record. There was simply no just cause for discipline in this matter, and certainly no basis to discharge the grievant. The union asked that the grievant be reinstated to his former position with full back pay and benefits.

QUESTIONS

1. Is a single incident of touching a woman's shoulder by a man just cause for discharge for violation of this company's policy against sexual harassment? Explain.
2. Are there mitigating circumstances present in this case? If so, what? How should these circumstances affect the outcome, if any exist?
3. Does the last-chance agreement make any difference in determining whether just cause exists for the discharge of this grievant? If so, explain.
4. Does the length of time between the two incidents make any difference in this case? Explain.

Case 65

Health Insurance Benefits for Same-Sex Domestic Partners

Employer Michigan State University, East Lansing, Michigan

Union Clerical-Technical Union of Michigan State University

BACKGROUND

The dispute that eventually resulted in this arbitration case began on June 10, 1994, when the union received notification that a bargaining unit employee, Norman Trace,[1] had been denied dependent coverage for a same-sex domestic partner under a university health benefits program. As a result, a grievance was filed protesting this action. The university denied any contractual violation, and the matter was not settled through the steps of the grievance procedure.

Most of the facts pertaining to the grievance were not in dispute. On or about May 10, 1994, Norman Trace, a full-time bargaining unit administrative employee with about 12 years of service, filed a "Record Change for Group Health Care Coverage" form with the university. In that form he requested the addition of a dependent, Rodney Brookings, as a "domestic partner" under the Physician's Health Care Plan. This plan was one of three health benefit plans available to bargaining unit members. Trace's application for dependent coverage for Rodney Brookings was returned to Trace with a cover letter dated May 12, 1994, stating: "The Physician's Health Care Plan . . . does not cover domestic partners, nor do any of the plans that MSU offers." This letter was signed by Kate Helms, assistant director of human resources.

TESTIMONY DURING THE ARBITRATION HEARING

The grievant, Norman Trace, testified that Rodney Brookings had been his domestic partner and husband for 10 years. They had purchased a house together. Brookings was in the process of a job and career change, and he was about to lose health coverage that he had with his former employer. Trace indicated that it was discriminatory for the university not to provide health/medical benefits to cover same-sex domestic partners who were committed to a long-term and lasting relationship.

Bettina Rivers, the second union witness, was a former president of the union. She testified concerning relevant contractual language and the intent of the parties in agreements between the university and the union going back to the early 1980s. Rivers noted how certain wording in these agreements had remained the same or changed over the years. She then testified concerning the 1994 negotiations that led to the current contract.[2] Rivers said that she was present when the union bargaining team proposed a number of changes in contractual language, including the term "domestic partner." In its

[1] Names of individuals are disguised.

[2] See appendix for relevant contractual provisions.

proposals, the union differentiated between "casual roommates" and "domestic partners." This latter phrase had not been used before in the collective bargaining contract, and it was first included in the 1994 proposals. Rivers stated that this partially reflected changing and more liberal attitudes in the university community and within society in general. She acknowledged that the 1994 negotiations marked the first time that the union specifically proposed to mention domestic partners in the contract. Rivers further acknowledged that none of the union's proposals were accepted by the university or became part of the master labor agreement between the parties. Norman Trace was the first bargaining unit member to apply for domestic partner eligibility for health benefits under the existing contractual language.

Testifying for the university was Kate Helms, assistant director for human resources assigned to the Benefits Unit office. According to Helms, the university had never provided benefits for same-sex domestic partners, since the employer's health plans did not cover such a relationship.

Testifying also for the university was Jason Neu, a representative with the employee relations office for the university. Neu identified the union proposals in the 1994 negotiations that would have specifically identified domestic partners to be eligible for health care benefits. He indicated that none of the union's proposed changes in this regard was acceptable to the university, and as a result, none of them became part of the collective bargaining contract.

POSITION OF THE UNION

The union asserted that the existing contractual language of Articles 4, 13, and 28 of the collective bargaining agreement required the university to make available health insurance benefits for same-sex domestic partners. The union particularly emphasized the language of Articles 4 and 28, which, according to the union, provided "clear and unequivocal language prohibiting unfair as well as illegal discrimination on the basis of sexual orientation and marriage status." Instead of that language being followed and adhered to, the university was attempting to argue that the mere submission and withdrawal of proposals during contract negotiations should deny the grievant, Norman Trace, of rights that already were inherent in the contract for quite a few years.

The union claimed that its proposals were brought to the collective bargaining table for "clarification" and "codification" purposes. The union's contract proposals were designed to more specifically define the domestic-partner relationship as well as to provide benefits for domestic partners that could have been even more expansive than what already were available under existing health coverage.

According to the union, the language of the contract in Articles 4 and 28 was so clear that precontract proposals and negotiations to revise that language should be irrelevant to this arbitration case. The union cited several prior arbitration decisions in analogous cases as being supportive of this contention.

The union pointed out that same-sex domestic partners were prohibited from entering into a legal marriage under Michigan state law. This effectively prohibited them from direct access to health insurance benefits provided only for legal spouses. This practice obviously had a disparate impact upon employees with same-sex partners by denying them access to a benefit provided only to those who entered into so-called legal marriages. The union cited a case involving the University of Vermont in which the Vermont Labor Relations Board, relying upon a U.S. Supreme Court case, ruled that such a practice violated Vermont University's anti-discrimination policy. According to the union, that case was nearly identical to this case at Michigan State University.[3]

The union cited the testimony of Bettina Rivers and other evidence concerning the negotiating background in which the language of Article 4 appeared in the first agreement (1980–83) between the parties. Bettina Rivers, former union president and member of the CTU executive board, had testified that the language of Article 4 was negotiated without any exclusions or exceptions. The intent of the parties was to prohibit discrimination in any form.

The union submitted that the denial of health insurance benefits for same-sex domestic partners of bargaining unit members violated Articles 4 and 28 of the agreement. It was a practice that was discriminatory and which had a disparate impact upon a group of individual employees protected under the agreement. The 1994 contract proposals were merely an attempt to secure additional benefits and to clarify existing contractual language.

The union requested that the grievance should be sustained. The university should be ordered to cease and desist from this discriminatory practice, and to provide health care coverage for the grievant, Norman Trace, and to his and other domestic partners of bargaining unit members.

POSITION OF THE EMPLOYER (THE UNIVERSITY)

The university first of all claimed that insufficient evidence had been submitted by the union to demonstrate a contractual violation. Through this arbitration, the union was attempting to obtain what it had failed to achieve at the bargaining table, that is, to secure health care benefits and other benefits for same-sex and other domestic partners. Within about three weeks after the current collective bargaining agreement was ratified by both parties in May 1994, Trace's grievance was filed on June 15, 1994. Having failed to achieve its goal in collective bargaining, the union was attempting to obtain that goal through arbitration.

The university emphasized that under Article 30, the parties to this dispute had agreed that no terms of the agreement could be changed or altered unless such a change or alteration was agreed to in writing between the employer and the union.

The university argued that for a number of years throughout the history of negotiations and relationships between the union and the university, the definition of the term "family dependent" had never included an unmarried person of the same sex. Likewise, it did not include an unmarried person of the opposite sex. The university had consistently administered its health care programs in accordance with the definition of spouse being a "partner in a legal marriage."

In summary, the university contended that based upon both past practice and negotiating history, it was clear that no articles of the contract required benefit coverage for same-sex or other domestic partners. The university urged that the union's grievance should be denied.

[3] The case cited was identified as Vermont Labor Relations Board, Docket #92-32 (June 4, 1993).

Appendix

Relevant Provisions of the Agreement

Article IV—Fair Employment Practices

I. The Employer and the Union are committed to a policy of non-discrimination on the basis of race, color, sex, religion, creed, national origin, age, political persuasion, sexual orientation, marital status, and handicap.

II. The parties are mutually committed to promoting respect, civility, teamwork and empowerment in the workplace.

* * *

Article XI—Leaves of Absence

V. B. Usage. . . .

4. An employee may use accrued sick leave credits not to exceed twenty-four (24) hours in a fiscal year for the illness of a member of the immediate family (as defined under Article 11.VII.A2) or member of the household. An additional sixteen (16) hours may be used for the care of dependent children, spouse or parents. The total number of hours shall not exceed forty (40).

* * *

VII.

Regular employees will receive funeral leave with pay to make necessary arrangements when a death occurs in the immediate family.

A. Time Allowed.

1. One (1) day in the case of the death of the employee's or spouse's uncle, aunt, nephew or niece, or member of the employee's household. For the purpose of this Article "aunt" shall include the uncle's wife, and "uncle" shall include the aunt's husband.

2. Up to three (3) days in the case of the death of spouse, child, parent, sister, brother, brother-in-law, sister-in-law, father-in-law, mother-in-law, daughter-in-law, son-in-law, grandparent, grandparent-in-law, grandchild, half-brother, half-sister, stepparent, stepchild, stepbrother, or stepsister.

* * *

Article XIII—Benefits Plans

Section I, I. A. Health Care Coverage.

* * *

7. If both husband and wife are eligible MSU employees, the spouse's (non-certificate holder) contribution may be applied toward the certificate holder's basic premiums.

* * *

11. Where applicable, the University will reimburse employees and/or spouses for Part B Medicare coverage when they become eligible for such benefits.

* * *

Article XXVIII—Rights of the Employer

Except as specifically abridged, delegated, granted, or modified by terms of this contract, the Employer shall retain all rights to exercise customary and regular functions, duties, and responsibilities of management, including, but not limited to, the right to hire, establish and change work schedules, set hours of work, establish, eliminate or change classifications, assign, transfer, promote, demote, lay off employees, and for just cause to discipline and discharge employees and otherwise maintain an orderly, effective and efficient operation. Further, the Employer retains supervision of all operations, methods, processes, means and personnel by which work will be performed and the right to determine and change the work to be done and the standards to be met by employees. The Employer may require employees to have a physical reexamination when directed by the University Physician. It is further understood that management shall not use its right to unfairly and illegally discriminate against an employee, group of employees, or the Union.

* * *

Article XXX—Scope of the Agreement

I. The Employer and the Union acknowledge that during the negotiations which resulted in this Agreement each had the unlimited right and opportunity to make demands and proposals with respect to any subject or matter not removed by law from the area of collective bargaining, and that the understandings and agreements arrived at by the parties after the exercise of that right and opportunity are set forth in this Agreement.

II. No provision of this Agreement, or any supplement thereto, nor the right of either the Employer or the Union under the terms of the Agreement shall be changed or altered in any way unless such change or alteration is agreed to in writing between the Employer and the Union.

QUESTIONS

1. (*a*) To what degree should the early negotiating history cited by the union be a significant determinant in the arbitrator's decision? (*b*) To what degree should the most recent negotiating history cited by the employer be a significant determinant in the arbitrator's decision?
2. Examine closely the relevant provisions of the parties' collective bargaining agreement. Should the nondiscrimination provisions of Articles 4 and 28 be interpreted to provide health benefits for same-sex domestic partners? Why, or why not?
3. In support of its position, the union cited a parallel case decided by the Vermont Labor Relations Board in regard to Vermont University. Does the Vermont case impose a precedent upon the arbitrator's decision in this case at Michigan State University? Why, or why not?
4. Should any social/moral values be part of the arguments and considerations in this case? Discuss.
5. If the arbitrator should decide in the union's favor, would this exceed the arbitrator's authority and be in violation of Article 30 of the agreement? Explain your reasoning.

Case 66

Arbitrability of the Scheduling Past Practice

Company Conoco, Inc., Moundsville, West Virginia

Union Local Union No. 864, International Chemical Workers Union

BACKGROUND

This production facility was purchased by Conoco from BP in January 1990. The established union continued to represent bargaining unit employees. Subsequently, some changes were agreed upon between Conoco and the union regarding the use of relief operators and the filling of temporary vacancies. A grievance arose regarding the manner in which the company scheduled the week of November 6, 1994, when one employee was on vacation and one was on extended sick leave.

The company facility operated 24 hours a day, seven days a week, requiring 21 shifts per week. There were five operator job classifications, with four employees in each classification. A regular workweek included five shifts; if four employees worked five shifts each, there remained a 21st shift each week needing to be covered. There were also two employees classified as relief operators, who were qualified to fill in when there were operator vacancies. If the 21st shift was covered by an employee within the classification who had already worked a five-shift week, that employee was paid overtime at the rate of time and one-half.

In late 1994, the Production Department consisted of seven job classifications: lead operator (4 employees), relief operator (2), Plant Operator 1 (4), Plant Operator 2 (4), Track Operator 1 (4), Track Operator 2 (4), and laborer (7). The procedures for filling vacancies in the three highest job classifications (lead operator, Plant Operator 1, and Plant Operator 2) differed from the procedures for filling vacancies in the lower classifications.

This dispute concerned the proper scheduling procedure to be followed in a situation where two employees were scheduled to be off on leave—one from the three higher classifications, and one from the Track Operator 1 position. During the grievance process, the parties could find only five occasions since 1990 when this situation had occurred.

On three prior occasions, the scheduling was done in accordance with the union's position, namely, that the two relief operators should be scheduled to cover the anticipated absences, and the 21st shift should be worked by the employee in the classification scheduled to be off and whose turn it was to work the overtime (called the "low employee off").

On one occasion in February 1993, the scheduling was done in the manner that was being grieved and which the company claimed was its right. The track operator vacancy was filled by having laborer(s) bump up; one relief operator covered the other scheduled absence; the second relief operator was used to work the 21st shift in four different job classifications.

The union claimed that this scheduling method violated a binding past practice, and grieved the issue to arbitration. During the arbitration hearing, the company and the union stipulated to the following factual background:

1. Prior to 1990, overtime on the 21st shift was usually scheduled to be worked by Operators from within the job classification where the work was to be done.

2. The utilization of the Relief Operators was modified by agreement of the parties after Conoco took over the facility to allow Relief Operators to cover the weekly 21st shift in addition to the other kinds of vacancies they traditionally had covered.
3. The parties negotiated a change in 1990 that permitted lower job classifications to bumpup to cover absences in the lower three classifications, as high as Track Operator 1.

As framed by the arbitrator, the issues for determination were stated as follows:

1. Whether the arbitrator had jurisdiction to consider the issue as presented by the union.
2. Whether the company violated a binding past practice by its method of scheduling the Production Department employees during the week of November 6, 1994.

THE PROCEDURAL ARBITRABILITY ISSUE

In its post-hearing brief, the company included in its arguments a contention that when the union initially submitted its grievance, the union had failed to cite the section of the parties' agreement alleged to have been violated and as required by Article VII, Section 1.[1] The company claimed that this failure of the union to adhere procedurally to the agreement created a jurisdictional issue that precluded the arbitrator from deciding on the merits of the grievance. The company urged the arbitrator to deny the union grievance on procedural grounds, citing several arbitral opinions that jurisdictional issues could be raised by either party at any time during a grievance-arbitration proceeding, including post-hearing.

In the union's post-hearing brief, the union did cite—for the first time—Article XXIII, which provided for continuation of past practices not in conflict with the agreement. The union contended that this case involved a long-standing past practice which the union claimed could not be changed unilaterally by management. The union did not address any arbitrability issue about the arbitrator's jurisdiction to decide the merits of the grievance.

POSITION OF THE UNION

The union's primary contentions were as follows:

1. A long-existing practice had been to use relief operators first to cover vacations and other "long-term" absences. Only if relief operators were not needed for such coverage were they used to cover the 21st shift.
2. It had only been in the last few years that relief operators were used to cover the 21st shift, a change brought about in recognition of the desire of some operators to have their day off instead of working an extra shift.
3. When the relief operators were covering absences, the 21st shift was to be covered by an operator from within the job classification of the "absentee"; this operator was paid at the overtime rate.
4. This had been the practice for many years over numerous contracts, and it had never been discussed in negotiations.
5. The fact that the company could find only one instance where relief operators had been used contrary to this practice supported the union's position about what was the normal and required practice.

[1] See appendix for relevant contractual provisions.

6. Filling vacancies by bumping up eventually created overtime in the lower job classifications, effectively shifting overtime from the higher classifications to the lower classifications.
7. The union acknowledged that there were occasions where vacancies needed to be filled by bumping up, and it was not grieving those occasions on which there had been agreement between the union and company.
8. The company was not authorized to accommodate employees who wanted their day off instead of extra work by violating an established past practice.

In summary, the union claimed that with the exception of the one instance in February 1993 that went unnoticed by the union, relief operators had never over the last 20 years covered the 21st shift when there were two "long-term" absences (vacation or sick leave) to be covered. The procedure had always been to assign the two relief operators to cover the scheduled absences for the week. In the last five years, the union had agreed that relief operators could be scheduled to cover the 21st shift if they were not needed to cover the scheduled absences. Otherwise, the 21st shift was to be worked as overtime by one of the operators from that job classification. About 5 years of the revised utilization of relief operators, combined with at least 15 years of pre-Conoco practice, created a consistent past practice of scheduling overtime for one of the operators within the classification for the 21st shift in such a situation.

The union urged the arbitrator to sustain the grievance. If the company had followed the required scheduling past practice during the week of November 6, 1994, one operator from each of four different classifications would have been scheduled for a 21st shift at an overtime rate. The union requested that these four operators—which the union further identified as "the grievants"—should be made whole for the overtime pay that they would have earned if it had not been for the company's improper scheduling during the week in question.

POSITION OF THE COMPANY

While maintaining that the arbitrator should dismiss the union grievance on procedural grounds, the company also addressed the merits of the case with the following primary contentions:

1. Article V, the management rights clause of the agreement, clearly guaranteed the company the authority and flexibility to schedule as needed and appropriate for efficient operations. The company retained the right to make work assignments, even if it hadn't exercised that right previously. Clearly expressed management rights in the contract outweighed any force of a past practice.
2. This same method of bumping up had been used over some four or five past years to cover emergencies, split vacations, and day-to-day absences in the three lower job classifications, nullifying the union's claim of a past practice to the contrary.
3. The company used this same scheduling method on a prior occasion in a similar situation (February 1993) without any objection from the union. This constituted a concurrence in the appropriateness of the method and negated the union's claim of a past practice to the contrary.

4. Prior to 1991, extra days were frequently scheduled for all job classifications. The need for overtime work was alleviated by the hiring of four additional employees in 1991.
5. During the 1990 negotiations, it was agreed to simplify bumping up into the lower three job classifications. In subsequent negotiations, the company's proposal for a similar change for the top three classifications was rejected, and so it had to rely on the relief operators to cover scheduled days off, absences, and vacations.
6. In the instance being grieved, no person was displaced.
7. All employees had access to "extra" overtime at their normal job classification pay rate periodically throughout the year. It was not the company's fault if employees in higher classifications did not wish to perform this work.
8. Many senior employees had often voiced their displeasure to the scheduler when he had had to schedule them for extra days. This was his attempt to help them to enjoy a day off as well as to develop a cost-effective work schedule.

In summary, the company argued that with the addition of more laborers and changes in the negotiated agreement regarding bumping up, an absence in the Track Operator 1 position could be filled by either of two methods at the company's discretion. The company could either assign one of the two relief operators to cover it, or it could allow a lower-classification employee to bump up into it. The company had done the latter on two occasions; the first time was in February 1993, which the union did not contest, and the second time was in November 1994, which led to the present grievance.

The company urged that the union grievance was devoid of merit. If the arbitrator should decide that the union grievance was procedurally arbitrable, the arbitrator should then deny the union grievance because the company had not violated either the contract or a binding past practice.

Appendix

Relevant Provisions of the Agreement

Article V—Management

Section 1. The responsibilities of the Company to manage its business within the broad meaning of that term and to make and implement decisions thereto shall be the same as those existing prior to the Company's recognition of the Union except as specifically limited and abridged by the express provisions of this Agreement, and the exercise of any such responsibilities of the Company shall not be subject to arbitration. The responsibilities of the Company include, but are not limited to, the right to manage, direct, and supervise its plant and business including all functions, operations, and methods of production . . . to define, change, and modify work assignments and classifications.

* * *

Article VII—Settlement of Disputes

Section 1. For the purpose of this Agreement, the term "Grievance" shall mean any difference, dispute, or complaint which an employee has with the Company concerning the interpretation, application, or claim of violation of any of the provisions of this Agreement. The grievance shall state the specific nature of the occurrence giving rise to the grievance, the Section or Sections of the Agreement alleged to have been violated, and the relief sought.

* * *

Section 2(3)(c). In reaching his decision, the arbitrator shall be restricted to the specific terms and provisions of this written Agreement, and he shall not add to, subtract from, or in any way alter any of the provisions of this agreement.

* * *

Article XXIII—Scope of Agreement

Section 1. This Agreement shall supersede all existing and previous Contracts and all local rules, regulations, and customs heretofore established in conflict with this Agreement. Prior practices and customs not in conflict with this Agreement may be continued. This Agreement covers the entire understanding between the parties hereto.

* * *

QUESTIONS

On the procedural arbitrability issue:

1. Why would the company wait until submitting its post-hearing brief to contest the union grievance on procedural grounds, that is, that the union had failed to cite a section of the agreement alleged to have been violated? Discuss.
2. Does the fact that the union did cite Article XXIII in its post-hearing brief mitigate the company's contention that the arbitrator should dismiss the grievance on procedural grounds? Why, or why not?
3. Is the procedural arbitrability issue a "smoke screen" being raised by the company, or is it a legitimate basis upon which the arbitrator may choose to dismiss the grievance? Discuss.

On the merits of the case:

1. If the arbitrator should rule that the union grievance was arbitrable and under the arbitrator's jurisdiction, evaluate carefully the various contentions presented by the union and the company. Which of these contentions do you find to be the most persuasive, and the least persuasive, and why?
2. The "force" of a past practice as compared to contractual managerial rights (such as in Article V, Section 1, of the parties' agreement) often is a basis for conflict between management and a union. How should an arbitrator decide when a past practice is binding upon the parties, even if it appears to be "contrary" to management's protected rights to manage its business in an efficient manner? Discuss.
3. If you were the arbitrator in this case, how would you decide, and why?

Case 67

How Should the Lead Skycap Be Selected?

Employer Andy Frain Aviation Services, Inc., operating at Seattle-Tacoma (Washington) International Airport

Union Local Union No. 6, Service Employees International Union

BACKGROUND

The employer operated at the Seattle-Tacoma International Airport (also known as Sea-Tac) in the provision of skycap and other services to airline customers. Before Andy Frain Aviation Services came on the scene at this location, skycaps now employed by Frain had been employed either directly by United Airlines, or by a competitor firm, Ogden Aviation Services, which had provided skycap services to Alaska Airlines. The employer and union negotiated their first Sea-Tac collective bargaining agreement covering skycap employees in 1994. Appended to the parties' labor agreement were separate seniority lists containing the names of those skycaps performing services for United Airlines and Alaska Airlines. The dispute in this case concerned only those skycaps appearing on the United Airlines seniority list.

Among other matters discussed during negotiations in late 1993 and early 1994 was the issue of the appointment of lead skycaps.[1] Throughout the parties' proposals, counterproposals, and discussions with each other, the employer wanted much more latitude to pick lead skycaps from among available employees than the union wanted to give. Ultimately, the chief negotiator for the employer, Arnie Epstein,[2] and the union's chief negotiator, Martin Kelly, agreed on contractual language proposed by the employer on May 2, 1995; this language eventually became Section 7.4 of the agreement.[3]

The union employees ratified the agreement containing that language on May 20, 1995. In the union's written summary of the tentative provisions of the agreement that was handed out to union members prior to the ratification vote, the union characterized the meaning of Section 7.4 as follows:

> Skycaps: . . . The lead skycap would be picked from those employees who otherwise would be eligible to work on the shift in question unless no one was willing to be lead or all employees had failed to perform lead duties adequately after having been given the opportunity.

THE DISPUTED COMMUNICATIONS

Subsequently, on May 31, 1995, Martin Kelly initiated a telephone conversation with Arnie Epstein regarding the intent and application of the Section 7.4 language. Kelly's

[1] Lead skycaps performed a number of "supervisory" duties at the same rate of pay as other skycaps. The lead skycap position had limited authority and was part of the collective bargaining unit.

[2] Names of individuals are disguised.

[3] See appendix for relevant contractual provisions.

recollection of this conversation was that he and Epstein agreed that lead skycaps would be selected from among those skycaps who actually bid into a particular shift rather than from among all skycaps eligible to bid. Epstein, however, while remembering a telephone conversation with Kelly, recalled no such discussion and agreement that skycaps would bid the shifts first before leads were selected. Kelly claimed that he and Epstein agreed that he (Kelly) would summarize their May 31 "accord" in a letter to Epstein, and that Epstein would not respond if Kelly's letter was agreeable. Kelly claimed that he sent such a letter both by facsimile and regular mail to Epstein. Epstein, however, testified that he did not receive such a letter either by facsimile or by regular mail. Epstein also denied that he had agreed that Kelly would put their "accord" into writing, and that he would not need to write back. The letter that Kelly testified he sent Epstein[4] stated in relevant part:

> Based on our conversation, my understanding with respect to the interpretation of Section 7.4, Skycap Lead, is that the Skycap Lead for an airline will be selected from among those employees who have seniority rights to have bid a position on the morning or afternoon shift in question, except as provided in situations "a" and "b" which are described in the later part of 7.4.
>
> Unless I am otherwise advised by you in writing, I will assume that you agree and that this is the manner in which the parties will interpret this section.

THE GRIEVANCE-ARBITRATION ISSUE

The parties' collective bargaining agreement took effect on June 6, 1995. Almost immediately, it became clear the parties were in disagreement concerning the application of the Section 7.4 contractual language. A union grievance was filed and was expeditiously moved to arbitration for a determination. The parties agreed that the issue to be decided by the arbitrator could be framed as follows:

1. Does the Employer retain the authority to assign lead skycap duties on a particular United Airlines shift to any employee on the United Airlines seniority list?
2. If not, what is the appropriate remedy?

POSITION OF THE UNION

The union argued that Section 7.4 of the agreement codified its intent that the decision concerning who would be "on the curb," that is, the bidding for shifts by seniority, was to be accomplished before the employer selected its lead skycaps. According to the union, this would preserve the valuable seniority right of employees to select their work shifts. The employer's choices for lead skycap had to be made from among the successful bidders as long as neither exception outlined in Section 7.4(a) and 7.4(b) occurred.

In the union's view, because the agreement did not specifically or accurately describe the parties' true intent, the arbitrator should interpret and "reform" Section 7.4 to reflect

[4] Martin Kelly had a photocopy of this letter in his files, but he did not have any facsimile transaction report to confirm that he had faxed the letter to Epstein. Arnie Epstein maintained that he had never received or seen a copy of Kelly's letter until after the union grievance had been filed.

the parties' intent and agreement in collective bargaining. The union urged the arbitrator to sustain its grievance.

POSITION OF THE COMPANY

The employer asserted that the agreement was precisely what the parties had agreed upon. Company management never assented to confining its lead selection process only to those employees who successfully bid a particular shift. The employer contended that it had to be free to assign the lead skycap position to employees of its choosing—so long as they were on the United Airlines seniority list—in order to meet the demand of its customer (United) that one skycap report to work a half hour early on each shift to meet with United personnel. Because the lead skycap position did not receive extra pay, some employees did not want the lead position's added responsibility. The employer contended that it retained and must preserve its authority to choose from skycap employees of any work shift in selecting its leads. This was essential to maintain proper customer service and efficiency. The employer urged the arbitrator to deny the union grievance.

Appendix

Relevant Provisions of the Agreement

Article XI—Seniority

11.2 Application of Skycap Seniority. For skycaps, seniority shall be the determining factor in shift selection, schedule selection, vacation selection, layoff and recall.

* * *

Article VII—Classification and Rates of Pay

7.4. The Employer shall have the right to assign lead workers to the morning and afternoon shift for each airline with which it contracts to provide skycap service. The Employer may assign any employee on a particular airline's seniority list to be the lead worker if:

(a) No employee working either the morning or afternoon shift respectively agrees to be the lead worker on that shift;

(b) All employees working either the morning or afternoon shift respectively have been the lead worker and their performance as the lead worker has been found by the Employer to be unacceptable.

QUESTIONS

1. What significance, if any, should the arbitrator give to the union's written summary of its interpretation of Section 7.4, which the union provided to bargaining unit members for contract ratification purposes?

2. What significance, if any, should the arbitrator give to either or both of the conflicting versions of the May 31, 1995, conversation and letter between the chief employer (Epstein) and union negotiators (Kelly)?
3. Closely scrutinize Section 7.4 of the parties' collective bargaining agreement. Are these provisions ambiguous, or are they clearly or predominantly supportive of the union's or the employer's position? Discuss.
4. If you were the arbitrator, how would you decide, and why?

Case 68

Post-Reinstatement Drug Testing

Employer City of Tampa, Florida

Union Local No. 1464, Amalgamated Transit Union

BACKGROUND

This case involved a grievance dispute between the City of Tampa, Florida, and the Amalgamated Transit Union, Local 1464. The union represented a bargaining unit of "blue collar" employees including the grievant, Adam Davenport,[1] a Services Attendant II, who worked in the Convention Center. Davenport was arrested on December 9, 1996, on a charge of domestic violence battery. He subsequently was terminated by the City on December 26, 1996. He did not grieve this termination.

Davenport was scheduled for trial on June 11, 1997. The victim in the case did not appear for trial, and thus the State Attorney's office dropped the charges against Davenport. On June 16, 1997, Davenport filed a grievance stating he should be reinstated to his former job in accordance with Article 7, Section 7.6, of the parties' labor agreement.[2] The parties held a third-step hearing on this grievance on July 17, 1997, and they settled the grievance by an agreement that Davenport would be reinstated to his former job position without any back pay.

On July 25, 1997, City management notified Davenport that he would be reinstated to his job as a Services Attendant II in the Convention Center effective 6:30 A.M. on July 28, 1997. Davenport also was told that the time he spent while being dismissed would be changed to reflect a leave of absence of 151 days.

After working nine days, Davenport was told that he would have to take a physical exam and drug test since he had been off work for a period exceeding six months. Davenport took a physical exam and drug test on August 8, 1997. He passed the physical exam, but he tested positive for marijuana in his drug test. City management then decided to suspend him from work. Davenport was told that he would be eligible for reinstatement at the end of a six-month period if he passed both his physical exam and drug test.

Adam Davenport filed another grievance on August 25, 1997, stating that it was improper to require him to take a physical exam and drug test after he was reinstated on July 28, 1997. In his grievance, Davenport indicated that the settlement at the third step of his first grievance did not mention any requirement for a physical exam or drug test. He requested immediate reinstatement and pay for lost wages and benefits. The City denied Davenport's grievance, and he remained off work for six months until he was again reinstated on February 9, 1998, after successfully passing a physical exam and drug test. The time he was off work was treated as a leave of absence without pay.

[1] Name is disguised.

[2] See appendix for relevant contractual provisions.

The union carried Adam Davenport's grievance to arbitration. Since Davenport was reinstated to his job, the parties agreed that the issue for the arbitrator's determination could be framed as follows:

> Did the employer properly handle the reinstatement of the grievant, Adam Davenport, in accordance with Article 7, Section 7.6, of the labor agreement? If not, what shall be the remedy?

POSITION OF THE EMPLOYER

During the arbitration hearing and in a post-hearing brief, counsel for the employer made the following arguments in urging the arbitrator to deny the grievance.

1. Adam Davenport's original reinstatement was contingent upon his passing a pre-employment physical examination, which included a drug test.
2. It had been a City practice for many years to require employees who had been off work for more than six months to pass a physical examination, including a drug test, before they could return to work.
3. City of Tampa Procedures and Standards B1.4(A)(2) states, "If the individual is reemployed within six months of termination, a physical examination is not required."
4. Tampa Civil Service Rules and Regulations Article E, Section 10 (b), states that employees who returned from a leave of absence status, or who were seeking reemployment, may be required to receive a satisfactory medical examination report before they were reinstated or reemployed.
5. Even though the City allowed Adam Davenport to work prior to the physical exam and drug test, it still regarded him as an applicant whose reinstatement was contingent upon passing the physical exam and drug test.
6. Since there was no language in the parties' labor agreement that mandated how to treat a former employee terminated for a felony arrest and who later becomes eligible for reinstatement, the City's long-standing practice, rules, and policies should be the controlling guidelines.
7. Nothing in the labor agreement mandated how the reinstatement was to be implemented, nor anything that required reinstatement with back pay. Thus, the arbitrator did not have the authority to reward the grievant with pay and benefits that did not exist in the labor agreement.

POSITION OF THE UNION

Counsel for the union during the arbitration hearing and in a post-hearing brief made the following arguments concerning why the union's grievance on behalf of Adam Davenport should be upheld.

1. The City did not have the right to require Adam Davenport to pass a physical examination and drug test prior to reinstatement.
2. The City did not notify Davenport that he was required to pass a physical exam and drug test before he could return to work.

3. The City did not mention any requirement to take a physical exam and drug test when the issue of reinstatement was discussed and settled in the third-step grievance hearing.
4. The grievant was not properly informed of his recourse if he disagreed with the results of his drug test. This is required under Florida Statutes, Chapter 112.0455.
5. There was no City policy that would require Davenport to wait six months before he applied for reinstatement following a positive drug test. The policy cited by the City referred only to new applicants.
6. If Davenport had been tested as a current employee, he would have been protected under the provisions of Article 42, Drug Free Workplace, of the parties' labor agreement.
7. Adam Davenport should be made whole in wages and benefits for the work time he lost following August 9, 1997, until the date of his reinstatement.

Appendix

Relevant Provisions of the Labor Agreement

Article 7—Disciplinary Action

7.6 Any employee who has been dismissed from the City of Tampa because of an arrest by any law enforcement agency will be reinstated to a comparable position in the City of Tampa provided that the employee is acquitted after a trial on the merits or all charges are dismissed by the State Attorney's office. The employee shall notify the Director of Administration in writing of his request for reinstatement within five (5) working days following the determination of acquittal and shall include proof of the acquittal.

Article 13—Leave of Absence without Pay

13.4 Reinstatement of Position. Upon the expiration of an approved leave of absence, the employee shall be reinstated to the position occupied at the time the leave was granted, or to a similar position in the same class at the same pay. Seniority, except as otherwise provided in this Agreement, rate of pay, and other benefits shall commence upon return to work. No position held by an employee who is on an approved leave of absence may be filled on a permanent basis; however, the position may be filled on a limited term basis.

13.6.5 Reinstatement. Any reinstatement shall require acceptable medical substantiation by the examining physician. If the employee's physical condition is such that the employee is able to perform the job, the employee will be reinstated to the position occupied at the time the leave was granted or to a similar class and at the same rate of pay. Reinstatement to any other position must take place through the application, certification, and selection process. All benefits shall commence again when an employee is reinstated to a former or new position.

Article 41—Employee Assistance Program

41.1 Purpose. The City of Tampa and the A.T.U. recognize that an employee's personal problems may result in a less than optimum, and even a declining, job performance.

These personal problems may include, but are not limited to, emotional or behavioral problems, marital or family problems, legal problems, financial problems, alcohol abuse, or drug abuse. In keeping with the mission of the City to provide the finest of services to the citizens of Tampa and recognizing the importance of the City's human resources, the City has established an Employee Assistance Program (EAP). The goal of this program is to restore the employee to full productivity by offering guidance and referral to qualified, professional providers. It is the City's policy that an employee's participation in the EAP will not jeopardize his or her future opportunities with the City, however, the EAP shall not replace, alter or be used to circumvent the City's discipline administration policy.

41.1.1 Eligibility. Employees enrolled in the City's group health insurance plan are eligible for EAP services. Spouses and/or dependents of employees are eligible if the employee is enrolled in the City's group health insurance program with family coverage. Any eligible employee or family member may directly seek EAP services for any personal problem. Such problems may include, but are not limited to: depression, anxiety, stress or psychiatric illnesses, difficulties stemming from alcohol or drug abuse or the emotional impact of problems of another person.

41.2 Program Access. Eligible employees or family members may access EAP services by:

A. Self-Referral. Employees or eligible family members experiencing personal problems may voluntarily and directly contact the EAP services with complete confidentiality (see Section 41.3).

B. Supervisor/Department Director Mandatory Referral. A supervisor/department director, noting a declining job performance on the part of an employee, may mandate referral of an employee to the EAP for assessment, further referral or counseling services.

(1) All mandatory referrals to the EAP must be coordinated through the City's Employee Relations Division.

(2) An employee's job will not be jeopardized by such a referral or by the employee's refusal to participate in the EAP. However, an employee's job may be jeopardized by failure to improve job performance, and such failure will be handled according to the City's Discipline Administration Policy.

41.3 Confidentiality. The confidentiality of EAP services is absolutely essential to the program's acceptance and success. Participants have the right to complete confidentiality concerning their use of the program, the content of the sessions, and all existing case information and records. Regardless of the nature of the referral, the EAP Counselor may not disclose any information about a participating employee to the City without the employee's written consent. In the case of a supervisory referral, the EAP Counselor may communicate to the City that the employee has or has not kept appointments. The EAP Counselor may also, with the employee's consent, work with the employee and the supervisor in defining the job performance difficulties and in setting work goals for improvement. All counseling records and information from employee visits are the property of the EAP.

41.4 Appointments. Appointments may be scheduled Monday through Friday between the hours of 9:00 A.M. and 5:00 P.M. An EAP staff member is available on a 24-hour basis by beeper service for life-threatening situations.

A. Employees and eligible family members may see an EAP staff member or other participating practitioner for up to three (3) sessions at no cost to the employee. Subsequent treatment sessions are available to the participating employee or family member. These services are generally at discounted rates and may be partially reimbursable under the City's Group Health Care Plan. The EAP will endeavor to refer participants to providers covered by the City's health insurance plan, including those listed as Preferred Providers.

(1) Supervisory referrals may be scheduled during the employee's work hours. Self referrals are to be scheduled during the employee's own time through the use of paid or unpaid leave, as applicable.

Article 42—Drug Free Workplace

42.3 Mandatory Referral for Substance Abuse Testing. The City has the authority to require an employee to complete physical examinations to ensure that the employee is fit for duty. This includes, but is not limited to, physical examination to determine if a specified employee is under the influence of alcohol on duty; to determine any abuse of prescription or non-prescription drugs; and, to determine any use of illegal substances.

(5) If an employee tests positive, the employee shall continue to be placed on sick leave (or a medical leave of absence if eligible when there is an insufficient leave balance) and shall be referred to the City's Employee Assistance Program (EAP) for counseling, further drug testing, and/or enrollment in an appropriate program. Upon completion of the program, the City shall require medical substantiation regarding fitness for duty and resolution of drug or alcohol use or dependency prior to reinstatement from sick leave or the medical leave of absence. Reinstatement shall be conditioned on continued monitoring and testing to ensure continued and complete recovery. Only one such referral to the Employee Assistance Program shall be permitted. An employee who fails to complete the program or who resumes use of said substances after the original reinstatement to work shall be dismissed.

QUESTIONS

1. Both the employer and the union cited state and city statutes in support of their respective positions. Should the arbitrator's decision in this case be influenced by application and interpretation of these statutes? Why, or why not?
2. Evaluate the arguments presented by the parties. Which of these do you find to be the *most* and the *least* persuasive? Why?
3. Why does a case of this nature place both the employer and the union in difficult roles as related to their responsibilities to the general public? Discuss.
4. Examine the relevant provisions of the parties' agreement. Which, if any, do you believe should be most relied upon by the arbitrator? Why?
5. If you were the arbitrator, what would be your decision? Explain.

Case 69

Conflict of Interest Rules and Discharge for News Photographer

Employer FOX Television Station

Union International Brotherhood of Electrical Workers, Local 69

BACKGROUND

There was no dispute that the employer has promulgated and enforces a conflict of interest policy. That policy required employees who made over $50,000 a year (which the grievant did) could not engage in any outside business or accept gainful employment with an outside business without disclosing that activity and receiving permission from the employer. However, there was a dispute concerning the applicability of the current policy in this case.

The grievant in this case had been employed as a news photographer by the local FOX television station for approximately five years at the time of his discharge. The employer provided the grievant with a copy of its statement on conflict of interest and required the grievant to sign for its receipt each year.

In early 2001, the grievant and two other persons decided to commence a business enterprise (ICNS). The record shows that the trio caused a website to be created describing the business and that description involved investigative news services—a business the employer was in. The record also shows with a preponderance of the evidence that the new company, ICNS, had purchased some video editing equipment and was seeking to purchase a video camera.

During the investigative interview with the grievant, two management officials allege the grievant admitted to being a director of the new company, ICNS, and that his primary function was to be the photographer and editor. The grievant denied he made this admission during the investigation.

The grievant's discharge was timely grieved by the union and the parties stipulated that this matter was properly before the arbitrator.

POSITION OF THE EMPLOYER

There was no dispute that the grievant, along with two other persons, started a business (ICNS) that would compete with FOX in the investigative news business. The employer investigated suspicions that the grievant was involved in the creation of this new venture and found evidence that he was. Upon questioning, the grievant admitted to the employer that he was a director of the new business and engaged in some work for this new company.

The grievant was warned every year while he worked for his employer that such competing businesses were a conflict of interest for which he would be discharged; even so he participated in the start up of ICNS.

After the discovery of his discharge for being involved with ICNS, but before this case came to arbitration, the employer discovered that the grievant misappropriate some of FOX's property for use in the new company. This evidence should be considered should the arbitrator deem any remedy is necessary in these proceedings.

The employer asked that the present grievance be denied as being without merit.

POSITION OF THE UNION

The union claimed that the employer failed to prove its charges against this grievant. The grievant had received numerous awards for his work at FOX and is, in every respect, an excellent employee.

It was the union's position that most of what the employer claimed is not true. There was a concept for a business called ICNS. However, that concept never came to fruition as the employer claims. The grievant did discuss the ICNS concept with management during the investigation, but the grievant told management the concept was "dead" and that he had done no productive work on behalf of ICNS.

The union also objected to the employer's claim that the conflict of interest policy, as modified in 2001, is applicable to this case. There were changes to the policy made unilaterally by the employer, and hence the policy is not valid and cannot serve as fair warning in this matter. The union never subscribed to the modified policy, and there were no negotiations concerning the 2001 edition.

For all of these reasons the union asked that the grievance be sustained, and that the grievant be returned to his former position with the employer with full back pay and benefits.

QUESTIONS

1. Does the employer have the right to modify its conflict of interest policy without negotiating with the union? Explain.
2. Is working for ICNS a dischargeable offense? Is being a director of ICNS a dischargeable offense? Explain.
3. If you were the arbitrator in this matter, how would you rule? Explain.

Case 70

Sickness and Accident Benefits Denied

Company Diamond Brands, Inc., Cloquet, Minnesota

Union Local No. 970, United Paperworkers International Union

BACKGROUND

The company plant manufactured various wood products. The parties had a collective bargaining agreement for many years, including group insurance provisions for employees and dependents.[1] One benefit was an income loss supplement for sickness and accidents (S&A). This case was over the denial of an S&A payment to an employee because of a payment she already received under her own no-fault auto insurance policy.

The Incident

In January 1998, Della Hester,[2] a production employee, was off work for one week due to an auto accident when her car went out of control under icy road conditions. After her return to work, Hester applied for a $185 per week S&A benefit. However, the company denied her claim on the basis that it was subject to an offset for the larger $250 a week payment she had received from her own no-fault auto insurance policy. This was provided in the company's policy with its carrier for S&A. In protesting the denial, the union cited that there was no such offset provision in the labor agreement. Della Hester had reported that the two payments together of the $185 S&A benefit and her $250 no-fault insurance amounted to much less than the weekly wage with her overtime that she was earning at that time.

The union filed a grievance on behalf of Della Hester that eventually was carried to arbitration. The issue for the arbitrator's determination was stipulated as follows:

> Did the company wrongfully deny the grievant her S&A benefit by applying her no-fault auto insurance payment as an offset for her accident income loss?

The Basis of the No-Fault Denial

Both the company and the union acknowledged that the company had paid full SA benefits for many prior years without any offset of a no-fault auto insurance payment, when an issue arose in 1996. In 1996, the company's new carrier (since 1994) denied an S&A claim of another employee by applying his no-fault payment as an offset under its 1994 policy with the company. The company ultimately was successful in persuading the carrier to pay the S&A benefit to this employee as an exception. In its December 5, 1996, letter to the carrier, the company cited the following reason for its request:

> Under the collective bargaining agreement (CBA) between Diamond Brands, Inc. and Matchmakers Local 970, there is no language that specifically allows for the offset of the

[1] See appendix for relevant contractual provisions.

[2] Name is disguised.

> weekly disability income benefit by benefits payable under the Minnesota No Fault Motor Vehicle Coverage law . . .
>
> When the short term disability plan was awarded to Canada Life on December 1, 1994, it was with the understanding of Diamond Brands, Inc. and our benefit consultant, W. A. Lang Company, that Canada Life plan would duplicate in form and substance the benefits of the two prior carriers, Fortis and The Hartford. Neither of these prior carriers considered No Fault Auto benefits as an offset to the weekly disability income benefits that they underwrote.

The company further indicated that at its next 1997 contract negotiations, management would negotiate with the union about the no-fault offset from S&A. Likewise, the company also gave notice to the union that effective with the expiration of the contract on May 1, 1997, it would apply the no-fault offset to S&A benefits and would discuss the matter in negotiations for a new contract at that time.

At the arbitration hearing, an insurance consultant stated that the no-fault offset was a common provision of most insurance contracts. The company also noted that such an offset was in accord with and allowed by a Minnesota statute, MSA 65B.61, subd. 1.3.

The Negotiation History

The union emphasized that there was no offset provision in the contract and that none was ever negotiated with the company. The union had never negotiated with nor participated with the company in its discussions with its insurance carrier. The S&A provision and the amount in the contract had always been a result of specific negotiations between the company and the union. Contracts back to 1967 contained language that the company's insurance program would remain in effect for the life of the contract. In 1973, contractual language made reference to the addition of negotiated changes in the insurance plan. In 1986, additional language was added that was contained in the current provision, which again made reference to negotiated improvements, and then specifically recited the benefit provisions including that for S&A.

The union noted that in the 1996 dispute with the other employee, while it accepted as a settlement the S&A payment finally made to the employee, it protested the company's reference to applying no-fault offset in the 1997 negotiations for a new contract term. In the 1997 negotiations that later occurred, there were no negotiations over the subject of a no-fault offset. Neither party made any proposal nor any mention of the subject. The only matter that arose was the union's request and the negotiated settlement of an increase in the amount of the weekly S&A payment benefit. The contract language otherwise remained as before for the new current contract term from May 1, 1997, to May 1, 2003.

POSITION OF THE UNION

Both during the arbitration hearing and in a post-hearing brief, the chief spokesperson for the union made the following contentions.

1. The group insurance benefits and provisions in the contract had been negotiated by the parties over many years. The contract language clearly required the payment of the S&A benefit and contained no provision for an offset reduction.

2. The company paid the full S&A benefit without any offset until the 1996 issue with the other employee when a settlement payment was made.
3. The contract required any changes through collective bargaining. In the 1997 negotiations, both parties presented a full agenda of their interests, and there were no negotiations whatsoever on the subject of a no-fault offset.
4. The clear and ordinary meaning of the contract language required that the full S&A benefit be paid without any offset. The union had other contracts in Minnesota, and the subject of a no-fault offset had never arisen in negotiations with other employers.
5. The union's position should be sustained, and the grievant, Della Hester, should be paid her S&A benefit of $185.

POSITION OF THE COMPANY

Both during the arbitration hearing and in a post-hearing brief, the chief spokesperson for the company made the following contentions.

1. The contract contained no language allowing the employee to collect an S&A benefit while also collecting no-fault insurance payments. The arbitrator was precluded from adding such a provision to the contract.
2. There was no contract language allowing the stacking of both S&A and no-fault income loss benefits.
3. Under the Minnesota no-fault statute, no-fault income loss payments are primary, and other entities are allowed to reduce their benefit by the amount of the no-fault payment to avoid stacking.
4. The union and employees had accepted that in the case of workers', compensation claims, the company would offset such income benefits from S&A.
5. The company's plan description given or made available to employees clearly indicated the no-fault reduction offset to S&A payments.
6. In the case of some lower-wage employees, the stacking of payments from both would provide more payout than their actual normal wage.
7. The prior past practice of not applying the no-fault offset was terminated by the company by its notice to the union in 1996 with the settlement of the other employee at issue.
8. The company's position was correct, and the arbitrator should deny the union grievance.

Appendix

Relevant Provisions from the Labor Agreement

Article 1—Agreement

. . . This Agreement can be changed or amended only by mutual consent of the parties . . .

Article 31—Scope of Agreement

This agreement contains the full and complete Agreement on all bargaining issues between the Parties . . .

Group Insurance Benefits

. . . the Employee Benefit Insurance Plan as herein after provided with negotiated improvements shall become effective . . .

Weekly Accident and Sickness Benefit

Payable: 1st Day—Accident

8th Day—Sickness or Pregnancy

Effective on ratification of 1997 contract $185/Week

Effective 5-1-98 $195/Week . . .

QUESTIONS

1. Evaluate the contentions of the union and the company in this case. Which do you find to be the *most* and the *least* persuasive, and why?
2. Did the company's notice to the union in 1996 that it would apply the no-fault offset to S&A benefits after the contract expired on May 1, 1997, cancel the previous past practice in this regard? Discuss.
3. Does the fact that the offset issue involved in this case was not discussed during 1997 contract negotiations bolster the company's position, the union's position, or neither's position? Why?
4. If you were the arbitrator, how would you decide this case, and why?

Case 71

Self-Defense or Excessive Use of Force?

Company ITT Industries Night Vision, Roanoke, Virginia

Union International Union of Electronic, Electrical, Technical, Salaried, and Machine Workers, Local 162

BACKGROUND

The grievant, Ms. H, worked for ITT Night Vision for nearly 15 years at the time of the incident that gave rise to her discharge. Ms. H's record was described by the union officials who defended her as excellent, with no prior discipline, confirmed by the human resource manager. There were several witnesses to the incident which occurred in December 2001.

The incident began with Ms. G approaching Ms. H with her hand raised in a threatening posture. There is no doubt in the description of the incident by the several witnesses that Ms. H's initial response to Ms. G was self-defense. The witnesses each described the initial phases of the incident as the beginning of a fight.

Ms. H responded to Ms. G's aggressive behavior with extreme prejudice. Ms. H responded to Ms. G with a series of vicious blows. Ms. H knocked Ms. G, a much smaller woman, to the ground, and then pounded Ms. G's head into the floor, eventually rendering her unconscious. Ms. H then continued to administer vicious blows on Ms. G long past a point where Ms. G was able to resist or to defend herself. These facts are virtually undisputed.

The record shows conclusively that Ms. G has a record of incendiary conduct. There is also evidence that sometime in 1989 there had been problems between Ms. G and the grievant. Ms. G is alleged to have struck Ms. H (when she was pregnant) in the stomach in 1989, allegedly causing Ms. H's baby to be stillborn. No disciplinary action was taken against Ms. G in that incident in 1989.

POSITION OF THE COMPANY

The company claimed, without rebuttal, that it had promulgated work rules against violence in the workplace. Employees knew that if they engaged in fighting on company property they would be disciplined, including discharge for such behavior. The company also claimed, without rebuttal, to have conducted a fair and thorough investigation of the subject incident. Having found the grievant engaged in violent conduct that was uniquely vicious, and well beyond any possible assertion that it was self-defense, the company decided that discharge was the only reasonable penalty to be assessed for this conduct.

The company had a responsibility to provide a safe and healthy work environment for its employees. Therefore, the company cannot tolerate such conduct that results in the vicious beating of a co-worker, such as the misconduct evidenced by this grievant in December 2001. The company urged the arbitrator to find just cause for the discharge and to deny the grievance as being without merit.

POSITION OF THE UNION

The union alleged that there had been a long history of the company not enforcing rules against violence in the work place. Ms. G attacked Ms. H in 1989 and management did nothing concerning this attack. Union witnesses also alleged that Ms. G threatened to cut their throats and nothing was done.

The union also alleged that Ms. G was the aggressor in the December incident. Ms. G came at Ms. H with her hand raised in a threatening gesture. All of the witnesses to the incident indicated they observed Ms. G come at Ms. H aggressively. Ms. H had a right to defend herself, and that was exactly what she did. To discipline an employee for self-defense is simply lacking in justice.

The record shows that management did not take into consideration any of the mitigating circumstances in this matter. There was a history of Ms. G attacking Ms. H. Ms. H had every reason to be extremely fearful of Ms. G. Further, Ms. H had an excellent, discipline-free work record that should serve to mitigate any penalty that management might believe was justified in this case. The union requested the grievance be sustained and that the grievant be reinstated with full back pay and benefits.

QUESTIONS

1. Can Ms. H's conduct toward Ms. G be properly characterized as self-defense? Why?
2. Does the history of violence between Ms. G and Ms. H serve to justify Ms. H's response to Ms. G's conduct? Explain.
3. Are there mitigating circumstances in this case? If so, what are they, and what weight would you assign them in this matter?
4. If you were the arbitrator in this matter, how would you rule? Explain.

Case 72

Egregious Horseplay

Company Trailmobile, Inc., Charleston, Illinois

Union Local No. 6-7591, Paper Allied-Industrial, Chemical and Energy Workers International Union

BACKGROUND

The Company manufactured over-the-road semi-trailers at its principal plant located in Charleston, Illinois. The grievant in this case, Marty Keller,[1] was employed by the company as a welder from July 12, 1994, until his discharge on May 8, 1998. Keller was discharged for throwing a six-pound sledgehammer on April 28, 1998, which struck another employee in the elbow, causing that employee to be injured. Keller first had been suspended pending investigation, and eventually he was discharged.

Failing to resolve the matter during the grievance procedure, the union requested arbitration of the matter.

TESTIMONY AND POSITION OF THE COMPANY

In opening statements and throughout the arbitration hearing, the company contended that there was ample just cause as required by the labor agreement to discharge the grievant, Marty Keller. Keller had violated widely published company "Policies and Rules" that specifically prohibited "throwing items either at or toward another person." The company argued that the grievant's offense was particularly "egregious," because in the workplace he threw a six-pound sledgehammer that struck another employee with enough force to cause serious injury.[2]

The company introduced testimony indicating that Marty Keller was well aware of company policies. Plant rules had been published for more than 10 years and were given to every new employee, salaried or hourly, at the time of hiring. In addition, all applicants signed a statement at their orientation program acknowledging, "My signature below certifies that I have been trained in each of the above and that I understand my responsibilities and rights under each." Keller had signed an orientation checklist on July 12, 1994. One of the elements on page 3 of the orientation checklist was "Rules of Conduct."

Company testimony verified the injury sustained by employee Mario Santiago. Santiago, a production worker, was taken to the hospital and his services were lost for the balance of his shift. Medical records showed that when Santiago was first seen by a physician following his injury, he had severe pain in his left arm and was diagnosed as having a contusion to the left forearm and elbow. An exhibit submitted in the hearing showed that Santiago described his pain as a "10" on a scale of 1 to 10. As a result of

[1] The names of all individuals are disguised.

[2] See appendix for relevant contractual and company rule provisions.

continuing pain, Santiago was ordered by physicians to observe a lifting limitation of 10 pounds when he again was seen by them on May 7, 1998, and May 21, 1998.

Testimony by Ray Smith, a supervisor, was that management conducted a thorough investigation. Smith testified that Santiago had described the incident to him and other managers. George Sell, manager of human resources, testified that during his interview with Marty Keller, Keller admitted throwing the sledgehammer. Sell stated that Keller was arrogant during the interview and "expressed no remorse." According to Sell, Keller had claimed that someone behind him had been throwing used welding tips at him while he worked. Keller said he responded by throwing the sledgehammer at a parts tub where three employees, including Santiago, were standing and smiling. Sell testified that he interviewed Mario Santiago, who denied throwing used welding tips at Keller or engaging in any other horseplay.

In summary, the company maintained that Marty Keller was guilty of "egregious" horseplay, and his discharge was for ample just cause. The company requested that the arbitrator find for the company and deny the grievance in its entirety.

TESTIMONY AND POSITION OF THE UNION

The union asserted that the company did not have just cause to discharge the grievant, Marty Keller. The company's own records, which were acknowledged and had been affirmed to by management witnesses, showed that Keller had compiled an exemplary record during his four years of employment with the company before his discharge.

Union witnesses testified that horseplay was a common occurrence at the company. According to Verna Links, the union's chief shop steward, horseplay was engaged in by both hourly and salaried employees. She testified that firecrackers were routinely brought into the workplace and thrown into places such as the toilet area. Links further testified that if employees reported horseplay or some type of harassment to management, the harassment of the reporting employee only increased. Links detailed an example of an employee who had quit the company because of harassment and intimidation. According to Links, the employee who quit worked within a 10-foot area of where Marty Keller had worked. Links stated that Keller did not have a reputation for engaging in horseplay. However, Mario Santiago, the worker who was injured when the sledgehammer was thrown, was known to engage in horseplay frequently.

Marty Keller testified on his own behalf. He claimed that when he arrived at his work station on the evening of the incident, he found stools stacked at his work area. This was a typical occurrence. He moved them to their proper location, but when he returned to his welding station, he found that the stools were back again and one had been welded to the floor. Keller stated that he broke the stool loose and kicked it to the side and went back to work. While he was welding, something kept striking him on the back of his neck and on his back and shoulders. Keller said that he kept stopping work and looking around. He found old used welding tips on the floor, and he believed that someone was throwing them from the parts tub area that was approximately 25 feet away. Keller said that he saw several employees "goofing off" and looking at him and smiling. He indicated that he then picked up the sledgehammer and threw it underhanded and hit the parts tub. However, it apparently bounced off and hit Santiago in the left arm. Keller claimed that he did not realize he had injured anyone and went back to work. Later he was summoned to the foreman's office, where he was told he was being sent home.

The union argued that the grievant, Marty Keller, was provoked into his action, and that Santiago had suffered the repercussions of his own acts of serious horseplay. In arguing that Keller had been denied due process, the union introduced testimony to the effect that the company failed to investigate the incident thoroughly. Ordinarily, the company would perform a complete investigation, and past practice was to discipline equally all those involved in horseplay. The union contended that it would be foolish to think that an employee with a good work ethic and no record of violence or ever being involved in a situation such as this would, unprovoked, throw a six-pound sledgehammer at another employee with the intent to hurt that employee.

The union requested that the grievance be sustained by the arbitrator and that the grievant, Marty Keller, be reinstated and made whole for all losses he suffered as a result of his unjust termination.

Appendix

Relevant Provisions from the Parties' Contractual Agreement

Article 3—Management

The Union recognizes those rights and responsibilities which belong to the Company. Those rights include, but are not limited to the following: the right to determine the size and location of the Company's plants and to extend, curtail, or terminate the operations of the Company; the right to determine the type of work to be performed and the products to be manufactured in its plant at any time, and to determine the type and amount of equipment to be used, the right to subcontract work, the right to determine production schedules, methods, standards, processes, means of manufacture, and to change existing methods or facilities; the right to establish new jobs and classifications, and to abolish, or change existing jobs and classifications, and to increase or decrease the number of jobs or classifications; the right to determine the number of shifts, the number of hours, and the days in the work week, the right to determine the number of persons to be actively employed by the Company at any time, and the right to hire employees of its own selection, and the right to determine the qualifications of its employees.

Except as specifically limited by the provisions of this Agreement, the Company retains the right to direct the working force, the right to maintain order and efficiency, the right to issue reasonable rules and regulations; the right to transfer employees and to assign employees to specific job assignments; the right to discipline, suspend and discharge employees for proper cause, to lay off employees, and the right to establish labor standards applicable to its manufacturing operations. All rights of a management nature except those specifically surrendered or modified by this Agreement are retained by the Company.

Relevant Provisions from Company "Policies and Work Rules"

Company Policies

At Trailmobile, we expect all our employees to conduct themselves according to the basic rules of good conduct. We want to provide a work environment which is productive, safe, pleasant and stimulating for all our employees. Politeness and integrity are qualities that help create a good working atmosphere and are readily communicated to other employees.

In order to achieve this, we are listing these work rules which we feel are absolutely necessary for the orderly and efficient performance of our work. These rules are not meant to be restrictive. Their purpose is to assist all of us in performing our work efficiently and pleasantly.

Violation of any of the following rules, while on Company premises, will be considered just cause for disciplinary action up to and including discharge. The Company also reserves the right to take disciplinary action up to and including discharge of employees for cause or violation of other commonly accepted rules of conduct not listed herein, or for repeated violation of several rules.

Threatening, intimidating or fighting on Company premises at any time.

Running in the plant, horseplay, scuffling, and throwing items either at or toward another person.

It is apparent that this list does not show a complete list of conduct violations. In the event of misconduct not mentioned, the Company will enforce such discipline as may be required in the interest and welfare of all employees.

QUESTIONS

1. Was the incident in this case "egregious" horseplay, or was it an unintentional consequence of questionable employee behavior on the job? Discuss.
2. Compare and evaluate the testimonies of Mario Santiago and Marty Keller. Whose testimony would you more likely believe to be credible, and why?
3. Why does a case of this nature pose a difficult problem for the union itself?
4. If you were the arbitrator, how would you decide, and why?

Case 73

No Reporting Pay

Company Whirlpool Corporation, Evansville, Indiana

Union Local No. 808, International Union of Electronic, Electrical, Salaried, Machine, and Furniture Workers

BACKGROUND

In 1998, the company was engaged in the manufacture of household appliances at its Evansville, Indiana, facilities. It used a just-in-time (JIT) system of delivery to receive parts from vendors. Other than parts and assemblies manufactured on the premises, essential parts for production would be in transit or in a transit warehouse waiting consolidation with other parts for respective company plants.

On August 7, 1998, second shift (3:00 P.M. to 11:30 P.M.) assembly employees were notified by supervisors of scheduled overtime for Saturday, August 8, 1998. An essential part in the assembly of refrigerators, a relay switch, was due into the plant on Friday evening.

The part was manufactured by a vendor in Mexico. Upon shipment, it moved to a "free trade zone" in Dallas, Texas, for U.S. Customs documentation. From there, it was picked up with the documentation for shipment to a local warehouse. Then in the normal course of events, it was transferred to a truck for shipment to La Vergne, Tennessee (south of Nashville), where many parts were consolidated for shipment to the Evansville plant.

The company became aware on Friday evening, August 7, that the part had failed to arrive. Management met to discuss the matter at 7:30 A.M. on Saturday. After several telephone calls to the manufacturer, which claimed the items were shipped, and trucking companies, which said they had no documentation, it was concluded that the items had been shipped but their location was unknown.

Management therefore decided that it would send home the first-shift employees after four hours of work (11:30 A.M.) when the inventory of onsite relay switch parts would be exhausted. Additionally, management decided that if the parts could not be located by 10:30 A.M., and the parts shipped in by 3:00 P.M., the second shift would be cancelled. At 10:30 A.M., the decision was made to cancel and notify second-shift employees, some of whom lived in three states and traveled as much as 60 miles one-way to work.

Esther Collins,[1] the manager of human resources, was the customary person to notify the media about plant closings, usually because of winter weather. There were 750 employees scheduled for the second shift whose work was cancelled. The first shift was sent home after four hours. As was her practice in the past, Collins called four television stations, where she received no answer at three and left a message at one. She successfully contacted announcers at four radio stations, who were advised of the second-shift cancellation and requested to broadcast the same. A facsimile message was sent to two other radio stations.

[1] The names of all individuals are disguised.

Additionally, Collins notified the Security Department and provided copies of a notice to be posted at several company gates. The notice said as follows:

> Whirlpool Evansville Division
>
> Second-Shift Assembly Cancelled
>
> Due to temporary shortage of a part critical to production of refrigerators, the previously scheduled overtime for Saturday, August 8, 1998, has been cancelled. Second-shift assembly and FIP should not report to work. The following departments should report to work on second shift:
>
> Press Shop
>
> Injection Molding
>
> Door Fabrication
>
> Metal Finish
>
> Maintenance is optional.
>
> Since we anticipate the arrival of the parts soon, production is scheduled to resume Monday.

The shipment of relay switches was discovered at 2:30 P.M. to be in a truck waiting to be unloaded at the La Bergne, Tennessee, warehouse.

Anton Kuhn, a production worker, lived in Uniontown, Kentucky, about 40 miles from the plant. At noon on Saturday, he and his brother had proceeded to the plant, having lunch on the way. They were listening to a radio station located in Owensboro, Kentucky, which was not on the list of media contacted by the company. It was a sunny summer day.

Upon arrival at the southwest gate, Kuhn noticed the parking lots were empty. He inquired of the guard if work was scheduled. Kuhn was informed by the guard that the day shift was sent home early, and that his (Kuhn's) "guess was as good as his." The guard did not direct Kuhn to any posted notice. Kuhn went into the plant, clocked in, and reported to his work area. There was no supervisor present. As other employees exited the plant via Kuhn's work area, he was told that second-shift production had been cancelled. Kuhn then clocked out and went home.

Several days later, the union filed a grievance on behalf of Anton Kuhn and 36 other employees who had reported to work and clocked in on August 8, 1998. These employees claimed that they were entitled to four hours of reporting pay. The grievance was carried to arbitration where the issue before the arbitrator was framed as follows:

> Did the Company violate the provisions of Article XV-85 by failing to pay the grievant and others four hours reporting pay? If so, what shall the remedy be?[2]

POSITION OF THE UNION

In summary arguments, the union contended that paragraph 85 of Article XV of the agreement was clear and unambiguous. The union asserted that the company failed to prove that proper notification or announcements had in fact been made that could reach all second-shift employees adequately. The union argued that the event causing the cancellation of work was not beyond the control of the company.

[2] See appendix for relevant contractual provisions.

The union urged that the grievance be upheld and that Anton Kuhn and 36 other employees who had reported and clocked in on August 8, 1998, be awarded four hours of reporting pay at their applicable hour rates.

POSITION OF THE COMPANY

In summary arguments, the company contended that both the notification requirement and four-hours' reporting pay requirement were excused because of causes beyond the control of the company. The company claimed that there was no way for management to anticipate the paperwork errors of its transportation company, thus making it impossible to track the parts. In the company's view, its method of communicating its notice of cancellation was reasonable, timely, and consistent with past practice. The union grievance should be denied.

Appendix

Relevant Provisions of the Labor Agreement

Article IV—Responsibility of the Company

6. The right to hire, the right to promote, and the right to discipline or discharge for cause is the sole responsibility of the Company, provided that claims of discriminatory promotions and of wrongful or unjust discipline or discharges shall be subject to the grievance procedure herein provided. The management of the business of the Company and the direction of its employees are the exclusive responsibilities of the Management, except as expressly modified by the terms of this Agreement.

Article XV—Hours

85. Any employee called to work or permitted to come to work without having been properly notified that there will be no regular work, shall receive a minimum of four hours available work at their regular hourly rate or be paid for four hours at their regular hourly rate, except in cases of labor disputes, machinery and power breakdowns, fire, flood, or other causes beyond the control of the Company.

QUESTIONS

1. Examine closely the provisions within paragraph 85 of Article XV of the agreement. In particular, what is meant by the phrase "*without having been properly notified, and other causes beyond the control of the company*"? Discuss.
2. In your opinion, did company management make *reasonable* efforts to notify second-shift employees about the shift cancellation? What other means of communication might have been utilized? Discuss.
3. Does the fact that only 37 employees reported and clocked in out of some 750 employees whose work was cancelled have any bearing upon the arbitrator's decision? Why, or why not?
4. If you were the arbitrator, how would you decide, and why?

Case 74

Who Decides If an Employee Is Unable to Work?

Company Akzo Nobel Coatings, Inc., Springfield, Ohio

Union United Automobile Workers, Local 402

BACKGROUND

The grievant in this case sustained two separate on-the-job injuries. The latest of these injuries was suffered on Friday, September 6, 2002. The grievant continued to work the remainder of that day, and reported for work the following Monday, September 9. The grievant worked for six hours, until the pain became too great to continue working. The grievant reported to the medical unit and was placed in "unable to work" status by the company's doctor.

Subsequently, in November 2002 the grievant furnished a medical slip from his personal physician indicating that he was physically able to return to work, with certain medical restrictions. The company, on November 25, 2002, refused permission for the grievant to return to work, citing concern for the grievant's physical well-being and risk of reinjury.

The union filed a timely grievance protesting the company's refusal to permit the grievant's return to work. The union contended the company had violated the collective bargaining agreement by refusing to allow the grievant to return to work. The parties stipulated that this case was properly before the arbitrator.

POSITION OF THE UNION

The union contended that the grievant complied with Article XXIV, Section 4, of the parties' collective bargaining agreement and should have been permitted to return to work. The union pointed to the fact that the grievant was allowed to return to work with more severe medical restrictions after his first injury prior to November 2002. Further, there was nothing in the grievant's current medical restrictions that precluded him from fulfilling any of the duties in the grievant's current maintenance classification job. The grievant's physician released him to return to work on November 25, 2002, in a medical slip dated November 21, 2002, and delivered to the company.

If the company believed the grievant was unable to perform his duties, the company could have referred the grievant to its own physician for examination. Further, Article XXV, Section 9 provided for the grievant exercising a right to transfer to a job he could do within his restrictions and in line with his seniority. None of this was done by the company.

It was the union's position that the grievant was entitled to return to his bid position and that he was entitled to be made whole for any lost earnings resulting from the company's violation of the collective bargaining agreement.

POSITION OF THE COMPANY

The company contended that Article XXV, Section 9, did not apply in this case. The company asserted it was the grievant's personal physician and not the company's doctor who determined the grievant was able to return to work with restrictions. However, Article XXV, Section 9, specifically required that the company's physician was to make such determinations with respect to the grievant's right to return to work.

Further, the company contended Article XIV, Section 4, makes clear that a position can be filled only by employees who are qualified to perform the duties of that position. The grievant's physician determined that he was unable to work from November 25, 2002, until May 2003. There are simply no contractual requirements that the grievant be paid for a period that his own treating physician determined that he was unable to work.

It was the company's position that this grievance should be denied in its entirety as being without merit.

Appendix

Applicable Contract Provisions

Article XXIV, Section 4—Sick Leave

1. Employees shall not be removed from the employ of the Company nor lose seniority standing when they are absent on account of disability or sickness provided the Company is notified within five (5) work days of such disability or sickness. . . .

5. Employees must have medical release and give twenty-four (24) hours notice prior to return to work (except Saturdays, Sundays, and holidays).

Article XXV, Section 9—Health and Safety

(Physicals) . . . Any employee may be required to take a physical examination . . . by any doctor selected by the Company to determine general health or physical fitness for certain work . . . If, upon recommendation of a Company doctor, the employee's present job is hazardous to the employee's health, the Company will remove him from the job and the employee may exercise his seniority to place himself on a job he is physically qualified to perform. Where there is a disagreement between doctors the Company shall bear the expense of an evaluation by a third physician . . .

QUESTIONS

1. May the grievant return to work with a medical slip from his own physician? If the company does not agree with the grievant's physician, are there contractual procedures for the company to follow to dispute that medical assessment? If so, what are they?
2. Does the record of evidence show when the grievant was released to return to work? If so when was that release date?
3. How would you decide this case? What remedy, if any, would you award in this matter?

Case 75

Internet Kiddie Pornography at Work: Just Cause for Discharge?

Company Xcel Energy

Union International Brotherhood of Electrical Workers, Local 160

BACKGROUND

Mr. N was issued a notice of termination on November 26, 2002, for violation of policies regarding the use of the company's computer network and the Internet. Specifically, Mr. N was charged with having spent approximately nine hours of his twelve-hour shift visiting child pornography sites on the Internet.

The company conducted an audit of Mr. N's Internet usage and found that he spent nine hours on October 17, 2002, visiting a site where sexually explicit photographs were shown of persons who had not yet reached puberty. Upon completing the audit and determining the nature of the site Mr. N had visited on October 17, 2002, he was interviewed by management personnel. Mr. N was placed on emergency suspension and a thorough investigation was made of the events of October 17, 2002. After due consideration of the facts and circumstances of this case management concluded that there was just cause for the discharge of Mr. N. Mr. N was subsequently discharged for his conduct on October 17, 2002.

A timely grievance was filed by the union on behalf of Mr. N protesting his termination. The grievance was denied, as were subsequent appeals through the grievance procedure. The parties stipulated that the matter was properly before the arbitrator.

POSITION OF THE COMPANY

The company contended it had just cause for the discharge of Mr. N. The company promulgated rules making it clear that illegal conduct and the use of company computers to visit pornographic sites, particularly involving children, would result in termination. During the hearing, Mr. N testified that he knew visiting the offensive site was wrong.

The company noted that it has had several cases in the past where employees were discovered visiting pornographic sites on the Internet, during working hours, and using company equipment. In each of the prior cases, the penalty assigned was termination, except in one case at a nuclear generating plant actually run by another company. That employee, who was not discharged, was given a long suspension, contrary to company policy. The management at the nuclear plant erroneously applied policies that were developed for nonunion employees, which resulted in an inappropriate penalty. Further, it is clear that Mr. N was viewing child pornography, which is a crime, and the employee receiving the suspension was viewing pornography where the models were adults; no children were involved.

It was the company's position that the clear and convincing preponderance of the credible evidence showed that Mr. N was guilty of the misconduct for which he was discharged, that the Company provided a fair and objective investigation, and that Mr. N was clearly warned of the penalty he could expect for this misconduct. The penalty assessed was administered even-handedly and was appropriate to Mr. N's misconduct.

The company contended that there was just cause for the discharge of Mr. N and that the arbitrator should deny the grievance in its entirety as being without merit.

POSITION OF THE UNION

The union contended that there was no just cause for the discharge of Mr. N. The union claimed that Mr. N was not fairly forewarned of the penalties for this type of conduct. It was the union's contention that discharge was not warranted for those who simply viewed pornographic material, and a written warning was all that was justified by this offense. For discharge, the material had to be transmitted or saved. Further, the Union argued that the rule barring visiting pornographic sites on company equipment and time was not clear, hence not enforceable.

The union claimed that the company conducted a faulty investigation. Management had its mind made up as a result of the computer audit, and hence Mr. N did not get an objective investigation. Further, the evidence presented at hearing did not show that Mr. N was guilty of the offenses he was charged with committing.

The union also alleged that the company had not applied its rules and penalties for their violation in an even-handed fashion. It is clear that at least one other employee engaged in similar conduct and received a lesser penalty. The company bore the burden to prove this case, and has failed to do so, therefore the union requested its grievance be sustained.

The remedy requested by the union was for Mr. N to be reinstated to his former position, and be made whole in all respects for the wrongful termination of his employment.

Appendix

Relevant Contract Language

Article 1, Section 2.

The right, in accordance with the provisions of this Agreement, to employ, promote, discipline and discharge employees and the management of the property are reserved by and shall be vested in the Company. The Company shall have the right to exercise discipline in the interest of good service and the proper conduct of its business. . .

Consequences of Violating Code of Conduct

An employee, who violates the law, the Xcel Energy Code or Xcel Energy policies will be subject to the Positive Discipline Process and possible termination of employment. Additional actions may include reassignment of work duties and limitation in future job opportunities. . .

Appropriate Use

Company information, electronic resources, and networks are provided for Company business purposes, not to satisfy curiosity or for personal gain, or for the direct or indirect gain of other companies or individuals. Incidental personal use is permissible if it meets the following requirements: Use does not violate the acceptable behavior outlined in the Code of Conduct. Use is not for the purpose of accessing, downloading, storing or otherwise processing information of a sexually explicit, violent, vulgar, or criminal nature or which otherwise offensively addresses age, gender, sexual orientation, race, religious, or political beliefs, national origin, or disability.

Disciplinary Guidelines

Termination [for] accessing Internet sites as well as saving and/or sending material that may be illegal (incest/rape/child pornography).

QUESTIONS

1. Did the company prove its case against Mr. N with a preponderance of the evidence? Explain.
2. Was the union able to provide proof supporting any of its affirmative defenses of this grievant? If so, which one, and what was the proof?
3. Was there a clear and applicable rule which Mr. N violated? Was there evidence that others violated that rule? If so, what was that evidence?
4. If you were the arbitrator in this case, how would you rule? Provide the reasons for your decision.

Case 76

Unilateral Changes to the Absence Control Policy

Company Conoco, Inc., Ponca City, Oklahoma

Union Local No. 444, International Brotherhood of Electrical Workers

BACKGROUND

The union bargaining unit's employees had been subject to an absence control policy (ACP) since approximately 1975. On July 23, 1998, the company presented the union with a revised ACP and requested that the union identify concerns with these proposed changes. The company agreed to meet with the union and to discuss the changes, but company management would not negotiate about them. The union responded by letter in which the union outlined numerous concerns over the proposed alterations. The parties met on September 22, 1998, to discuss the changes. In another meeting on November 6, 1998, the company advised the union that the revised ACP would go into effect on December 1, 1998. By a letter dated November 12, 1998, the union demanded the right to bargain over the changes to the ACP. The company did not respond, and management unilaterally implemented the revised policy on December 1, 1998. Consequently, the union filed an unfair labor practice charge against the company with the National Labor Relations Board (NLRB) alleging that the company had failed in its statutory duty to bargain (Sections 8(a)(5) and 8(a)(1) of the National Labor Relations Act (NLRA) as amended).

Subsequently, the NLRB deferred the unfair labor practice charge to the grievance and arbitration procedure of the parties' collective bargaining agreement. When the parties agreed to submit the issue to arbitration, the issue before the arbitrator was asserted by the union in its submission as follows:

> On or about December 3, 1998, the Employer, by its officers, agents, and representatives, failed in its duty to bargain in good faith with IBEW Local 444 by unilaterally implementing an absence control policy without providing the Union a meaningful opportunity to bargain. Since about November 12, 1998, the Employer has failed to supply information necessary and relevant to the Union with regard to changes in the absence control policy.

POSITION OF THE UNION

The union contended that the National Labor Relations Act (NLRA) made it a mandatory duty for employers to bargain with representatives of employees regarding wages, hours, or other conditions of employment. Further, the NLRB had consistently affirmed that plant rules affecting working conditions—such as attendance control—are a subject that employers have an affirmative duty to negotiate with the authorized representative of the employees. Many labor agreements contain a "management rights" provision that specifically permits the employer the right to unilaterally create and enforce reasonable rules and regulations. But in this plant, the labor agreement did not contain a "management rights" provision. Therefore, the union contended that the company had a duty imposed by the NLRA to negotiate the ACP, because the ACP specified conditions of employment. At the very least, the union had a retained right to challenge the revised ACP on grounds of "reasonability." The union asserted that a collective bargaining agreement, unless a contrary intention was agreed to by the parties, should carry forward for its life the major terms and conditions of employment that existed at the time the contract was agreed upon.[1]

It was undisputed that an absence control policy (ACP) had been in effect for approximately 25 years. Company managers claimed that they made unilateral changes to the policy during those years without negotiating with the union. As identified and discussed during the arbitration hearing, the union claimed that those changes were minor and procedural and could hardly be called "significant." They were not the type of alterations to which the union objected. Such minor unilateral changes made by management did not constitute a waiver by the union of its right to request collective bargaining over subsequent changes to the ACP. In contrast to previous alterations, the ones that the company instituted in 1998 were of a significant nature, and they should not be unilaterally imposed by management upon bargaining unit employees. Absent a clear waiver by the union of its right to bargain over changes in wages, hours, and other terms of employment, the company had a duty to negotiate major changes in the ACP and whether such changes were reasonable.

The union requested that the arbitrator direct the parties to negotiate any changes to the absence control policy. If they were unable to settle on a revised policy, then the ACP should revert to its former provisions until such time as the entire collective bargaining agreement was open for renegotiations.

POSITION OF THE COMPANY

The company noted that in 1975, the refinery experienced a work stoppage by its represented workers. Among the issues at the center of this dispute was the company's right to unilaterally promulgate and modify its absence control policy. The conclusion of this strike did not produce any restrictions on the company that required negotiations or mutual agreement between the parties to maintain or modify the ACP. The union did not dispute this fact.

During the years since 1975, management had made several changes to the ACP. None of these alterations came as a result of negotiations, and all were unilaterally implemented. The company normally would discuss and/or notify the union of the changes before they were implemented, but they were not the subject of negotiations. This fact was agreed to in the arbitration hearing by the union's only witness.

In early July 1998, the company notified the union of its intent to modify the ACP because of an ongoing high absenteeism rate. Thereafter, a few meetings were held with the union to discuss and clarify the changes. However, it was made clear to the union that these alterations were not the subject of negotiations. The sole purpose of these "preparatory" meetings was to collect whatever input the union might care to supply, and to apply those suggestions if management considered them to be meritorious. However, the company never waived its right to implement whatever alterations to the ACP it deemed necessary. Some of the union's suggestions were incorporated into the policy, while others were not. On December 1, 1998, the company implemented the revised ACP.

[1] See appendix for relevant contractual provisions.

The company pointed out that the parties' collective bargaining agreement had never contained a "management rights" clause. Absent any restrictions in the collective bargaining agreement, management had always exercised its "residual rights" to initiate and enforce rules and regulations. This included many additional policies other than the ACP. The union offered no evidence to suggest that management's "residual rights" had been changed or reduced by collective bargaining over absence control. An employer has the fundamental right to manage its business, including the basic right to develop and implement an absence control system. In short, there was nothing that limited management's right to make unilateral changes in the ACP. Therefore, the union grievance should be denied.

Appendix

Relevant Provisions of the Agreement

Article II—Union Recognition—Work to be Performed

Section 1. The Company recognizes the rights of its employees to bargain collectively through representatives of their own choosing. Local Union No. 444 of the International Brotherhood of Electrical Workers is recognized by the Company as the exclusive representative for collective bargaining for all of its hourly employees classified as electricians, electrician apprentices and helpers in the mechanical and operating departments of its Ponca City, Oklahoma, refinery.

Article VII—Benefits

Section 1. The Company agrees that it will not withdraw any of the present Conoco plans for the benefit of employees, namely:. . . Comprehensive Disability Income Plan . . .

QUESTIONS

1. Why do you think the National Labor Relations Board (NLRB) deferred the union's unfair labor practice charge to arbitration in this case? (*Suggestion:* Search for NLRB literature regarding NLRB decisions where unfair labor practice charges were deferred to arbitration and the reasons for such deferral.)
2. Evaluate the union's reasons for asserting a right to negotiate the absence control policy (ACP) as being part of "conditions of employment." Should the union have a right to challenge and negotiate over the "reasonability" of changes in the ACP? Discuss.
3. Evaluate the company's contentions that its position was supported by: (a) past practices, and (b) "residual rights" of management.
4. If you were the arbitrator, how would you decide, and why?

Case 77

Wage Concession: Contract Violation or Authorized Wage Freeze?

Company National Carbide Die

Union United Steelworkers of America, Local 5852-14

BACKGROUND

In October 2002 the parties negotiated a memorandum of agreement which called for union wage concessions (presented in the appendix to this case). The parties agreed that as of July 1, 2003, the company's business did not appreciably improve and the company was still making losses. The company did not restore the $.45 per hour conceded by the union in the October 2002 agreement when requested to due so in July 2003. The union filed the following grievance:

> In June 2002, the Company requested a meeting with the Union as to the Company's finances. The parties met and agreed to wage and benefit concessions for that specific year with the understanding that if the Company's financial position improved they would restore the wages but not the benefit reduction.
>
> The parties met in March 2003 and discussed the financial conditions of the Company. During the meeting, the Company requested the Union to freeze the $.45 per hour increase effective July 1, 2003. The Union Committee responded in the negative but would submit the Company's request to a secret ballot vote. The Company's request was overwhelmingly defeated, and the Company was so notified.
>
> The Union requests the Company to cease and desist such arbitrary, capricious, and unreasonable action and restore the $.45 per hour wage increase effective July 1, 2003, retroactively, plus the interest.

The contract contained a narrow arbitration clause that limited the arbitrator's authority to interpretation and application of the contract, without adding to, subtracting from, or modifying the parties' collective bargaining agreement in any way.

The company denied the grievance, and the parties stipulated that the present matter was properly before the arbitrator.

POSITION OF THE UNION

The union contended that the agreement between the parties, as modified by the concession agreement, clearly barred the company from denying the bargaining unit employees their $.45 per hour wage increase effective July 1, 2003. The union claimed that items 2 and 3 of the concession agreement unequivocally supported the union's position and required the company to implement the July 1, 2003, increase and pay interest for the delay in paying the increase.

The union pointed to the parties' arbitration clause and emphasized that the arbitrator had no authority to add to, subtract from, or modify the provisions of the parties' agreements. Therefore, the union believed that the grievance should be sustained and the remedy requested by the union granted.

POSITION OF THE COMPANY

The company claimed that the union's position was simply without merit. The plain meaning, expressed in the clear language of the parties' October concession agreement, together with the bargaining history of that document, demonstrated the mutual intent of the parties. The union knew or should have known that it was deferring the collective bargaining agreement's July 1, 2003, pay increase until July 1, 2004.

The company urged that the only logical construction of the concession agreement's language was that the Union and the bargaining unit employees agree to defer the disputed increase by adopting the concession agreement as an amendment to the parties' collective bargaining agreement. The company therefore requested that the arbitrator deny this grievance as being without merit.

Appendix

Concession Agreement

This Agreement dated as of October 16, 2002, amends the July 1, 2002, Agreement between the parties as follows:

1. Effective August 1, 2002, reduce salaried and hourly wages by 10%. Approximate monthly savings:

a) Salary - $ 7,000
b) Hourly - $13,000

2. In March 2003, review financial status with Bargaining Unit Representative. If Company earns $100,000 in pre-tax income in 2002 income in 2002, reinstate ½ of salary and wage reductions effective April 1, 2003. Salary and wage increase effective 7/1/03 will also be addressed at that time.

3. If financial performance is acceptable, effective July 1, 2003, return salaries and wages to July 1, 2002, levels. Subsequent hourly increases deferred to 7/1/04 and 7/1/05.

QUESTIONS

1. Is the language of the concession agreement clear and unambiguous with respect to hourly increases being deferred to July 1, 2004, and July 1, 2005? What, if any, are the conditions that result in these hourly increases being deferred? Explain.
2. What does the concession agreement require concerning the $.45 of hourly wages frozen in October 2002? What is supposed to happen to these deferred increases? Explain.
3. If you were the arbitrator, how would you rule on the union's grievance? Explain.

Case 78

Layoff of the Higher-Seniority Employees

Company Yale Hoists, Forrest City, Arkansas

Union Local No. 5681, United Steelworkers of America

BACKGROUND

The facts in this case were not in dispute. Yale Hoists, located in Forrest City, Arkansas, and Local No. 5681 of the United Steelworkers of America were signatories to a collective bargaining agreement effective from May 6, 1995, through May 6, 2000. The company had purchased the Forrest City plant in October 1996. The purchase was an asset-only acquisition. Previously (1988–1996), the plant had been owned by Spreckles Industries of Pleasanton, California. Three other companies owned the plant between 1957 and 1988. When Yale Hoists acquired the plant in 1996, it totally replaced the corporate and local management.

Production and maintenance employees were represented by the union under the present and prior owners. During the tenure of the prior owners, collective bargaining agreements similar to the current agreement were negotiated. At the time the company acquired the plant, company representatives met with representatives of Local No. 5681 and advised them that the company would agree to accept and follow the existing agreement. The company did not exempt from its acceptance any provision of the agreement.[1]

Plant operations were not profitable after the company's acquisition. Following two changes in local general managers, the company hired a new general manager for the plant in November 1998. This new general manager, Herman Schotte,[2] immediately instituted a number of cost-reduction measures, including a layoff of 21 salaried employees (approximately 23 percent of the salaried workforce).

Shortly thereafter, Herman Schotte concluded that a reduction in the bargaining unit labor force was also necessary. On January 26, 1999, company management posted a notice advising employees that a layoff of bargaining unit employees would become effective on February 1, 1999. Forty-two hourly employees were affected by the layoff (21 percent of the bargaining unit). In its notice to the union, management explained that under Article VII, Section 2, of the agreement, if senior employees were not able to step into and begin performing the work being performed by junior employees, then the senior employees would not be retained and junior qualified employees would remain employed.

When the union learned that senior employees would be displaced by junior employees in the course of the layoff, a grievance was filed which stated as follows:

> Company in violation of contract by not laying off by seniority.
> This is unfair labor practice.

[1] See appendix for relevant contractual provisions.

[2] Name is disguised.

Settlement requested in grievance: The company should pay back pay to the employees wrongfully done, pay damages done caused by this layoff.

The case was processed through the grievance procedure and was carried to arbitration.[3]

POSITION OF THE UNION

Both during the arbitration hearing and in a post-hearing brief, the chief spokesperson for the union made the following contentions.

1. In the union's view, the company had violated the nature and intent of a binding past practice that had been followed for many years at the plant.
2. The past practice at the Forrest City plant had been that layoffs were made by strict seniority. The only exceptions to this were those indicated in the agreement, Article VII, Section 2, pertaining to the layoff of electricians, maintenance mechanics, or tool and die apprentices. None of the junior-seniority employees retained by the company following the announced layoff in January 1999 were among the exceptions stated in Article VII, Section 2.
3. The company's suggestion that it did not "agree" to be bound by the past practice concerning the retention of the most-senior employees during a layoff was not a valid contention. At no time during negotiations of the purchase of the plant did company representatives state that they would not follow the applications of the seniority provisions of the agreement that had been in place at the plant for many years.
4. At the arbitration hearing, management did not dispute that the union's interpretation of the relevant language of Article VII had been followed at the plant for many years. The company's acquiescence to the "existing agreement" showed that it also acquiesced to the existing past practices interpreting the language of the current agreement. Thus, the company was bound by the prior practice of laying off employees in accordance with seniority.
5. For all of these reasons, the union grievance should be sustained. The six higher-seniority employees affected by the improper layoff should be reinstated to the workforce and returned to work and made whole for all losses they suffered as a result of their improper layoff.

POSITION OF THE COMPANY

Both during the arbitration hearing and in a post-hearing brief, the chief spokesperson for the company made the following contentions.

1. It was undisputed that in a nondisciplinary grievance of this nature, the burden of proof must be borne by the union. The union must show by a preponderance of the evidence that the company violated the agreement. Since the union failed to produce a preponderance of evidence in support of its position, the grievance must be denied.

[3] At the time of arbitration, the parties agreed that six higher-seniority employees had been laid off as a result of the company's actions.

2. The contention that the company was bound by the union's and the prior owner's interpretation and application of Article VII of the agreement was not supported by the facts. To the contrary, at no time following the acquisition of the Forrest City plant and prior to the current layoffs did the company ever agree or acquiesce to the union's interpretation of what the language of Article VII would mean at the time of a layoff.

   More importantly, during negotiations for the renewal of the agreement in 1977, which the union contended its current interpretation of Article VII was confirmed, there was no attempt to remove the clear language from Section 1 and 2 of Article VII, which specified that qualifications to perform classification unit work on day one of the displacement of another employee were required. Yet the union now was contending that the clear language of Sections 1 and 2 should be overruled by the single sentence added in 1977 that provided that least-senior employees would be laid off first.
3. In reviewing the manner in which the company conducted the layoff on February 1, 1999, the company complied with the language of Article VII, Sections 1 and 2. These two sections of the agreement, when read together, clearly and unambiguously require that in a workforce reduction, a senior retained employee must be minimally qualified to perform the standards for the job to which he or she moves in his or her classification unit without extensive retraining. The company was not bound by any "seniority alone" practice that may have been followed by other owners in the past.
4. In addition to the language of the agreement, the arbitrator should look to the economics of the plant's operations and the effect the union's interpretation of Article VII would have on the continued viability of the plant. If seniority alone were used as the determinative factor in this layoff, the company would have incurred significant retraining costs for the senior retained employees. The cost of retraining the senior employees would have been approximately $450,000, which would have dealt a serious blow to the economic viability of the plant. If the company had been required to retrain all the senior employees who were displaced, all of the months of profit that the plant had shown since February 1999 would have been erased or substantially diminished.
5. None of the six more-senior grievants who were laid off had ever performed the jobs in question, whereas the retained junior employees had previously performed these jobs. These junior employees did not require any retraining, whereas the senior employees, if they had been retained, would have required between 45 and 90 days of retraining.
6. The basic rationale for any reduction in force is to save costs. Management does not like to lay off employees, but it must make decisions that contribute to and guarantee the continued operation of the plant. If the company cannot rely upon clear contract language concerning qualifications to step into jobs, but must engage in extensive retraining to avoid laying off senior employees, no cost savings whatsoever could be realized from a reduction in force. Maintaining the same labor costs following a reduction in force as those existing prior to the reduction in force would defeat the central purpose of a cutback in the size of the bargaining unit workforce. The language of the agreement should not be read to require the company to incur no cost gains or experience negative cost gains during a reduction in force.

7. The Forrest City plant was in a "survival" mode from the time the company acquired it in 1996. Had management conducted a layoff in the manner urged by the union, the plant probably would not have survived. The company's interpretation of the agreement and the plain language of Article VII, Sections 1 and 2, was a more reasonable interpretation. The union failed to prove that the company acquiesced to or otherwise agreed to accept the union's view that under Article VII "seniority only" controlled a layoff. For these reasons, the grievance was not well founded and it should be denied.

Appendix

Relevant Provisions of the Labor Agreement

Article IV—Rights of Management

Section 1. The Union agrees that the function of Management belongs solely to the Company, and that it will not interfere with the Company's free exercise of this function, subject to the provisions of this Agreement.

Section 2. The function of Management includes, among others: the right to select and to hire new employees; to direct the working force; to formulate the plant rules and to discipline or discharge for just cause; to transfer or relieve employees from duty because of lack of work or other reasons consistent with efficient operation; to assign work to employees; to decide the number and location of its facilities; to determine the products to be manufactured, including the means and processes of manufacturing; to determine methods of work measurements; to establish standards of performance and to introduce new or improved methods or facilities.

Article VII—Seniority

Section 1. Seniority is defined as the length of an employee's service with the Company from the latest date of hire and will apply within the established lines of progression, within the classification units, a copy of which is hereto attached and made a part of this Agreement. In all cases of promotions, layoffs, and recall, the following factors shall be considered in accordance with the established lines of progression:

(a) Length of continuous service.

(b) Ability to perform work.

(c) Physical fitness.

Where factors (b) and (c) are relatively equal, length of continuous service shall govern. Where the Company fails to recognize length of continuous service, it shall consult with the employee involved and advise him of its position on the employee's lack of relatively equal ability to perform the work or relatively equal physical fitness.

Section 2. In the event an employee is laid off from his classification in a unit under Section 1 above, he shall replace the employee with the least Company service who is assigned to the classification in the same labor grade and then lower labor grades, in the classification unit, provided he has more seniority than the employee he replaces, and that he can perform in accordance with the standards of the job.

* * *

In cases where reduction in forces causes layoff from the plant, the least senior employee(s) will be laid off first; except electricians A, maintenance mechanics A, tool and die makers, and tool and die apprentices will be laid off only if there is a reduction in their classification. At that time they will be subject to the normal layoff procedure.

QUESTIONS

1. When the company acquired the Forrest City plant in 1996 and accepted the existing labor agreement between the union and the prior ownership, was the company obligated to accept and follow any existing past practices? Why, or why not?
2. Examine carefully each of the contentions of the union and the company. Which do you find to be the *most* and *least* persuasive, and why?
3. Discuss the economic justification arguments presented by the company. Should the arbitrator be influenced by the economic concerns of the company in deciding this case? Why, or why not?
4. If you were the arbitrator, how would you decide, and why?

Case 79

Cash Same as Stock? The Case of the 401k Contributions

Company Weyerhaeuser Co., Indianapolis, Indiana

Union PACE International Union, Local 6-0154

BACKGROUND

Weyerhaeuser took over the Indianapolis operations from Willamette. When Weyerhaeuser took over Willamette operations, including the Indianapolis facility, Weyerhaeuser management terminated the Willamette 401k programs and replaced those with the Weyerhaeuser 401k plan.

The collective bargaining agreement that existed between the union and Willamette contained a 401k program at Article XI of the agreement. All provisions of the 401k program that existed in the Weyerhaeuser program exists in the Willamette program that contained the parties' agreement, save one provision. The provision changed by management in this case was that rather than matching $1.00 of the employee contribution to the 401k plan with $.50 in cash as the contract requires, Weyerhaeuser would match $1.00 of the employee contribution with $.50 worth of stock. All other aspects of the 401k plan remained the same.

There were no procedural matters in this case, and the parties stipulated that this case was properly before the arbitrator.

POSITION OF THE UNION

The union's position was simple and straightforward. Weyerhaeuser is the successor company in this contract, in that Weyerhaeuser took over the Indianapolis facility from Willamette which negotiated the current collective bargaining agreement with the union. At the time Weyerhaeuser acquired Willamette, Weyerhaeuser agreed to honor the totality of the Willamette contract with the union. At the time Weyerhaeuser took over it kept every aspect of the contract in force, with the exception that Weyerhaeuser changed one provision of the 401k program: making the company contributions to the plan in stock rather than in cash (cash is what the Willamette program required for the company contribution).

The record shows that Weyerhaeuser never informed the union of its intent to change the nature of its contribution. Weyerhaeuser never requested negotiations with the union over the retirement program. Weyerhaeuser simply unilaterally changed from cash contributions, similar to the programs it negotiated in Weyerhaeuser programs, and discontinued the cash contributions required by this contract.

The union contended that this unilateral change was a violation of the successor company's obligations under the collective bargaining agreement it inherited from Willamette. The union requested the arbitrator sustain this grievance in its entirety. As remedy, the union asked that the company be ordered to return to cash contributions as required by the current collective bargaining agreement between the parties.

POSITION OF THE COMPANY

It was the company's position in this case that Willamette had reserved the right to amend the negotiated 401k plan at any time. It was management's position that when the Willamette 401k plan ceased to exist, on Weyerhaeuser's acquisition of the company, it was replaced by the Weyerhaeuser 401k plan. The Weyerhaeuser plan is identical to the Willamette plan except that under the Weyerhaeuser plan company contributions are made in stock and not in cash.

The plain truth of the matter is the company may amend the plan, as it did in this case. Because Willamette no longer exists, its 401k plan no longer exists, and it is prudent and reasonable that a new 401k plan be adopted in its place. In this case, the 401k plan adopted by Weyerhaeuser provides for everything the Willamette program did. The fact that stock is used rather than cash for the company contributions does not diminish the value of the contribution.

It should be clear to the arbitrator that there has been no contract violation, and that the present grievance should be denied in its entirety as being without merit.

Appendix

Contract Language

Article XI—Retirement

The Employer and the Union have agreed to a pension and a 401k plan for employees of the Employer working under the jurisdiction of this Agreement with said Union, the terms of which are set forth in a separate summary plan description booklet.

(The booklet describes the details of the Plan, and says nothing of any obligations or rights of the Employer rather than the details of the plan.)

QUESTIONS

1. Is a successor company bound by the terms of the contract negotiated prior to its acquiring the firm? If so, how might a successor company change the provisions of an inherited collective bargaining agreement?
2. Is Article XI of the collective bargaining agreement binding on Weyerhaeuser? Does that also bind the company to the provisions of the 401k plan contained in the booklet cited in Article XI? Explain.
3. If you were the arbitrator in this matter, how would you rule? If you granted the grievance, what remedy is appropriate in this case?

Case 80

Vacation, or Layoff, During a Shutdown

Company USS, Division of USX Corporation, Gary Works, Gary, Indiana

Union Local No. 1014, United Steelworkers of America

BACKGROUND

Due to low orders, the company decided to shut down plate mill operations for one week in February 1999, and to perform a major construction project that previously had been scheduled for a later date. On February 1, 1999, plate mill management posted a notice addressed to production employees that stated:

> Subject: One (1) week shutdown period
>
> Please be advised that the plate mill will be shut down commencing February 12, 1999, to install a new main mill drive armature, AGC hydraulic cylinders, and cooling bed roller grating. This shutdown period will end February 22, 1999, in accordance with section 12C-2-D of the February 1, 1994, basic labor agreement. This notice is to fulfill the less than 60 days' notice. All affected employees will have the right to select one of the following options:
>
> 1. Schedule a week of vacation during the shutdown.
> 2. Elect to be placed on layoff during the shutdown.

Union representatives, who previously had been informed by management of the probability of such a shutdown, advised employees not to make an election. The union considered the company's offer to be in violation of the Employment Security Plan (ESP) in Appendix G of the basic agreement.[1] When informed of the union's decision, management then notified the union that employees who failed to communicate their election (i.e., choice from the two options) to management by February 11, 1999, would be scheduled on vacation.

In response, some bargaining unit employees elected to take either a week's vacation or week's layoff. However, the overwhelming majority did not choose either option, and they were scheduled by management for a week's vacation during the shutdown period. A consolidated group grievance was filed by the union on March 1, 1999, which stated the following:

> We, the undersigned and on behalf of all affected employees, contend that management violated our contractual rights when they forced us on layoff, or arbitrarily placed us on vacation.
>
> *Remedy Requested:* Make all affected employees whole in every way and cease and desist this violation.

The consolidated group grievance was on behalf of employees in the plate mill at Gary Works. The grievance protested that these employees were improperly placed on

[1] See appendix to case for relevant contractual provision.

layoff, or on vacation, during a one-week shutdown for the week beginning February 14, 1999. Of these, 237 were employees who were scheduled on vacation either based on their choice or not making a choice, and 26 were employees who elected to be laid off.

Since the facts of the case were not in dispute, the parties decided to submit the case directly to a Board of Arbitration[2] without having an arbitration hearing. Both the company and union submitted and exchanged original briefs, followed by a reply brief, in which their respective positions were presented.

POSITION OF THE UNION

The union contended that the Employment Security Plan, Appendix G, provided an unambiguous guarantee that employees would not be laid off, and this express provision superseded and overrode the company's Section 12-C-2-d right to require employees to choose between layoff with the attendant loss of income, and using vacation that may have previously been scheduled for a more desirable time.

The union stressed that Appendix G-B-1 expressly guaranteed that employees would not be laid off, subject to certain exceptions that did not apply in this case. Therefore, any inconsistent provision of the agreement was overridden. The company cannot *require* employees to choose between vacation and layoff, because that would render the no-layoff guarantee of the ESP merely an illusion. The company cannot *offer* such an option because of the provision in Appendix G-G abolishing voluntary layoff practices and agreements. The only contractually permissible action was to follow the procedures agreed to at Gary Works for placement of employees in other jobs (by seniority) who otherwise would have been laid off.

The union contended that the company impermissibly placed employees in a position of either having to lose a week's pay by electing layoff, or giving up an important contractual right (i.e., the right to exercise their seniority in the selection of vacation periods and to retain their previously scheduled vacations when the company failed to give 60 days' advance notice of a shutdown). The company should not be rewarded for its failure to give 60 days' notice by being allowed to avoid its obligations under the ESP. In short, the choices imposed on the employees by management were not contractually permissible.

As remedies, the union requested that: (1) employees improperly laid off receive back pay for the week they should have been scheduled to work in accordance with the ESP; (2) employees improperly scheduled on vacation (i.e., who did not make an election) be allowed to take their vacations as previously scheduled; and (3) employees improperly forced to select vacation during the shutdown should have the option of a week's pay, or restoration of eligibility for vacation as previously scheduled.

POSITION OF THE COMPANY

The company contended that Section 12-C-2-d expressly authorized vacation scheduling during a shutdown period of the type at issue here, and provided that the applicable

[2] The Board of Arbitration consisted of one company representative, one union representative, and a neutral arbitrator selected by these representatives and who served as chairperson.

remedy when the company fails to provide 60 days' notice is that the employee has the option to elect layoff instead of vacation. In the company's view, Appendix G did not override or eliminate this provision.

The company argued that Appendix G-H-1 expressly established the parties' intent to preserve other existing contract language, and that Appendix G and Section 12-C-2-d can and should be read as consistent contractual provisions. As set forth in Appendix G-B-7, the guarantee of "employment security" is simply the opportunity to earn 40 hours of pay (including vacation pay) during a payroll week. In this case, the only action taken by the company was to reschedule vacation in accordance with its rights under Section 12-C-2-d, which provided employees with at least 40 hours of pay. Thus, it was essentially employee actions that resulted in layoffs. An employee who elected layoff had the opportunity to earn 40 hours of pay by taking a vacation. By electing layoff, the employee declined the opportunity to earn at least 40 hours of pay through vacation. Thus, the company's action was fully consistent with Appendix G.

The company insisted that the union's position, in effect, would render meaningless part of Section 12 from the labor agreement by preventing the company from scheduling a vacation shutdown with less than 60 days' notice. This would be contrary to the preservation of existing rights in Appendix G-H-1. Nothing about the provisions of Appendix G could possibly lead to a conclusion that its purpose was to preserve vacation preference.

The company reiterated that the union's reliance on Paragraph G of Appendix G was misplaced. Appendix G-G-1 merely eliminated local voluntary layoff agreements and practices, and provided a means by which new voluntary layoff agreements could be effectuated. This provision obviously had nothing to do with other express provisions of the agreement, including Section 12-C-2-d.

Finally, the company asserted that in the event the Board of Arbitration should find that the company's actions somehow were in violation of Appendix G, there was no basis for awarding any of the remedies sought by the union. Any questions of remedy should be reserved, if necessary, for future negotiations between the company and union.

Appendix

Relevant Provisions from the Labor Agreement

Section 12—Vacations

* * *

C. Scheduling of Vacations

* * *

1-c. Vacations will, so far as practicable, be granted at times most desired by employees (longer service employees being given preference as to choice); but the final right to allot vacation periods and to change such allotments is exclusively reserved to the Company in order to insure the orderly operation of the plants.

2. Vacations

* * *

d. In case Management desires to schedule vacations for employees eligible therefore during a shutdown period instead of in accordance with the previously established vacation schedules for that year, Management shall give affected employees sixty days' notice of such intent; in the absence of such notice, an affected employee shall have the option to take his vacation during the shutdown period or to be laid off during the shutdown and to take his vacation at the previously scheduled time.

Appendix G—Memorandum of Understanding on Employment Security Plan

* * *

B. Guarantee

1. Employees eligible for this ESP may not be laid off during the term of this Agreement except as provided below . . .

* * *

7. The guarantee provided to active eligible employees by this ESP. . . is defined as the opportunity to earn forty (40) hours of pay (including hours paid for but not worked, . . .), during any payroll week. . .

* * *

E. Job Assignments from the Employment Security List

The local parties at each plant have reached agreement on the placement of employees who would have been laid off but for this ESP. Those agreements, as set forth at Appendix U of the February 1, 1994, Settlement Agreement, are made part of this ESP, and may not be changed except as agreed to by the plant Leadership Committee.

* * *

G. Voluntary Layoff Practices and Agreements

1. Upon the effective date of this ESP, all existing practices, agreements, or working conditions which permit voluntary layoffs, other than those continued pursuant to Section E of this ESP, will be abolished . . .

H. Existing Rights

1. Except as expressly provided in this ESP, nothing in the ESP shall interfere with, limit, detract from, or adversely affect in any way the rights and obligations of the parties set forth in other provisions of the Basic Labor Agreement . . .

QUESTIONS

1. Why do you surmise that the company and union decided to submit this case directly to arbitration without having a hearing? Discuss.
2. Examine carefully the disputed contractual language at the core of this case. Which provisions do you believe override (or supersede) other provisions that may seem to be in conflict with each other? Why?
3. Evaluate the company's assertion that there was no basis for awarding any remedies sought by the union in the eventuality that a Board of Arbitration majority should rule that the company in some way had violated the labor agreement.
4. If you were the *neutral* arbitrator, how would you decide, and why?

Case 81

Discharge for Job Abandonment?

Company Coca-Cola Enterprises, Inc.

Union Teamsters, Local 414

BACKGROUND

The grievant in this matter was a route driver employed by Coca-Cola. The grievant's regular workweek was Monday through Friday, with a start time of 6:00 A.M. The grievant volunteered to work an overtime shift on Saturday, January 3, 2004. The grievant failed to report for work for the overtime on Saturday, and subsequently missed his next two regularly scheduled shifts on Monday, January 5, and Tuesday, January 6.

The grievant had been arrested early Saturday morning January 3, 2004, for domestic battery. He was taken to jail, from where he called his father, collect, and asked him to call his employer and report that he would be unable to report for work for a couple days due to a "family emergency." The grievant's father subsequently called Coca-Cola and reported what his son had asked him to report. The grievant was arraigned on Tuesday and that afternoon posted bail and was released from jail. Upon his release from jail, the grievant called his supervisor informing him that he had been in jail and that he had a court appearance scheduled for January 7, 2004. The supervisor informed the grievant that he was not to report to work for the remainder of the week.

In a letter dated January 12, 2004, the grievant was informed he was terminated for having been absent for "three consecutive working days without notifying the Company." Section 4.10 c. of the parties' collective bargaining agreement states that "Seniority and the relationship of the Company and employee shall be considered broken and terminated when . . . an employee is absent three consecutive working days without notifying the Company." The company also has a unilaterally promulgated attendance policy which states that employees will be subject to progressive discipline for failing to report for work without notifying the employer prior to the start of their shift. The first offense is subject to reprimand, the second to a three-day suspension, and the third offense to discharge.

The grievant filed a timely grievance—which was denied—as were subsequent appeals through the parties' negotiated grievance procedure. The parties stipulated that the present matter was properly before the arbitrator.

POSITION OF THE COMPANY

The company's position was that the grievant's seniority had been broken pursuant to Section 4.10 c. of the parties' collective bargaining agreement. The company contended that the issue of just cause for the discharge of the grievant was only relevant should the arbitrator find that the grievant did not violate Section 4.10 c.

The company's position with respect to Section 4.10 c. was that the notification requirement had a well-established practice of requiring there to be personal notification by the employee that he would not be coming to work. The company offered the testimony of several management personal indicating that they had always required personal notification. The company also argued the grievant's personally reporting an absence a week before this incident indicated his knowledge and acceptance of this practice.

The company further contended that should the arbitrator not find a violation of Section 4.10 c. the discharge was still proper. The record shows that the grievant failed to call in prior to his absence on Saturday, thereby earning a reprimand. He failed to call in Monday for his second offense under the company's attendance policy. Finally, the grievant failed to call in Tuesday, thereby earning his discharge under the attendance policy. Therefore, employing the just cause standards under the company's attendance policy there is still proper cause to remove this grievant.

Further, the company contended that there are no reasons to mitigate this penalty, and that the union failed to prove its contentions that there was disparate treatment of this grievant. The company therefore urged the denial of this grievance.

POSITION OF THE UNION

The union contended that Section 4.10 c. did not apply to this matter and that there was no just cause for the discharge of this grievant under the company's attendance policy. The company had failed to show that the grievant violated either.

With respect to Section 4.10 c., there was nothing in the written language of the contract or in the bargaining history which even suggested that notification of the absences to the company had to be in any particular form, let alone communicated personally by the employee. Even management's own witnesses testified that they were unaware of a single employee being discharged because the notice of their absences weren't in a particular form under Section 4.10 c. The arbitrator is bound to apply the clear and unambiguous language of Section 4.10 c. which states notice must be given, and this grievant twice informed his employer within the three-day window that he was not able to attend work.

The union also contended that the disciplinary rules also did not apply in this case. The employer's own witnesses all testified that a written reprimand is never issued to an employee until after their fifth absence. This grievant had not reached his fifth absence in a year's period of time and had not earned the first level of discipline under the company's attendance policy.

The facts are not in dispute and the language of both the contract and attendance policy is clear and nowhere requires personal notification. The arbitrator is bound by that clear language and must sustain this grievance and order the grievant reinstated with full back pay and benefits.

QUESTIONS

1. Is Section 4.10 c. clear and unambiguous with respect to notification of the employer? If so, does it require personal notification?
2. Is there any requirement in the attendance policy that the grievant personally notify his employer of his absences?
3. Was there any evidence that past practices existed in this matter? If so, what are they? How do they affect the applicability of the contract or attendance policy? Explain.
4. Did the grievant abandon his job? Was there just cause for his discharge?